Novels of Everyday Life

Novels of Everyday Life:

The Series in English Fiction, 1850–1930

LAURIE LANGBAUER

Cornell University Press

ITHACA AND LONDON

First published 1999 by Cornell University Press
First printing, Cornell Paperbacks, 1999

Printed in the United States of America

Library of Congress Cataloging-in-Publication Data

Langbauer, Laurie.
    Novels of everyday life : the series in English fiction, 1850–1930
/ Laurie Langbauer.
        p.   cm.
    Includes bibliographical references and index.
    ISBN 0-8014-3497-1 (cloth : alk. paper). — ISBN 0-8014-8501-0 (paper : alk. paper)
    1. English fiction—19th century—History and criticism.   2. Popular literature—Great
Britain—History and criticism.   3. English fiction—20th century—History and criticism.
4. Manners and customs in literature.   5. Series (Publications)   I. Title.
PR878.P68L36   1998
823'.809355—dc21   98-39544

Cornell University Press strives to use environmentally responsible suppliers and materials to
the fullest extent possible in the publishing of its books. Such materials include vegetable-
based, low-VOC inks and acid-free papers that are recycled, totally chlorine-free, or partly
composed of nonwood fibers.

Cloth printing   10 9 8 7 6 5 4 3 2 1
Paperback printing 10 9 8 7 6 5 4 3 2 1

Contents

Acknowledgments

I am indebted to the many institutions that have supported work on this project: the American Association of Learned Societies, the Institute for Advanced Study in the Humanities at the University of Edinburgh, Swarthmore College (for both an ongoing Faculty Research Grant and a George M. Becker Fellowship), and the University of Utah Humanities Center. I especially thank Lowell Durham and Lynne Rasmussen for making me feel completely at home while I was in Utah. I am grateful to the University of North Carolina at Chapel Hill, my real institutional home, for grants from the University Research Council and the Dean's Office in the College of Arts and Sciences for assistance with scholarly publication.

It's impossible to convey my thanks to the many people who have commented on various drafts of this project; they helped make it a much stronger book. Their time and attention means more to me than I can say: Lisa Aldren, Betsy Bolton, Jane Burns, Jonathan Crewe, Jane Danielewicz, Judith Farquhar, Megan Matchinske, Elsie Michie, Patricia Spacks, Ann Stewart, Melissa Zeiger. James Thompson read everything I gave him long after I should have stopped. The intellectual community at the University of North Carolina at Chapel Hill has kept me thinking and made me happy: William Andrews, Darryl Gless, Joy Kasson, John McGowan, Susan Navarette, and Beverly Taylor have been instrumental in making the English department truly congenial. The faculty seminar of which I was part at the Institute for the Arts and Humanities promises support from and debate with colleagues throughout the University for years to come. I thank especially Peter Filene, Jacquelyn Hall, Laurie Maffly-Kipp, and Ruel Tyson. Linda M. Shires provided encouragement and advice at a critical stage. I thank as well various audiences at the University of Edinburgh, UNC—Chapel Hill, and the University of Utah: they helped me think further through some of the issues I explore here. Margaret Homans, Mary Jacobus, Karen Lawrence, Mary

Poovey, Harry Shaw, and Barry Qualls provided valuable assistance in keeping me going and in bringing the project to completion. Their scholarship and generosity provide a model I can only strive to meet. I thank Bernhard Kendler for his inimitable blend of integrity and wit. I am aware of just how lucky I have been to be able to work with him twice. I have been lucky, too, in working with Kay Scheuer on this book; I hope some of her talent has rubbed off on it. Without Kapila Basnet, Arabel Elliott, Cheryl Fahrner, Liz Farley, Christine Faughan, Carolyn Holman, Charity Miller, Phoebe Polk, and Jessa Sacco, this book would never have been written. Without Terrence Holt, there wouldn't have been a reason to write it. I also want to remember the people who are no longer here since I began the book: William Richard Langbauer, William E. Holt, and Rachel Merritt. I owe a debt of love to those who remember them with me: Alyce B. Langbauer and Constance Holt. MacLean Tobias Holt showed up somewhere in the middle of the book, and made it all worthwhile.

A part of the Introduction appeared in different form as "Cultural Studies and the Politics of the Everyday" in *diacritics* 22 (1992): 47–65; a small section of Chapter 1 is also included in "Absolute Commonplaces: Margaret Oliphant's Theory of Autobiography," in *Margaret Oliphant: Critical Essays on a Gentle Subversive*, ed. D. J. Trela (London: Associated University Press, 1995), 124–34. Chapter 3 was published in *differences* 5.3 (1993): 80–102. The last section of Chapter 4 appeared as "Feminist Literary Criticism and Cultural Studies," in *"Turning the Century": Feminist Theory in the 1990s*, ed. Glynnis Carr, special issue of the *Bucknell Review* 36 (1989): 219–43, and is reprinted by permission of that journal.

L. L.

Novels of Everyday Life

Introduction

Why this book?

Although I didn't know it at the time, I started it to try to understand what had made me read nineteenth-century novels in the first place—what seemed their two salient, absolutely defining characteristics for me when I was a hopeful, earnest, young woman determined to tackle the classics in my teens: the first, not only that they went on forever (and the longer the novel the better in those empty Illinois summers) but that they went on again and again. Long after I had outgrown *Little House on the Prairie* and Louisa May Alcott's more curiously connected "Little" books, it was still not quite cheating to read these enormous stories that unfurled themselves into (almost) endless series, novel leading into novel in a protracted chain. Even novels that weren't connected I read as if they were, running straight through Austen's fiction—all just the various adventures possible to one exceptional heroine who (unlike me) had pushed past the threshold of life to find herself in the midst of it, unprotected, breathless, but completely equal to it.

That such books threw you into the midst of life was their second attraction. That they were so long already and seemed to go on forever in a series meant I was plunged into a world whose repetitiveness and minuteness of detail substituted for a dailiness I felt at the time I lacked, shut away day after day in a succession of strange and remote houses as I was growing up. Given the caprices of my family, who seemed to move at a moment's notice to places that were unfamiliar but somehow just the same, my own life was blank and alien, at one and the same time completely unpredictable and inescapably humdrum. Although I didn't have the words then to call what I liked about those novels "the series" and "the everyday"—and although I didn't have the critical tools to work out how those two categories went together—I think they gave me the framework that kept me sane during a lonely and uncertain adolescence.

A quarter of a century later, made who I am by that past, I started this book. When I began it, all I knew was that I was interested in something about Victorian novels it took me a couple of articles to learn to call "the everyday." I knew it was a particular property of realism—one that located verisimilitude in the ordinary and domestic—but it was also enough like the way I had come to see my own world and the place I had come explicitly to locate my happiness in it (those small, meaningless moments at my job, with my husband or my son—a certain rhythm and repetitiveness to life like the hum and tap of a sewing machine) that it took me a while to recognize that "the everyday" wasn't some essential reality, made uniquely grounded and certain just because it was my own. It was a convention. It had a theoretical history—all the issues I explore in this book. It took me even longer to see that "the everyday" was the special province of a particular form—that precisely because of their expansiveness, their repetitiveness, their complication of closure, those linked novels that are part of extended series seem to mirror and carry properties often defined as essential to everyday life: that it's just one thing after another, going quietly but inexhaustibly on and on. I think I was especially obtuse about all this even as it fueled my interest in my project because I didn't want to admit that I'd undertaken an exercise in self-punishment, every chapter of which entailed absorbing not just one fat and unwieldy novel but sometimes ten or even (with Trollope) twenty. Like the series novels I was reading, like the everyday they represented, my work on this project just kept steadily—it seemed eternally—continuing.

But I believe too that my own blindness to the link between the series and the everyday, even when it kept insisting on itself for years, is at least to some degree exemplary. Not that I finally get to become some kind of exceptional heroine in this story: on the contrary; what that blindness exemplifies is an ideological—a cultural—blindness, common to a shared subject position, the bourgeois self. The very categories of the everyday and the series further that blindness by insisting on their own invisibility, by swamping us with their plausibility. The critics who have come closest to revealing a connection between the series novel and the everyday have been materialist, all Marxists to some degree (although none has made exactly that connection, many theorists have done the work that has allowed me to make it). It follows from Marx's legacy of exposing how the social ordering of our material world cloaks us in false consciousness in order to perpetuate itself: the everyday we take for granted, and mimic (as well as enforce) in our own literature, is not some kind of natural, transparent, preexistent experience, but the product of a social system on which that system rests, through which it circularly generates itself.

That understanding is at the heart of this book. But my interest in the series and the everyday is informed as well by the deep belief that our consciousness, even when we wish to call it false, is nothing we can shed. All we can ever do is mark the paradoxes in which we are caught, only indicate the

contradictions in the system that produces us—not transcend it. Such paradoxes are all the more palpable to me in a study of the two categories that not
only (I will argue here) crucially inform the bourgeois subject but also most
particularly seem to me to have made *me* who I am. But just because I love
the quiet moments that make up my own personal myth of the everyday—
largely domestic, but also professional (for isn't most of an academic's life
constituted of a series of steady, repetitive, unheralded daily chores? I find a
fund of pleasure and discovery in the proliferating stacks of notecards and
photocopies, always on my desk, that can never be winnowed down over the
years no matter how much I throw away, the same books read for the hun-
dredth time each term, the students' faces, perennially young but always different, that keep the courses I offer year and again from ever getting stale;
it's these small pleasures that to me make the job rewarding)—just because
I find pleasure in these moments, doesn't mean that this everyday isn't a myth.
Yet I am interested that one reaction to the everyday can be pleasure—and
not just with the banalized tedium that someone like Henri Lefebvre or Max
Horkheimer and Theodor Adorno wants to locate in serial production (as I
recount in my chapters on Holmes and on Oliphant and Yonge). My version
of the everyday brings me lasting comfort, deep and abiding joy (and in ways
that go beyond the strategic cleverness that theorists like the situationists or
Michel de Certeau want to accord the everyday).

This difference of attitude to the series and the everyday seems to me to
have to do with gender. Pleasure too demands interrogation; feminists, along
with theorists of sexuality, have given us the most consistent reminders of
that. What does it mean to associate pleasure with the everyday, and to declare that that connection has something to do with gender? To answer questions like these, I need to turn to the series novel. This book is a reading of
both fiction *and* contemporary theory because the ways that the fiction—
especially by women novelists—reflects on and augments the theory are important to me. The theory is too silent about too much: linked novels that
make up a series have gotten no serious critical attention as a literary form.
Any interest theorists of form devote to them comes simply as a footnote to
a related but very different discussion, an analysis of serial production, of individual novels published in installments. Those feminist critics who are best
about the relations of the novel's form and women's concerns in nineteenth-
century England—Elaine Showalter, Sandra Gilbert and Susan Gubar, Mary
Poovey—even when they talk about serial publication never mention series
fiction at all. This is all the more surprising since, by the later part of the
nineteenth century, the series seemed to its contemporary readers and critics
the prevalent mode. By the 1850s (partly because of the unspoken influence
of French fiction, such as Balzac's *Comedie Humaine*) it seemed that, except
for George Eliot, almost every (supposedly) major English novelist—Scott,
Thackeray, and Dickens (in the link, through *Master Humphrey's Clock*, between *The Old Curiosity Shop* and *Barnaby Rudge*)—had tried his or her

hand at the series. For the novelists that followed in the latter half of the century—Trollope in his Barsetshire and Palliser series, Oliphant with Carlingford, Yonge's family chronicles, Doyle's stories linked by Holmes, Galsworthy's Forsyte saga, and on into Bennett's Five Towns, Hardy's Wessex, and Conrad's stories about Marlow—some kind of linkage between works practically seemed required. Although modern theory remains largely silent about this form, the fiction of the time was not. Reflecting on its manner of presentation was an important element of later Victorian novels. And what those novels determined as they meditated on it was also that the series had to do with gender.

As this book demonstrates, gender was so necessary to the series's formulation that it could be called on in absolutely contradictory ways; its explanatory power was in excess of sense. Doyle, for instance, displays how the tradition attempts to co-opt the infinite repetitions implied by the series as an analogy for male immortality, a transcendence of the corrupt and mortal flesh that women represent for culture. At the same time, women novelists such as Oliphant and Yonge get mocked for writing series fiction as a means of wallowing in the corporeal. Their critics claim that women writers use series fiction for meaningless replications, a prolificness that simply repeats but (because it is feminine) cannot lead anywhere. Trollope's, Richardson's, and Woolf's fiction shows the ways that these associations of the series with gender can be used to buttress assumptions about race and class as well. All these writers reveal a lively debate about the series taking place around gender which engages directly with topics that are central to political criticism today.

Similarly, although there is a firmly established critical background discussing "the everyday," Victorian series fiction and its successors help supply the missing place of gender in it. Those theorists who come to mind when we think of the everyday—Sigmund Freud and *The Psychopathology of Everyday Life*, Lefebvre, with his *Critique of Everyday Life* as well as *Everyday Life in the Modern World*, de Certeau and *The Practice of Everyday Life*—even when they associate women and the everyday are still largely uninterested in women except as they tell them something about men. It is important to keep in mind this heritage of gender exclusion (among others) in the theoretical history of the everyday because it continues to have political ramifications in the current use of the term.

Those exclusions provide another reason I got interested in this topic: the suspicion that a very effective strategy of dominance is to enforce one particular definition of the everyday on everyone. The power involved in just who gets to define the everyday provided one standard sitcom plot of the 50s and 60s and an ongoing issue in my parents' own lives: the hushed and shining home to which the husband returned each weekday at 5 for his cocktail erased the signs of his wife's daily labor, turned the home into one more peaceful reception area or the corner office to which he aspired, deceptively transformed her everyday into the promise of his own. My father was never allowed that illusion, either at work (his kind of work could never offer him a corner office) or at the place he felt he ought to have more control, his home. Until she went off to work herself, my mother never tried to mask each visceral detail of life with small children: the smell of the diaper pail, the vista of dirty dishes, the loud, unsatisfiable, endless desires. On TV, when Dad took over the home to see what Mom really did all day, the children turned back into animals, the kitchen nearly exploded; he was more than happy to hand the job back over to her (which was okay, since she had failed miserably during her time at his office as well). But as a child I knew the father's experience as no monitory vision of a home mishandled but simply as my daily life. That was the way it always was; my mother could do no better than that chaos herself (who could?), although everyone told her she ought to. And that was the point: because culture couldn't sanitize or annul our daily experience (happily, small and very unruly children are almost completely resistant to ideology), its norms pathologized where they couldn't mask. It is a truism now of feminism that stressed 50s housewives never organized because all over the country they hid from each other the anarchy and squalor of their daily lives. My mother felt angry about the impossible demands on her, but also inadequate because she failed to meet them.

That story is meant as a parable not so much about what the everyday *is*, but how it operates. Although, as a woman in America, I often experience the everyday as the repetitive and banalized routine of life with small children (and I cling tenaciously, politically, to that understanding of it as well, since that kind of drudgery seems to me vital, absolutely incomparable in value to most of the work we do under capitalism), I know that it is just one—and a highly stereotypical—story of everyday life. Everyday life has been associated with everything from forgetfulness to housework to walking (think of Freud, Lefebvre, de Certeau); what interests me is just how it gets defined differently in different contexts—not what it *is* but how it *works*. That is a standard poststructural approach that has been crucial to my work since I first undertook it. But I realized during the course of writing this book that something else is crucial as well: not just *how* a term operates, but the attitudes it carries with it, how we *feel* about it.

The writers I consider here all tell different stories about what they think the everyday might be and how it might operate (one impulse behind the series could be the urge to keep telling the same story over differently, to keep trying to account for the everyday). But what began to interest me more was the difference those various stories made to their tellers. The radically opposed attitudes taken to the tedium of the everyday by the men and women I consider in my Holmes chapter, for instance, make all the difference—in whether we see the everyday as simply another (perhaps the most exemplary) site of ideological constraint and indoctrination, or also as the arena for some kind of political struggle. In seeing it as both, I build on the Marxist-inspired theory which forms the bulk of the theory of the everyday I examine in this book. But the novels that I study ask me to transform those theorists' dialectical model, with its emphasis on transcendence—the belief that those contradictory attitudes get synthesized into some new and transformative unity—to resituate it, recontextualize it back within an everyday whose loop, the series shows us, keeps cycling us back within its compass. Their stories don't locate us in some seamless elsewhere but insist upon the manifest and divided here and now in which we must make do—not only because we have no other choice but because our politics might be better (more considerate and responsive to those in the same boat, more tolerant of difference) if we do.

My own feelings about the series and the everyday are mixed, like those of all the writers and theorists I examine. Although I recognize the problems of associating women and the everyday, I also see that category as a place of great theoretical richness for feminism; although I see the danger in any fixed definition of the everyday, I still consider it the most sustaining arena of my personal life, perhaps because I can't really pin it down. When I started this book I didn't realize I was going to study what now seems to me the—completely unstable—ground of my identity. As I finish it, I seem to be laying some crucial part of my past to rest in that ground. What the series impulse suggests to me is the ways we just keep telling different versions of the same story until our particular series finally has its run. It is clear to me now how this is the continuation of my first book, completely opaque how the next will grow out of this. Because in my own understanding of nineteenth-century fiction the everyday and the series are inseparably entwined, impossible to think outside or beyond, I try to express here how they provide one of the vital connective links forging identity and culture in that fiction.

This book considers the series novel and the everyday in the late Victorian period and the years immediately following because that was arguably the time when that form and that topic had their greatest cultural presence. Another study might attempt to sketch the social and historical reasons why the later Victorians got so interested in these categories. Linda Hughes and Michael Lund, in *The Victorian Serial*, try to account for serial production in this way, for instance.[1] In this introduction instead I examine the literary and theoretical background of these terms in order to provide a context for them: not so much for their appearance in Victorian fiction as for our current recognition and understanding of them there. If this book is in any way

[1] Linda Hughes and Michael Lund, *The Victorian Serial* (Charlottesville: University Press of Virginia, 1991), 1; all future references to this book will appear in the text. For the standard history of Victorian serial publication, see Richard Altick, *The English Common Reader: A Social History of the Mass Reading Public, 1800–1900* (Chicago: University of Chicago Press, 1957). See also Robert Patten, *Literature in the Marketplace: Nineteenth-Century British Publishing and Reading Practices* (New York: Cambridge University Press, 1995).

a cultural history, it is one (as my chapter on modernism shows) that wants to emphasize the constructedness of that history, the mediation of the Victorians' concerns through our own.

Because it seems important to me to recognize the ways we have come to think, what structures our perception and understanding, this book's focus is on the theory of the series and the everyday. And it reaches that focus by reading those English novels that make the connections between these terms apparent and provide some suggestions about how it might be crucial. More than anything, this book means to stage a dialogue—between novels and criticism written a century ago and modern theory that lets us recognize such topics in them in the first place. Rather than emphasizing the supposed facts of history, I'm more interested in the ongoing theorization of the series and the everyday as important cultural categories—and their theorization by novels as well as by more strictly defined "theory." The novels, in fact, often seem to do better than explicit analysis in keeping these terms open, continuing to question what they mean and how they work, resisting turning theory into fact. And since, as I argue, the series and the everyday are important to culture because they perform as some of its most effective ideological carriers, the ability to resist any closed or fixed definition of them—to whatever degree possible—seems one way of marking ideology's transparency, exposing ideology if not combating it.

In order to undertake a reading of the series and the everyday, and their connection, in Victorian fiction and beyond, I first explore some strands of the current critical background of those terms. The Marxist heritage of criticism on the series and the everyday stems from Marx's own emphasis on the serial replications of capitalism—the endlessly producible commodities of the factory system, the similarly stamped-out and undifferentiated workers and consumers, whose own mass production is hidden behind the illusion of enlightenment individualism. Marx was also especially concerned with how the assumptions and needs of capitalism infiltrate and condition the most ordinary details of people's lives, so that that economic system gets taken for granted, comes to seem natural, the only system which is even possible. Because Marx helped make notions of seriality and the everyday visible, if not also in need of ruthless critique, critics who have considered these topics have tended to do so in a generally materialist way; they examine the hidden economic and social factors that define the series and the everyday and cause us to think in (while remaining at the same time largely unaware of) these categories.

This introduction charts the Marxist etiology of those terms, but in the framework of a more recent poststructural response to it, which especially attempts to revise it in terms of gender (and, to some degree, race). I'm interested not so much in delivering a history as in exploring that history's ongoing process of revision. I therefore consider, first, the series and, then, the everyday in terms of their separate theoretical histor*ies*, before beginning to suggest some of the connections between them that I chart in this book.

⁂

By series fiction I mean quite simply successive novels or stories that are linked together, usually by recurrent characters or settings. There can be all kinds of discriminations within the term; in discussing particular kinds of succession, critics have attempted to differentiate sequels, say, from the series. Sharon Russell quotes one such distinction from James Robert Parish's *Great Movie Series*; at least when it comes to movies, Parish sees the sequel as a distinct unit—it follows "a self-contained film that spawns continuation follow-up films"—while the series is more messily intermixed, ongoing, and open-ended; it contains "a basic set of characters, governed by a particular backlog of events which control but do not hinder the future tide of their happenings."[2] Russell argues that, with the advent of television, what may have seemed historically like two different forms have merged: episodes in TV shows can often be related to each other as parts of a series as well as sequels. And they can also be serial in the sense that each episode "have an open ending" which is particularly "a state of crisis" (128) ("Thus a serial is defined not just by a lack of closure," Russell writes, "but by the way in which closure is refused" [128]). That focus on *how* the particular properties of the serial and the series impulse work—and how they work differently in different contexts—seems to me crucial to an understanding of the form.

Proponents of the strictest definition of series fiction might hold that it is not serial, since each narrative unit ends not with a crisis, a cliffhanger, but with a climax resolved through its denouement into regular closure, a closure which is then breached at the start of the next story. Anthony Trollope was already playing with these conventions in his Barsetshire series, however, by leaving the future of Lily Dale and Johnny Eames open (in what his readers at any rate saw as a state of crisis) at the end of *The Small House at Allington*, before settling it finally in *The Last Chronicle of Barset*. Dorothy Richardson's experiments in suspense and irresolution in her twentieth-century series, *Pilgrimage* (her third novel ends abruptly and without explanation with the suicide of her heroine's mother), continue what we might already see as a tradition of experimentation with open-endedness within series fiction. Such experiments in closure suggest that the series and seriality (as this introduction, and this book, assume) are also ultimately indistinguishable.

And, when it comes to nineteenth-century fiction, it is seriality (rather than the series) that has gotten most critical attention—especially the serial

[2] Sharon Russell, "Narrative Closure in Series and Serials," *Purdue University: Seventh Annual Conference on Film*, ed. Marshall Deutelbaum (West Lafayette, Ind.: Purdue University Press, 1983), 127–32; 127; all future references to this essay will appear in the text.

defined in terms of serial publication, of what Terry Eagleton has called a "literary mode of production," a "material practice" "constituted by structures of production, distribution, exchange, and consumption."[3] Hughes and Lund define the serial—they see it in terms of part-publication, "a continuing story over an extended time with enforced interruptions"—as the dominant literary mode of the Victorian era. They argue that serial publication was so effective in Victorian England because "the serial was attuned to the assumptions of its readers" (4). Eagleton sees such concurrence as the necessary effect of capitalism's workings: "Every literary text in some sense internalises its social relations of production . . . every text intimates by its very conventions the way it is to be consumed, encodes within itself its own ideology of how, by whom and for whom it was produced. Every text obliquely posits a putative reader, defining its producibility in terms of a certain capacity for consumption"(48). Literary form, as Bill Bell suggests, precisely because it is a "consequence of market and technological forces," becomes the very "articulation of the values of the age."[4] And serial publication was especially effective during Victorian capitalism because it constructed a mass readership that could supposedly afford to buy fiction on this installment plan.[5] Norman Feltes writes that serial publication is in this way the necessary literary manifestation of the rising industrial capitalism of the time because "industrial capitalism changed the market by 'enabling production—within certain limits—to expand its own markets, if not actually to create them.'"[6]

Materialist critics of the serial argue that the form of the novel as manifested through the mode of part-publication not only reflected the ideological assumptions of the time but did the work that installed and consolidated that ideology; the serial's most important ideological work was to produce and determine an audience for itself. The mass readership created by serial publication provided an effective arena for ideological schooling. Mary Poovey makes this case, for instance, in considering the supposed origin of popular serial publication, the myth of Charles Dickens's instant success with *The Pickwick Papers* because of its appeal to a "common human-

[3] Terry Eagleton, "Categories for a Materialist Criticism," in his *Criticism and Ideology: A Study in Marxist Literary Theory* (New York: Verso, 1976), 44–63; 45, 44, 47; all future references to this chapter will appear in the text.

[4] Bill Bell, "Fiction in the Marketplace: Towards a Study of the Victorian Serial," in *Serials and Their Readers, 1620–1914*, ed. Robin Myers and Michael Harris (New Castle, Del.: Oak Knoll Press, 1993), 125–44; 125.

[5] Hughes and Lund, *Victorian Serial*, argue that "rising literacy rates, urbanization, and growing prosperity played an essential role in making the serial a characteristic nineteenth-century form . . . affordable to a mass audience" (4); Eagleton, "Categories," that "the capitalist mode of production develops its dominant LMP by increasing the population, concentrating it in urban centres where it is within the reach of the mechanisms of literary distribution, and permitting it limited degrees of literacy, affluence, leisure, shelter and privacy" (49–50).

[6] N. N. Feltes, *Modes of Production of Victorian Novels* (Chicago: University of Chicago Press, 1986), 4.

ity." The part-publication Dickens hit on with that book was not new, but it succeeded—according to the standard account of the rise of the serial mode—because he had just the touch to uncover the shared attitudes within very different groups, bringing them together into one audience. Poovey maintains instead that serial publication succeeded because it provided an efficient mechanism for *creating* those attitudes: "the argument that Dickens 'comprehends' what makes his readers alike actually creates this likeness." [7] Rather than appeal to a likeness between different groups that was already there, Dickens's fiction "generate[d] the effect of describing the value it actually helped create" (108). It marks the outline of a readership that gives identity and meaning to those who assume it.

This interpellation of a mass audience marks the creation of the bourgeois subject—a subject made to feel an individual precisely so that it will be unaware of how it operates for capitalism as part of a mass (and will therefore continue to do so unthinkingly, rather than critically—a blindness necessary to the system since, as Marx suggests, a critical stance could ultimately lead only to revolution against capitalism). Jennifer Wicke considers Dickens's part-publications as themselves commodities; she contends that they represent a new literary mode (just like the new kind of advertising they mirror and promote), the very purpose of which is "to suggest new needs." [8] And, partly because there are always new ones, these needs are markedly unsatisfiable; they are always in excess of any particular object. The modern individual created by literary forms such as serial publication is the ideal consumer who is made endlessly to desire whatever capitalism wants to sell.

The serial works as an exemplary tool of capitalist production (specifically its self-production, its self-generation by forming the subjects that perpetuate it) through its own replications of the same: the ongoingness, the repetitiveness of serial publication. In this way, this literary mode reflects the ideological underpinnings of capitalism, which, Rachel Bowlby suggests, has always been seen by its materialist critics as itself serial in nature. She cites George Lukács's critique of the "episodic structure" of some nineteenth-century novels (which he finds "'only a thread . . . a superficial . . . fortuitous sequence'"—a critique to which I will return in my chapter on Woolf).[9] Such episodicness in novels underlies "the seriality of fashion in the endless appearance of new images of 'the new' and . . . the cycle of 'monotony' and 'novelty'" within culture (14); it is part of the logic that keeps capitalism going, that ensures that its "social reality . . . appears simply as a succession of separate images or scenes" (16). Horkheimer and Adorno also, like Lukács,

[7] Mary Poovey, *Uneven Developments: The Ideological Work of Gender in Mid-Victorian England* (Chicago: University of Chicago Press, 1988), 109; all future references to this book will appear in the text.

[8] Jennifer Wicke, *Advertising Fictions: Literature, Advertisement, and Social Reading* (New York: Columbia University Press, 1988), 29.

[9] Rachel Bowlby, *Just Looking: Consumer Culture in Dreiser, Gissing, and Zola* (New York: Methuen, 1985), 13; all future references to this book will appear in the text.

place a disconnected and meaningless seriality at the heart of what they see as the void of capitalist culture (as I explore more fully in my chapter on Oliphant and Yonge). Under capitalism, they argue, "everything has to run incessantly, to keep moving," and "the result is a constant reproduction of the same thing."[10] This means not just that capitalism is always and only about itself (it is "the meaningful content" of every cultural production [124])[11]; for Horkheimer and Adorno too, capitalism also perpetuates itself through the lure of unsatisfiable desires ("The culture industry perpetually cheats its consumers of what it perpetually promises" [139]). For bourgeois subjects, "the supreme law is that they shall not satisfy their desires at any price" (141). In this view, serial publication becomes so prevalent in the Victorian era as the effect of capitalism finally establishing its dominance; it is just one version of a series impulse essential to the self-perpetuation of that system.

That series impulse is what links the specific material character of serial publication to the more amorphous identity of series fiction in general. Marx's emphasis on the brute force of necessity, on the crucial role of economic forces in the formation of social identity, has meant that materialist critics of the serial focus on it largely as a material mechanism—a kind of literary manifestation and enforcer of an economic mode. But critics working from other theoretical groundings continue to consider the series impulse as a crucially informing factor in the constitution of modern culture and the production of subjects. A Foucault-influenced critic such as D. A. Miller turns, however, from serial publication in particular to series fiction in general (especially Trollope's). Just as Foucault's emphasis is on a more general and diffuse system of power (rather than a particular form of economics), Miller is interested in the less rigorously linked novels in a series, whose connections are not regimented by the demands of a production schedule (as are those of a single novel produced serially). More disseminated, harder to predict, the connections between such novels, their echoings of one another's characters, plots, and settings, reflect Foucault's notions of the intimate, but barely locatable, workings of power.

The relaxing of closure between novels in a series seems especially to perpetuate those workings. Miller writes of Trollope's Barsetshire series that "it is not that a novel like *Barchester Towers* quite deserves to be called 'open-ended,' though like very few nineteenth-century English novels, it both has

[10] Max Horkheimer and Theodor Adorno, "The Culture Industry: Enlightenment as Mass Deception," in their *Dialectic of Enlightenment*, trans. John Cumming (New York: Herder and Herder, 1944), 120–67; 134; all future references to this essay will appear in the text.
[11] Under capitalism, art forms have "ceased to be anything but style" (131)—a style which recycles nothing but more capitalism: "Amusement under late capitalism is the prolongation of work" (137). Popular art, for instance, in its own "cyclically recurrent and rigidly invariable types" (125) "occup[ies]" men's senses from the time they leave the factory in the evening to the time they clock in again the next morning with matter that bears the impress of the labor process they themselves have to sustain throughout the day" (131).

and is a sequel." [12] What I want to establish instead is that such relations were not "very few"; they were not isolated—many Victorian novels were part of a series, and all were probably read to some degree in relation to this predominant form. But Miller seems right when he suggests that the series form is continuous without being quite "open-ended," and that it arises precisely because of the system of power. Like Lukács, or Horkheimer and Adorno, Miller argues that Trollope's ironized endings ensure "the absence of [a] strong teleology," "a meandering succession of episodes" (122), which is important to the self-perpetuation of Trollope's fiction. It is what allows him to turn out novel after novel in a series: "while a strong sense of an ending may get the novels sold, it is a weak sense of one . . . that gets them written in lucrative quantities" (122–23). The ongoing prolificness embodied in the series is continuous with the politics of the social order which the series underwrites: "What at the phase of novel production is the superior efficiency of relaxing teleological construction . . . shows up in the finished novel-product as the viability of a social order that . . . no more foresees a resolution to the 'problems' that in fact sustain it than it envisions its own coming-to-an-end" (123). Foucault's notion of the social order also emphasizes that its motive force is to keep itself going. In this reading as well, the series becomes just another mechanism for self-continuation; it exemplifies the self-sustaining, self-generating dynamic of power.

The formal properties of the series represent a cycle of perpetuation and revitalization of the status quo. The series relaxes teleology and complicates closure while still to some degree preserving them; each novel in a series does end even as it leads to the next, and the series at some point stops, even if only because its author dies. This view of the series is like Horkheimer and Adorno's notion of capitalism, which gives the illusion of progress even if nothing in it ever really changes. Trollope's *Barchester Towers*, for instance, replays the plot of *The Warden* (Trollope, in fact, calls the second novel "Hiram redividus") [13] even though the story of Mr. Harding's relation to Hiram's Hospital seemed adequately settled the first time. The importance of the continuing repetition of something the narrative of Barsetshire has supposedly outgrown—and moved beyond—is marked by Mr. Harding's seemingly unnecessary retelling of this old story once again in *The Last Chronicle of Barset*, and to Adolphus Crosbie of all people. Although Crosbie cares nothing for Mr. Harding's story, he is perhaps made to hear it because he is formally bound by a similar structure; he is only in *The Last Chronicle* at all because it repeats the earlier story (from *A Small House at Allington*) of his courtship of Lily Dale.

Catherine Gallagher believes that this repetition which gets nowhere, this empty proliferation of the same thing, reflects culture's anxiety about the un-

---

[12] D. A. Miller, *The Novel and the Police* (Berkeley: University of California Press, 1988), 122; all future references to this book will appear in the text.

[13] Anthony Trollope, *Barchester Towers* (New York: Penguin, 1987), 420.

groundedness of value, the way language simply multiplies meanings like "the unnatural generation of money, which, in usury, proliferates through mere circulation, but brings nothing qualitatively new into being." [14] The series points to a social order based on the multiplication of mere signs, not real things, a realm of exchange divorced from the illusion of production. Gallagher thinks that writing in the nineteenth century came predominantly to represent this anxiety because of its serial character (specifically "the development of cheap serial publication" [43]). In this way, series fiction, even as it underwrites the social order, plays up its anxieties and, hence, exposes its illusions. That exposure may not lead to any effective resistance against the ideological assumptions that order the series and the system of power in the first place. Gallagher, who, like Miller, insists on a Foucauldian revision of Marx, would probably want to argue that the exposure is just another mechanism for the continued maintenance of power. My book, however (as my chapter on Holmes suggests), considers the series instead to explore the faultline between its perpetuation and its exposure of the logic of dominance, to suggest the ways that this tension can take on different political meanings and have different political effects in different contexts (a reading that seems to me to reflect the complexities of Foucault's own suggestions). This stance needn't translate into the inelastic liberatory politics of the version of deconstruction that Miller and Gallagher position themselves against: what the series seems to me to suggest through its very form is the way such political attitudes remain unfixed and changing, and keep posing us ongoing questions.

In one of the few books to engage directly with series fiction as a form (in her discussion of the *roman-fleuve*), Carol Collatrella maintains that the seeming open-endedness and continuousness of the series are not its only important characteristics; its sheer length, its expansiveness, its pushing past boundaries are also important. Such expansiveness demands a panoramic understanding, an emphasis on the way things take their meanings within a larger, always shifting, never quite determinable context. For Collatrella, this means that the subject of the series is by definition history (just as for Horkheimer and Adorno it was by definition capitalism)—and especially history understood as "the realistic portrayal of the multiplicity of society." [15] An emphasis on multiplicity seems to her a function of history, of nineteenth-century assumptions: "The founding principle of the *roman-fleuve*, the interrelatedness of novels in series, resembles the biological principle that all species are related. Although the metaphor of the natural world as a 'web of affinities' was later coined by Darwin, early evolutionists, in-

---

[14] Catherine Gallagher, "George Eliot and *Daniel Deronda*: The Prostitute and the Jewish Question," in *Sex, Politics, and Science in the Nineteenth-Century Novel*, ed. Ruth Bernard Yeazell (Baltimore: Johns Hopkins University Press, 1986), 39–62; 40; all future references to this essay will appear in the text.

[15] Carol Collatrella, *Evolution, Sacrifice and Narrative: Balzac, Zola, Faulkner* (New York: Garland, 1990), 7; all future references to this book will appear in the text.

cluding Buffon, also subscribed to a theory of nature that emphasized the interdependence of organisms" (15).

In a dispute with D. A. Miller about the inevitability of ideological containment in Trollope's series, George Levine, like Collatrella, sees the evolutionary principle of "gradualism . . . that change takes place primarily through 'imperceptible gradations'" over a long span of time, as underlying the interconnections of nineteenth-century fiction.[16] Levine sees this emphasis as tactical, a "conservative principle that allowed . . . revolutionary leaps" (543). Imagining change as occurring over a large sweep of time (such as evolution's eons or the several impossibly thick novels of a nineteenth-century series) seems to defuse the effect of that change, to hide the fact that it still might be radical in its consequences. Seen in this light, the expansiveness of the series might actually encode a kind of seditious politics, that can be tolerated, or imagined at all, because they are projected onto the long *durée*.

I explore the way the expansiveness of the series allows it to become a kind of cultural repository, to act as its political unconscious; simply because it represents so much, the series is bound to contain at least a trace of any conceivable cultural dilemma or fantasy. The series's multiplicity is crucial. Although D. A. Miller argues that a "wide, highly variegated network, with multiple and mutually correcting jurisdictions" (128) only leads to a more total and effective functioning of power, Levine contends that nineteenth-century science already teaches us something more difficult and complex about theory (and power): it helps us see the importance of retaining the "capacity to imagine a system that at crucial moments remain[s] unpredictable, inexplicable, beyond control" (549). The series, especially through its connection with the everyday, is the focus of this book because their mutual alignment seems to provide a site where we come closest to doing—where (despite its seeming impossibility) we keep trying to do—that kind of theory.

The paradox of the series is that, in seeming in its expansiveness to enclose *so* much, it exposes that totality as only an illusion. It highlights instead that there is simply more than we can ever enclose. Something must always be left out. Generating (from the series) a theory that has as one of its informing principles its inability to account for everything allows us to address what are otherwise closed questions: to engage, for instance, with other genders, sexualities, cultures, without attempting to define or speak for them. Homi Bhabha, for example, considers how serial repetitions begin to complicate distinctions between the same and the other. The uncanniness of our ultimate inability to tell apart things that we want to hold as distinct allows us, he suggests, "to face Progress with some unanswerable questions."[17] Rather than attempting to settle such questions, he writes, we might work instead

---

[16] George Levine, "Charles Darwin's Reluctant Revolution," *South Atlantic Quarterly* 91 (1992): 525–55; 539; all future references to this essay will appear in the text.

[17] Homi Bhabha, *The Location of Culture* (New York: Routledge, 1994), 238; all future references to this book will appear in the text.

to recognize where they come from, the ways they are tied to "a vision of social contradiction and cultural difference" (238). In this book that means an attention to gender in terms of the class issues raised by the materialists' economic critique of the series, but also in terms of issues of race. For just as the series is inextricably bound up with economics, it is also intimately bound to imperialism. As J. M. Coetzee writes: "One thought alone preoccupies the submerged mind of Empire: how not to end, how not to die, how to prolong its era." [18] This study accounts less for questions of sexuality, which modern theorists such as Judith Butler have clearly connected to issues of seriality, through her emphasis on performativity and iterability. Sexuality is one of the major unanswered questions here that keep this project ongoing and only partial, even as the writing of this particular book comes to an end. What's important about the series (seen as cultural repository) and the everyday (seen as the very medium of culture) is that they don't ever allow us to stray very far in our formal and thematic considerations from the specific social contradictions and cultural differences—such as gender, race, or sexuality—that make such considerations important.

❧

The everyday" as a term owes a great deal of its currency and vitality to the field of cultural studies. "Cultural studies" (like "feminism") seems to me actually not to designate a discrete field so much as to mark a place of exciting conflict about what "culture" means and how it might be studied. Some of the roots of this amorphous field—and, I think, this contradictory one (that's its strength)—lie in the social sciences: sociology, anthropology. From them, it has taken its focus on daily life (often the working definition in them, in fact, of culture). Some of the critics working within cultural studies don't want to see it as amorphous, however; they want to contain its conflict. This attempt to lay claim to the whole of cultural studies seems to have taken something else from the social sciences: a positivist attitude that relies on an immutable and absolute truth, that assumes that its way of studying culture is scientific, objective, the *only* way. My own critical approach rests on the belief that that kind of positivist stance wherever it arises is actually a kind of political strategy. What interests me here especially is the way that "the everyday" is called upon to legitimate that stance.

The revival of "the everyday" as a keyword in cultural studies is rich and exciting. This book couldn't have been written without it. Yet some strands of cultural studies call on the everyday as a kind of given, supposedly transparent. The series novels that I explore in this book show us, however, that an invocation of the everyday is a rhetorical strategy. The very attempt by a

[18] From *Waiting for the Barbarians*, quoted in Jane Marcus, "Britannia Rules *The Waves*," in *Decolonizing Tradition: New Views of Twentieth-Century 'British' Literary Canons*, ed. Karen Lawrence (Urbana: University of Illinois Press, 1992), 136–62; 136.

positivist cultural studies to ensure its authority through an everyday it assumes without questioning demonstrates the rhetorical use of the term. One way to map the rhetorical effects of "the everyday" is to investigate the various histories constructed for it as a conceptual category. One version of that history is in the work of Continental thinkers such as the historian Henri Lefebvre, which has been rediscovered and translated perhaps because of the rediscovery of the everyday by cultural studies.[19] Another important part of current cultural studies locates its own history differently. It sees itself as growing directly out of the Centre for Contemporary Cultural Studies at the University of Birmingham in England: the work of Raymond Williams, as well as that of critics such as Stuart Hall (a later director of the Centre), embodies this heritage for them.

And heritage, in the sense of direct descent, is for them the critical term: the question for them is not of the various histories of cultural studies, but primarily of one account. In the Routledge anthology *Cultural Studies*, for instance, which sets its task precisely as the definition and embodiment of that field, the editors claim they are interested in mapping "the diversity of positions and traditions that may legitimately lay claim to the name" of cultural studies.[20] They go on to locate that heritage squarely in Birmingham. Their anthology (drawn from a conference, to which they invited the contributors) is meant, in part, to combat what they see as ignorance of the roots of "cultural studies" in the Centre (which worked for a long time without recognition and with few resources) by those they think willing to "simply rename what they [are] already doing to take advantage of the [present] cultural studies boom" (10–11).[21] Yet associating the field's history with metaphors of pa-

---

[19] Lefebvre's 1967 *Everyday Life in the Modern World* has been available in English translation since 1984. Verso brought out the first English translation of his 1947 *Critique of Everyday Life, Vol. One* in 1991, and Blackwell published the first English translation of his 1974 *The Production of Space* in that year as well. I will discuss Lefebvre's *Critique* in more detail in the chapter on Doyle.

[20] "Cultural Studies: An Introduction," *Cultural Studies*, ed. Lawrence Grossberg, Cary Nelson, and Paula Treichler (New York: Routledge, 1992), 1–16; 4; all future references to the editors' introduction (abbreviated "Cultural Studies") will appear in the text.

[21] The editors are careful throughout their introduction to emphasize the ways that cultural studies "draw[s] on multiple methods simultaneously" (3). They list as only some of these methods: "textual analysis, semiotics, deconstruction, ethnography, interviews, phonemic analysis, psychoanalysis, rhizomatics, content analysis, survey research" (2). And they stress that "even when cultural studies is identified with a specific national tradition like British cultural studies, it remains a diverse and often contentious enterprise, encompassing different positions"(3). At the same time, however, they stress that "we believe it matters how cultural studies is defined and conceptualized. . . . cultural studies cannot be just anything" (3). As the bulk of the citations supporting their understanding of cultural studies (mostly to Stuart Hall, but also to Raymond Williams and Richard Johnson) suggests, they believe the best understanding of cultural studies lies in the British tradition: "It is the Centre for Contemporary Cultural Studies at Birmingham that adopted, constructed, and formalized the term cultural studies as a name for its own unique project. Some United States academics are willing to generalize about cultural studies in complete or virtually complete ignorance of the work that runs from Williams to many of the contributors in this book. It is hard to think of another body of work where that level of ignorance could be sustained unchallenged" (8–9). That history for them is important because, in part, it moved cultural studies away from "the extreme deconstructive possibilities of some

trilineage and inheritance, in the sense of laying claim to a legitimate name, begins to suggest effects that threaten the very diversity the editors support. A lot of the discussion after the presentations at the original conference (which, to their credit, the editors include in the anthology) is precisely about whom this particular view of cultural studies excludes in its attempts to define the term.[22] Michelle Wallace's query at the conference about why only two African American women were invited to speak points to one inadvertent, but perhaps inescapable effect, of defining cultural studies in terms of laying claim to legitimacy.[23]

Many of the essays in *Cultural Studies* refer often to the category of the everyday (a very rough count finds around a hundred references to it—one for every other page). The editors explicitly associate their focus as "the everyday terrain of people" (11) from the start. Yet neither their introduction nor any of the essays that follow, except for Meaghan Morris's, examines this category in any detail.[24] In the rest of this introduction, I go on to consider some of the ways "the everyday" is used by the figures in the Birmingham Centre—Williams, Hall, and others—taken for its significant ancestry by the introduction to *Cultural Studies*. The history I offer here is only partial; I'm more interested myself in kinds of cultural studies that see themselves as unconstrained by or excluded from such notions of heritage. What's exciting to me about cultural studies is precisely its current explosion and all the new things that various approaches attempt to do with it (a lot of recent work also questions the need for the field's consistency and cohesion[25]). Even in the late 1980s, Gayatri Spivak and Meaghan Morris (as I discuss here) suggested that the abrogation of difference remains a specter in any attempt to constitute culture as a field of study. Such work helps us revise the category of the everyday within cultural studies from a (seemingly) unproblematic ground supporting shared experience, theoretical consistency, and ultimate social harmony to a site of irresolvable difference, of conflict whose resolution is not simply delayed, but theoretically impossible.

The attempt to open the field to a range of approaches is often misinterpreted as attack. As Gayatri Spivak has observed, the poststructuralist critique of cultural studies can be "misread as 'postmodern modesties re-

versions of poststructuralism" (9). For a related critique of this anthology, which comes at it from a different angle, see Fredric Jameson, "On *Cultural Studies*," in *The Identity in Question*, ed. John Rajchman (New York: Routledge, 1995), 251–95.

[22] See especially "Discussion: Stuart Hall," (286–94) after Stuart Hall, "Cultural Studies and Its Theoretical Legacies" in Grossberg, *Cultural Studies*, 277–86.

[23] See "Discussion: Michelle Wallace"(664–71; 667) after Michelle Wallace, "Negative Images: Towards a Black Feminist Cultural Criticism," in Grossberg, *Cultural Studies*, 654–64.

[24] Meaghan Morris, "On the Beach," in Grossberg, *Cultural Studies*, 450–73.

[25] See the more recent anthology collected by one of the editors of *Cultural Studies*, which includes many of that book's contributors: *Disciplinarity and Dissent in Cultural Studies*, ed. Cary Nelson and Dilip Parameshwan Gaonkar (New York: Routledge, 1996); see also an essay that reflects in part on the conference from which *Cultural Studies* was drawn, Renato Rosaldo, "Whose Cultural Studies? Cultural Studies and the Disciplines," in *Mass Culture and Everyday Life*, ed. Peter Gibian (New York: Routledge, 1997), 26–33.

plac[ing] Marxist certitudes.' . . . This is the risk that one must run in order to understand how much more complicated it is to realize the responsibility of playing with or working with fire than to pretend that what gives light and warmth does not also destroy."[26] What poststructural skepticism might add to the study of culture is a perpetual self-questioning: how do all critics repeat the universalizing moves we wish to put into question? In what ways do we annul difference and invoke consensus at the moment that our theories conjure up that talisman of the real, the everyday? This approach demonstrates a very different utility for "the everyday" than the one an empirically influenced cultural studies claims for it: rather than an essence grounding a system, "the everyday" becomes a construction whose exposure as such calls that system—and its politics—into question.

By politics here I mean more than the idea of change, often associated with social intervention and collective action. One poststructural revision of this term has been Barbara Johnson's, who associates politics instead with undecidability, the very province often dismissed as apolitical: "There is politics precisely because there is undecidability," she writes.[27] Perhaps another way to think about politics is to associate it with conflict: not with settling conflict (which usually means domination anyway) but with sustaining it. Politics can also mean contestation, the fight not to nullify but to assert disagreement—the struggle to be heard rather than silenced, to uncover the vision of unity and harmony as what seeks to silence, to show it up as somebody else's ideal. It is precisely the promise of this politics that makes the idea of cultural studies exciting and compelling to a critic concerned with race and gender as well as with class, such as bell hooks (who, not incidentally, felt uncomfortable and out of place at the *Cultural Studies* conference, to which she was invited).[28] She writes: "Usually scholars in the academy resist engagement in dialogues with diverse groups where there may be critical contestation, interrogation, and confrontation. Cultural studies can serve as an intervention, making a space for forms of intellectual discourse to emerge that have not been traditionally welcomed in the academy."[29] To do so may require undoing the complacencies of commonalty; to allow for difference may mean continually destroying the sense of shared goals that the editors of the Routledge anthology understandably enough want to see as connecting and defining some entity that could be called "cultural studies." Seen in this light, "the everyday," a site where a great deal of cultural studies has tra-

[26] Spivak, "Constitutions and Cultural Studies," *Yale Journal of Law and the Humanities* 2 (1990): 133–47; 145–46. All future references to this essay (abbreviated "Constitutions") will appear in the text.
[27] Johnson, "Apostrophe, Animation, and Abortion," *A World of Difference* (Baltimore: Johns Hopkins University Press, 1987), 184–99; 194.
[28] See her comments in "Discussion: Stuart Hall," 293–94.
[29] hooks, "Culture to Culture: Ethnography and Cultural Studies as Critical Intervention," *Yearning: Race, Gender, and Cultural Politics* (Boston: South End Press, 1990), 123–34; 125. This essay goes on to reflect on hooks's discomfort at the *Cultural Studies* conference (134).

ditionally located those commonalties, also refuses them, and, in this sense, keeps politics going.

"Culture can no longer be conceived outside the everyday." [30] So writes Henri Lefebvre, identifying the study of culture with the study of the everyday. Although British cultural studies has in a sense paralleled Lefebvre—Edward Ball suggests that an emphasis similar to Lefebvre's on "*la vie quotidienne* may be familiar to English readers as the target of critique within the body of 'Cultural Studies' that has grown up in Britain since the 1950s"—Lefebvre's discussion of "the everyday" doesn't just inform such work:[31] it also helps us to reflect on and problematize it. Just what is the everyday—or culture for that matter—and what might Lefebvre (or any cultural studies) mean by the relation between them?

Such questions are difficult to answer because their terms seem undefined. And, according to Lefebvre, that is the point: defining "the everyday" is not easy. People meet with a certain opacity in the term "the everyday"; they experience a resistance to comprehending it that, he suggests, is part of its meaning. Lefebvre can only gesture to it: for him, the everyday is "the unrecognized" ("Leftist" 78); it is what "is practically untellable." [32] Invoking the everyday is an attempt to invoke "lived experience" ("It is lived experience [*le vécu*] elevated to the status of a concept and to language" ["Leftist" 80]). Yet, in equating the everyday with the "real, empirical, practical" in *Everyday Life in the Modern World* (11), Lefebvre also recognizes that "the real" is precisely what cannot be represented. Everyday life eludes metaphor, "evades the grip of forms" (182). "Writing can only show an everyday life inscribed and prescribed" (8) because "everyday insignificance can only become meaningful when transformed into something other than everyday life" (98). Although in his *Marxism and Totality* Martin Jay singles out Lefebvre as one of the Western Marxists to whom the concept of totality is central, in Lefebvre's discussion of the everyday the possibility of such totality is also put in question;[33] with the introduction of the everyday, Lefebvre's structuralism becomes poststructuralism.

[30] Lefebvre, "Toward a Leftist Cultural Politics: Remarks Occasioned by the Centenary of Marx's Death," trans. David Reifman, *Marxism and the Interpretation of Culture*, ed. Cary Nelson and Larry Grossberg (Chicago: University of Illinois Press, 1988), 75–88; 82. All future references to this essay (abbreviated "Leftist") will appear in the text.

[31] Ball, "The Great Sideshow of the Situationist International," *Yale French Studies* 73 (1987): 21–37; 29.

[32] Lefebvre, *Everyday Life in the Modern World*, trans. Philip Wander (New Brunswick, N.J.: Transaction, 1984), 24; all future references to this book (abbreviated *Everyday*) will appear in the text.

[33] Jay, *Marxism and Totality: The Adventures of a Concept from Lukács to Habermas* (Berkeley: University of California Press, 1984). This is a contradiction in Lefebvre's work that Jay attempts to resolve with the—to me similarly contradictory—idea of an open and indeterminate totality (296–99). Jay emphasizes Lefebvre's other work, but barely mentions *Everyday Life in the Modern World*, perhaps because it begins to deconstruct the very structures Lefebvre elsewhere constructs.

The opacity of the everyday, then, is crucial: it reflects the poststructural recognition that all anyone can do is gesture to the real; subjects can't experience it unmediated and untransformed by expectation, by representation, by their own attention to it. By making the invisible visible, by giving a form and content to an experience so vague and so seemingly natural that part of its significance is that its subjects can't define it, defining—*theorizing*—the everyday transforms it into what it is not: "It is not possible to construct a theoretical and practical system such that the details of everyday life will become meaningful in and by this system" *(Everyday,* 98).

Yet an attention to the everyday is important because it is there that we can see how society works. Lefebvre argues that "daily life is the screen on which our society projects its light and shadow, its hollows and its planes, its power and its weakness" *(Everyday,* 64–65). The everyday's "irreducibles, contradictions and objections" (75) are crucial to Lefebvre, however; the everyday encodes society's power, but also its weaknesses. To make the everyday into an object of study carries with it "the distinct advantage of orienting oneself toward the future" (76). An attention to it therefore becomes a form of "cultural revolution" (204). It marks a change that is utopic in the way that *"we are all utopians,* so soon as we wish for something different" (75). This utopia grows out of an attention to the everyday—a defamiliarization of it—because, for Lefebvre, such defamiliarization is itself what revolutionizes culture: "a revolution takes place when and only when . . . people can no longer lead their everyday lives" (32). The very attempt to put the everyday into a system, constantly refined by its refusal and deconstruction of that system, becomes a model of representation—of theory—transformed by the resistant and elusive real that it also transforms, and provides Lefebvre with what he considers an adaptive and creative political practice; he insists that "the limitations of philosophy—truth without reality—always and ever counterbalance the limitations of everyday life—reality without truth" (14).

In insisting on a system, Lefebvre still gestures to totality, but his system continually calls its own notion of totality into question. Although his strategy is to "gather together culture's scattered fragments for a transfiguration of everyday life" *(Everyday,* 38), the stylistic twists and turns of Lefebvre's own mercurial prose, his emphasis on contradiction, suggest that part of that transfiguration is a stubborn refusal of coherence. Emphasizing such "contradictions of lived experience" is (Alice Kaplan and Kristin Ross suggest) how Lefebvre's work helps us find "the Political, like the purloined letter, . . . hidden in the everyday." [34] Yet Lefebvre's work is not free of the explicit attempt to resolve such contradictions into coherence. The need for totality asserts itself strikingly in places where a different politics, or a politics of difference, makes Lefebvre recodify and stabilize the political and theoretical flexibility his treatment of the everyday opens up.

[34] Alice Kaplan and Kristin Ross, "Introduction," *Yale French Studies* 73 (1987): 1–4; 3.

The difference of gender in particular seems to renew such restrictions. Considering the everyday, Lefebvre argues, allows him to focus on the collective subject—no less than all of mankind: "*Homo sapiens, homo faber* and *homo ludens* end up as *homo quotidianus*" *(Everyday,* 193).[35] Yet a curious division goes on within this supposedly unified collective; mankind, perhaps not surprisingly, comes to mean man in particular. Lefebvre admits that everyday life actually "weighs heaviest on women. . . . they are the subject of everyday life and its victims or objects" (73). But he also argues that "because of their ambiguous position in everyday life . . . they are incapable of understanding it" (73). According to the old logic that women can't understand something because they embody it, the contradictions of the everyday, which make it opaque to everyone (but in which also lies its oppositional potential), make it particularly so to women. Women become responsible for a constraint that afflicts some people more than others. In fact, Lefebvre suggests that mankind's "conditioning, seeping through the channels of a highly organized everyday life, succeeds mainly on the level of woman or 'femininity.' Yet femininity also suggests feminism, rebellion and assertiveness" (67).

For Lefebvre, the feminine indoctrinates mankind into a dominant culture whose terms of everydayness it also teaches those subjects not to contest, even though "femininity" is itself an ambiguous term that carries with it an oppositional force—"feminism"—it might put to better use. The implication is that because women can't understand such ambiguity, don't recognize their contradictory position, they squander that feminism; it turns into mere "assertiveness." Lefebvre writes of women's attempts "to escape by the roundabout method of eluding the responsibilities of consciousness, whence their incessant protests and clumsily formulated, directionless claims" *(Everyday,* 92). In refuting this (failed) feminism, Lefebvre reasserts notions of teleology with a vengeance; yet the roundabout and directionless protests of women he condemns, rather than eluding responsibility, may instead be precisely the place to locate a different politics.

In blaming women for people's unconscious relation to the everyday, Lefebvre casts women in another too-familiar role: both women and the everyday are smothering. They come to stand for an overwhelming totality. Each, for him, represents the very forces that create subjects, both in literally producing them and then normalizing them into culture; this meaning of the everyday helps to explain its collapse with culture ("Culture can no longer be conceived outside the everyday"). Women and the everyday in this sense represent that definition of culture as a medium embracing its subjects, one sustaining and shaping them (people can't conceive *outside* it). In this chain

[35] And, despite the contradictions implied by the decentering of the subject, for Lefebvre, such a collective subject remains an entity nonetheless: "A class cannot be considered as a philosophical 'subject' any more than can a society; but they possess unity, wholeness, totality, in a word 'system'": Lefebvre, *Everyday,* 41–42.

of synonyms, the everyday, synonymous with culture, also becomes synonymous with ideology: "Ideologies are made of understanding and interpretations . . . of the world and knowledge plus a certain amount of illusion, and might bear the name of 'culture'" (*Everyday*, 31).[36] Such ideology is not false consciousness, but what creates and determines consciousness itself. The everyday becomes the term for the embracing totality that tends people, molds them, makes them into subjects.

Lefebvre himself seems to try to elude such a determining force in a roundabout way when he bars *women* from effective agency and critical consciousness. In making the lack of critical consciousness and agency an issue of gender (of essential—biological—lack), Lefebvre repeats the old dodge that asserts that man—somehow naturally more complete—might have more power, and might more easily escape constraint. But this line of argument is one the everyday also complicates, if not resists. Rather than posing a dilemma one might settle, an either/or in which some subjects are constrained while others go free (that scapegoats some into constraint in order to provide the illusion of freedom for others), the contradictions of the everyday in Lefebvre's account make it stand instead for a more *complex* political relation of the subject to culture and ideology. It marks the site not only where people are determined in ways they can't see, but where they project and imagine (as Lefebvre suggests, utopically) how to think outside and elude what determines thought and imagination. Considered in this light, the difficulty of defining the everyday comes to reflect the very impossibility of thinking outside the structures of our thought.

This unraveling of Lefebvre's discussion suggests that "the everyday" doesn't magically provide a stable ground. It's not simply that the meaning and value of "the everyday" change depending on the needs of the system that invokes it (although, of course, such changes do occur). More than that, the shifts and contradictions in its meaning demonstrate the complications of fixing one simple or stable relationship between culture or ideology and the subjects they create, of encompassing culture and ideology within a single field, call it politics, or theory, or cultural studies. For Lefebvre, the everyday enforces a constraining politics when it keeps people from recognizing it as political. Yet Lefebvre only dances around the understanding that to bring things to consciousness—to put them in a system—does not dispel the (political) unconscious. Part of the complexity of the everyday is that it represents at one and the same time conflicting registers and assumptions; it charts a fault-line between the conscious and unconscious, between determining powers people can see and those they can't, between theories that seek change and those that enmesh their subjects in determinism. It marks a site of conflict that makes consensus—about lived experience as well as about that experience's transformative potential—difficult if not impossible.

---

[36] Or, as he writes later: "ideologies, institutions, in one word culture" (*Everyday*, 198).

The everyday becomes a crucial category because its consolidations and de-constructions touch directly on the subject's relation to ideology and culture.

In the history of British cultural studies that the editors of the Routledge anthology believe is crucial to any understanding of "cultural studies," the use of "the everyday" draws on Marxism differently. Yet it still maintains this tension between totality and conflict. Just *whose* claim best reflects the Marxist totality—*whose* theory most coherently describes culture's coherence—is the focus of an early debate between Raymond Williams and E. P. Thompson. To read their work in this way might itself seem to be a poststructural commonplace: it's accepted now (the argument might go) that the illusion of coherence is a repressed part of *any* theory, a product of the desire to account for everything. The explicit claim for totality and coherence is just an early (insufficiently theorized) position of the new left—especially of those like Thompson who were particularly hostile to theory. Yet this early position is still an enduring one. The claim to be able to account for everything continues to inform discussions of cultural studies such as Stuart Hall's and Richard Johnson's, both later associated with the Birmingham Centre.

One of the texts this cultural studies most frequently invokes as it constructs its genealogy is an early essay of Williams's, "Culture Is Ordinary" (the Routledge anthology, for instance, sees it as key; the work I consider here by Hall, Johnson, and Brantlinger refers to it too). This essay unites questions of culture and the everyday (as lived practical experience), foregrounding the everyday in the study of culture. Where Lefebvre's treatment of the everyday emphasizes its fracturing possibilities, Williams's focuses on the ordinary for its power to unite and integrate: to Williams, the everyday reveals that culture is not just Culture, not just the special province of the arts and learning, but "a whole way of life." [37] As for Lefebvre, for Williams the role of the critic is to bring recognition of the everyday to critical consciousness, but this recognition means a recognition specifically of synthesis: people need to see that culture is ordinary "so that the whole actual life, that we cannot know in advance, that we can only know in part even while it is being lived, may be brought to consciousness and meaning" ("Ordinary," 9).

But such totality precludes difference, especially the difference of gender. Although Williams acknowledges that the understanding of the "whole actual life" can only be partial, such failure to understand it does not devalue the whole itself; the achievement of that total knowledge become a promise, a (historical) process in which individuals and society are always engaged: the influence of Marx on Williams here is clear. The sense of "culture as a process," culture as "the cultivation of something," a kind of "'long revolution' . . . [a] sense of a movement through a very long period," which

[37] Williams, "Culture Is Ordinary," *Resources of Hope* (New York: Verso, 1989), 3–18; 4. All future references to this essay (abbreviated "Ordinary") will appear in the text.

Williams later emphasizes in his more complicated definition of the term in *Keywords*, is already implicit in this early essay.[38] In "Culture Is Ordinary," Williams especially identifies the ongoing process of ordinary culture with legitimacy—with the very process of genealogy itself in a kind of male-linked series: Williams locates culture in generations of descent, with a specific patrilinear inheritance that moves from his grandfather to his father to himself:

> Culture is ordinary: that is where we must start. . . . To grow up in [my] family was to see [its] shaping of minds. . . . My grandfather, a big hard labourer, wept while he spoke, finely and excitedly, at the parish meeting, of being turned out of his cottage. My father, not long before he died, spoke quietly and happily of when he had started a trade union branch and a Labour Party group in the village, and, without bitterness, of the "kept men" of the new politics. I speak a different idiom, but I think of these same things. ("Ordinary," 4)

Although Williams does gesture to a few women in this essay, they're denied this pattern of relation and connection. The inheritors of the whole way of life—shaped by the everyday but also shaping it—are men. They forge its history and bring it to critical consciousness.[39]

Yet Williams's oedipal narrative actually puts into question his idea of ordinary culture as a whole way of life. Williams's most famous critic, E. P. Thompson, immediately questioned this allegory of the everyday. Thompson was bothered particularly by Williams's sense of a shared tradition built on relation and commonalty. For way of "life" Thompson wants to substitute way of "conflict" or way of "struggle," and, by so doing, he argues, really focus on "activity and agency" rather than the impersonal continuity of life implied by generational progression.[40] Yet ultimately that emphasis on agency actually lays to rest Thompson's own sense of conflict; caught in the perpetual paradox of all criticism (mine included), in seeming to disagree with Williams, Thompson winds up sounding a lot like him.

Thompson too uses gender to clinch his own argument, simply continuing the oedipal progression Williams charts. Once again woman stands for a culture she embodies but doesn't share, specifically for the (male) Tradition of

[38] Williams, *Politics and Letters: Interviews with "New Left Review"* (New York: Verso, 1979), 154, 155.

[39] *This* view of culture as an active process played out by men is actually very similar to Lefebvre's; Lefebvre too constructs culture as a process, a narrative in which men are heroes. To him, it evokes an image "of Sleeping Beauty. She does not doze on flowers and on fragrant grass but on a thick mattress of texts, quotations, musical scores—and under a vast canopy of books, sociological, semiological, historical, and philosophical theses. Then one day the Prince comes; he awakens her and everything around the forest comes to life along with her—poets poetizing, musicians musicking, cooks cooking, lovers loving, and so on. . . . Culture is not merely a static palimpsest of texts; it is lived, active, which is what the fable of the wakened princess suggests to me" ("Leftist," 81–82). Like Williams, Lefebvre here gives culture a tradition ("the vast canopy of books"), and suggests how that tradition through the intervention of the cultural critic (who else is the Prince?) comes alive, is seen to be lived, active, everyday: poets poetizing, but also cooks cooking.

[40] Thompson, "The Long Revolution," *New Left Review* 9 (1961): 24–33; 33. All future references to this essay (abbreviated "Long") will appear in the text.

(high) Culture itself ("Burke, Carlyle, Mill, Arnold" and Eliot), the reverence for which Thompson feels occludes conflict in Williams's account. He writes:

> At times, in *Culture and Society*, I felt that I was being offered a procession of disembodied voices—Burke, Carlyle, Mill, Arnold— . . . the whole transmitted through a disinterested spiritual medium. I sometimes imagine this medium . . . as an elderly gentlewoman and near relative of Mr. Eliot, so distinguished as to have become an institution: The Tradition. There she sits, with that white starched affair on her head, knitting definitions without thought of recognition or reward . . . and in her presence *how one must watch one's LANGUAGE!* The first brash word, the least suspicion of laughter or polemic in her presence, and The Tradition might drop a stitch and have to start knitting all those definitions over again. ("Long," 24–25)

A derided tradition becomes an elderly gentlewoman, whose near relation to Eliot (another kept man?) points up his effeminacy—and, through him, the effeminacy—the passivity—of the rest of the tradition. The burlesque of this passage wrests the fate of history out of the hands of this harmless Clotho, a monitory figure only to those still scared by women; a polemic so brash that she would drop her yarn completely, Thompson implies, is the very antidote to the outdated and elitist malaise of history this figure represents. And, through her unattractiveness, Thompson rids the oedipal line of history of the need for a woman altogether. Williams's allegory for ordinary culture still implies some woman (wife, mother) as a vehicle through which the generations of men must pass. By personifying high culture as a maidenly old woman (by suggesting that the tradition's writers are themselves somehow old-maidenly), in dispelling the need for high culture, Thompson gets rid of the need for woman too.

Woman is a scapegoat that allows Thompson to dispel Williams's Leavisite reliance on the great tradition, to assert instead a culture that he thinks really is ordinary. In attacking the great tradition, Thompson admonishes Williams for the homogenizing tendency implied in it: "He must resist the temptation to take his readers and himself into the collective 'we' of an established culture, even when he uses this device to challenge assumptions which 'we' are supposed to hold (and yet which have been under challenge from a minority for over 100 years)" ("Long," 26). He asserts that the picture Williams gives of the 1840s is very different from his own and that the principles Williams sees ordering the social totality of the time are "an arbitrary selection" (28). Yet such ambiguities and uncertainties do not, for Thompson, point to any underlying problems in the writing of history, especially in conceiving of it as a totality. On the contrary, if Williams "has not yet succeeded in developing an adequate *general* theory of culture," it is simply because his understanding of it is not Thompson's own—or, rather, not really Marx's (28). For Thompson, an adequate tradition does exist, "notably that tradition which originates in Marx" (30)—especially in Thompson's own kind of Marxist history; any other "synthesizing discipline will

very soon make imperialist claims. . . . Now if Williams by 'the whole way
of life' really means the *whole* way of life he is making a claim, not for cultural history, but for history" (31). Such history somehow elides the problems of imperialism implicit in synthesis because it focuses on the ordinary,
the everyday: "the working people's daily 'way of conflict.'"[41]

Thompson was an early and influential critic of imperialism. As part of
that critique, he suggests here that "unless we insist upon the role of minorities and of conflict in the process of making [the whole way of life] we
might get an unpleasantly conformist answer" about what that culture looks
like ("Long—II," 36). Yet minorities and conflict have a hard time modifying his own account as well. Criticizing a fragment of Williams's language ("a
society which had changed its economy, which under pressure was changing
its institutions, but which, at the centres of power, was refusing to change its
ways of thinking"), he suggests that "certain difficulties in Mr. Williams'
style . . . arise from his determination to depersonalise social forces. . . . if
Dame Society was changing all these garments, who or what bewhiskered
agent was standing outside the boudoir and forcing her to this exercise?"
("Long," 26). By gendering society as female, Thompson places himself out
of it and becomes the bewhiskered agent of male potency (for Thompson
also wants to effect some changes in society; the thrust of his argument is
that his kind of Marxist synthesizing will allow such agency, while Williams's
will not). In Thompson's version too, woman is excluded from a role in the
making of the whole way of life (she just passively embodies it, and is acted
upon). This is indeed unpleasantly conformist (it is a too-familiar tale that
such radical thinkers as Williams and Thompson could so unconsciously uphold the gender conformity of their era). And what of the other "minorities"
so excluded as not even to figure in this drama? Can any synthesis keep from
being imperialist? If the need to take "into account the culture of Congo ex-
ploiters" (which Thompson says Williams has not done) to bring things into
a properly *"whole* view" demands "the taking of sides," will that in itself
change anything? Isn't the problem instead that even the best-intentioned desire to take the side of the exploited doesn't prevent using such groups nonetheless to embody and underwrite the ordinary dramas of white male agency,
in the way that woman does here?[42]

An astute critic, Williams himself, of course, sees these dangers. His later
work takes Thompson's criticism into account, especially in the attempt to
theorize the role of conflict and difference within a common culture.[43] "The
idea of a common culture," Williams writes, "is in no sense the idea of a simply consenting, and certainly not of a merely conforming, society. One returns, once more, to the original emphasis of a common determination of
meanings by all the people, acting sometimes as individuals, sometimes as

[41] Thompson, "The Long Revolution—II," *New Left Review* 10 (1961): 34–39; 38. All future references to this essay (abbreviated "Long—II") will appear in the text.
[42] Thompson, "The Long Revolution—II (Addendum)," *New Left Review* 11 (1961): 70.
[43] See his direct response to this critique, in *Politics and Letters*, 134–36.

groups, in a process which has no particular end, and which can never be supposed at any time to have finally realized itself, to have become complete."[44] Yet Williams remains committed to this idea of common culture, unlike later poststructurally inspired Birmingham critics, such as Kobena Mercer (who, as I discuss in my Trollope chapter, suggests a hybrid culture instead). Underlying the need for commonalty is an unspoken privileging of wholes, the assumption that one must criticize "that divided and fragmented culture we actually have" ("Idea," 35) because division and fragmentation are somehow in themselves bad (why?). As Stuart Hall notes, rather than modifications and qualifications in Williams's thought, "one is struck by a marked line of continuity through these seminal revisions."[45] Discontinuities, fragmentation, contradiction, conflict—all just become subsumed within a larger cultural totality, which the form of Williams's own writing reflects.[46] Hall argues that, throughout his life, Williams continued to stress "the interactivity of practices and . . . the underlying totalities, and the homologies between them" ("Two Paradigms," 61). When Williams writes, then, that "culture is ordinary: through every change let us hold fast to that" ("Ordinary," 6), he holds fast as well to an identification of the everyday with some ultimate totality.

Although clearly outlining what he calls the "totalizing movement" in Williams (and Thompson), Hall, by accepting their assumptions about a desired wholeness, echoes that movement in his own definition of cultural studies. Within the Birmingham Centre, Hall was a significant force, an incisive and nuanced critic of racism in the study of culture.[47] Yet his understanding of culture as ideally unified ultimately restricts his critique and damps the diversity of cultural studies by suppressing its conflict. In "Cultural Studies: Two Paradigms," an essay that cites "Culture Is Ordinary" (59) and is itself often cited by others in defining cultural studies, Hall's stated purpose is to find out "around what space [are culture's] concerns and concepts unified?" ("Two Paradigms," 59).[48] He spends this essay charting how the divergent strands of what he calls Williams's and Thompson's "culturalism," and a

---

[44] Williams, "The Idea of a Common Culture," *Resources of Hope*, 32–38; 37. All future references to this essay (abbreviated "Idea") will appear in the text.

[45] Hall, "Cultural Studies: Two Paradigms," *Media, Culture and Society* 2 (1980): 57–72; 60. All future references to this essay (abbreviated "Two Paradigms") will appear in the text.

[46] Hall writes that for Williams (and Thompson), "'culture' is those patterns of organization . . . which can be discovered as revealing themselves—in 'unexpected identities and correspondences' as well as in 'discontinuities of an unexpected kind'—within or underlying *all* social practice" ("Two Paradigms" 60). Discontinuities are important because they point to the larger pattern.

[47] For a testament to the powerful influence of Hall's work, see *Stuart Hall: Critical Dialogues in Cultural Studies*, ed. David Morley and Kuan-Hsing Chen (New York: Routledge, 1996).

[48] Hall elsewhere identifies "culture" and "totality"; see his "Cultural Studies and the Centre," in which he writes: "Perry Anderson has—in our view correctly—argued that such a [Parsonian] sociology could produce no concept of 'totality' and, without that, no concept of 'culture' either": "Cultural Studies and the Centre: Some Problematics and Problems," in *Culture, Media, Language: Working Papers in Cultural Studies, 1972–79* (London: Hutchinson, 1980), 15–47; 21. All future references to this essay (abbreviated "The Centre") will appear in the text.

"structuralism" he associates with Lévi-Strauss and Althusser, are actually "integrated" into one another (59). Hall *is* interested here in structuralism, which he associates elsewhere with the everyday; the early Barthes and Lévi-Strauss are useful, he argues, because they bring "the term 'culture' down from its abstract heights to the level of the anthropological, 'the everyday'" ("The Centre," 30). He is interested in structuralism, however, because it "has the conceptual ability to think of a unity which is constructed through the *differences* between, rather than the homology of, practices" ("Two Paradigms," 68); when structuralism shades over into poststructuralism, he balks ("Of course, the stress on difference can lead—and has led—the structuralisms into a fundamental conceptual heterogeneity, in which all sense of structure and totality is lost" [68]). He wishes instead somehow "to think of the 'unity' of social formation as constructed, not out of identity but out of *difference*" (68). Crucial to Hall is retaining the model of unity, which he recasts as "unity-in-difference," "complex unity" (68), some way of incorporating differences "without losing . . . grip on the ensemble which they constitute" (69).

The paradox of "unity-in-difference" is interesting as a utopic ideal; Hall's writing is moving, and has been influential, precisely because of the optimism and idealism propelling it. In practice, such a paradox may look very much like Mercer's "hybridity." Yet Hall's own work reveals the insidious pressures that keep trying to subsume difference *under* unity, to impose a hierarchy, to resolve the paradox. Hall refers elsewhere to "the contradictions of everyday life" (a particular emphasis of feminism, he suggests), but the goal remains to resolve them;[49] although contradiction might seem to emphasize difference rather than coherence, these contradictions (according to Hall) are banished at those abstract heights in which culture is somehow made whole again, as it has been in the early "culturalism" that Hall, in this sense, repeats, more than modifies.

Hall's colleague Richard Johnson also acknowledges, but still attempts to synthesize away, the troubling heterogeneity of difference. In his essay "What Is Cultural Studies Anyway?" Johnson works to give "an account of the whole."[50] Attempting to preserve the idea of unity or coherence, he observes that "a lot hangs, I think, on the *kind* of unity or coherence we seek" (38) and argues for a coherence that would somehow connect yet preserve fragmentation. He would do this, it seems, by a substitution of terms: "We need ways of viewing a vigorous but fragmented field of study, if not as a *unity* at least as a whole" (41). For Johnson, cultural studies provides this kind of wholeness; no "one discipline or problematic [can] grasp the objects of culture as a whole," but cultural studies, encompassing all disciplines, can

---

[49] Hall, "Introduction to Media Studies at the Centre," *Culture, Media, Language,* 117–21; 121.

[50] Johnson, "What Is Cultural Studies Anyway?" *Social Text* 16 (1986/87): 38–80; 73. All future references to this essay will appear in the text.

(41). Within cultural studies, conflicting approaches and readings of culture harmonize, "all [become] true"; "theoretical and disciplinary fragmentations" join together (45–46). (In a diagram, Johnson maps cultural studies as a connecting circle.) Just as for Thompson, who argues that a focus on synthesis will allow "the New Left to gain in intellectual coherence" ("Long—II" 37), for Johnson too a theoretical valorization of wholeness somehow upholds his theory's own completeness.

The challenge of integrating the complexity of everyday life into this circle, Johnson argues, provides cultural studies with its focus. In his history of it, cultural studies began when its practitioners "turned [their] assessments from literature to everyday life" (38). It is precisely because everyday life seems so ambiguous—"In everyday life, textual materials are complex, multiple, overlapping, co-existent, juxta-posed, in a word, inter-textual" (67)—that it needs to be embraced within cultural studies. He writes: "Cultural studies is a heightened, differentiated form of everyday activities and living. Collective activities of this kind, attempting to understand not just 'common' experiences but real diversities and antagonisms, are especially important, if they can be managed, and subject to the caveats which follow" (79 n51). Johnson's caveats, however, transform the threat of antagonism back into commonalty. For instance, although Johnson admits that attempts by ethnographers to map the intertextuality of everyday life into a coherent pattern have seemed to annul differences within the everyday—such ethnographies fit "the Other" into their own patterns, thereby "pathologising subordinated cultures" (70)—for Johnson, such problems are simply temporary: in their understandable enthusiasm for the social totality, such ethnographies have forgotten that "fundamental social relations have not [yet] been transformed" (70). And Johnson himself synthesizes the differences of various other critics into his own approach, downplaying the way feminism and critiques of racism have directly criticized the ethnographic mode he maintains here, and recasting feminism as a handmaiden to cultural studies (40). For Johnson, feminism and critiques of race become supportive (not at odds with him, or within themselves), and what they especially support is this idea of synthesis that they supposedly act out in everyday practice; in this way, "feminism and anti-racism" are important not so much in themselves but because they "have kept the new left new" (40); their differences from Johnson's position are incorporated within it.

It is precisely this process of unification through incorporation that Patrick Brantlinger highlights in his summary of the work of the Birmingham Centre: "One of the disabling aspects of academic work cultural studies aimed to overcome was the alienation of the disciplines from each other: knowledge should be made whole again."[51] Like Hall and Johnson, Brantlinger qualifies his insistence on synthesis (he writes that cultural studies is "a coa-

---

[51] Brantlinger, *Crusoe's Footprints: Cultural Studies in Britain and America* (New York: Routledge, 1990), 62; all future references to this book will appear in the text.

lescing movement, a sort of magnet gathering the various theories that now go under the label 'theory' into a problematic and perhaps impossible synthesis" [10]). Still, he takes that synthesis as an ideal goal nonetheless. One subtext of *Crusoe's Footprints* is an attempt to defend the version of cultural studies that comes from the Birmingham Centre against the fragmenting influence of poststructuralism.[52] To Brantlinger, despite poststructural attacks on "the (supposedly) failed Enlightenment project," "*some* version of history and of the social totality is necessary for there to be *any* form of social criticism"; it is in Marxism that one can find an "effective concept of social totality that would unify the cognitive field in a rigorous manner" (72).

Just what can happen when you work toward "*some* version of . . . unification" (73) is perhaps clearest in Brantlinger's treatment of those groups considered other, exactly those groups he feels cultural studies can empower. Despite his own excellent summary of the problems of the assimilationist model underlying the early construction of American studies, the route Brantlinger suggests to empower those others works through their rhetorical assimilation into the dominant culture.[53] Brantlinger's reading of marginalized groups concludes that not only are the "Crusoes . . . ourselves; so are the Fridays" (11). Implicitly opening up Marx's reading of *Robinson Crusoe* to include Friday, Brantlinger is in a sense too inclusive: in Brantlinger's syntax at least, Friday becomes another projection of, a part of, dominant culture. When Brantlinger writes "ourselves," he doesn't mean for that group to represent dominant culture. He means, I think, what Homi Bhabha suggests too when *he* writes "The 'other' is never outside or beyond us; it emerges forcefully within cultural discourse, when we *think* we speak most intimately and indigenously 'between ourselves.'"[54] But Thompson's criticism of Williams applies here too: this utopic gesture to commonalty unwittingly echoes one of dominance because that gesture annuls conflict. It doesn't admit subject positions to whom its own best-intentioned desires for connection still seem oppressive (admittedly, the very contradiction that has

[52] Yet he is worried that even Stuart Hall has fallen prey to this influence; he writes of one essay in which "Hall himself offers a history of British cultural studies as a sort of French dependency. This is undoubtedly the weakest version of the story" (63). Just what is wrong with poststructuralism is actually quite shifting and contradictory in Brantlinger's account. On the one hand, even though he is in favor of his own version of totalism, he criticizes deconstruction for being too totalistic; in Derrida's account (he writes) "there is 'nothing outside the text' or beyond the field of our representations. As with totalistic versions of ideology, representation conceived as consciousness as such makes critique difficult or impossible: starting from Derrida's position, there seems to be no way to distinguish more or less accurate representations from misrepresentations, truth from falsehood, reality from fiction" (104). On the other hand, what is dangerous about deconstruction is that it is fragmenting; he writes elsewhere of "the deconstructionist 'abyss' of completely indeterminate 'difference'" (116).

[53] See 26–33. Here he criticizes "the American rhetoric of unifying the plural and harmonizing differences," and the attempt by American studies to reconcile different disciplines and create social harmony (27). A "'balance' or unity that minimizes conflict" is the liberal goal of American studies, according to Brantlinger.

[54] Homi Bhabha, "Introduction: Narrating the Nation," in *Nation and Narration*, ed. Homi Bhabha (London: Routledge, 1990), 1–7, 4.

also wrenched and educated a well-intentioned, white, middle-class feminism, whose liberal gestures on its own terms haven't been enough). Brantlinger's statement that Friday is "ourselves," despite his best intentions, similarly risks the appropriation of other races and cultures that programs such as African American as well as women's studies have worked to overcome: it doesn't acknowledge how the other (black people, for example, or women) might have its own many voices, in sharp discord with anyone else's sense of "ourselves."

Valuing connection over division has certain effects; Brantlinger uses the undefined practice of the everyday as a benchmark to reject approaches that might otherwise be divisive to collective harmony, especially feminism. Associating the everyday with women and feminism, he refers directly to Lefebvre's association of women and the everyday (138) and quotes Michele Barrett's contention that "feminism has politicized everyday life—culture in the anthropological sense of the lived practices of a society" (136). An identification of women and the everyday as lived experience is crucial because, when feminism strays from such experience, it ceases for Brantlinger (just as for Lefebvre) to function as feminism. Only an attention to the everyday, Brantlinger argues, can rescue feminism from poststructuralism: he quotes Catherine Stimpson to blame the breakdown of feminist solidarity on deconstruction's fragmenting of "consensus" (130).

Brantlinger's differences from deconstruction are fine. After all, I am arguing that disagreements about the study of culture are precisely what make that study interesting. Yet Brantlinger misrepresents poststructuralism when he dismisses it as apolitical (because not predicated on collective unity), rather than seeing in it an alternative politics, a form of politics different from his own. To him, it is poststructuralism's arrogance about matters of the everyday that makes it apolitical; he writes that Derrida is actually trapped in the metaphysics he wishes to deconstruct, "a metaphysics which (as Derrida recognizes) tries to look over the heads of most people and to transcend everyday language use, and therefore overlooks the fact that 'culture is ordinary'" (41). Poststructuralism increases the "distance between theorist and 'the masses'—real people, 'lived experience,' 'the practice of everyday life'" (170)—which he assumes as the given that legitimates his own approach. Not only does such supposedly elitist theorizing weaken feminism's consensus, but it is just such fragmentation that makes feminism politically neutral enough to succeed where Marxism fails (for Brantlinger, a very backhanded compliment). According to him, the very lack of unity within feminism, by blunting its political effect, has been the means to its acceptance within the (conservative) academy (136–37). What is especially interesting about this claim is not whether it's wrong or how much it simplifies, but that Brantlinger makes it in the midst of his own attempt to establish cultural studies within the academy too. The everyday in this account, rather than preserving difference, becomes the means to annul other theories of culture. And this criticism of poststructuralism and feminism seems to me an overstatement of Brantlinger's position, at odds with the invaluable work he has himself done. His own many-faceted scholarship has rightfully established him as a major influence on the constitution of Victorian studies in the American academy, making it a field in which issues of gender and race are central. The need to trace a "legitimate" heritage of British cultural studies imposes a kind of closed family circle, a patriarchal inheritance that ignores the contradictory impulses within even those who invoke it around the name of the everyday.

It is precisely to open the hermetic and insular definition of cultural studies that feminists such as Gayatri Spivak and Meaghan Morris redefine the category of the everyday. In her feminist critique, Gayatri Spivak, putting American borrowings of British cultural studies in their own cultural context, implies that the particularly American dependence on the idea of a united "we" helps explain the recent attraction here of one particular version of cultural studies, codified through a gesture to its British heritage.

Just as those dominant politically offer the illusion of something called "We the People," promising through this consensus an agency supposedly not available to the electorate in their everyday lives,[55] for Spivak this kind of cultural studies is itself also involved in the production of a managed and controlled category of the "we."[56] Part of "the academic's [unexamined] social task" ("Making," 782), Spivak writes, is this very same "production of something called a 'People'" ("Constitutions," 134). But, Spivak argues, in participating in this production, cultural studies must ask questions about its own "constitution" ("Constitutions," 144). Critics need consciously to recognize and intervene in their own production of this illusion of consensus—to recognize especially just how the formation of cultural studies or indeed any other program as a field depends on problematic assumptions about unity and consensus.

Such consensus needs especially to be called into question because the dominant powers use the consensus they create as a way to define themselves as coherent and unified in the face of unsettling difference. For Spivak, however, the dynamic that unsettles such power already lies "dormant and un-

---

[55] Spivak writes: "The electoral mobilization of We the People provides an alibi for crisis management among the powers by allowing the party to claim 'A People's Mandate,' while the citizen's political everyday life operates without the necessity of his/her participation": Spivak, "The Making of Americans, the Teaching of English, and the Future of Cultural Studies," *New Literary History* 21 (1990): 781–98; 782. All future references to this essay (abbreviated "Making") will appear in the text.

[56] In making her argument, Spivak is working from Derrida's deconstruction of "We the People" as the origin for a political state that is itself actually their origin: "Derrida points out that 'the good People of these Colonies' in whose name the representatives sign the American Declaration of Independence do not, strictly speaking, exist. As such they do not yet have the name and authority before the Declaration. At the same time, they are required to produce the authority for a Declaration which gives them being" ("Constitutions," 142). Derrida argues that "this outrageous thing [is] quotidian" ("Constitutions," 142)—and, as both normal and exceptional, it begins to put its own logic into question.

critical in the everyday" ("Making," 782); critics need to bring such contradictions into consciousness, especially through the attempt explicitly to
insert women or people of color into the reigning consensus, thereby fracturing it. Such terms cannot easily be introduced into this equation: introducing
women, who function in culture as pluralized subjects ("Constitutions,"
145), introducing African Americans, already represented within the Constitution's discussion of representation not as complete but as fractional (as
slaves, counted as "three fifths of all other persons" ["Constitutions," 136]),
both put the notion of completeness and coherence into question. One way
to modify Spivak's perhaps overly optimistic deconstruction here might be
by recognizing that such corporate entities do constitute themselves precisely
by writing such fractured subjects into their very Constitutions. Is simply
pointing up such contradictions enough? Might those contradictions help
form, rather than undermine, the constructions that write them in the first
place?

Spivak argues that the everyday as a category is especially useful when
attending to the differences excluded from stories of consensus; she in fact
redefines the everyday, not as lived experience, some "real" underlying consensus, but as the ongoing deconstruction of that illusion of experience. Spivak argues that such an illusion is still necessary to the self-definitions of
women or people of color: "It cannot be denied that the best and the worst
in the history of the feminist movement . . . entails the presentation of *woman*
as unified representative subject" ("Making," 795). Yet such unification must
be endlessly interrogated—can't help but be interrogated she thinks by postcolonial subjects like herself caught between cultures—even as it is assumed:
"This impossible 'no' to a structure, which one critiques, yet inhabits intimately, is the deconstructive philosophical position, and the everyday here
and now of 'postcoloniality' is a case of it" ("Making," 794).[57] Feminists, in
deconstructing the unity they appeal to, as well as the unity appealed to in
culture and a cultural studies that emphasize integrity, need to play upon the
tension between the need for consensus, and the price paid for that (temporary) wresting into a collective. To construct entities like "cultural studies"
and "feminism," while they may be useful and effective, "is thus not an unquestioned teleological good but a negotiation with enabling violence"
("Constitutions," 146).[58]

Spivak attempts in this essay to work carefully between deconstruction and

[57] For those feminists not defined as third-world or women of color, Spivak writes: "U.S.
women . . . are in a unique and privileged position to continue a *persistent* critique of mere
apologists for their Constitution, even as they use its instruments to secure entry into its liberating purview. Favorite sons and daughters who refuse to sanctify their father's house have their
uses. Persistently to critique a structure that one cannot not (wish to) inhabit is the deconstructive stance" (Constitutions," 147).

[58] The utopia inscribed here within cultural studies becomes its recognition of its interventions as provisional, limited, incomplete: "Indeed, the hoped-for future of everything written in
the name of cultural studies today must, I think, be the classroom staged as intervention, too
painfully aware of its limits to dream only of integration" ("Making," 796).

construction, to unsettle the foundation of dominant powers while providing some ground for political action (her politics, like Barbara Johnson's, rest in that very unsettling). To recognize the illusion of consensus as an illusion (even while invoking it), so that the recognition becomes part of everyday life, seems to be the major strategy of these politics. But just what Spivak's enabling "everyday here and now" is remains to be deconstructed; it is a category Spivak herself cannot help assuming, the very category to which it remains impossible to say no. Though refusing a notion of harmony and coherence, Spivak's cultural studies is similar to British cultural studies in this: the everyday remains the locus and grounding of her construction of culture and politics; the intransigence of the everyday's aura of referentiality in two such different approaches (it permeates my own thinking as well) stresses the rhetorical power of the term.

For Meaghan Morris, what different versions of cultural studies share in their use of the category of the everyday is a tendency to attempt to discredit their opponents with it. In "Banality in Cultural Studies," she argues that in this regard both the Continental and British—poststructural and humanist—practitioners of supposedly progressive cultural studies become practically indistinguishable.[59] "It is remarkable," Morris writes, "given the differences between them . . . that neither . . . leaves much place for an unequivocally pained, unambivalently discontented, or *aggressive* theorizing subject" (20)—the kind of subject Morris locates in feminism or radical left politics: "there is an active process going on in both of dis-crediting—by direct dismissal . . . or by covert inscription as Other . . . —the voices of grumpy feminists and cranky leftists" (20).[60] Anything that insists on itself as the only cultural studies works these exclusions specifically in attempting to define "an appropriate theoretical *style* for analyzing everyday life" (6); it begins "to define and restrict what it is possible to do and say in its name" (4). The aim to dismiss or inscribe opposition becomes the attempt to extinguish politics.

[59] Morris, "Banality in Cultural Studies," *Discourse* 10 (1988): 3–29; all future references to this essay will appear in the text. In describing her "irritation about two developments in recent cultural studies" Morris writes that one of them is Continental theory, including "Jean Baudrillard's revival of the term 'banality' to frame a theory of media. It is an interesting theory that deals in part with the tele-visual relationship between everyday life and catastrophic events. Yet why should such a classically dismissive term as 'banality' re-appear, yet again, as a point of departure for discussing popular culture?" (3). The other is British cultural studies ("the program of the Birmingham school in England" [5]) which she associates especially with the work of Ross Chambers and John Fiske: "the thesis of cultural studies as Fiske and Chambers present it runs perilously close to this kind of formulation: people in modern mediatized societies are complex and contradictory, mass cultural texts are complex and contradictory, therefore people using them produce complex and contradictory culture. To add that this popular culture has critical and resistant elements is tautological—unless one . . . has a concept of culture so rudimentary that it excludes criticism of and resistance from the practice of everyday life" (19). Morris wishes to "frame a comparison" (11) between these two groups.

[60] Morris suggests that British cultural studies "most often proceeds *from* admitting class, racial, and sexual oppressions *to* finding the inevitable saving grace" (20).

The attempt by a field calling itself "cultural studies" to create "a collective subject, 'the people'" (17) Morris thinks, must record the price of this endeavor in its ethnographies of the everyday; when the ethnographer fails to take into account her or his own investment in (and production of) this collective, "the people" actually just becomes the ethnographer's mask, circularly "both a source of authority for a text and a figure for its own critical activity," in part a figure for *its* own coherence and completeness (17). If critics take seriously the ways the everyday "'can reorganize the place from which discourse is produced'" (as de Certeau has argued), then—to Morris—that "means being very careful about our enunciative and story-telling strategies—much more careful than most cultural studies (and feminist writing) has been in its mimesis of a popular—or 'feminine'—voice" (24). Morris's own "our" here shows that it is difficult to be careful enough; my own rhetoric too demonstrates that it is probably impossible to keep from creating a sense of collective endeavor in the very act of critiquing that move.[61] But what's involved for her in making the attempt is a revision of the everyday that "may also come around eventually in a different, and as yet utopian, mode of enunciative practice" (27).

It is the way "'everyday practices . . . alternately exacerbate *and disrupt* our logics'" (23) that Morris wishes cultural studies to make explicit—to open cultural studies up to politics which already disrupt it, to "dilemmas, which . . . no modern critical mode can resolve" (7). And it is, ultimately, that incompatibility between the logics of poststructuralism and British-influenced cultural studies that has been the point of my argument too. The kind of cultural studies that locates its history within the Birmingham Centre has much to offer and is in no way as unified or schematic as its own self-presentation or my recasting of it implies (after all, Hazel Carby, Kobena Mercer, and a range of "joyous and inventive practitioners" of cultural studies have come through that Centre). The actual richness and diversity of cultural studies—and British cultural studies in particular—can be read in the introduction to another, more recent, Routledge cultural studies anthology. In *The Cultural Studies Reader*, Simon During writes:

> Cultural studies is increasingly drawing attention to . . . "everyday life." Ironically, however, cultural studies . . . derives the notion from an avant-garde tradition which turned to everyday life not as a basis for reassuring consensus but as an arena capable of radical transformation. . . . There can be little doubt that everyday life does provide an area where imaginative intellectual analysis and description may produce liberating effects. . . . None the less, theory which grounds itself on a sense of the everyday does not avoid . . . problems. . . . Most relevantly, within a discipline that has globalized itself through affirming other-

---

[61] That this "our" leaves some people out gets pointed up by bell hooks's explicit criticism of Morris as one poststructural feminist who doesn't mention writing by women of color; hooks, "Postmodern Blackness" in *Yearning*, 23–32; 24.

ness, it is important to remember the obvious point that everyday life is not everywhere the same. . . . [T]he everyday does not possess a single history. It exists within multiple histories. . . . So it is not as though appeal to everyday life can avoid the intractable questions . . . which cultural studies began by addressing. But the fact that textualizing and historicizing everyday life, with all its seduction, leads to these kinds of difficulties is another sign that the discipline has real vitality. There remains much work to do.[62]

This is the work that essays such as Spivak's and Morris's begin to tackle. The very difficulty of their essays, the difficulties of teasing out from them the implications of the everyday, reflects (as it does in Lefebvre's work) the complications of keeping questions open, of eschewing resolution for an as yet undefined alternative: this is an approach whose ambiguities seem to its critics a weakness rather than a strength. The very openness of their work seems to me, however, to be its promise. It complicates the assumption of legitimate descent, linear progression, as the only narrative model—just as series fiction does.

The meeting of the series and the everyday—the insistence of this formal principle and this topic that they be thought together—seems to me exciting precisely because it is a linkage that at the same time resists formulation; it remains unpredictable if only because of its own vastness and multiplicity. The entwining of the two describes a system that cannot account for everything precisely because it holds so much. It marks the place where writers attempt to imagine a kind of cultural infinity: the endless replication of what is already the very universe people take for granted around them, a firmament within which they can consciously locate themselves only (and only fleetingly) through a cognitive wrench. Each of the chapters that follows attempts to make such a breach in the fabric of unconsciousness.

❧

Most of this book focuses on mid- to late-Victorian fiction: Oliphant's Carlingford Chronicles appear in the 1860s and 1870s; Yonge writes about the same time; Trollope's series span the '50s through '80s, and Doyle writes from the '80s clear up into the next century. But, although the later Victorian period emphasizes the series impulse and the everyday, I don't mean to argue that such formal and thematic issues are somehow restricted to that period. Just the opposite. But what do we make of the appearance of these issues in other periods? Other critics, such as Hughes and Lund, as we've seen, argue that the Victorians felt a peculiar interest in the series for historical reasons, their place in the rise of capitalism most particularly. Yet, for me, the entwining of the series and the everyday puts into question any un-

[62] Simon During, "Introduction," to *The Cultural Studies Reader*, ed. Simon During (New York: Routledge, 1993), 1–25; 24–25.

examined notion of history as teleology, rise, growth, or progress. That doesn't mean that I think that we should do away with history. As I've noted, constructing a history for cultural studies has powerful effects. Constructing a *provisional* literary history can certainly also be useful. To some degree, my project seems to follow this form: I treat these writers in chronological order, reflecting on the earlier writers by considering Dorothy Richardson (*Pilgrimage* was published between 1915 and 1938 and completed posthumously), Virginia Woolf, and John Galsworthy (themselves writers primarily of the teens, 1920s, and 1930s). The appearance of the series and a focus on the everyday within modernism might, through contrast, seem to flag just what is telling about the Victorians' interest in them. But it is important to remember that what that contrast is actually telling us about is our own particular construction of history, which, no matter how compelling, is just one way of putting things together; we need to foreground and examine the form producing the supposed facts of history as much as we do those facts themselves. Just as it questions the *way* cultural studies constructs its history, my book, then, no matter how much it conforms to the expected conventions of historical progress—or at least continuance—also questions those conventions. I wish us to question our assumptions of literary history as one long series.

The form we give history is constituted to a great extent by the same impulse giving rise to the series form in the Victorian novel, and in narrative itself. The very history of the novel that literary criticism constructs is tied to notions of seriality. The early works we tend to see as key emphasize it: in distinguishing its own realism from previous romances, *Don Quixote* is intrigued explicitly with how a principle of replication works itself out within the heart of narrative—how that principle in fact seems to inaugurate a new tradition—an interest that helps explain that work's own extension into two novels. The sequels to *Pamela* and *Robinson Crusoe* similarly enact an impulse to repeat, to persist beyond closure. Such sequels might be said only to gesture toward the series form the Victorians would directly explore; as Peter Brooks has argued, two isn't enough—"three . . . is perhaps the minimum repetition [necessary] to suggest series and process." [63] And even in these earlier novels, this interest in expansiveness beyond closure is also tied to an interest in the everyday. The writing-to-the-moment of Pamela's correspondence to some degree performs an emphasis on dailiness that Defoe also attempted to capture through Crusoe's inventories on his island. Our historicizing, as it constructs its own series, can find elements of the series impulse or the everyday that it labels nascent or prototypical, supposedly waiting to develop fully with the growth of the form.

One Victorian reaction to such supposed predecessors might be articu-

[63] Brooks, *Reading for the Plot: Design and Intention in Narrative* (Cambridge: Harvard University Press, 1984), 9.

lated through an understanding of the category of series *as* process, as history in the sense of going on. We might highlight Scott's Waverly Novels, organized through the loosely associated, infinitely expandable frame, *Tales of My Landlord*, as the first important series, providing the Victorians with a bridge between what the eighteenth century saw as narratable and their own definition of narrative possibility. Here, especially, the sense of what can be narrated has everything to do with the definition of history: the series as a mode of narrative connection combines in Scott with an antiquarian interest in preserving the ongoing sweep of history, explicitly through an attention to the details of people's everyday life and speech. He cannot think series and history apart, and the everyday is the glue that connects them.

Thackeray is often cited as the next serious series writer; Trollope certainly saw Thackeray as his most direct antecedent.[64] Thackeray's historical fiction (and Scott was an important influence on Thackeray) seems to reveal how the mid-Victorians retain a notion of the series as history. Submerged within the "nineteenth-century commonplace" that "*Henry Esmond* was the best *historical* novel ever written" lies that novel's relation to the series impulse;[65] although it was one of the few novels that Thackeray did not publish serially, *The History of Henry Esmond* grows out of "a series of burlesque novelettes" that he published previously in *Punch*, and itself gestures to the series through its sequel, *The Virginians* (recurring characters in other Thackeray novels, including the narrator Pendennis, connect *Pendennis*, *The Newcomes*, and *Philip* into a kind of series as well).[66]

But Thackeray's historical novels also provide a good example of the constructedness of history. And that constructedness suggests that we might see the series (and with it, history) in another light: not as a pattern of genealogy and development, but as what imperils those connections. George Lukács complains that Thackeray doesn't really give us *history* because of Thackeray's insistence on exposing the artifice of literary and historical construction. Thackeray's antiheroism in particular seems to Lukács to degrade what he thinks ought to be the "organic integral components" of narrative, by which he means the narrative of Marx's plot of history; the explicit constructedness of Thackeray's history punctures the illusion of history's inevitable progress, its transcendent relation to an underlying reality. Because Lukács refuses to see (his version of) history's transcendence as an illusion, Thackeray's self-conscious artifice seems threatening. Lukács dismisses it as jaded and alienated. For Lukács, the "vividly seen connections" of true history vanish in Thackeray's work into mere seriality.[67]

---

[64] Trollope, of course, wrote a monograph on Thackeray for the "English Men of Letters" series (1879).

[65] John Sutherland, "Introduction," to *The History of Henry Esmond* (New York: Penguin, 1972), 7–24; 7.

[66] Sutherland makes the point about *Punch* (11).

[67] George Lukács, *The Historical Novel*, trans. Hannah Mitchell and Stanley Mitchell (London: Merlin Press, 1962), 205; all future references to this book (abbreviated *Historical*) will appear in the text.

As Lukács writes elsewhere about the naturalists (dangerously close to whom he feared Thackeray veered): "The so-called action is only a thread on which the still lives are disposed in a superficial, ineffective, fortuitous sequence of isolated, static pictures."[68] This bankrupt sequentialness is for Lukács part and parcel of the everyday; Thackeray's "distortion of history" comes through "its degradation to the level of the trivial and the private"; he satirizes historical characters precisely by depicting them within the everyday, revealing "no more than the normal, sociable habits of everyday private life," in which great men are exposed as just men after all (personally motivated—drunks, liars, windbags), and history exposed as story (*Historical*, 204).

Yet, despite Lukács's claims, it seems to me that Thackeray doesn't totally do away with the notion of history as some kind of certain or master narrative—or even with an understanding of that narrative in terms of growth. Thackeray's demystification of history may serve to mystify something else: *his* own "greatness" within literary history. Thackeray's view of history may cut others down to size, but it does so by subjecting them to his measure. By presenting his own pastiche of eighteenth-century style in *Henry Esmond* (down to such typographical archaisms as the yoked double-s's), Thackeray literally *creates* his own literary history too. John Sutherland suggests "It is quite feasible to see in *Henry Esmond* the nineteenth-century mind tracing the genealogy of its civilization in the eighteenth century."[69] (Even Lukács agrees that "the literary traditions of the eighteenth century lend cohesion to [Thackeray's] works," [*Historical*, 206]). Thackeray assumes a nineteenth-century notion of history as inevitable evolution that allows his work to grow out of this past, while also correcting and perfecting what it has discovered to be inchoate stirrings within earlier narrative—as well as redirecting contemporary fiction back to what he wants to define as its proper lineage. By placing himself at this series's end, he forges the path of its history. In Thackeray's work, what the eighteenth century produces is Thackeray.

Later Victorians, as I explore, begin to dismantle the optimism of inevitable progression embodied in Thackeray. Marx's work may be the premier example of such dismantling; his very genius might have been to appropriate Victorian myths of evolution as the means with which to undo them. The poststructural theory inspired by Marx with which I explore the fiction in this book emphasizes not progression but sheer succession— the nightmare of the empty replications of industrial capitalism's assembly line. To these theorists, the series impulse and the everyday in this fiction specifically expose the workings of dominant ideology; one thing Lefebvre or de Certeau implies is that an explicit emphasis on the series and the everyday should take us beyond simply perpetuating dominant ideology; the unexamined logic of capitalism encourages an unthinking replication which

[68] George Lukács, "Narrate or Describe?" in his *Writer and Critic and Other Essays*, trans. Arthur D. Kahn (New York: Grosset & Dunlap, 1970), 110–48; 144.
[69] Sutherland, 21.

such analysis is meant to foreground, trouble, perhaps unravel. But what does it mean that the nineteenth-century novel in which both theorists locate the beginning of this critique doesn't mark the end of literary history (or of ideology for that matter), at least when it comes to the series and the everyday? Just as the novel doesn't stop with Thackeray, the series and the everyday don't stop with later Victorian fiction. In my later chapters I ask: what might responses to that fiction—figured in terms of its immediate successor, a modernism that still seems obsessed by it—tell us, not just about its refraction of the series impulse and the everyday, but about literary history in general?

This book considers Dorothy Richardson, for instance, because her *Pilgrimage* continues what other critics might see as a Victorian emphasis on the series and the everyday. To have the literary history of the series form lead to *Pilgrimage* already puts that history into question because Richardson's work has remained to a great degree unrecognized by (because so problematic in) literary history. *Pilgrimage* both is and isn't modernist because it explores what literary history wants to claim as modernism's defining preoccupations—the breakdown of closure, for one, and its relation to the decentering of the self—but it does so through what that history (in order to construct itself as a history at all) needs to make an archaic hold-over from a past age: *Pilgrimage* opens up the self through the breakdown of closure accomplished by the series impulse.

That series's central character, Miriam, may seem properly modernist in breaking down the fixity of identity, blurring the boundaries between self and world, but Richardson achieves that effect by expanding the character to fill her multivolume, open form—a collapse of series with character that had already to some degree been suggested by Trollope's Palliser series and Doyle's Sherlock Holmes. The status of *Pilgrimage* is also vexed because, like that of Trollope (and Oliphant and Yonge), Richardson's emphasis on the series has meant just too much for the tradition to take in; she saw each novel that made up *Pilgrimage* as "a single chapter of one book."[70] As critics have noted, even after her work had stretched to thirteen volumes (and several thousand pages), Richardson continued to insist on its incompleteness.[71] For

[70] Gillian Hanscombe, "Dorothy Richardson versus the Novel," in *Breaking the Sequence: Women's Experimental Fiction*, ed. Ellen G. Friedman and Miriam Fuchs (Princeton: Princeton University Press, 1989), 85–98; 85.

[71] Ellen G. Friedman, "'Utterly Other Discourse': The Anticanon of Experimental Women Writers from Dorothy Richardson to Christine Brooke-Rose," *Modern Fiction Studies* 34 (1988): 353–70; 357. Elaine Showalter writes: "Most of all, Richardson's art is afraid of an ending. Looked at from one point of view, her inability to finish is a statement in itself, a response to the apocalyptic vision of Wells and Lawrence. If men were so obsessed by their sense of an ending that they could not understand the present moment, women were outside of time and epoch, and within eternity. But as Richardson grew older, her relationship to *Pilgrimage* became more obviously possessive and anxious. The book was an extension of herself; to complete it was to die. When Dent published an edition of *Pilgrimage* in 1938, Richardson was deeply upset to read that critics thought this was the whole book. From 1939 to 1951 she worked on a final section of *Pilgrimage*; after her death the manuscript (published as *March Moonlight*) was discovered among her papers; presumably it was still unfinished. Her concep-

some critics, the lack of closure that strings it from volume to volume makes it "a landmark text in early modernism."[72] Other critics find in *Pilgrimage* a "failed" modernism because its relentless emphasis on a single conscious-ness represents "a *closure* rather than a revolutionary rupture" with a sense of fixed identity and the past forms depicting it.[73] I argue that the series im-pulse within Victorian fiction already questions whether the refusal of clo-sure is particularly modernist to begin with.

And in questioning that, I begin to question the assumptions of literary history too. How do we categorically impose a difference between Victori-anism and modernism? In *Pilgrimage*, the series puts into question a literary history that wants to impose stable meanings on periods and forms (as if the series's extra-ordinary length, for instance, could only be mimetic of the pos-itivist assumptions of encyclopedic documentation, say, rather than of a de-construction of closure). My own book deviates from that sense of (literary) history by maintaining instead that the series can and does do both at the same time.

For it is not that the series ever disappears as a novelistic form. D. H. Lawrence, after all, was another modernist who continued to make use of it. And one could argue that the series has become even more prevalent today as a popular form, in endless detective, adventure, and romance fiction. Hughes and Lund suggest, for instance, that it leaves the canon outright and becomes simply a popular form: movies, radio, soap opera, science fiction, mystery novels, romance sagas—these are the contemporary places we lo-cate the series.[74] What marks the difference of the series now—and keeps Richardson on the outskirts of the tradition—is *how* we regard it. Although the Victorians regarded it as a popular form too (see my chapter on Oliphant and Yonge), we see it as solely popular, in no way serious. Lawrence's lugubri-ous trumpeting of the seriousness of his gender may have been a defense pre-cisely against an otherwise automatic dismissal of his form as trivial.

My project's excursion into literary history, then, emphasizes the extension of—not the break with—a Victorian heritage by writers such as Richard-son. My point here is not so much that *Pilgrimage* is neglected because, rather than being shockingly new, it insisted on a form that the new century wanted to see as outdated. That remains, I think, an important point. But I'd like to

tion of the book as a continuous process was the myth that enabled her to publish at all": Elaine Showalter, *A Literature of Their Own: British Women Novelists from Brontë to Lessing* (Prince-ton: Princeton University Press, 1977), 261.

[72] Lynette Felber, "A Manifesto for Feminine Modernism: Dorothy Richardson's *Pilgrim-age*," in *Rereading Modernism: New Directions in Feminist Criticism*, ed. Lisa Rado (New York: Garland, 1994), 23–39; 36.

[73] Michele Barrett and Jean Radford, "Modernism in the 1930's: Dorothy Richardson and Virginia Woolf," in *1936: The Sociology of Literature, Volume 1—The Politics of Modernism*, ed. Francis Barker, Jay Bernstein, John Coombes, Peter Hulme, David Musselwhite, and Jen-nifer Stone (n.p.: University of Essex, 1979), 252–72; 265, 269.

[74] Linda K. Hughes and Michael Lund, "Linear Stories and Circular Visions: The Decline of the Victorian Serial," in *Chaos and Order: Complex Dynamics in Literature and Science*, ed. N. Katherine Hayles (Chicago: University of Chicago Press, 1991), 167–94.

take it even further, to assert *Pilgrimage*'s seeming archaism in order to argue something else: that the series form itself militates against the very sense of history as something that progresses, especially something that progresses through abrupt revolution and rupture. It may work against a sense of history altogether if we need to understand history in terms of change, in terms of historical difference. Raymond Williams actually offers another model of history: history as accretion, sedimentation—encoding elements defined as emergent or residual depending on our placement in it.[75] A contemporary of Richardson's, John Galsworthy, makes clear in his novels that identity is a function of history in this sense, a function of where one stands within the rip-tides or whirlpools of generational connection (and it bears remembering too that Richardson objected to the phrase "stream of consciousness" because she thought human existence more like a deep pool).[76] All Galsworthy's characters—the supposedly succeeding generations of "young" and "very young" progeny—don't actually succeed, but repeat an almost mythic pattern (the conflict between Soames and Irene) at the same time that they alter it. The expansiveness of the series, of a work like *Pilgrimage* or the Forsyte saga, may swamp any attempt at conventional historical distinctions. That unsettling explains the inutility, if not threat, of *Pilgrimage* to a literary movement such as modernism whose very name proclaims its desire to set itself apart from the past. It explains why Virginia Woolf had so vehemently to separate herself from Richardson (and Galsworthy).[77]

In criticizing *Pilgrimage*, Woolf finds in it "something which has the shapeliness of the old accepted forms" [78]: the series form so prevalent in the Victorian period. Although Woolf seems to want to imply that, unlike Richardson, she at least is doing something new, she actually doesn't reject the notion of series altogether. For Woolf, English literature is itself an unbroken series, the path along which time has traveled ultimately to arrive at *her*; it is "an immeasurable avenue . . . which tapered out indistinguishably upon the furthest horizon. If I looked down at my book I could see Keats[,] and Pope behind him, and then Dryden and Sir Thomas Browne—hosts of them merg-

---

[75] Raymond Williams, "Base and Superstructure in Marxist Cultural Theory," in his *Problems in Material Culture* (London: Verso, 1980), 31–49.

[76] Richardson hated the phrase "stream of consciousness" precisely because of its implied linearity: "Stream of consciousness is a muddle-headed phrase. It's not a stream, it's a pool, a sea, and ocean. It has depth and greater depth and when you think you have reached its bottom and there is nothing there, and when you give yourself up to one current, you are suddenly possessed by another": Vincent Brome, "A Last Meeting with Dorothy Richardson," *The London Magazine*, June 1959, 29; quoted in Felber, "A Manifesto," 25.

[77] See, for example, Woolf's famous dismissal of Galsworthy, Arnold Bennett, and H. G. Wells in her "Character in Fiction," in *The Essays of Virginia Woolf*, vol. 3, 1919–1924, ed. Andrew McNeillie (London: Hogarth, 1988), 6 vols. projected, 4 vols. to date (1986–1994), 420–38. According to David Holloway, upon Galsworthy's death, Woolf "recorded in her diary her thankfulness that 'that stuffed shirt' had died," but I have been unable to confirm this from existing editions of Woolf's diary; David Holloway, *John Galsworthy* (London: Morgan-Grampian, 1968), 1.

[78] Virginia Woolf, "The Tunnel," *Essays*, 3:10–12; 12.

ing in the mass of Shakespeare, behind whom, if one peered long enough, some shapes of men in pilgrims' dress emerged."[79]

That literary history should trundle along to arrive ultimately at "her book" may be a slightly different claim for Woolf to make—more radical, less self-aggrandizing—than for Thackeray, since *A Room of One's Own* is all about the ways in which women writers have been left out of the tradition (in fact, at the beginning of *A Room of One's Own* Woolf's narrator is denied admission to the "famous library" that represents the male tradition when she wants to get in to have a look at the manuscript of *Henry Esmond*). Even though she is the daughter of the compiler of the *Dictionary of National Biography* (who was, at one time, Thackeray's son-in-law), *A Room of One's Own* is all about Woolf's sense that she can annex literary history's genealogy only outrageously. Yet, at the same time (and perhaps also because of her own genealogy), she still shares Thackeray's sense of that history as genealogy, as series.

Rather than hewing to the traditional position and arguing that the series vanishes altogether within the literary history of the twentieth century, I will (in Chapter 4) trace the series's remnants in Woolf. It seems important to me that—in spite of her claims to the contrary—Woolf's work retains a trace of the series, connects it with the everyday. Even though Woolf may have spent her writing career searching for a new form with which to capture the intricacies of shifting and unstable identity, the shadow of the (supposedly Victorian) series remains in her own depiction of recurrent characters—most particularly Clarissa and Richard Dalloway, as they appear in *The Voyage Out* and *Mrs. Dalloway* and give shape to a series of short stories published as *Mrs. Dalloway's Party*.[80] It may be that we can maintain the illusion of modernism and modern history only by breaking with the series. Horkheimer and Adorno want to uphold the distinction between the high literary and the popular, which they see collapsing in the twentieth century (I argue in my first chapter that the collapse of the two has actually always been attractive to many women writers). Modernism specifically tries to preserve that distinction by differentiating itself from the seriality of popular forms. In reading Galsworthy in my conclusion—in reading current African American women writers in my chapter on Woolf—I consider an alternative literary history that we must confront when we retain the ideas of seriality and the everyday in our critical readings.

Although all the writers I consider explore the linkage of the series and the everyday, each charts the ways they meet and merge differently—gives his or

---

[79] "Reading," *Essays*, 3:141–62, 142.

[80] Woolf's dissatisfaction with the traditional novel form per se comes across in her claims that she often doesn't know what to call her individual works: "I have an idea that I will invent a new name for my books to supplant 'novel.' A new— by Virginia Woolf. But what? Elegy?": "Saturday 27 June 1925," *The Diary of Virginia Woolf*, vol. 3, 1925–1930, ed. Anne Olivier Bell (New York: Harcourt Brace Jovanovich, 1980), 34.

her readers a slightly different window into the dreamlike obscurity (so blank because so familiar) that makes up their daily lives. What I hope the readers of this book will see is the energy, the determination, the desperation with which these writers try to peel back the curtain of that opacity because they recognize what it hides as determinative, vitally informing. Part of that process means that these writers also insist on their failures; they point to the juncture of the series and the everyday as what resists and flees their best attempts to map it.

For Oliphant and Yonge, the coming together of the series with the everyday exposes the arbitrariness of the principles that guide the fashioning of the literary tradition. Their yoking—especially through the devaluing of women writers both as mere spinners of endless tales and as cartographers of the quotidienne—makes visible the politics guiding the construction of the canon. But what it also makes visible is the way those politics themselves cannot be fixed or contained, remain in excess of definition or control. Such irresolution suggests neither subversion nor containment, but instead the inability systematically to predict or ensure either result.

The juncture of the series with the everyday in Trollope's novels exposes a kind of cultural delusion of omnipresence, omniscience, omnipotence. His novels display how the desire to account for everything—whether in a theoretical system or a sovereign state—is one of the motive forces underlying the serial replications of imperialism, wherein the dominant group attempts to impose its own sense of the daily on the universe around it. The attempt to account for everything breaks down, however, at those moments where it encounters the differences of gender and race; although the figure of the woman of color in Trollope's novels eludes culture's ability even to imagine her, her opacity promises her neither freedom nor indenture. It attests only to her hidden centrality in the ongoing circulation of signification.

Doyle's stories, too, explore the line between the series and the everyday as opening up another kind of delusion—the dream of immortality that provides culture with its patrilineal outlines. A masculinist attempt to escape the boredom of the mundane—already an apotropaic translation of its dread of (supposedly) feminine corruption and fleshly decay—is met in his fiction by a different kind of feminine boredom: an indifference so radical it threatens the very terms of the system itself. As the overly familiar Sherlock Holmes stories themselves attest, the everyday becomes the terrain in which a strategic recycling and repetition of the overfamiliar provides an alternative practice, one that dispenses as well with the terms of subversion or containment that have become so customary they are meaningless in critical discourse.

Modernist fiction traces the outlines of the connection between the series and the everyday in the late Victorian fiction that precedes it by attempting to redefine their relation—partly by seeming to refuse it. Yet Richardson's and Woolf's fiction remains organized by the overlapping of these two categories. In exposing its continued implication in the very structures it wishes to criticize, this fiction provides an example of the kind of open and unfixable politics central to my study—one displayed most particularly in its treatment of class and race. In using contemporary African American women's fiction in its own retrospective relation to a modernist writer such as Woolf, I try to end this book by pointing to a future constructed out of the series and the everyday that itself remains open.

Finally, in a brief afterword, I consider John Galsworthy's Forsyte saga, in order to reflect on the inevitable repetitions of critical discourse. Our approaches to literature and meaning-making become a series of avoidances and denials—but also recapitulations—of perspectives different from our own. Sigmund Freud's attention to the everyday as the site that betrays the powerful unconscious forces that determine identity provides a useful model with which to consider the repetition compulsions of critical rhetoric.

This book yokes these particular novelists with various theoretical approaches (such as Freudian psychoanalysis) that explore the connections of the everyday with the series. In my first chapter, Horkheimer and Adorno, as well as such poststructuralists as Gilles Deleuze and Félix Guattari, and Jean Baudrillard, provide one debate about high culture that discusses it in terms of these categories. I consider Trollope's attempts to represent all of culture by revisiting the supposedly unbridgeable divide between poststructuralism (represented by Derrida and Bhabha) and empiricist cultural studies, suggesting similarities as well as differences in their treatment of seriality and the everyday. The Continental thinkers who made the category of the everyday available to debate—Lefebvre, de Certeau, and the situationists—help me locate its patrilineal heritage in my discussion of Sherlock Holmes. And I return to Lukács and Bhabha, this time in connection with the work of Slavoj Žižek and Frantz Fanon, when exploring the literary history constructed around the series and the everyday in fiction that reflects on the Victorian series.

My engagement with the theory we most typically associate with the everyday, however, is informed throughout by various strains of poststructural feminism—though no label can herd these rowdy and disparate approaches into a common camp. In my first chapter, I consider the work of Julia Kristeva and Teresa de Lauretis, especially as it has been elaborated by Tania Modleski and other theorists of that women's serial, the soap opera. Feminists concerned with an antiracist critique, including Spivak, Hortense Spillers, and Deborah McDowell, inform the gender analysis within my Trollope chapter. I consider the intersection of poststructural critics such as Naomi Schor with cultural feminists in my Sherlock Holmes chapter, which also rests on the cultural readings done by Susan Stewart and Donna Haraway. Haraway is crucial in the final chapter as well, as are a host of feminist critics who have analyzed the modernism of Richardson and Woolf— including the analyses by the authors Alice Walker, Paule Marshall, Barbara Christian, and Bernice Reagon. The critical writing of all the women novelists I consider in this book significantly informs its theory. What I intend here above all is to suggest the ways that, through its necessary defamiliarizations—the cognitive wrench that happens when you shove the white, male subject out of the middle of the universe—feminism provides us with the best way to see the seemingly banal repetitions that make up the world around us.

It felt as if it might go on for ever, and yet the very sentiment that inspired it made separation and convulsion inevitable—one of those strange paradoxes which occur every day.

—Margaret Oliphant, *Phoebe Junior*

I *Minor Fiction, Endless Progress*
Toward a Feminist Ethics

In the hotly contested debate about the canon and about literary value, what does it mean that almost half a century—for some, a whole lifetime—can be considered a minor period? We treat the second half of the Victorian era—especially regarding the novel—as decidedly minor. During the latter part of the century, Dickens, Eliot, and Thackeray stop writing; near the beginning of the next, Conrad and Hardy take their place, but continue long enough into the twentieth century to be classed comfortably with the modernists. The novelists that did the bulk of the writing during the mid- to late-nineteenth century—novelists such as Margaret Oliphant, Charlotte Yonge, and Anthony Trollope—are exemplary not just for their contemporaries' but for our own current critical attitude to them: they figure as highly popular but definitely minor writers. Yet as minor writers in a period of minor writers, they ask us to rethink our very notion of the minor.

More than that, such writers as Oliphant and Yonge may be instructive about our construction of the minor because they, at least, openly embraced their status as minor. Although she had written nearly a hundred novels, many popularly acclaimed, along with histories and biographies, and was a similarly indefatigable reviewer, Oliphant used her autobiography to promote the image of herself as a mother forced to write incidental hack fiction simply to feed her children. Yonge's father allowed her to publish her seemingly innumerable novels (including runaway best-sellers like *The Heir of Redclyffe*), histories, inspirational tracts, and books for children only after she had renounced any private ambition or desire for gain; as a writer, she presented herself as merely a humble member of the church and an educator of youth.

These postures had, of course, to do with gender:[1] given the cultural gate-

---

[1] One conceptual pathway that allowed ideological discord to assume this particular shape was, as I will be implying in this chapter, the Victorian crisis of faith, which provided a whole (by this time conventional) impetus and vocabulary with which to reject and transform such

keeping that admitted women writers to the canon rarely, and then only on certain terms, many women writers learned to adopt an equivocal stance. They dealt with their exclusion from the canon by attempting to co-opt it, as Nina Baym and Annette Kolodny have argued, renouncing any ambition, claiming satisfaction with a marginality that allowed them to address a simply popular and domestic audience, an audience of other women, similarly excluded from recognized social positions by their gender. Baym and Kolodny see this as a political strategy: behind such demurrers, they argue, hide a canny appraisal and implicit critique of gender inequity.[2]

What might also be hidden there, as I maintain in this chapter, is a radical skepticism about any ideal or essential literary greatness, which amounts to a covert redefinition of the shifting, contextual, relational—and in that way inescapably biased—basis of canonical evaluation. Yet Oliphant's and Yonge's very different explicit politics (Oliphant's liberal tendencies are brought into sharp relief by Yonge's conservatism) make the specific gender politics of claims to the minor difficult absolutely to pin down. Feminists such as Baym and Kolodny assume too quickly that an emphasis on the minor has a particular politics (for them, it's progressive). This may seem an understandable, if not also laudable, effect of their own political commitment. Yet theorists of the minor who little care for feminism, such as Horkheimer and Adorno (the politics of the popular are for them, as we will see, backward and abhorrent) or Deleuze and Guattari (who find its politics, once again, progressive), also decide and attempt to secure the politics of the minor. As Oliphant's and Yonge's examples suggest, however, rather than fix a certain politics, an emphasis on the minor instead opens up the very question of the political itself.

---

notions as "genius" and "canon." The minor is a vital topic not just because it comprises all these debates, but also because it suggests how to think about them. I'm not quite sure it matters what exactly is causal here—behind anxiety of influence and conceptual precedent do lie motive forces that have to do with food, and sex, and power (economics, gender, race), but our very notions of things like hunger, pleasure, and force too (think of how religious ecstasies transfigure all these things) are mediated by the kind of decisions we make as to what is primary and what minor, as to whom we accept as ultimate authority and what we decree as that god's canon.

[2] Baym, for instance, writes: "The notion of the artist, or of excellence, has efficacy in a given time and reflects social realities. . . . We can all think of species of women's literature that do not aim in any way to achieve literary excellence as society defines it. . . . Until recently, only a tiny proportion of literary women aspired to artistry and literary excellence in the terms defined by their own culture. There tended to be a sort of immediacy in the ambitions of literary women leading them to professionalism rather than artistry, by choice as well as by social pressure and opportunity": Baym, "Melodramas of Beset Manhood: How Theories of American Fiction Exclude Women Authors," in *The New Feminist Criticism: Essays on Women, Literature, and Theory*, ed. Elaine Showalter (New York: Pantheon, 1985), 63–80; 65. Baym argues that the male tradition deliberately misread the pressures upon and the different standards of women's fiction in order to set it up as a foil to sanction men's endeavor; it became not just different, but inferior, second-rate, its supposed insufficiencies a threat to the integrity of male high art. Kolodny finds this minor fiction's politics in the "self consciousness with which writers . . . perceived themselves as excluded from the dominant literary tradition and as writing for an audience of readers similarly excluded": Kolodny, "A Map for Rereading: Gender and the Interpretation of Literary Texts," in Showalter, 46–62; 49.

In this chapter I rethink the politics of the minor by considering their relation to the category of the everyday in late Victorian fiction. One argument contemporary reviewers made about Oliphant's and Yonge's novels (as well as about Trollope's, and also those of the score of that period's other novelists whom we barely remember) is that, although enormously popular, they must be by definition minor because they took as their subject the banalities of everyday life. One definition of the domestic realism practiced by most women writers of the time (as well as by most male writers, however) is simply its attention to the everyday, what that poet of the exotic, Edward Fitzgerald (perhaps feeling superseded), called "Books about the Daily Life which I find rather insufferable."[3] Summing up the literary endeavors of women writers of the time, Elizabeth Helsinger, Robin Lauterbach Sheets, and William Veeder write in *The Woman Question*: "Most novelists publishing under women's names were pursuing a tradition of domestic realism that was already established when Victoria came to the throne. Since the late eighteenth century, commentators like Hannah More had argued that women had a particular gift for writing about the everyday experiences of heart and home."[4] But, as these critics emphasize, aligning women writers with the everyday experiences of domestic fiction was also a way of undercutting them, displacing onto women the everyday's supposedly trivial valence, drawing off onto *them* canonical minority per se. They quote an 1860 reviewer who applauds women writers for their attention to the everyday, to "heaps of conventional commonplaces which men generally overlook, or are incapable of appreciating," but concludes from this that "the female novelist who keeps strictly to the region within which she acquires her knowledge may never produce a fiction of the highest order, but she will be in the right path to produce the best fiction of the class in which she is most likely to excel."[5] According to this (old) logic, because women's popular domestic fiction could only be about their everyday lives, it couldn't at the same time also be important or major.

The everyday region to which women writers get circumscribed is a limbo of the popular that Oliphant notes. She asks:

> Where do those battered, dog's-eared, unlovely wrecks of popularity go? Do they rest in a limbo as dark as that of those who live in the infernal suburbs, *senza*

---

[3] Quoted in Amy Cruse, *The Victorians and Their Reading* (New York: Houghton Mifflin, 1914), 59. The entire relevant passage reads: "I cannot get on with Books about the Daily Life which I find rather insufferable in practice about me. . . . I can't read the *Adam Bedes* and *Daisy Chains*, etc., at all." The lumping together of Eliot and Yonge here suggests the way the category of the minor shifts to meet various demands. Although in theory Eliot is part of the canon, especially when she treats of theoretical and abstract topics (which explains why she felt pressured to write books like *Romola*), she can be as insufferable in practice—and hence as trivial—as Yonge when she acts as a woman and attends to the unimportant trifles of daily life.

[4] *The Woman Question: Society and Literature in Britain and America, 1837–1883*, ed. Elizabeth Helsinger, Robin Lauterbach Sheets, and William Veeder, 3 vols. (Chicago: University of Chicago Press, 1983), 3:48.

[5] Reviewer for the *London Review*, quoted in ibid., 53.

infamia e senza lodo—dusty dark in endless acres of untouched shelves? . . . We remember an old library in the days before Mudie, which, but that all was silent, would have made a sufficiently good representative of Dante's Limbo. What if there might be hopeless souls about whose fate it was to go on and on reading the old novels? It might form a chapter of purgatorial literature not without originality—but very alarming to the producers of many novels. . . . How many centuries, we wonder, would it take an unhappy fictionist to get through all the dead and gone novels of his country alone!—the Pamelas and the Rose Matildas, the sporting, and, ah me! the detective books. Repent, oh novel-writers, while there is time![6]

Without infamy but also without praise, these writers endlessly circulate in a gray area of exclusion and neglect. And Oliphant traces the logic by which this endless circulation spins out into palpable form: the rows upon rows of unread books, the unproductive reader, doomed to track from one book to another, without hope of reaching the end. Charles Dickens and Wilkie Collins also describe a reader caught in a similar loop:

> A young and charming lady, previously an excellent customer at the circulating libraries, read this fatal domestic novel [Charlotte Yonge's *The Heir of Redclyffe*] on its first appearance some years ago, and has read nothing else ever since. As soon as she gets to the end of the book, this interesting and unfortunate creature turns back to the first page, and begins it again. Her family vainly endeavour to lure her away to former favourites, or to newer works; she raises her eyes for a moment from the too-enthralling page, shakes her head faintly, and resumes her fascinating occupation for the thousandth time, with unabated relish.[7]

This loop is also reflected in one of the most popular formal devices of later Victorian fiction. In this period, the formal expression of an attention to the everyday meant more than the mode of domestic realism. It also meant the elaboration of that mode in novel after novel, in the linked novels that form the famous chronicles or series of the period: Trollope's Barchester and Palliser series, Oliphant's Carlingford Chronicles, Yonge's family sagas. Series novels simply take the same story one step further (as *Barchester Towers* repeats the story of Mr. Harding's relation to Hiram's Hospital from *The Warden*, say), literally embodying Max Horkheimer and Theodor Adorno's notion of progress without change. Susan Willis argues that they see history under capitalism as an "abhorrent and bleak sameness . . . propelled by the notion of progress, but going nowhere . . . Everything transforms but nothing changes."[8] The series postpones any ending with the illusion of the same continuing endlessness our own lives seem to have to us.

[6] Margaret Oliphant, "The Looker-On," *Blackwood's* 67 (June 1895): 902–29; 925.

[7] Charles Dickens and Wilkie Collins, "Doctor Dulcamara, MP," in Charles Dickens, *Uncollected Writings from Household Words, 1850–1859*, ed. Harry Stone (Bloomington: Indiana University Press, 1968), 619–26; 622.

[8] Susan Willis, *A Primer for Daily Life* (New York: Routledge, 1991), 35–36.

For the Victorians, series fiction, like the serial publication it usually relied upon, echoed the perceived form of everyday life; according to the authors of *The Victorian Serial*, the long *durée* of installment after installment (and, I would add, of novel after novel) insisted upon the everyday: "A work's extended duration meant that serials could become entwined with readers' own sense of lived experience and passing time . . . within the busy context of everyday life . . . [because] readers repeatedly were forced to set aside a continuing story and resume everyday life." [9] Hughes and Lund contend that this duration and expansiveness were part of the spirit of the age; they "promised more to come, and the richness of detail and expansion of the text over time suggested a world of plenitude. . . . Indeed, the confident capitalistic framework during the booming years of the nineteenth-century economic expansion had a kind of literary analogue in the serial form." [10] Such a neat fit between the period's self-image and this formal—serial—expression might have had everything to do with the enormous popularity of the series novel during this time; its very everydayness would ensure the naturalness of supposed capitalist progression, make it seem for the Victorians not the illusion of ideology but a fact that could be taken for granted. Yet this isn't the only effect of the series impulse, as the disparagement of minor fiction shows. The passages from Oliphant and Dickens that I've quoted suggest how the series might also have worried capitalism: staying too long in circulation, co-opting it entirely, they disrupted capitalism's throw-away economy (so that previously excellent customers, trapped within the series, stop buying and become "alarming to [new] producers"). Or, at any rate, the series may encode the attempt to manage this risk. It translates the reader's desire to repeat into a form available to commodity capitalism. The same story is not so much efficiently recycled as it is repackaged and marketed anew as the next installment.

In Dante, as Oliphant, herself a chronicler of the afterlife, knew well, the gyrations of Limbo actually reflect the motive force of the entire system—of

[9] Linda K. Hughes and Michael Lund, *The Victorian Serial* (Charlottesville: University Press of Virginia, 1991), 8–9. They are not the only critics to locate in popular later Victorian fiction a series impulse and an emphasis on the everyday. R. C. Terry, for instance, argues that the realism of the popular fiction of this period is based on "the externals and 'realities' of daily life": R. C. Terry, *Victorian Popular Fiction, 1860–80* (Atlantic Highlands, N.J.: Humanities Press, 1983), 55. Sally Mitchell goes further, finding that such references to the "everyday world" (32) in this popular fiction usually get chronicled into "a series of events, often repetitive" (31): "Situations are repeated in different novels and, even more strikingly, within the same novel. An event happens, then some people talk about it, and then one of them tells someone else about it. The repetition is often badly managed in a technical sense; it does not reveal how different people interpret the same happening, but simply allows the event to be experienced again": Mitchell, "Sentiment and Suffering: Women's Recreational Reading in the 1860s," *Victorian Studies* 21 (1977): 29–45; 34. The repetition, in other words, seems to have no other point but itself, to stay the text's sense of progress, or, perhaps, as Horkheimer and Adorno might suggest, to point out the actual bankruptcy of the so-called progress within traditional (capitalist) narrative.
[10] Hughes and Lund, *Victorian Serial*, 4.

heaven, in the endless hosannas of the celestial host (their exultation comes from their eternal life which allows them eternally to repeat their praise), but of hell too, in its circles within circles, so clearly seen in the examples of Sisyphus and Tantalus, where the conservation of energy is what is actually hellish: that souls cannot die but must eternally repeat. In contrast to such black and white realms, Limbo is gray because there are no clear choices there; it is inside neither heaven nor hell, neither one thing nor the other. Exposing the workings of the system is threatening to it for a simple reason: Limbo shows that such spiraling circuits have no *essential* meaning or value. The minor calls the transcendent into question, emphasizing the importance of context, the changing status of supposedly immutable truths.

The everyday may be the vehicle for this because, as recent theory of the everyday has suggested, as a political and philosophical category, it is one that breaks down the easy dichotomies of either/or. Henri Lefebvre and Michel de Certeau (as I discuss in my chapter on Holmes) see the everyday as the place where the mundane and the utopic meet. The traditional denigration of the everyday and the minor as simply mundane—degraded, inauthentic, alienating—is meant to bracket or occlude such troubling paradoxes. And Oliphant's and Yonge's contemporaries aren't the only ones who practice the evasion. Even in our own century, when the Victorian myth of cultural progression heavenward has been increasingly discarded, the relation between the series and the everyday, and their connection with the popular, especially as degraded and minor, remain. It is by now a Marxist truism that serialized activity is characteristic of mass culture.[11] Horkheimer and Adorno predicate their enormously influential 1944 essay "The Culture Industry: Enlightenment as Mass Deception" on this assumption. For them, however, the value of such succession is very different from what it traditionally seemed to the Victorians (or to most Victorians except Marx); they see capitalism as perniciously perpetuating itself through the endless and unsatisfied promise of what amounts to sterile repetition. "The totality of the culture industry . . . consists of repetition" (16) they write:[12] "The culture industry perpetually cheats its consumers of what it perpetually promises. . . . [T]he promise, which is actually all the spectacle consists of, is illusory: all it actually confirms is that the real point will never be reached. . . . In front of the appetite stimulated by all those brilliant names and images there is finally set no more than a commendation of the depressing everyday world it sought to escape" ("Culture," 139). For Horkheimer and Adorno, the seriatim stream of capitalism's bankrupt everyday life is reflected and perpet-

[11] Tania Modleski, for instance, assumes what she calls "the serialized activity that Jean-Paul Sartre saw as characteristic of mass culture": *Feminism without Women: Culture and Criticism in a 'Postfeminist' Age* (New York: Routledge, 1991), 42. All future references to this book (abbreviated *Feminism*) will appear in the text.

[12] Max Horkheimer and Theodor Adorno, "The Culture Industry: Enlightenment as Mass Deception," in their *Dialectic of Enlightenment*, trans. John Cumming (New York: Herder and Herder, 1972), 120–67; 136; all future references to this essay (abbreviated "Culture") appear in the text.

uated by its cultural forms: "cyclically recurrent and rigidly invariable types" ("Culture," 125) that go on and on, leading to no satisfaction or resolution: culture's unsatisfied promises are the lure that conducts each subject deeper and deeper into capitalism's hell.

These theorists clinch their essentialization of the drab succession of the everyday by associating it with gender: "The escape from everyday drudgery which the whole culture industry promises may be compared to the daughter's abduction in the cartoon: the father is holding the ladder in the dark. The paradise offered by the culture industry is the same old drudgery" ("Culture," 142). Yet although it is the daughter here who seems to wish to escape the everyday into some romantic utopia, Horkeimer and Adorno make clear that it is actually women (so easily, ever since Eve, deceived) who are to blame for culture's downfall: "The description of the dramatic formula by the housewife as 'getting into trouble and out again' embraces the whole of mass culture from the idiotic women's serial to the top production" ("Culture," 152). The "idiotic women's serial" epitomizes mass culture for these theorists (and note how such a women's form is for them even *more* minor than mass culture's "top productions"). And the trouble that women get into and out of again and again eternally, endlessly luring men into sin and mortality, is reflected in women's (supposedly) essentially sexual nature: culture suggests that

> what repeats itself is healthy, like the natural or industrial cycle. The same babies grin eternally out of the magazines. . . . In spite of all the progress in reproductive techniques, in controls and the specialities, and in spite of all the restless industry, the bread which the culture industry offers man is the stone of the stereotype. It draws on the life cycle, on the well-founded amazement that mothers, in spite of everything, still go on bearing children and that the wheels still do not grind to a halt. ("Culture," 148–49)

The reproductive techniques of art and sexuality merge. Horkheimer and Adorno, repelled by women's unremitting generation, indict it for progress's exhaustion. Woman, the passive dupe of culture, is the vehicle that keeps culture going, endlessly spinning its wheels. As Andreas Huyssen argues, in "Mass Culture as Woman: Modernism's Other," his response to Horkheimer and Adorno, for them mass culture gets stigmatized as minor and depleted precisely through this alignment with women. And the implicit denigration of women (for these critics, the idiotic serial shows that formally the series is really, essentially, a *women's* form, like her runaway childbearing) goes hand in hand with a denigration of the everyday: "The repudiation of *Trivialliteratur* has always been one of the constitutive features of a modernist aesthetic intent on distancing itself and its products from the trivialities and banalities of everyday life."[13]

---

[13] Huyssen, "Mass Culture as Woman: Modernism's Other," in his *After the Great Divide: Modernism, Mass Culture, Postmodernism* (Bloomington: Indiana University Press, 1986), 44–62; 47.

Yet even when critics attempt to bind the minor to the opposite political pole, the effects of their argument (especially when it comes to women) remain the same. Unlike early twentieth-century Marxists including Horkheimer and Adorno, the later poststructuralists Deleuze and Guattari, in their *Kafka: Toward a Minor Literature*, argue that minor literature, rather than perpetuating the economic and social system of power, instead describes "the revolutionary conditions for every literature." [14] Deleuze and Guattari write: "The three characteristics of minor literature are the deterritorialization of language, the connection of the individual to a political immediacy, and the collective assemblage of enunciation" (*Kafka*, 18). Minor literature, written in the dominant language as if in a foreign tongue (much the way we could argue that the Scottish Oliphant might have regarded English), makes the confines of that language strange, "deterritorializes" it into a defamiliarized if not utopic/dystopic space. The spareness of its text, what critics often regard as its clumsiness or obviousness, makes its politics inescapable. And it records the vox populi: "in it everything takes on a collective value. Indeed, precisely because talent isn't abundant in a minor literature, there are no possibilities for an individuated enunciation that would belong to this or that 'master'" (17). Yet, when it comes to gender, a hint of mastery returns in this argument for subversion. While never explicitly engaging with gender, their general argument as I have just outlined it relies directly on gender assumptions. Like Horkheimer and Adorno, Deleuze and Guattari too connect women with the formal principle of series fiction that for them also demarcates the minor.

In considering Kafka's fiction (their example of revolutionary minor work), for example, these theorists concentrate on images and lines of narrative that seem to spin out past individual stories into other texts; the effect of such disrupted containment or closure is so great that they suggest that "from now on, there will be no reason for a novel to end" (*Kafka*, 55). Such formal impulses are coded by gender: "women mark the start of a series or the opening of a segment that they belong to; they also mark its end" (67–68). For Deleuze and Guattari, these series marked by women are actually the source of the revolutionary potential of minor fiction. Their formal disruptions suggest and provide a route to shatter what seems the impasse of the subject mired within an ideology he cannot imagine how to get beyond: "the first characteristic of these proliferating series is that they work to unblock a situation that had closed elsewhere in an impasse" (53). Taking narrative beyond closure, these series "tend to distribute themselves along a line of escape, to take flight on this line" (55). And such a formal impulse is for them *essential* to—a defining characteristic of—minor literature: "Production of intensive quantities in the social body, proliferation and the precipitation of

---

[14] Gilles Deleuze and Félix Guattari, *Kafka: Toward a Minor Literature*, trans. Dana Polan (Minneapolis: University of Minnesota Press, 1986), 18; all future references to this book will appear in the text.

series, polyvalent and collective connections brought about by the bachelor agent—there is no other definition possible for a minor literature" (71). Although, unlike Horkheimer and Adorno, Deleuze and Guattari see the series impulse of degraded fiction in a politically positive light, their understanding of woman's relation to the series remains basically similar: although not idiotic per se, she does remain somehow both responsible and passive, the vehicle for political effects that are important because they affect the (male) bachelor.

Deleuze and Guattari recognize to some degree that this reassertion of (sexual) mastery is an imaginative construction on their part, an apotropaic response meant to resolve and stabilize an uncertain dilemma: "Since there is no way [from inside ideology] to draw a firm distinction between the oppressors and the oppressed . . . one has to seize all of them in an all-too-possible future, hoping all the while that this act will also bring out lines of escape, parade lines, even if they are modest, even if they are hesitant, even if—and especially if—they are asignifying" (*Kafka*, 59). I like especially Deleuze and Guattari's image here of oppressor and oppressed eerily blending. It provides, I think, one of the most useful, if not also horrific, understandings of our uneasy and uncertain subject positions. The political strategies they draw from it are critical precisely because they require confronting this horror and unease. Deleuze and Guattari acknowledge the series impulse as a (perhaps meaningless) response to this irresolvable ideological impasse. Nevertheless, they attempt elsewhere in the book to make it mean something, to resolve this impasse in favor of subversion, revolution, escape. And they make use of a reliable cultural scenario content with who traditionally oppresses and who is oppressed; as Andreas Huyssen suggests, male theorists find easy to protest in their arguments what they can take "for granted on an experiential level in everyday life."[15] Women remain a convenient vessel, a manipulable symbol, with which these theorists convert their own significances into truth.

The force of tradition in essentially aligning (and disparaging) women, the serial, and the everyday remains so strong in Western culture that it influences even those theorists who resist it—and resist it not only implicitly (as we might argue Deleuze and Guattari mean to do), but explicitly as well. According to Tania Modleski (who elsewhere in her work on the soap opera is perhaps the most influential recent critic on the series impulse), Jean Baudrillard is the theorist who makes women's connection to mass culture something more than passive: he praises "the masses, rather than condemning them on account of their putative femininity" (*Feminism*, 30). Or, rather than transforming women into active cultural agents, Baudrillard transforms the very significance of the mass cultural passivity Horkheimer and Adorno deplore; it becomes a resistant, if not revolutionary, strategy. The

[15] Huyssen, "Mass Culture," 46.

masses "annihilate everything that seeks to control them, not by their strength of will but by their very will-lessness and passivity" (*Feminism*, 31) through "engaging in the same 'excessive fidelity to the law' that characterizes Hegel's eternal feminine, the same 'simulation of passivity and obedience' that 'annuls the law governing them.' It is the mute acquiescence of the masses to the system—the silence of the majority—that renders them most feminine" (*Feminism*, 32). Yet (as Modleski also recognizes) in attempting to clinch his own claims of resistance through the connection of women and the popular, Baudrillard doesn't just expose, but assumes (assumes that it exists and attempts himself to borrow it) a familiar cultural construction: the passivity of the eternal feminine.[16]

What interests me is that this is the *eternal* feminine. This mass cultural strategy that culture deems feminine—for Baudrillard, it is women's "simulation"—is directly aligned for him too with the notion of the series. In *Simulations*, Baudrillard argues that the very notion of simulation itself (the organizing principle of his theory of culture) arises from the reproduction of the series, "the *serial* repetition of the same object," endemic to late nineteenth- and twentieth-century industrial production, characterized by proliferating and unmoored repetition, "the end of all original reference" or possible conclusion.[17] For Baudrillard, this impulse of pure serial replication, one out of control and without reference, inheres in everyday life: "today it is quotidian reality in its entirety—political, social, historical and economic—that from now on incorporates the simulatory dimension" (*Simulations*, 147). The feminized masses resist the system through the very serialized activities of the everyday that carry them along in their passivity; in defining this as the "banality" of the everyday, Baudrillard claims:

> It is at the extremities of this monotony, this insignificance, this indifference of our systems, that the sequences, unfoldings, and processes—which no longer proceed from cause and effect—appear; a challenge that is immanent in the very unfolding of things. This challenge is neither religious nor transcendent, and if there is a strategy here, it is no one's. . . . Here things operate as though there were a will to challenge, as opposed to a willing servitude: a genius of indifference, which victoriously opposes itself to all enterprises of meaning and difference, but which cannot be attributed to one group, one class, or to particular individuals.[18]

As a poststructuralist, Baudrillard, like Deleuze and Guattari, recognizes the impasse of ideology; like them too he helps to expose the series impulse of

---

[16] For an indictment of Baudrillard's textual misogyny (which really doesn't go far enough), see Jane Gallop, "French Theory and the Seduction of Feminism," *Paragraph* 8 (1986): 19–24.

[17] Jean Baudrillard, *Simulations*, trans. Paul Foss, Paul Patton, and Philip Beitchman (New York: Semiotext[e], 1983), 99–100, 136; all further references to this book will appear in the text.

[18] Jean Baudrillard, *The Ecstasy of Communication*, trans. Bernard Schutze and Caroline Schutze, ed. Sylvere Lotringer (New York: Autonomedia, 1988), 85–86.

the everyday as a response to questions that cannot be resolved through individual volition or agency. He explicitly denies the claims of religion; yet the fact of "genius" still appearing somewhat archaically within his vocabulary suggests that the series and the everyday remain tied up with issues of the canon and of value even when we try to move beyond the assumptions of humanism, and of transcendence and truth, in which such issues are usually grounded.

In treatments of the feminized masses, the ideological impasse that Deleuze and Guattari and Baudrillard all note—one performed in the debate between them and Horkheimer and Adorno, so that the series and the everyday can represent at one and the same time the conservative and radical effects of mass culture—gets transformed in these male exchanges into women's passivity, scapegoated onto women. Essentializing this way has a rhetorical force that does more than just attempt to ground these arguments, make them appear right and true. In them, women also begin not just to reflect but also to be to blame for capitalism's idiocy. And making *women* responsible for the problems of ideology implies that (in spite of everything) those problems are resolvable; they are not outside human exchange or control.

Yet, through the series and the everyday, Oliphant and Yonge suggest another response to ideological impasse. Though perhaps no less wishful, their response is at least more witting in that it doesn't just seek magically to annul such contradictions, but formally preserves them, even when it tries imaginatively to construct some utopia beyond them. Following Nancy Miller's earlier essay on this topic, "Emphasis Added: Plots and Plausibilities in Women's Fiction," Penny Boumelha stresses that the refusal of closure typical of the endings in later nineteenth-century women writers' novels actually addresses the ideological cul-de-sac in which women found themselves at this period.[19] Boumelha's and Miller's arguments suggest that, although women writers of this period had developed a complex critique of women's social and literary inequity, they still recognized themselves as the products of that society, constructed by its very forms—and some of those forms, most important for such writers, were the narrative conventions of the novels that they wrote, conventions which grew out of the very ideology they used their novels to critique. How within this double-bind might they imagine a different future for women? How could they imagine a different end for them using the very ways of thought that had trapped women in the first place? For Boumelha and Miller, such insoluble dilemmas get marked by the impossible endings of women's fiction, where narrative stutters, breaks down, breaks out into wild flights. And, I would also argue, it may be why women writers were so attracted to series fiction. Rather than providing the lines of escape that

[19] Penny Boumelha, "Realism and the Ends of Feminism," in *Grafts: Feminist Cultural Criticism*, ed. Susan Sheridan (New York: Verso, 1988), 77–91; 87. Nancy Miller, "Emphasis Added: Plots and Plausibilites in Women's Fiction," in Showalter, *New Feminist Criticism*, 339–60.

Deleuze and Guattari optimistically posit (or the inescapable mire described by Horkheimer and Adorno), by repeating and extending, going on and on, delaying any final conclusion (although ultimately coming to some kind of end, if only by trailing off), the series mulls over and reworks women's double-bind, insists directly on this problem, emphasizing especially the powerful but *still unsatisfied* desire to get beyond it.

And one reason the series may be so closely connected with the everyday for these writers of domestic realism is that the everyday seems to refuse ideal solutions. It insists that there is no utopia outside of ideology's confines. An emphasis on the everyday may provide instead a way of inhabiting those confines, working within them, without simply overlooking them or accepting them as natural. In both assuming a degree of freedom that allows them to recognize to some extent their constraints and admitting that a full analysis (and remedy) of those constraints must remain a future goal, such writers engage in what for Tania Modleski is the most important practice of feminism: "feminist critical writing is simultaneously performative and utopian, pointing toward the freer world it is in the process of inaugurating" (*Feminism*, 48). Through an emphasis on the series and the everyday, women writers transform their double-binds into contradiction that *remains* contradiction—always both confining *and* generative.

Like the formal impulse of the series, the politics such contradiction generates remain necessarily open-ended. Oliphant's and Yonge's fiction can help us as readers in questioning any essential political charge within the series's contradiction and lack of closure. And, as feminists, we stand in need of such help; just like other theorists, we keep trying to assert our meanings as not simply better but also true. It is against such impulses that Julia Kristeva has argued in her essay "Women's Time." This essay provides an important background treatise for current notions of seriality; it has been highly influential in shaping feminist notions of the series impulse.[20] Yet, because of its criticism of feminist bids for transcendence, it has been rejected by some as antifeminist altogether.

In "Women's Time," Kristeva argues that culture has traditionally associated women with a kind of seriality; for culture, women's time "essentially retains *repetition* and *eternity* from among [time's] multiple modalities," so that, rather than seeming linear, women's time appears "cyclical and monumental," necessitating women's very "*refusal*" of the history into which it also inserts them—a doubleness Kristeva finds beneficial.[21] Kristeva sees the cultural connection of women with this kind of seriality especially played

---

[20] This essay seems in fact to have prompted Tania Modleski's earliest thoughts about the serial; she discusses it in detail in her first essay about this topic, "Time and Desire in the Woman's Film," *Cinema Journal* 23 (1984): 19–30. Interestingly, although her later, much better known essays retain the very terms of this discussion, she omits from them all direct reference to this problematic Kristevan text.

[21] Julia Kristeva, "Women's Time," trans. Alice Jardine and Harry Blake, *Signs* 7 (1981): 13–35; 16, 17, 20; all future references to this essay (abbreviated "Women's") appear in the text.

out in women's fiction, where the everyday and utopic meet: "Why literature? . . . [B]ecause it makes a game, a space of fantasy and pleasure, out of
the abstract and frustrating order of social signs, the words of everyday communication" ("Women's," 31). Yet many feminists find the performative and
utopian effects of Kristeva's own space of fantasy and pleasure here disturbing; in editing this essay, Alice Jardine admits "The following article will be
judged by many as antifeminist. I cannot possibly deny that it is." [22] In this
essay, Kristeva criticizes feminism as a political position, criticizes it for humanism, an anthropomorphism which "blocks the horizon of the discursive
and scientific adventure of our species" ("Women's," 35); by essentializing
women's identity, feminism not only itself becomes "a kind of inverted sexism" (27), scapegoating men, but also claims a kind of transcendence: "In its
present form, is not feminism in the process of becoming [a religion]?" (33).
Kristeva's challenge to a feminism she still finds wanting is for it to transform
that religion: to demystify its own tendency to metaphysics, to seize and
transform women's traditional association with the series and the everyday
so that the utopias contained within them are not the same old dreams of
transcendence. In doing so, feminism would find within the "aesthetic practices" (35) of its literature a new kind of responsibility and a "new ethics"
(35). Like Jardine, I cannot deny that Kristeva's redefinition of feminism in
this essay is at one and the same time both feminist and antifeminist (although it's important that her rejection of a traditional and essentialized
feminism here is exactly opposite to the antifeminism we will see played out
in Yonge, who doesn't find feminism religious or metaphysical *enough*); but
Kristeva's emphasis on seriality and the everyday allows a critique of feminism's politics, and allows a politics of her own, that put the very notion
of simple "progressiveness" into question. What we can learn from Kristeva
is that simply to promote these categories is not necessarily to promote
feminism.

A whole generation of scholars working on the women's serial—especially
Tania Modleski and those critics responding to her, including most promi-
nently Sandy Flitterman-Lewis and Christine Gledhill[23]—have (mistakenly,
I think) taken Kristeva's association of women with seriality almost as bible,
to argue for a kind of feminist subversion somehow built into the series's resistance to closure. In their emphasis on seriality, Deleuze and Guattari too
insist on the revolutionary potential of the minor. Rather than the "one
single dream: to assume a major function," these theorists admonish writers instead to "create the opposite dream: know how to create a becoming-

[22] Alice Jardine, "Introduction to 'Women's Time,'" *Signs* 7 (1981): 5–12; 12.
[23] Modleski's best known work appears in her *Loving with a Vengeance: Mass-Produced
Fantasies for Women* (New York: Methuen, 1982); Sandy Flitterman-Lewis, "All's Well That
Doesn't End—Soap Opera and the Marriage Motif," in *Private Screenings: Television and the
Female Consumer*, ed. Lynn Spigel and Denise Mann (Minneapolis: University of Minnesota
Press, 1992), 217–26; Christine Gledhill, "Speculations on the Relationship between Soap
Opera and Melodrama," *Quarterly Review of Film & Video* 14 (1992): 103–24.

minor" (*Kafka*, 27) in order to abolish mastery and oppression. By explicitly embracing their minor status, popular series writers like Oliphant and Yonge seem to enact such insurgent tendencies, consciously to personify the vox populi of dispossessed women. It may indeed be strategically useful sometimes, as Baym and Kolodny, Deleuze and Guattari, Modleski and others do, to link the category of the minor with the oppressed position of minority groups (if women can be considered a minority). In my reading, however, Oliphant's and Yonge's example shows the continued political problems of ascribing fixed position and value to literary forms, no matter what our intentions. Rather than simply flipping the hierarchy to make minor status somehow resolve ideological impasse and thus solve the problem of the political, the intention of the formal explorations in these series of novels may be to keep questions open—and in the face of culture's and tradition's desire to the contrary.

One reader of women's serials traces the traditional cultural condemnation of the series impulse at least as far back as Saint Paul, who inveighs against "fables and endless genealogies, which minister questions rather than godly edifying."[24] Such a sentiment may explain why the score of popular and expansive minor women writers working in the nineteenth century was for Hawthorne and his literary fraternity a "*damned* mob of scribbling women." But if ministering questions was what kept them from being edifying within the logic of mastery that allowed the male fraternity to declare its canon godly, then it might behoove us as feminists to resist turning our own ethics into a religion, as Kristeva suggests—to resist closing off questions, to resist insisting on an essential charge for minor fiction, and to explore instead the way it redefines the political and keeps it open.

❧

"Now it was all over. The romance was ended, the hero gone, and life had begun anew."[25] In stubborn refusal of the Aristotelian properties of narrative, so Margaret Oliphant's stories always begin. But what is the new life she chronicles in them? As she emphasizes throughout *The Doctor's Family* and throughout her work, it is simply the unremarkable—and unnarratable—succession of what Oliphant calls "the world and the everyday hours," that commonplace unvarying routine which (it has been a tenet of literary criticism at least since the *Poetics*) narrative is supposed to disrupt.[26] Oliphant's series of novels, the Carlingford Chronicles, include a short story,

[24] Timothy 1:4, quoted in Mary Ellen Brown, "Motley Moments: Soap Operas, Gossip, and the Power of Utterance," in her anthology *Television and Women's Culture: The Politics of the Popular* (Newbury Park, Calif.: Sage, 1990), 183–98; 184.

[25] Margaret Oliphant, *The Doctor's Family* in *The Rector and the Doctor's Family* (New York: Penguin/Virago, 1986), 138; all future references to this novella (abbreviated *Doctor's*) will appear in the text.

[26] Margaret Oliphant, *The Perpetual Curate* (New York: Penguin/Virago, 1987), 16; all future references to this book (abbreviated *Perpetual*) will appear in the text.

"The Executor" (1861), two novellas, *The Rector* and *The Doctor's Family* (published in *Blackwood's Edinburgh Magazine,* 1861; in book form, 1863), and four novels, *Salem Chapel* (1863), *The Perpetual Curate* (1864), *Miss Marjoribanks* (1866), and *Phoebe Junior* (1876). And, in Carlingford, the relentless succession of the everyday ultimately swallows up any disruption, in an inexorable process: "Affairs went on in Carlingford with the usual commonplace pertinacity of human affairs. Notable events happened but seldom in anybody's life, and matters rolled back into their ordinary routine, or found a new routine for themselves after the ordinary course of humanity" (*Doctor's,* 77). This is also a description of Oliphant's narrative method in this series—or, rather, of her critique within it of narrative. The problem of these novels—and the reason they get stretched out into a series—is not to disrupt stasis but to tell it, to recount the everyday.

In his meditation on how to recount the ordinary, Stanley Cavell suggests that the *"Annales* historians' idea of the long time span" also describes the impulse behind "the altogether extraordinary spans of narrative time commanded by serialization."[27] He uses the example of a heart monitor—"a graph of the normal, or the establishment of some reference or base line, a line, so to speak, of the uneventful" (258)—to capture the idea of the serial's formal principle: "serial procedure can be thought of as the establishing of a stable condition punctuated by repeated crises or events that are not developments of the situation requiring a single resolution, but intrusions or emergencies . . . each of which runs a natural course and thereupon rejoins the realm of the uneventful; which is perhaps to say, serial production is undialectical" ("Fact," 258). The undialectical lack of progress, in which seeming change gets reabsorbed as momentary disruption, is Horkheimer's and Adorno's synecdoche too for capitalist culture. And Oliphant also sees the form of culture in terms very similar to Cavell's, although the affect she gives to this is much different. In discussing the "homely clear successions of everydays" that make up for her the steady state of history, Oliphant writes:[28]

> There is nothing more remarkable in all contemporary histories of a troubled era than the quiet tenor of everyday, which, after all, public events agitate so little. . . . Daily human life, which can make nothing of the seven-league boots of history, but must tread on its ordinary pace with its prosaic ordinary footing, walks through revolutions blindfolded, nor ever finds out what . . . pitfalls it has escaped, till long after looking back upon them, in the light of recollection, when many a time the pulse quickens and the heart beats to perceive dangers at the time unknown.[29]

[27] Stanley Cavell, "The Fact of Television," in his *Themes Out of School: Effects and Causes* (San Francisco: North Point Press, 1984), 195–268; 262; all future references to this essay (abbreviated "Fact") will appear in the text.
[28] Margaret Oliphant, "Evelyn and Pepys," *Blackwood's Edinburgh Magazine* 76 (July–Dec. 1854): 32–52; 37.
[29] Ibid., 37, 41.

Rather than abandoning this succession of the uneventful, however, Oliphant wishes to dwell on it, to dwell in it in her own histories of Carlingford, in the series impulse itself: "Real life has no ending save in death," she writes in one review; "it is a tangle of breakings off and addings on, of new beginnings overlapping the old." [30] One of the talents she recognizes in a new writer— Henry James—is the attempt to capture such endless circulation narratively:

> When now and then some artist of special endowments refuses the bondage of art, abandons the necessities of dramatic completeness, and throws us into a vague eternity of wistful suggestions . . . going through all the anguishes and excitements, which ought to bring a conclusion of one kind or another, but always breaking off, never attaining, beginning again in endless and listless renewal, finding every occasion *manqué*, and every new turn of the wheel as continuous yet as incoherent as before—the effect of his delicate perversity is great. [31]

And Oliphant's critical judgment—always acute (even when, as here, somewhat ironic)—has been confirmed. The literary tradition has accepted James's narrative perversity as "great," while Oliphant's, if considered at all, has been considered definitely minor. Part of the problem for Oliphant is context: considered against the supposed certainties of the Victorian world view and the stated requirements for tightly knit endings of the Victorian three-volume novel, her own narrative experiments in inconclusiveness have been overlooked or misunderstood. The literary tradition has never quite known what to do with Oliphant's novels, which is why they keep (not quite) disappearing, hovering at the edges of the canon (Virago Press, for instance, has reprinted all the Carlingford novels, but they are no longer available in the United States). Despite various attempts to rescue them (Elaine Showalter's is one of the best known), they keep getting redefined and dismissed as minor. [32] As the continued interest of feminist presses in Oliphant's writing suggests, part of the reason she has been overlooked in the past has to do with gender: Oliphant's novels themselves provide a cultural analysis that links the scapegoating of women with the kind of dissatisfaction heaped onto serial production that we find in cultural critics like Horkheimer and Adorno. By also linking such problematic relations with the everyday, they provide a theory with which to account for their own vexed relations to literary tradition.

In trying to fix some rules of conduct with which to guide herself, one of Oliphant's heroines realizes that what she is up against is the problem of the everyday. Faced with any number of potentially problematic activities (walks

---

[30] Oliphant, "New Novels," *Blackwood's* 128 (Sept. 1880): 378–404; 382.

[31] Oliphant, "New Books," *Blackwood's* 129 (July 1879): 88–107; 101.

[32] Showalter, *A Literature of Their Own: British Women Novelists from Brontë to Lessing* (Princeton: Princeton University Press, 1977), 20, 47. Oliphant's novels have been difficult for the literary tradition to discuss because we haven't had a ready vocabulary for them. I want to argue that we can find that vocabulary if we look for it, for it is one that Oliphant herself supplies, the vocabulary of the everyday.

with young men, ice-skating), she comes to realize that it is not so much the content that matters, but the form—"Once or twice [almost anything] was possible, but not every day."[33] When it comes to narrative convention, Oliphant's novels explore the way readers too will tolerate the extraordinary but not the everyday event. In doing so, these novels identify their audience with the traditional view—both with the recognized tenets of the canonical tradition and with the ordinary, somewhat narrow-minded authority of Carlingford, ever ready to judge her heroine's conduct (although Oliphant often ultimately supports Carlingford's judgment). For just as Oliphant's heroine has a problem categorically fixing rules, it is difficult to fix a clear distance between the tradition and what it wishes to project outside itself (or between it and the dissident wishing to claim such distance). Paradoxically, Carlingford, so ready to condemn the everyday, is also its site. One thing about the everyday, Oliphant implies, is that we are loath to see it, especially to recognize it in ourselves, to see ourselves as what we are so willing to condemn and reject as the "vulgar routine" in others.[34]

The indivisible connection of the everyday to its seeming opposite explains what critics have disparaged as another problem with Oliphant's writing, what they read as a flaw that *also* keeps it minor: the inability of her everyday domestic realism to avoid a cheap sensationalism.[35] In her literary criticism, Oliphant recognizes that sensationalism, just as much as the everyday, is also characteristic of the minor as far as tradition is concerned: "all our minor novelists, almost without exception, are of the school called sensational," she writes.[36] She locates this sensational impulse in two sources. The first is serialization. "The violent stimulation of serial publication—. . . with its necessity for frequent and rapid recurrences of piquant situation and startling incident—is the thing of all others most likely to develop the germ and bring it to fuller and darker bearing," she argues[37] (a century later Cavell also finds serialization linked "with the idea or the fact of the popular" ["Fact," 250]). Second, Oliphant connects the sensational with the proliferation of women novelists writing at the time; "Out of the mild female undergrowth, variety demands the frequent production of a sensational monster to stimulate the languid life."[38] As the last passage suggests, however, unlike her critics, Oliphant argues that a demand for the extraordinary comes

[33] Margaret Oliphant, *Phoebe Junior* (New York: Virago/Penguin, 1989), 225; all future references to this book (abbreviated *Phoebe*) will appear in the text.

[34] Margaret Oliphant, *Salem Chapel* (New York: Penguin/Virago, 1986), 24; all future references to this book (abbreviated *Salem*) will appear in the text.

[35] See for example Terry, *Victorian Popular Fiction*; Vineta Colby and Robert Colby, *The Equivocal Virtue: Mrs. Oliphant and the Victorian Literary Marketplace* (n.p.: Archon Books, 1966). For a concise overview of the critical reception of Oliphant's work from her death to the present, see Joseph O'Mealy, "Mrs. Oliphant, *Miss Marjoribanks*, and the Victorian Canon," *The Victorian Newsletter* 82 (Fall 1992): 44–49.

[36] Oliphant, "Novels," *Blackwood's* 102 (Sept. 1867): 257–80; 258.

[37] Oliphant, "Sensation Novels," *Blackwood's* 91 (May 1862): 564–84; 568.

[38] Oliphant, "Novels," *Blackwood's* 94 (August 1863): 168–83; 168.

directly out of an attention to the everyday: "that mere desire for something startling which the monotony of ordinary life is apt to produce."[39] As she suggests in her meditation on history that I previously quoted, the same events that are part of the everyday can, seen in another context, inspire our pulses to quicken and our hearts to beat. And even her critics admit that Oliphant's recourse to the extraordinary is contradictory; Helsinger et al use Oliphant, in fact, as exemplary of the paradoxes underlying the definition of the sensational, and, through it, the everyday.[40]

Such contradictoriness has everything to do with minor status. As one critic complains, Oliphant's "resort to the *kitsch* factors of sensationalism, conventional plotting, and so on, as guarantors of popular esteem, comes with curious readiness."[41] The impossible division of the sensational from the everyday domestic realism of Oliphant's fiction remains an important part of her writing precisely because it is part of the way she embraces her status as minor, explores and works through the relation of the popular to the canon. Oliphant's very distinction as a woman writer, she claims, is specifically that she represents the popular: "Twenty literary and other exceptional women in London may speak for a hundred or two more of their like, scattered over the kingdom; but we speak for the mass, which is not exceptional."[42] It is this embrace of her minor status—both when it comes to the everyday and when it comes to the sensational that the canon sees as its opposite, and also condemns—and her recognition of this contradiction within the tradition's definition of the minor, that distinguish Oliphant's different relation to the canon from that of James. As one of her characters asserts about Carlingford: "we never have any High Art down here."[43]

Just as Horkheimer and Adorno argue that capitalism's long duration is punctuated by striking events that seem momentous but only reveal that nothing ever changes, so the lack of high art in Carlingford's everyday dreariness is punctuated nevertheless by extraordinary events. Oliphant's series is really a compendium of all the old plots, conventions, and even character names current at the time. In her novels, Oliphant tackles not just sensationalism, but drawing-room comedy, Tractarian conversion, electioneering, and so on. Yet rather than conflict with her emphasis on the everyday, such

[39] Oliphant, "Novels" (Sept. 1867), 275.
[40] Helsinger et al., *The Woman Question*, 3:135–45.
[41] Valentine Cunningham, *Everywhere Spoken Against: Dissent in the Victorian Novel* (Oxford: Clarendon Press, 1975), 233.
[42] Oliphant, "The Great Unrepresented," *Blackwood's* 100 (Sept. 1866): 367–79; 379. Oliphant's views about the franchise were to change over the course of her life: see, for instance, her statement that "I think it highly absurd that I should not have a vote, if I want one" (708), in "The Grievances of Women," *Fraser's Magazine* 101 (May 1880): 698–710, an essay in part about the ways men "coerce" women "every day of their lives" (700). But it is hard to cast Oliphant's early stance against the vote in "The Great Unrepresented" as antifeminist; it is more, like Woolf's *Three Guineas*, radically (and wishfully) separatist.
[43] Oliphant, *Miss Marjoribanks* (New York: Penguin/Virago, 1988), 433; all future references to this book (abbreviated *Miss*) will appear in the text.

a proliferation of modes and topics furthers it. By the sheer tour de force with which her realism is able to take off every literary commonplace going, Oliphant shows them up as commonplaces, reveals them as conventions, rather than supposed "reality." And she also shows the literary audience's desire for them. Her novel *Salem Chapel* provides a pastiche of Wilkie Collins, which it takes up for a while and then lets drift off, as if bored by it (and which Oliphant's editor, Blackwood, thought kept the novel from greatness). Blackwood was right that such sensationalism makes no sense in Carlingford, but that may be the point. Inserted into Oliphant's novel, a sensational view of the world can only mean "the utter chaos and disturbance of ordinary life" (*Salem*, 331) depicted there. But Oliphant's use of this plot is like her cleric's use of the sensational in a sermon, which prefaces her subplot's own sensational events:

> Mr. Vincent perceived the effect of his eloquence, as a nursery story-teller perceives the rising sob of her little hearers. When he saw it, he awoke ... to feel how unreal was the sentiment in his own breast which had produced this genuine feeling in others, and with a sudden amusement proceeded to deepen his colours and make bolder strokes of effect. His success was perfect. . . . His hearers drew a long breath when it was over. They were startled, frightened, enchanted. If they had been witnessing a melodrama, they scarcely could have been more excited. (*Salem*, 102–3)

Oliphant includes sensational elements in her realism but constantly calls attention to them as overly conventionalized moments—"This is too extraordinary" (*Phoebe*, 103), her characters cry repeatedly.[44] By turning sensationalism into kitsch, Oliphant both preserves and overturns it, returns it to everyday life.

In Oliphant's fiction, as Cavell suggests, such intrusions return to the steady state of the ordinary. The interpolation of the everyday into events we try to make distinct from it is part of the impulse of Oliphant's chronicle. In one of the early Carlingford stories, by an extraordinary plot twist, one of

[44] The old narrative chestnut about the mysterious will, which begins the first Carlingford story, "The Executor," is shown to be "extraordinary" even as Oliphant makes use of it; she calls it that three times on the first page alone. See Oliphant, "The Executor," in *The Doctor's Family and Other Stories* (New York: Oxford University Press, 1986), 1–33; 1; all future references to this story will appear in the text. Similarly, in *The Perpetual Curate*, the subplot about the long lost brother, with its own wills and forgeries, is insistently "extraordinary"—"It's a very extra-ordinary revelation that has just been made to us" (*Perpetual*, 338; see also 345, 364, 368). At an overly coincidental meeting required by the plot in *Phoebe Junior*, the characters exclaim "'This is too extraordinary'" (*Phoebe*, 103). The loss of Miss Marjoribanks's fortune is also "extra-ordinary" (*Miss*, 411, 412), and the tired plot about the adventurer Mr. Cavendish has that character himself protest "'These are very extraordinary accusations'" (*Miss*, 315; see also 156). What critics want to see as evidence of Oliphant's minorness—they cast her recourse to such extreme conventionality as a kind of narrative shallowness or amateurness—actually seems to me a sign of her great irony and narrative self-reflexiveness. But just as Oliphant tells us that Dr. Marjoribanks's Scottish wit is usually lost on the slower-witted Englishman of Carlingford, keepers of the canon don't often seem up to her own sense of fun.

the characters blighting the heroine's life is conveniently killed off; when his corpse is brought sensationally into her parlor, however, we are told that it is laid down amid "the accessories of her own daily life and work" (*Doctor's*, 115), not so much invading them (as the outraged hero protests) but already part of them, for to maintain this burdensome relative has been the focus of the heroine's daily drudgery. In *Salem Chapel*, the audience that think themselves rapt outside "the everyday familiar world" (306) by Vincent's sermon are deluded, like Oliphant's own critics and readers distracted by her sensationalism. The bitter murderess of that novel's sensational sub-lot looks down on the congregation, the commonplace Carlingford burghers, thinking that she in her extraordinary iniquity is "among the dreadful wastes of life, of which these poor fools were ignorant" (*Salem*, 383). Yet the novel makes clear that such wastes are not the province of murderous passions alone, but also reside in what it calls the everyday "killing anxieties of life" itself (*Salem*, 372).

Despite whatever extraordinary dramas Oliphant invents in these novels, sooner or later, all her Carlingford matrons know, things will settle down "in their ordinary way" (*Miss*, 430): "Those commonplace unalterable days . . . it seemed impossible that such heavy hours could last, and prolong themselves into infinitude, as they did; but still one succeeded another in endless hard procession" (*Doctor's*, 107–8). Those characters who remain dissatisfied in Carlingford, always yearning for events to transfigure the everyday, are left (like Oliphant's own audience, she suggests) "with anticipations which were far from cheerful, and a weary sense of the monotony and dulness of life" (*Perpetual*, 437). For, from the start of the series, the figure for that "dread monotony of life" ("Executor," 26) is Carlingford itself, with its rows of houses "doleful and monotonous" ("Executor," 7). As the series goes on and on, what Oliphant leaves with her reader is the steady state of Carlingford, the same characters simply aging, some of them dying, from book to book. The desire for meaning and resolution prompts Oliphant's audience to keep pace with the unalterable succession of her own books as they appear in the series; her audience was always, in fact, clamoring for more, but her critics' ultimate dissatisfaction with the series may register the way the everyday drives readers on because it suspends satisfaction; it is beyond the pleasure principle. The Carlingford novels tease the reader with localized, extraordinary incidents, only to let them drift away. Bereft of the extraordinary, her audience finds itself like her characters plunged into the banalities of Carlingford: "[after that] climax, it would have been a kind of bathos to plunge into ordinary details" (*Miss*, 438).

Yet that is where Oliphant's novels plunge us, substituting the endlessness of the everyday for what we think is the tide of our desire. The balked sensation plot in *Salem Chapel* partly echoes (and, in its own failure, debunks) the hero's misguided daydreams: foolishly convinced that he is loved by a lady of rank and wealth, this poor Dissenting minister "plunged into his lecture, nothing doubting that he could transfer to his work that glorious tumult of his thought; and, with his paper before him, wrote three words, and sat three hours staring into the roseate air, and dreaming dreams as wild as any Arabian tale . . . of the romance that never ends" (*Salem*, 60). Vincent's daydreams, of course, are never realized; he never wins his lady. For his romance that never ends, Oliphant substitutes the endless everyday realism of her own chronicles. Oliphant's irony about Vincent here (he hasn't yet realized that life consists of unsatisfied hard work) is partly meant to show too that within what Horkheimer and Adorno call the "everyday drudgery" of capitalist culture, novel writing is part of "that same old drudgery" ("Novels are part of the industrial system of England," Oliphant writes elsewhere).[45] But unlike Horkheimer and Adorno, Oliphant doesn't insist on everyday drudgery simply to condemn or wish it away, but instead to partake of and explore it.

By insisting on the endless hard work of the everyday, Oliphant provides a perspective to consider the utopic impulse in Horkheimer and Adorno (as well as Deleuze and Guattari). The everyday—to the extent that it is undialectical, as Cavell argues—comments on the dialectical impulse that would transfigure it, turn its tedium into something else, something supposedly authentic and integrated, something which is, Oliphant suggests, not the place of European High Art (as Horkheimer and Adorno would have it), but a utopia, a romance, a nursery tale. That modern theorist of utopia, Paul Ricoeur, has suggested that such imaginary constructions provide a place from which we can think ourselves beyond the thoughts that have constructed us, "an empty place from which to look at ourselves": "The kernel idea of the nowhere implied by the word 'utopia' . . . [means] a place which exists in no real place, a ghost city. . . . What must be emphasized is the benefit of this special extraterritoriality. From this 'no place' an exterior glance is cast on our reality, which suddenly looks strange, nothing more being taken for granted. The field of the possible is now open beyond that of the actual; it is a field, therefore, for alternative ways of living."[46] In her supernatural tale *A Beleaguered City*, Oliphant gives us her own treatment of "a ghost city"; interestingly, it is the one book critics have repeatedly argued deserves a place in the canon, continuing the implicit cultural connection between utopia and high art.[47] But Oliphant emphasizes in that novel that the town of Semur, taken over for several days by the dead, is absolutely bourgeois, common-

[45] "New Novels," 379.

[46] Paul Ricoeur, "Introductory Lecture," in his *Lectures on Ideology and Utopia*, ed. George H. Taylor (New York: Columbia University Press, 1986), 1–18; 15, 16.

[47] See, for example, Robert Colby and Vineta Colby, "*A Beleaguered City*: A Fable for the Victorian Age," *Nineteenth-Century Fiction* 16 (1962): 283–301; they conclude even this appreciation of Oliphant's work with faint praise: "In this, her finest story, in which she was able to distill so much of her experience . . . her emotions, mind, and imagination were all for once fully engaged, and . . . she created a labor of love that should endure among the minor classics of our literature" (301).

place, ordinary. Although, as critics have suggested, the story's extraordinary events seem "the sudden intrusion of the strange and marvellous into the everyday lives of ordinary people," what Oliphant calls the "life of everyday" doesn't change.[48] There is no epiphantic transfiguration of the everyday at story's end—the story, in fact, simply trails off.

A Beleaguered City is not only a supernatural tale, marking a generic departure from Oliphant's Carlingford series, but an extension of Carlingford as well. If either town marks a utopic (or dystopic) site, it does so in terms of the kind of radical redefinition of utopia that Teresa de Lauretis finds inhering within the "practices of daily life."[49] In "the ongoing effort to create a new space of discourse . . . a view from 'elsewhere,'" she argues, we need to recognize that that elsewhere is already and also here in the everyday: "For that 'elsewhere' is not some mythic distant past or some utopian future history: it is the elsewhere of discourse here and now, the blind spots, or the space-off, of its representations. I think of it as spaces in the margins of hegemonic discourses . . . in the micropolitic practices of daily life and daily resistances."[50] By remaining firmly grounded in the everyday, the elsewhere of Oliphant's imaginative constructions encompasses both the relentless oppression of culture and the resistance to it.

It may have been this effect of her emphasis on the everyday that made her contemporaries most want to define her as minor, to relegate her away from important questions by decreeing that the everyday must be unimportant. Most reviewers wished to see Oliphant—as a woman writer especially—as being properly outside or innocent of the ideological, and the politics it implies; they argued that it was her very emphasis on the everyday that kept her so: "She did not deal in novels with a purpose. She frankly assumed, in her old-fashioned way, that people read novels for amusement, and not because they wanted to know more about Karl Marx or Schopenhauer. She wrote about ordinary persons in ordinary circumstances."[51] But Oliphant focuses on the everyday *because* she sees it as the site of the kind of ideological questions also entertained by such theorists as Marx (who, like her, was interested in nothing so much as ordinary persons in ordinary circumstances). For Oliphant, the everyday is precisely what indoctrinates us within, and also makes us wrestle with, ideology, as she insists when discussing another mode of serial publication, the daily press—"that almost irresistible force of a persistent voice going on from day to day," she calls it.[52] "Whatever is persistently in the papers day after day attains a certain credibility, and imposes itself upon us, whether we will or not."[53] Oliphant's own relentless series

[48] Ibid., 285, 284–85.
[49] Teresa de Lauretis, *Technologies of Gender: Essays on Theory, Film, and Fiction* (Bloomington: Indiana University Press, 1987), 2.
[50] Ibid., 25.
[51] "Mrs. Oliphant," London *Daily News*, June 28, 1897.
[52] Oliphant, "The Looker-On," 903.
[53] Ibid., 906.

publication might have been an attempt to identify with authority, impose her own truths, but at the same time it provided her with a space to counter others' indoctrinations.

These emphases in Oliphant suggest that she is not so much interested in portraying the everyday as in investigating our construction of it. Rather than fundamentally defining the everyday herself, deciding that it is the vehicle for our constraint in or escape from social power, Oliphant instead uses her series of novels to locate the everyday as the site for just such debate, for political and ideological struggle. In the recent discussion of the series impulse in soap opera narrative, critics have veered close to the kind of essentializing notion of the everyday that Oliphant refuses. In arguing for the serial's resistance to closure and preservation of enigma, critics including Modleski and Sandy Flitterman-Lewis have risked decreeing it as by definition a resistant and subversive form. Michele Mattelart, Deborah Rogers, and Patricia Holland, on the other hand, insist on its conservatism, emphasizing the speciousness of a form that makes the daily grind seem pleasurable in order to appropriate subjects to it.[54] The impulse of Oliphant's fiction (as of modern soap operas themselves, I would speculate) is instead to keep the question open, to theorize the everyday as a shifting, complex realm.

Oliphant's heroine Phoebe Junior, for instance, when she finds herself among the commonplace mercantile grandparents from whom her parents have worked hard to distance her, tries to solace herself that she is not so ordinary, tries to transform the everyday as it applies to herself: "she took her place at [the table], and poured out tea for the old people, and cut bread-and-butter with the most gracious philosophy. Duchesses did the same every day. . . . it cannot be told what a help and refreshment this thought was to Phoebe's courageous heart" (*Phoebe*, 88): "Look at that cup," she says to one of the refined gentlemen she must nervously entertain in her grandparents' presence, "and fancy grandmama having this old service in use without knowing how valuable it is. Cream Wedgwood! You may fancy how I stared when I saw it; and in everyday use!" (182). But rather than validate Phoebe's view of her own specialness (part of her would like to think that, although maintained by her grandparents, she is too precious for their banal tastes to recognize, forced unnaturally to be useful within the everyday), Oliphant insists on the everyday as that which cannot be transcended. Phoebe's guest makes a pretty speech in reply that gets in his own implicit claim to be above the usual: "A set of fine China is like a poem—every individual is necessary to the perfection of the whole. I allow that this is not the usual way of looking at it; but my pleasure lies in seeing it entire, making the tea-table into a

---

[54] Michele Mattelart, *Women, Media, and Crisis: Femininity and Disorder* (London: Comedia, 1986); Deborah Rogers, "Daze of Our Lives: The Soap Opera as Feminine Text," *Journal of American Culture* 14 (1991): 29–41; Patricia Holland, "Review of *Television and Women's Culture* and *Women and Soap Opera*," *Screen* 33 (1992): 122–26. See also Lynn Spigal, "Detours in the Search for Tomorrow: Tania Modleski's *Loving with a Vengeance: Mass-Produced Fantasies for Women*," *Camera Obscura* 13–14 (1985): 215–34.

kind of lyric, elevating the family life by the application of the principles of abstract beauty to its homeliest details" (183). But Oliphant has Phoebe's honest grandmother debunk both their pretensions—especially such privileging of abstraction and transcendence—by being unashamed of her own humbleness: "Old things like this as might have been my granny's, they're good enough for every day, they're very nice for common use; but they ain't no more fit to be put away in cupboards and hoarded up like fine china, no more than I am" (184).

As the realm in which all relations actually take place, the everyday is to be ignored at one's peril. It is from there that Mr. May, another character in this novel, draws his power; his petty demands are what keep him a tyrant in his own family, as he deliberately provokes his daughters by the most common expedients "every day of their lives" (72) for his own sadistic pleasure. Oliphant suggests how such cruelties are powerful through their very pettiness: "Love, patience, charity, after all, are but human qualities, when they have to be held against daily disgusts, irritations, and miseries" (*Doctor's*, 136). Yet Mr. May's power is also overthrown through the everyday. His forgery (that staple of sensation fiction) is revealed as a banality arising from the most everyday of motives and causes. The narrator charts its humdrum course, pointing out to the reader who might lose track of its mundaneness every "trifling incident [that] had its influence upon after affairs" (*Phoebe*, 155). May simply nickels and dimes his money away, the very banality of his desperate circumstances screening them from him ("Well, he said to himself," as he squanders his money on the last small purchase that makes his debt irrevocable and his forgery inevitable, "who could call it extravagance? . . . a thing which was a necessity, not for luxury, but everyday use?" [*Phoebe*, 246]). Oliphant's humbling lesson for Phoebe is that May's sensational crime arises from everyday use and not from something extraordinary: "What could he have done it for?" Phoebe wonders. "Mere money, the foolish expenses of every day, or what would be more respectable, some vague mysterious claim upon him, which might make desperate expedients necessary?" (294). For her readers too, Oliphant is highlighting the difficulty—and danger—of attempting to separate power and resistance, the extraordinary and the everyday.

Oliphant's work also emphasizes the difficulty of fixing limits when it comes to canonical evaluation. In the backings and fillings that spin out the self in her *Autobiography*, she both insists on her minor status and implies that her work has been underestimated nonetheless. Both are possible simultaneously because the standards of tradition are not fixed or immutable: in an essay on canon formation, "Modern Novelists—Great and Small," Oliphant asserts just that. "Greatness is always comparative," the essay begins. "There are few things so hard to adjust as the sliding-scale of fame." [55]

---

[55] Oliphant, "Modern Novelists—Great and Small," *Blackwood's* 77 (1855): 554–68, 554; all future references to this essay (abbreviated "Modern") will appear in the text.

Literary rank is a hierarchy—a sliding scale—that depends on a relative position: greatness must be compared to something else. The point of the essay is that the sign is arbitrary: as the essay begins, Oliphant's narrator is musing on greatness while she turns the pages of an autograph book. Yet she admits she recognizes few of the supposedly famous names in it, and "we flatter ourselves that we were not inferior in this particular to the mass of the literature-loving public" ("Modern," 554). The negative here complicates questions of inferiority, turns them on their head—Oliphant is not inferior to the mass, who, the essay goes on to suggest, are not so inferior either: so-called minor writers, writers of "the second rank," remain familiar and "well-known names," and "to have remained so long in possession of the popular ear is no small tribute to their powers" (554, 555). Such popular minor writers, writers for mass culture, undermine those great names we no longer recognize and even some "grand names of unquestionable magnitude and influence" who have become obscure in another way—"the secret of whose power we cannot discover in anything they have left behind" (554).

Established culture wishes to deny such relativism because in losing the ability to ordain greatness (defined in its self-image) it loses its own previously uncontestable claim to it. Horkheimer and Adorno deplore the way mass culture rests on sterile repetition, simulacra without reference, precisely for this reason; although in the dizzying proliferation of his own writing, Baudrillard aggressively exploits such loss of original reference as the inescapable logic of culture, his arguments retain a nostalgia for a lost real nonetheless. Even Julia Kristeva, in critiquing traditional feminism for essentializing certain qualities as feminine (such as the repetitive and endless cycles of nonlinear time), objects that we find in feminism's relation to masculine culture a logic of face-off, in which opposition becomes only the simulacrum of what it opposes ("Women's," 28) (assuming at least to some degree an impossible realm outside such relational definition). Although Oliphant criticized what she called "the bubble reputation" of many of her fellow minor authors, and although she directed against others a criticism often made about her own works—that the Victorian three-decker, especially in its serial mode, was an empty and repetitive form, spun out of control[56]—her emphasis on the everyday largely prevents ultimate recourse to some ideal greatness. Her novels accept, and also recognize the power of, the ungrounded system revealed by the everyday. They suggest that, just as the place within which to confront ideology is not elsewhere but here, so too the system of simulacra, although empty and arbitrary, no longer certain or true, is still meaningful and very effective. Although the system may be arbitrary, it still nevertheless constructs us, and with palpable—if not often painful—effects.

[56] For the first phrase, see ibid., 562; for Oliphant's criticism of the form, see "New Novels," for instance, where she says of Meredith's *Egoist*, "had he confined it to one volume, it might have been a remarkable work" (404).

Taking the everyday for granted, disparaging it, failing to understand its importance, is what makes us pawns in this struggle.

When it comes to the canon, Oliphant herself provides a symbol of the destabilization that threatens to undermine literary hierarchy. Perhaps because he made it into the canon, Henry James was aware of the reasons that Oliphant got left out; he explains her problematic status in exactly those terms. "Criticism has come to the pass," he writes, "of being shy of difficult cases."[57] In their obituary essays about her, critics attempted uneasily and unsuccessfully to give Oliphant her literary rank—was she above Trollope but below George Eliot?—simply continuing what had been their discomfort with her all along: she remained unrankable, a limit case of the tradition. Their response to Oliphant's work may have been to some degree shaped by Oliphant. Just as they jumped willingly to take at face value her own ironic self-evaluations of her work in her *Autobiography* (as Oliphant predicted there they would), the gatekeepers of literary tradition may ultimately have dismissed Oliphant's case as undecidable because that is what her own work told them to do.[58] Esther Schor has considered the way that Oliphant, very aware of herself as arbiter of culture in her own role as literary critic, continually called into question her own critical authority, thematized its instability in her fiction: "What does it mean, [her] fictions ask, to use a rhetoric of distinctions, decisions and determinations to account for a literary text? to assimilate one's mixed and perhaps irreconcilable responses to a single, morally viable and socially responsible position? to authorize and canonize the reading of a single reader?"[59] Schor finds the inconclusive and undecidable ending of *A Beleaguered City* a metaphor for Oliphant's refusal of fixed and certain standards that directly puts into question not just the role of the critic but the tradition in which he or she must operate.

But Oliphant's audacity goes further than simply emphasizing such uncertainty; she also stipulates that, whether her contemporaries recognize it or not, it is the spirit of her age, "an unheroic age, which will not suffer a man to be absolutely sure of anything" (*Perpetual*, 33; see also 242)—the

---

[57] Quoted by Q. D. Leavis, "Introduction," *Autobiography and Letters of Mrs. Margaret Oliphant*, ed. Mrs. Harry Coghill (Leicester: Leicester University Press, 1974), 9–34; 9.

[58] "Death of Mrs. Oliphant," *Standard*, June 28, 1897: "Though it would be wrong to speak of her as in any sense belonging to the very first rank of contemporary writers, no estimate of the literature of the Victorian epoch can ever be complete which does not reckon with her works. . . . If we were asked to say what rank Mrs. Oliphant will take among novelists since Scott and Miss Austen, we should be inclined to ascribe her a high place—higher, possibly, than Trollope, and certainly than Charles Reade, though, of course, unmeasurably lower than either George Eliot, Dickens or Thackeray." "The Death of Mrs. Oliphant, a well-known Novelist," *Pall Mall Gazette*, June 28, 1897; both in National Library of Scotland Oliphant Collection. As Oliphant says in her *Autobiography*: "I feel that my carelessness of asserting my claim is very much against me with everybody. It is so natural to think that if a workman himself is indifferent about his work, there can't be much in it that is worth thinking about": *The Autobiography of Margaret Oliphant*, ed. Elisabeth Jay (New York: Oxford, 1990), 15.

[59] Esther Schor, "The Haunted Interpreter in Margaret Oliphant's Supernatural Fiction," *Women's Studies* 22 (1993): 371–88; 385.

presumption behind Oliphant's unheroic and everyday realism. She locates such undecidability directly in the everyday: "It is one of the paradoxes of which nature is full," she writes, "that the more close we come to the absolute commonplace, the more difficult it is to understand it."[60] The everyday is that which it is impossible categorically to fix; one of her women artists, musing on the panorama of Carlingford, suggests as much: "it was a very ordinary scene. . . . if only any painter could have transferred to his canvas the subdued musical hum of surrounding life" (*Miss*, 272). In ironic self-aggrandizement, Oliphant implies that such everyday pictures are the most elusive and formidable, such everyday fictions not so commonplace after all.

At the same time, Oliphant exposes her audience's discomfort with the vagueness of the everyday, its lack of certainty. In *The Perpetual Curate*, the curate's brother becomes a convert to Rome exactly because there is no room there for "conflicting doctrines and latitude of belief": "If you but knew the consolation," he says, "after years of struggling among the problems of faith, to find one's self at last upon a rock of authority, of certainty—one holds in one's hand at last the interpretation of the enigma" (*Perpetual*, 435). The curate, however, knows his brother's consolation is an illusion; "'outside lies a world in which every event is [still] an enigma,'" he tells him, as he "looked back on his memory, and recalled, as if they had been in a book, the daily problems with which he was so well acquainted" (*Perpetual*, 436). The book in which such daily problems are written is Oliphant's own—and written in a way to refuse authority and cleave to the uncertainty of the everyday. This aspect of Oliphant's fiction especially troubled her critics; one reviewer regrets "the somewhat aggravating pathos of the *denouement* [of one story] which failed to explain the inscrutable mystery on rational grounds."[61] Another blames Oliphant's minor status as much on such ambiguous doubleness—her "deep, pervading sense of irony"—as on her relentless emphasis on the "ordinary commonplace."[62]

Such undecidable everyday questions are for Oliphant specifically questions of gender. In "Modern Novelists—Great and Small," the novelists of second rank she sees the canon construct (in order to define itself against them) are by definition women writers, who are thought to have "a *natural* right or claim" to this status (555; emphasis mine). (Referring to such essentialist assumptions about women's nature, Oliphant writes: "we are not men spoiled in the making, but women."[63]) From the beginning of the Carlingford series, what characterizes the gender struggle for Oliphant is men's attempt to deny being part of the everyday. In her early novella *The Rector*, that sheltered don who has somehow made his way to Carlingford can only ask "what was he doing here, among that little world of human creatures

[60] Oliphant, "Men and Women," *Blackwood's* 157 (April 1895): 620–50; 645.
[61] *Times*, June 28, 1897.
[62] *Standard*, June 28, 1897.
[63] "The Great Unrepresented," 376.

who were dying, being born, perishing, suffering, falling into misfortune and anguish, and all manner of human vicissitudes, every day?"[64] Arthur Vincent, the hero of *Salem Chapel*, also is horrified by Carlingford because "amid [its] rude luxuries and commonplace plenty, life could have no heroic circumstances" (*Salem*, 16). It takes a failed romance (in terms of both his unrequited love and the frustrated sensation plot) for him to learn, to the degree he ever does, that this is the lesson of Oliphant's world.

Women's acceptance of the everyday, even their enslavement to it, is what distinguishes them from men, one of "those indefinable peculiarities of difference that exist between the mind of woman and that of man" (*Miss*, 194) and also "one instance of the perennial inequality between the two halves of mankind" (*Perpetual*, 461). Their connection with the everyday makes women incomprehensible to men. Vincent simply cannot understand his mother, the way she "took all the common cares of life with her into her severest trouble" (*Salem*, 162) because he still wishes to hold apart the everyday and the extraordinary (doing so also allows him conveniently to overlook his mother's drudgery and sacrifice):

> "You women are incomprehensible," said the young man, with an irritation he could not subdue—". . . if the world were going to pieces you must still be intent upon . . . trifles."
>
> ". . . Oh, Arthur, it is often the trifles that are the most important." (*Salem*, 358)

Oliphant translates the tension between women and men into the tension between the resignation to life's inevitable and persistent vicissitudes and the resistance that hopes to wrap up or resolve them: "*She* was a dutiful woman, subdued by long experience of that inevitable necessity against which all resistance fails, and he a passionate young man, naturally a rebel against every such bond. They could not understand each other" (*Salem*, 162). Yet although Oliphant poses the question of the status of the everyday in this opposition—women/men, age/youth, the serial/closure, restraint/escape—she will not maintain the unequivocalness of these terms or resolve the opposition; she will not settle what remains an unsettled debate. Oliphant may be interested in the question of the everyday because it opens up the question of women's construction as much as of the tradition's—categories, she stresses, informed by contradiction. Rather than simply support or undercut the view of women ventriloquized through Vincent's view of his mother, Oliphant leaves it as a question: "Woman's weaker nature, that could mingle the common with the great; or woman's strength, that could endure all things—which was it?" (*Salem*, 190).

Throughout her series, such contradictions remain part and parcel of

[64] Oliphant, *The Rector*, in *The Rector and The Doctor's Family*, 1–35; 26; all future references to this novella (abbreviated *Rector*) appear in the text.

Oliphant's alignment of women and the everyday. Even her last Carlingford heroine, her (almost) new woman, Phoebe Junior, remains riven by them. Like Oliphant's male characters, Phoebe too has wished (for reasons of class) to rise above the everyday. But Oliphant sympathetically details the way that Phoebe is torn between a desire to join a High Culture that ignores her and to revise it:

> She was very well got up in the subject of education for women, and lamented often and pathetically the difficulty they lay under of acquiring the highest instruction; but at the same time she patronized Mr. Ruskin's theory that dancing, drawing, and cooking were three of the higher arts which ought to be studied by girls. It is not necessary for me to account for the discrepancies between those two systems, in the first place because I cannot, and in the second place, because there is in the mind of the age some ineffable way of harmonizing them which makes their conjunction common. (*Phoebe*, 17–18)

Oliphant's maintenance of paradox—"it is the form her wit takes, a sympathetic relish for contradictions"[65]—reflects her political strategy: to hold a problem open, to maintain debate and conflict, not to elude authority but to query it. Such a strategy led her to her own problems with authority; no less a critic than Queenie Leavis, herself heavily invested in the great tradition, argues it kept Oliphant from ever being the editor of a journal, although almost every male editor in England was happy to pay her cheaply for her talents (another reason they may have cheapened them on the market). The literary fraternity thought such skepticism as Oliphant's, along with her gender, debarred her from their ranks.[66]

If we want to say that Oliphant's strategy makes her a political revolutionary (as some recent critics claim),[67] then we need to observe her own use of the term "revolution," as well as of "politics." For Oliphant both remain an ongoing, never-ending struggle. Her heroine Lucilla Marjoribanks is paradoxically distinguished from the rest of Carlingford in that she doesn't attempt by any act of will to distinguish herself; she doesn't try to make anything else out of the everyday life given to her, but, in accepting it, finding it engrossing and important, gains her influence and efficacy. Oliphant emphasizes that this is expressly a *political* capability: Lucilla's drawing room is the site of consummate political maneuvering both in terms of supposedly commonplace and trivial feminine questions ("To be sure the men did not even find out what it was that awoke the ladies' attention; but then, in delicate matters of social politics, one never expects to be understood by *them*" [*Miss*, 122]) and in terms of Lucilla's decisive management of Carlingford's Parlia-

---

[65] Penelope Fitzgerald, "Introduction," *The Rector and The Doctor's Family*, v–xvi; xv.

[66] See Leavis, "Introduction," *Autobiography*, 15–16, and especially 21.

[67] See *Margaret Oliphant: Critical Essays on a Gentle Subversive*, ed. D. J. Trela (Selinsgrove, Pa.: Susquehanna University Press, 1995), and Margarete Rubik, *The Novels of Mrs. Oliphant: A Subversive View of Traditional Themes* (New York: Peter Lang, 1994).

mentary election ("for she had come to an age at which she might have gone into Parliament herself had there been no disqualification of sex" [*Miss,* 394]). Yet at the same time Oliphant also stresses that Lucilla is not the kind of woman "to 'make a protest'" (395) even though she almost continually calls her a "revolutionary" (44, 67, 73, 100, 213, 218, 229, 230, 274, 311, and so on). Lucilla's kind of revolution, the one politically effective in Carlingford, is connected with the ongoing undramatic succession of Oliphant's own series production, literally with the long durée of evolution. To understand Lucilla, one must understand all Carlingford up until her time, Oliphant tells us at the start of her narrative, which "is something like going back into the prehistoric period—those ages of the flint, which only ingenious quarrymen and learned geologists can elucidate—to recall the social condition of the town before Miss Marjoribanks began her Thursday evenings" (41). Oliphant is interested in revolution not just as a sudden break but also a repeated cycle.

The evolution of Lucilla's political strategy then does not guarantee progression in the traditional sense; it (like Oliphant's series) culminates in no grand climax. What ends Lucilla's story, in fact, is "one of the very commonest sounds of everyday existence—a cab driving down Grange Lane" (*Miss,* 469–70). This sound heralds the arrival back on the scene of Lucilla's very commonplace lover, who hasn't figured at all in the plot, and who ends it by the most banal expedient of marrying the heroine. Blackwood found this an anticlimactic and disappointing ending, converting a promising book into another minor failure. But Oliphant's narrator at the novel's end predicts just such a reaction, forecasting that Carlingford itself will want to turn a "commonplace conclusion" into "a distinct bit of romance" in order to keep "the blank of ordinary existence" from settling down on them again (495); throughout the story the novel has been well aware that "the ordinary routine did not satisfy Lucilla's constituency" (152). Oliphant proposes instead that the everyday is where they—and we—ought to locate their politics. It is in this light perhaps that we should read Oliphant's sharp rejoinder that she "is concerned about nothing except the most domestic and limited concerns" when Blackwood tells her that he hopes to see her in "the first rank of novelists."[68] By insisting on her role as the writer of minor and everyday struggles that never end, Oliphant relocates politics abidingly in the minor and everyday.

In "Modern Novelists—Great and Small," Oliphant's treatise on minor literature, she is especially interested in the production of women writers.

[68] Margaret Oliphant, *Autobiography and Letters,* ed. Mrs. Harry Coghill (New York: Dodd, Mead, 1899), 198.

And she singles out one writer especially to associate with the repetition and proliferation that Horkheimer and Adorno connect not just with women but with the form of the series and with the minor. Of Charlotte Yonge's many novels, Oliphant writes: "There is no accounting for the wonderful rise of the 'bubble reputation' in many instances; but though we cannot admit that these books deserve *all* the applause they have got, they are still very good books, and worthy of a high place" ("Modern," 562). Yonge's best-selling *Heir of Redclyffe* was one of what Oliphant elsewhere called "the numerical successes in literature of the present day, when edition follows edition, and thousand thousand." [69] Besides the young ladies of the circulating library, politicians, Oxford undergraduates, artists such as William Morris, and soldiers in the Crimea were all said to have wept over the death of its pious hero. And although they may not have spun out quite so many editions, Yonge's chronicles of the Mays, the Underwoods, and a host of other huge families spawned a network of linked novels that she couldn't write quickly enough to satisfy her readers. It is this series of endless production that stands out about Yonge even for the very prolific Oliphant. Oliphant (always aware of her own enormous production; she once bet Trollope that she had written more novels than he—and won) [70] wrote of what she called Yonge's "series of books" that "we had almost said [that she had produced] hundreds of narratives of a similar character." [71] Yet Oliphant was always careful to praise this highly prolific and popular writer, who, she felt, like herself, included within her work "much shrewd appreciation of common life ("Modern," 562).

Except for this common focus on the everyday, no two writers might seem more different than Charlotte Yonge and Margaret Oliphant. Traditional authority downplayed Oliphant's novels for their cynicism and irreverence, for an ironic and pointed feminism that questioned the very grounding of tradition and authority. Yonge's novels suffered for the opposite reason. Even some of her admirers recognized that her moral views were orthodox and sanctimonious. Reverence for traditional authority led her to such conservative disclaimers about her pictures of domestic realism and meditations on women's lives as: "Not that I have anything new to say—only that which is so old that it may seem new. I have no hesitation in declaring my full belief in the inferiority of woman, nor that she brought it upon herself." [72] Yet such dogma seems to have done little for her when it came to the authorities; contemporary reviewers piously acknowledged her piety while dismissing her

---

[69] Oliphant, "The Sisters Brontë," in *Women Novelists of Queen Victoria's Reign: A Book of Appreciations"* (London: Hurst & Blackett, 1897), 3–59; 5.

[70] Referred to, for instance, in "Death of Mrs. Oliphant; By an Old Friend," *Daily Telegraph,* Monday, June 28, 1897.

[71] Oliphant, *The Victorian Age of English Literature,* 2 vols. (New York: Tait, 1892), 1:493–94.

[72] Charlotte Yonge, *Womankind* (New York: Macmillan, n.d.), 1; all future references to this book will appear in the text.

artistry because of it. To the tradition, she was simply the writer of a didactic fiction fit only for women and children. Even in this century, Queenie Leavis still felt the need aggressively to assert that view, to defend the tradition from what it saw as Yonge's assault—the very onslaught of her massive output—"before the canon of English Literature finds itself permanently burdened with one of the prolific fiction-writers whom time alone has already expelled."[73]

Oliphant was well aware of Yonge's priggishness and hypocrisy and was a more trenchant analyst of it than any of these critics. The family named May in *Phoebe Junior* directly burlesques Yonge's famous family of that name (as one of Oliphant's younger Mays says about Yonge's family: "We are not a set of prigs like those people" [*Phoebe*, 141]). The world of Carlingford doesn't care much about these Mays, but is interested in a much more commonplace figure, a kind of dull, selfish boy called Clarence Copperhead, whom the title character ultimately marries. The heroine tries to explain her own preference for Clarence to Reginald May:

> "He is not the fascinating pupil of a church-novel. There's nothing the least like the Heir of Redclyffe about him."
> "You are very well up in Miss Yonge's novels, Miss Beecham."
> "Yes," said Phoebe . . . "All that I know of clergymen's families I have got from her. I can recognize you quite well, and your sister, but the younger ones puzzle me; they are not in Miss Yonge; they are too much like other children, too naughty. . . . See how much I have got out of Miss Yonge. I know you as well as if I had known you all my life; a great deal better than I know Clarence Copperhead; but then no person of genius has taken any trouble about him."
> (*Phoebe*, 175)

Oliphant's parody of Yonge registers (however backhandedly) the influence of an alternative women's tradition, Oliphant's indebtedness to Yonge ("See how much I have got out of Miss Yonge"). Oliphant's ironic disclaimer—"no person of genius has taken any trouble about" Clarence (of course, *Oliphant* is the writer troubling herself with his depiction)—may ironically spoof Yonge's (and her own) claims to genius (even while asserting them), but is actually more irreverent about the tradition itself. Oliphant's parody of this fellow minor writer of series fiction is neither simple nor dismissive:

---

[73] Q. D. Leavis, "Charlotte Yonge and 'Christian Discrimination,'" *Scrutiny* 12 (1944): 152–60; 152. In "Charlotte Yonge as a Chronicler," Edith Sichel argues that "the annals of commonplace virtue are not more tedious than the annals of commonplace vice. Miss Yonge is as lengthy as you choose, but what can be more lengthy than a modern realist novel?" *The Monthly Review* (May 1901): 88–97; 88. E. A. Bennett also talks of Yonge's "fabulous fecundity"—her "length is prodigious": Bennett, *Fame and Fiction: An Enquiry into Certain Popularities* (New York: Dutton, 1901]), 49, 51. As Bennett's language suggests, the disapproval of Yonge's "fecundity" buttresses itself (as did Horkheimer and Adorno's dismissal of mass culture) with gender. Leavis also discusses Yonge as a prolific writer who is really sterile, not truly pregnant, unhealthy, while she accords to male writers a vital and potent sexuality (see "Charlotte Yonge," 153–55).

she knows what is at stake in reactions to Yonge—that the tradition willingly sacrifices writers like her (no matter how devoutly she upholds it) in order to sanctify the very establishment of its canon.

The tradition here, as in Oliphant's case, opposes its claim to High Art against what critics call "the everyday social life [Yonge] represents."[74] Almost every reviewer emphasized that an attention to the everyday ("you are admitted every day to almost every room," one of them wrote)[75] formed the gist of Yonge's domestic realism: "Prosaically considered, *The Daisy Chain* is a matter-of-fact chronicle of the trivial daily doings of the eleven motherless children of a doctor in a country town."[76] Henry James argued that Yonge's emphasis on everyday life had originated a school of realist fiction in England—a school that focuses on what one critic called "the faithful representation of commonplace things"[77]—to rival Zola and Flaubert. Strange as it may seem to us now, critics often compared the brute naturalism of such French writers to Yonge's everyday chronicles (chronicles of what Queenie Leavis at any rate saw as sexless upper-class snobs endlessly concerned with events like Confirmations and each other's adherence to sectarian principles—an odd contrast to the prostitutes and roués of French fiction).[78] Their emphasis on the everyday was enough for Yonge's contemporaries to connect if only by contrasting these otherwise so seemingly antagonistic kinds of fiction. And that connection highlights how the everyday cuts right to the heart of the problem of tradition for those attempting to maintain it. No matter how (overly) moral, how masochistic even in their obeisance to prestige and domination, Yonge's novels become for the tradition equivalent to its French rivals when they pay attention to a realm of experience traditionally deemed invisible, insignificant; they begin in spite of themselves to expose the relational base of power.

Which is not to argue that the everyday life in Yonge's chronicles represents a subconscious subversive impulse of license and latitude. On the contrary, in keeping with Tractarian principles, she emphasizes the everyday as

[74] Margaret Mare and Alicia Percival, *Victorian Best-Seller: The World of Charlotte M. Yonge* (New York: Chanticleer, 1948), 237.

[75] Anon., "The Author of Heartsease and Modern Schools of Fiction," *The Prospective Review* 10 (1854): 460–82; 461.

[76] "Literature and Science: Miss Yonge," *The Guardian*, Dec. 2, 1896: 1931–32; 1931.

[77] Both the reference to James's claim and the passage cited are in Barbara Dennis, "The Two Voices of Charlotte Yonge," *The Durham University Journal* 34 (1973): 181–88; 182, 184.

[78] In "Charlotte Yonge as a Chronicler," the reviewer asserts that "the secret of Charlotte Yonge's strength lies in this: she plucks the heart out of the obvious—she evokes the familiar. . . . if we are to make a preposterous analogy, Miss Yonge is, on the whole, more like Zola than Homer in her methods" (89–90). Amy Cruse quotes a contemporary of Yonge's, Henry Sidgwick: "Did you ever read Madame Bovary? It is a very powerful book, and Miss Yonge reminds one of it by force of contrast. It shows how the ennui of mean French domestic life drags down women, whereas Miss Yonge makes one feel how full of interest the narrowest sphere of life is" (*Victorians and Their Reading*, 55). Perhaps the most famous comparison of this kind is Rhoda Broughton, who said "I began life as Zola, I finish it as Miss Charlotte Yonge" to describe the way her originally shocking work came over time to seem tame (Cruse, 58).

the proper ground for discipline, duty, authority. As she tells the readers of her little magazine "The Packet," she wrote in order to "help you to perceive how to bring your religious principles to bear upon your daily life."[79] As she emphasizes in *Womankind*, her misogynistic treatise on women, "the original meaning of the word Religion is 'rule'" (73), and "to set a watch before the lips, and to examine oneself daily, is the rule laid before every Christian" (159). The everyday, especially for womankind, involves "daily obligation" (77): "make it a duty to learn something, practise something, obtain some step in self-improvement every day" (84). If Yonge's domestic realism makes a utopia out of the everyday—and one critic asserts that her "domestic interiors . . . prefigur[ed for her readers] a Victorian paradise"[80]—her better world is one, like de Lauretis's, in the here and now. Yet (and this puts the inherent progressiveness of arguments like de Lauretis's into question) what exists in that space is the order and restraint of a celestial autocracy.

In defending the canon from the burden of Yonge's seriality, Leavis also defends it from what she calls Yonge's "orthodoxy."[81] To modern readers, this argument seems unexpected, coming from what we consider the very orthodox Leavis, but the logic is actually plain: the obviousness of Yonge's orthodoxy might give away the canon's own, might make clear that the great tradition is not essential, unbiased, outside time or interest (as Leavis would claim) but constructed by a body of adherents who profit from its strict and narrow limits. In fact, in their discussions of the canon, "minority" critics such as Henry Louis Gates Jr. and Gayatri Spivak, rather than aligning the everyday with the oppositional stance of the minor, associate it with a traditional, canonical impulse.[82] As the paradoxical and conflicting associations of the everyday in current theory, and Oliphant's and Yonge's examples, show, rather than marking some certain essence, some stable and utopic realm, the everyday—like the canon itself—remains a shifting construct that takes its meaning from its context.

"Oh! why will not the rights and wrongs of this world be more clearly divided?" Yonge's narrator demands in the midst of one of her chronicles.[83] Part of the impulse that keeps Yonge endlessly writing novels is the endless attempt (always unsuccessful) to negotiate this divide, to pin down the dizzy-

---

[79] Quoted in Georgina Battiscombe, *Charlotte Mary Yonge: The Story of an Uneventful Life* (London: Constable, 1943), 67.

[80] Dennis, "Two Voices," 182.

[81] Leavis, "Charlotte Yonge," 156.

[82] Spivak finds the constitution of things like the canon, which she locates within the everyday, "normative and privative"; see her "Constitutions and Cultural Studies," *Yale Journal of Law and the Humanities* 2 (1990): 133–47; 145, as well as her "Making of Americans, the Teaching of English, and the Future of Cultural Studies," *New Literary History* 21 (1990): 781–98. In "The Master's Pieces: On Canon-Formation and the African-American Tradition," Gates calls the canon "the commonplace book of our shared culture": *South Atlantic Quarterly* 89 (1990): 89–11; 92.

[83] Charlotte Yonge, *The Trial: More Links of the Daisy Chain* (New York: Appleton, 1865), 124; all future references to this book will appear in the text.

ing ramifications of every trivial action within this everyday world. Yonge's reaction to this moral explosion is to extend her proliferating series (and, even more than her contemporaries, she pushes this logic past its limits; her series spin out of control in every direction, as her chronicles mushroom to include two, three, even four extended families, all intermarrying, begetting new members, invading each other's novels). The critics' alarm about the sterile repetition of such seriality—about Yonge's "ardent admirers who read and reread her fiction repeatedly" [84]—like Leavis's derogation of its unhealthy refusal of sexuality seems itself an apotropaic response to the rampant production in Yonge's writing. This proliferation is meant to swamp her own doubt; it grows out of an impulse to assuage her own discomfort about the promiscuous intermingling of opposites that only repeats it.

Just as Horkheimer and Adorno do, Yonge's contemporaries blame such promiscuity on women. One reviewer found all Yonge's work too dilatory— "she constantly repeats . . . [which] unnecessarily swells the book." [85] An emphasis on the everyday is what makes such expansion mere dilation rather than something monumental or great: "Humanity may, indeed, disclose itself after long intercourse, by constantly peeping through the holes and crevices of every-day manner. . . . But, on the whole, the larger kind of character can only be delineated by help of special emergencies." [86] The larger kind of character (of course) equals "men, more especially men of deep character"; their qualities live not in the everyday but "far beneath the surface of ordinary action: only a rare emergency will bring them to the surface." [87] Here, according to the cultural assumptions Kristeva outlines, men supposedly progress linearly through extraordinary climaxes; women's generative power repeats itself to no clear end within the repetitive cycles of women's time. The overheated language with which this review describes Yonge's plots, with their swellings and peepings and crevices, is reminiscent of the narrative patterns set forth by critics such as Peter Brooks and Susan Winnett which attempt to identify plot trajectories with supposed male and female patterns of sexuality.[88] That is an essentialism I wish expressly to reject partly because Yonge herself upholds the ideology behind it, transforming the cultural view of men's and women's time into fixed evaluations. She has one character counter her mother's objections to her behavior ("I don't think your father would have wished it") with: "He would have gone on with the spirit of the times, mother; men do, while women stand still." [89] In Yonge's work, the everyday world of what she casts as women's time gets translated into what

---

[84] "Literature and Science: Miss Yonge," 1931.

[85] "The Author of Heartsease," 464.

[86] Ibid.

[87] Ibid.

[88] Peter Brooks, "Freud's Masterplot," *Yale French Studies* 55/56: (1977): 280–300; Susan Winnett. "Coming Unstrung: Women, Men, Narrative, and Principles of Pleasure," *PMLA* 105 (1990): 505–18.

[89] Quoted in Mare and Percival, *Victorian Best-Seller*, 72.

she, with approval, calls "the feminine conservative element" (*Womankind*, 290)—the same element which keeps conserving her narrative, allowing it to channel itself from one novel into another with little loss or resolution.

Yonge attempts to redefine "larger character" by redefining heroism and heroinism ("no words have been more basely misused")[90] in terms of the everyday: "plenty of more really gallant things happened every day, and were never heard of" (*Clever*, 179), instead of in terms of the rodomontade of special emergencies. For Yonge, the register of true heroism lies in the everyday, for "after all, it is the discipline and constant duty that make the soldier, and are far more really valuable than exceptional doings" (*Clever*, 179). Many of Yonge's heroines initially try to refuse the everyday—the most famous is Ethel May: "little, simple, everyday matters did not come naturally to her as to other people"[91]—because the everyday realms Yonge sketches in her books are separate and unequal for men and women. Ethel, for instance, has to learn to accept this, to learn when she comes to womanhood to devote herself to everyday domestic concerns and no longer to try to match her brother in his studies. It is a hard lesson, "and her eyes filled with tears. 'We have hardly missed doing the same every day since the first Latin grammar was put into his hands!'" (*Daisy*, 181). It is partly her ultimate acceptance of woman's place in the second rank that makes Ethel's novel seem to Yonge's critics so plotless—nothing special ever happens to this unmarried heroine, which is exactly what Yonge wants to portray.

Rachel Curtis of *The Clever Woman of the Family* is another heroine who tries to refuse the everyday, as Yonge warns her readers in the opening epigraph to that novel:

Thou didst refuse the daily round
Of useful, patient love,
And longedst for some great emprise
Thy spirit high to prove. (*Clever*, 1)

Rachel, however, does so by trying to refuse the traditional marriage plot; while her sister "had contented herself with the ordinary course of unambitious feminine life, Rachel had thrown herself into the process of self-education" (6). Yet what Yonge makes Rachel learn in her novel is that heroism comes from accepting woman's traditional and everyday role:

"I did think I should not have been a commonplace woman," [Rachel said] and she shed a few tears. . . . "I used to think it so poor and weak to be in love, or to want any one to take care of me. I thought marriage such ordinary drudgery, and ordinary opinions so contemptible, and had such schemes for myself . . . [and love] has only made me just like other women." (283)

[90] Charlotte Yonge, *The Clever Woman of the Family* (New York: Penguin/Virago, 1985), 81; all future references to this book (abbreviated *Clever*) will appear in the text.
[91] Charlotte Yonge, *The Daisy Chain or Aspirations: A Family Chronicle* (London: Virago, 1988), 629; all future references to this book (abbreviated *Daisy*) appear in the text.

Yet, although Rachel does marry, that marriage brings no climax or epiphany: Her life, and her novel, simply continue. For Rachel and Ethel , tears of renunciation signal nothing extraordinary but an everyday sacrifice, signal their heroic devotion to an everyday that allows their stories to keep going, allows what Yonge thinks of in fact as life eternal.

There may be some unintentional feminist energy in this—many of Yonge's women readers want to argue that she has her heroines willingly take up their cultural yoke because that at least gives them a story and allows them a sphere of activity; it demonstrates what ordinary women's lives are really like. The argument might also be made that Yonge highlights and exposes women's traditional role by hewing to it so resolutely and insistently. Yonge, more than almost any other women writer of her time (her model for this might have been sensation fiction), goes out of her way to trope up women's passivity: in a fitting figure for their own lack of progression, her novels are filled with invalids lying with fixed cheer upon couches. That one of her most heroic and saintly invalids is also centrally a writer (Ermine Williams in *The Clever Woman* writes very successfully under the pen name of The Invalid in *The Traveler's Review*) suggests that Yonge's emphasis on the ways such women must school themselves in their everyday duty, learn to accept their own marginalization and the slights of others, is meant to tell us something about the tradition. R. H. Hutton, a leading critic of the day, used just such imagery in his evaluation of Yonge's work: he finds overly ethical—didactic—fiction like Yonge's a "deformity" which prompts readers to prefer "the merest realism of every-day life." [92] Patrice Petro has seen the split between activity and passivity as another of the founding oppositions on which the canon tries to rest: as we have seen with Horkheimer and Adorno, high art tries to validate its own claims by securing their supposed relation to true progression; the popular, on the other hand, is only escapist, entrammeling. [93] Yonge's extreme interest in female invalids may not really subvert the cultural logic that associates women and passivity, but even in accepting it she begins to explore the limits within which the tradition—and the minor— are constructed.

To modern feminists like myself interested in different issues from Hutton, ethics still seem important. Yonge's antifeminism is what seems to determine her ethics, what critics like Leavis (herself pretty antifeminist) call her orthodoxy. Yet in what some critics see as her own antifeminist tract, Julia Kristeva continues to associate women and ethics, noting the "sacrificial contract" which culture has made women embrace; the problem with feminism for Kristeva is that it has too willingly provided another similar contract, made itself over into an alternative religion for women, in that way accepting the cultural logic it thinks it is contesting ("Women's," 25). If Yonge's

---

[92] Hutton, "Ethical and Dogmatic Fiction: Miss Yonge," *National Review* 12 (1861): 211–30; 213.

[93] Petro, "Mass Culture and the Feminine: The 'Place' of Television in Film Studies," *Cinema Journal* 25 (1986): 5–21; 6.

novels—which remain highly readable and almost unpleasantly attractive (especially to an unbelieving reader like myself; I especially can't believe how enjoyable they remain in spite of everything)—are in any way feminist, it seems to me they become so in this negative ironic way. That seems to mean, in part, that we must subject feminism to the same critique to which we want to subject the canon—even though (and precisely because of a canonical impulse within feminism) we might run into the same resistance that Kristeva's essay meets. To prefer the skeptical impulse within the writing of an author like Oliphant may be utopic; Oliphant can herself be conservative and orthodox enough at times. Part of keeping feminism from resolving into its own authorized tradition may be admitting that we must, in spite of ourselves, stake out an ethics for it, as long as we remember that its utopias remain constructed, imaginary places—not ends so much, but, like series fiction, a process. Part of this process also means trying to complicate evaluations of bad and good as well (evaluations which are, after all, the mainstay of the very tradition we want to deny), trying to read an often disheartening writer like Yonge along with a more sympathetic writer like Oliphant, to find in *both* a useful unraveling of canonical logic. Both writers expose the relational construction of categories such as the minor and the everyday in an endless oscillation that keeps such questions from ever being fixed. The only ethical position may be to learn to live with contradiction every day.

I wish Mr. Trollope would go on writing Framley Parsonage *forever. I don't see any reason why it should ever come to an end, and everyone I know is always dreading the last number.*

—Elizabeth Gaskell to George Smith

2 *The Everyday as Everything*

Pushing the Limits of Culture in Trollope's Series Fiction

An important move in recent oppositional criticism has been the attempt to complicate terms made univocal—abstracted, simplified, universalized—in our own practice. Some of the critics who argue for this move, however, want to blame earlier criticism—especially the deconstruction of binaries—for inadvertently keeping us trapped in the logic of opposition, of either/or, by emphasizing binaries even if only to break them down. Rather than focusing on and rebutting the ways culture tries to define woman as not-man, or black as the shadow of white, these critics wish to *construct* other critical models instead. They mean to build these out of complex interconnections—those within and between conventional political terms. Rather than addressing categories such as "woman" or "race," the questions become more tangled: how do lesbian, heterosexual, working- and middle-class, adolescent and elderly women give shape to one another and to our notion of "woman"? And how is the category of "woman" informed by, and how does it itself inform, a notion of "race" that means more than Caucasian, Hispanic, Asian, and so on? Could such a notion also undo the seamlessness of those divisions by admitting into them such factors as nationality and class—while recognizing the ways those factors too are multiple and fractured? These are the kind of questions I want to think about it this chapter; but in thinking about them, I want also to question whether emphasizing terms as hybrid and contingent alone is sufficient. What are the politics involved in doing so? In what ways exactly can that emphasis provide for something more than a critique of constraint within signifying systems, systems of power?

This emphasis on the way "difference relates," as Fredric Jameson writes, is, as he sees it, a product of our particular "cultural logic."[1] Such a relation to culture may explain why this strategy is claimed by various kinds of cul-

[1] Jameson, *Postmodernism, or, The Cultural Logic of Late Capitalism* (Durham: Duke University Press, 1991), 31.

85

tural studies as the initiative that distinguishes them from other fields of study. Edward Said's contention at the end of *Culture and Imperialism* that "survival in fact is about the connections between things," becomes in part the very rationale for cultural studies, an expression of why we might need such a program in the first place.[2] In his introduction to his Routledge cultural studies reader, for instance, Simon During claims that culture is "an important category because it helps us recognize that one life-practice . . . cannot be torn out of a large network constituted by many other life-practices."[3] In their Routledge cultural studies anthology, Lawrence Grossberg, Cary Nelson, and Paula Treichler agree:

> Certainly, within the fragmented institutional configuration of the academic left, cultural studies holds special intellectual promise because it explicitly attempts to cut across diverse social and political interests. . . . As Lata Mani notes in her essay in this volume, in its utopian moments cultural studies sometimes imagines "a location where the new politics of difference—racial, sexual, cultural, transnational—can combine and be articulated in all their dazzling plurality."[4]

For these editors such possibilities are not entirely utopian nor vexed; cultural studies, they assert, in emphasizing "the interrelations between supposedly separate critical domains," already begins to achieve them: "Cultural studies proposes neither a 'mantra of subordination' in Kobena Mercer's phrase, nor a politics of an ever-expanding list of subordinate positions based on such identities as class, race, sex, etc. Instead it looks for the relations that exist among these positions in specific contexts, and the ways these positions are themselves produced by context."[5] The emphasis cultural studies places on "specific context" aims to make the interrelations of these positions concrete and available for study.

Yet at least one contributor to this anthology doesn't find the interrelations sketched by the contexts interrogated within it all that accessible or certain. In her postscript to the book, Angela McRobbie identifies as one of the authorizing crises of cultural studies "a turning away from binary relations in favor of what Derrida describes as 'an indefinite series of differences.'"[6] Although she concedes that deconstruction's "move away from binary oppositions . . . [can] be seen as opening up a new way of conceptualizing the political field and creating a new set of methods for cultural studies" (721), she

[2] Said, *Culture and Imperialism*, (New York: Vintage, 1993), 336.
[3] "Introduction," *The Cultural Studies Reader*, ed. Simon During (New York: Routledge, 1993), 1–25; 1.
[4] "Introduction," *Cultural Studies*, ed. Lawrence Grossberg, Cary Nelson, Paula Treichler (New York: Routledge, 1992), 1–22; 1.
[5] Ibid., 11 and 18.
[6] Angela McRobbie, "Post-Marxism and Cultural Studies: A Post-script," in ibid., 719–30; 719; all future references to this essay will appear in the text.

regrets that the results in this anthology are so indefinite. But, for McRobbie, that problem is actually poststructuralism's. She contends that poststructuralism is to blame for the indeterminacy troubling this collection, despite most of its contributors' suspicion or outright rejection of it (she, in fact, quotes with approval Stuart Hall's assertion in the anthology "that deconstruction can 'formalize out of existence the critical questions of power, history, and politics'" [720]). She blames Derrida in particular for having complicated the question of certainty; she sees "Derrida's insistence on the relational and unfixed nature of meaning" (720) as the primary source of such complications. Although McRobbie understands cultural studies as focusing on interrelations too, Derrida's unmoored "relational" meanings are not the ones she wants. She finds that the collection, in its focus on "textual or discursive" relations, ignores the interconnections of what she calls "real existing identities" (730). Those interconnections are especially located within the "lived experience" (721) of an everyday, as opposed to the merely empty textuality of poststructuralism. McRobbie ends her essay with a call for attention to "the relational interactive quality of everyday life" (730) as a way to explore the concrete and determinable interconnections of culture.

In this chapter, I'd like to consider how we might indeed think about culture by locating an "indefinite series of differences" in "the everyday." Yet rather than asserting some unbridgeable opposition between cultural studies and poststructuralism, I want to consider their interrelations as well. This means, in part, complicating Derrida's relation to cultural studies—and precisely in terms that call into question the wish for a fixed and certain ground of reality—a ground we have seen so often meant to be conjured by reference to "the everyday."[7] In the introduction to his book *The Location of Culture*, Homi Bhabha also calls for "a movement away from a world conceived in binary terms, away from a notion of the people's aspirations sketched in simple black and white . . . a shift of attention from the political as a pedagogical, ideological practice to politics as the stressed necessity of everyday life—politics as performativity."[8] In "the move away from the singularities" of categories like gender and race (1) to what he calls

---

[7] While excepting some poststructural theorists like Bhabha and Spivak, whose theory (probably because of these theorists' supposed identity politics) happens to lead to politics, McRobbie argues that "what has worried me recently in cultural studies is when theoretical detours become literary and textual excursions" which ignore what she calls "the everyday world and everyday culture all around me" (721). Just how we might define the everyday which seems so obvious to her apparently doesn't inform McRobbie's dismissal of theory; nor does the additional problem that various cultures' "everydays" are highly theorized and not so obvious to each other.

[8] Bhabha, "Introduction: Locations of Culture," to *The Location of Culture* (New York: Routledge, 1994), 1–18; 14–15. Bhabha is careful to point out that interconnection does not mean the end of conflict: "How are subjects formed 'in-between,' or in excess of, the sum of the 'parts' of difference (usually intoned as race/class/gender, etc.)? How do strategies of representation or empowerment come to be formulated in the competing claims of communities where, despite shared histories of deprivation and discrimination, the exchange of values, meanings and

"hybridity"—"the emergence of the interstices" (2)[9]—Bhabha insists, however, that we recognize in the everyday "a return to the performance of identity as iteration" (9)—that is, he sees the opening up of the study of culture through this category as inseparable from poststructuralism. For categories like "iteration" or the "performative" themselves come to current criticism directly from the work of Derrida—specifically from his debate with John Searle about the politics of the formal structuring of meaning implied by the speech acts of what J. L. Austin calls ordinary language. What notion of the everyday gets offered by this debate about ordinary language theory and how might it contribute to our understanding of the working of culture?

This chapter suggests that another way to ask these questions might be: what politics do we find in an attention to culture that doesn't see culture as real and certain, but as textual, formally constructed? To consider that question I turn to the workings of what Anthony Trollope defines as ordinary language as he constructs his series fiction. In attempting in those series to imitate culture as a discursive text, mediated by various registers of language, Trollope makes a direct connection between the formal principle of the series—iteration—and the everyday. Especially given his own cultural prejudices, Trollope's fiction provides a useful arena for considering the tension in our models of culture between a desire for fixity, closure, and totality, and a gesture to openness. By arguing that—given the seeming endlessness of his proliferating series—Trollope's form is in excess of any particular vision of culture he attempts to impose in those series, I want to try to imagine what such a structure of deferral might mean for cultural studies. The problem series fiction like Trollope's poses to ideological critique is how to comprise all the various and endless registers involved in politics: how imagine a cultural studies as complex and inexhaustible in its aim as Trollope's fiction? And Trollope's fiction is especially useful here because it seems so vehemently apolitical: the ability to see that within his fiction's relentlessly asserted ordinary workings lie questions of hierarchy and power gives us access to a radical critique, even if they don't help us construct some new world in its stead.

This critique need not assume that the politics of either Trollope or a particular poststructuralism like Derrida's are somehow essentially progressive or enabling (any more so than are the politics of the version of cultural studies that reifies certainty, no matter how much it too may claim an implicit

---

priorities may not always be collaborative and dialogical, but may be profoundly antagonistic, conflictual and even incommensurable?" (2).

[9] He calls this hybridity elsewhere a traumatic moment—"the indeterminate or the unknowable . . . around which the symbolic discourse of human history comes to be constituted. . . . The margin of hybridity, where cultural differences 'contingently' and conflictually touch, becomes the moment of panic which reveals the borderline experience": "By Bread Alone: Signs of Violence in the Mid-Nineteenth Century," *The Location of Culture*, 198–211; 207.

progressiveness). The problem for this chapter is how to critique that post-structuralism while also making use of it. The other chapters in this book focus on the everyday to expose the constructedness of a category that gets passed off as the real itself, as well as to engage with theoretical systems that—through equating the "everyday" and the "real"—attempt to determine how the everyday and the real should look and work. But in turning to the poststructural refraction of ordinary language theory, this chapter must also ask what is (for this book) a more difficult question: what about post-structuralism? What are the politics involved in bids to the everyday that fully recognize and treat it as a construction? In considering this, I'm considering the complications of a position I also find to be necessary—for what is this book if not also mobilized by and relying upon its own gesture to the everyday as a formal category, even by analyzing it, showing it up, laying it bare? In doing so, I'm face to face with what seems to me the problem peculiar to the study of culture: how to negotiate its network with no hope of political purity, with only a choice of methods that have been inescapably shaped, in various ways, by its logic.

In this chapter I will investigate Trollope's series fiction—especially through his Barsetshire novel *Framley Parsonage*, set in the context of his travel books—to see how these politics of cultural performance work, to see what the everyday and the series tell us about our attempts at reading the web of cultural interconnections. The limitlessness of context in Trollope's fiction forecloses the possibility of thinking everything at once politically: my hope is that Trollope's intricate mesh of endlessly interwoven relations as he imitates the workings of culture will at least point to a method with which we should persevere nonetheless—one that in emphasizing the how rather than the what, the process rather than some end, makes the attempt to do the impossible still indispensable. Trollope's own politics in depicting colonialism's role in the fretwork of culture are often predictable and disturbing. That doesn't mean that form has an essential politics, however: rather, although form in Trollope always *has* a politics, the importance of context in determining it makes simple determinations unfixable. Precisely by problematizing context, making it impossible to fix any context's limit, Trollope's series fiction keeps formal possibilities open.

Trollope's series of series, by depicting the boundlessness of culture, demands from us a cultural studies similarly open. Cultural studies—as represented by Said or those anthologies—might usefully delimit specific contexts, in order strategically to fix the circumstances by which we can evaluate the interrelations of various subject positions (if only to deplore Trollope's culturally hierarchical views, for example). Yet the work of Derrida can suggest how cultural studies can do so while also remaining aware of the risks of exclusion and the hierarchization that comes through the attempt to fix culture's limits. How to generate a contiguous and self-modifying politics from within the contradictions of *that* connection—marking provisional limits that, at the same time, we immediately call into question—is the challenge this chapter explores.

In doing so, however, my argument also needs to put into question the relation of what Bhabha and Kobena Mercer call "hybridity" to the cultural web of dominance that such hybridity is supposed to unsettle. To Mercer, the hybrid subject offers a cultural critique, if not an outright transformation of culture, by the very fact of its polymorphous identity: its "profusion of rhizomatic connections . . . implies another way of conceiving 'the role of the intellectual,' not as a heroic leader or patriarchal master, but as a connector located at the hyphenated intersection of disparate discourses and carrying out the task of translation." [10] Bhabha too seems to find a saving grace in the very fact of hybridity. Hybridity, as he uses the term, registers not just the inescapable multiplicity of postcolonial identity but the deconstructive slippages within any cultural constitution. It is not just that a given culture happens to be made up through the conflict and relation of incommensurable identities whose politics overlap and clash, but that identity itself—the constitution of *anything*, including culture—is necessarily produced within this amorphous, unfixable, in-between space. Yet, although Bhabha recognizes that the management of this in-between space produces both dominant *and* dissonant cultures—it is what produces colonial power and also provides for its undoing, he argues—the tendency of his argument (one he borrows from Derrida, it seems to me) is to highlight hybridity's unsettling and occlude its production of power.[11]

Rather than recognize that hybridity and interconnection can provide useful strategies, however, we might also question how they encode the logic of a cultural network—one that Marxists like Jameson call global capitalism, and critics via Foucault see as an increasingly totalizing grid of power. However we account for it, we can find the beginnings of this network's cultural logic at least as far back as the later nineteenth century, as it gives rise to series fiction like Trollope's that is predicated on its continuum. The interconnections of Trollope's series show that an emphasis on hybridity may indeed cut to the heart of cultural power (whether by doing so it dislodges it is another question). Yet hybridity is a useful term only because a strategy of interconnection is what by this point makes up the very fabric of power: what Trollope's form demonstrates about culture is the way capitalism relies on patriarchy, for instance, and how both are necessary to and dependent on

---

[10] Kobena Mercer, *Welcome to the Jungle: New Positions in Black Cultural Studies* (New York: Routledge, 1994), 30; all future references to this book (abbreviated *Welcome*) will appear in the text.

[11] See, for example, his discussion in "Signs Taken for Wonders: Questions of Ambivalence and Authority under a Tree outside Delhi, May 1817," *The Location of Culture*, 102–22, especially 112–15.

imperialism, with its foundational racism, and on and on. Rather than contradicting or annulling one another as they might through the unevenness of their registers, these various grammars of dominance—what Bhabha calls "the great connective narratives of capitalism and class" (6), for instance— seem to dovetail effortlessly, to collude with and further one another. Such cultural logic probably has everything to do with the precedence of empire at this time, in its need, as it forges global connections, to appropriate, translate, subsume, to retool every new site into another node through which to conduct its own business. And perhaps the answer that Mercer's postcolonial hybrid subject makes to a waning imperialism—"*we are here because you were there*"—is precisely the way to explode its logic from within, to convert its omnivorous hegemony into a different kind of reciprocity (*Welcome*, 7). But the political valence of cultural hybridity and interconnection cannot simply be assumed. Given that culture has for some time asserted dominance through mutually enabling, mutually implicated, systems of oppression, the assertion by some cultural studies of its own emphasis on contingency and imbrication does not in and of itself provide a different politics (and thinking that an emphasis on relationality provides this is where poststructuralism and cultural studies are alike). Part of what this chapter explores is how to strive for connections that don't just repeat the logic of relationality, but also do something more.

※

Poststructuralism has always been interested, to some degree, in the way culture's logic is self-generated, context-bound. The antecedents in linguistics of current poststructuralist theory suggest that terms take meaning within a context, that the workings of form chart a network; in so doing, this theory implies the fine cultural interconnections of entities (such as the liberal, bourgeois self) that have traditionally been considered discrete and autonomous. Given this post-Saussurian logic, political categories such as race, class, or gender—unmoored from essential reference, understood as constructions themselves, products of the social text—can take meaning only through reference to and contiguity with each other. Yet, given the assault on totality that is also implicit within a poststructuralist critique, how can we chart those connections? How might we identify a politics of form that would allow for what Susan Bordo has called a "view from everywhere"—that would somehow preserve the differences in such constellations of political terms while drawing their interconnections? Bordo's point is precisely that such a view is impossible—which seems, of course, unarguable. But is that enough? Bordo's contention (which is also part of the assumptions behind this chapter) is that the larger context cannot be fixed—there will always necessarily be something left out. What might it mean, however, if we attempted to trace interconnections while emphasizing this interminable slide?[12] Through its very impossibility, that attempt might give us the most useful map of culture's unchartableness.

In Trollope's *Phineas Redux*, Madame Max Goesler meets Lady Glencora Palliser's request for a favor with an adage: "If it is simply difficult it is done. If it is impossible, it shall be done."[13] In its utopian optimism, Madame Goesler's proverb suggests the utility of the impossible to enable everyday practice. Tania Modleski locates within a political criticism such as feminism "a performative dimension—i.e., to be *doing* something beyond restating already existent ideas and views." Political criticism, she argues, must be both performative and utopian: through an impossible circularity—by assuming what it also takes to be its goal—such criticism will point "to the freer world it is in the process of inaugurating."[14] What I suggest in this chapter is that when exposed as a formal construction, the everyday in its relation to the series also begins to trace one of these impossible utopian sites. And it is a site that sees the everyday precisely as a practice, a performance, and one that works at the level of ordinary language, especially in its identity as colloquial, vernacular—proverbial. When countering the archdeacon's overmastering reasoning in *The Warden* (successfully, it turns out), the gentle Mr. Harding tells his daughter: "There is a great deal of truth in all he says—he argues very well, and I can't always answer him; but there is an old saying, Nelly: 'Everyone knows where his own shoe pinches!'"[15] Not *what* is said here, but *how* it is said—the everyday as ordinary, proverbial, commonplace—might be just what provides a different kind of cultural logic. What is important about this logic is that it is ongoing: it points to what shall be done. Because the archdeacon thinks his argument is incontrovertible, he can't recognize that Mr. Harding continues to answer him nevertheless. He doesn't even hear the everyday register in which the dialogue continues; precisely because he thinks the argument is over, Mr. Harding is able to surprise and ultimately resist him.

---

[12] Susan Bordo, "Feminism, Postmodernism, and Gender-Skepticism," in *Feminism/Postmodernism*, ed. Linda J. Nicholson (New York: Routledge, 1990), 133–56. Bordo's essay is particularly helpful in taking issue with a carping criticism that attempts to invalidate any political analysis by pointing out what it *doesn't* do, criticizing any attention to gender that doesn't deal absolutely equally with sexuality or with race, and on and on. Such criticism is a kind of easy spoiling that has probably at some point left everyone engaged in political analysis feeling helpless and tired. Yet, poststructuralism, instead of being perniciously invalidating (it becomes rather curiously the culprit in Bordo's argument—as in McRobbie's—the source of such one-upmanship), seems to provide the means by which we might imagine a constructive way to talk about interconnection.

[13] Anthony Trollope, *Phineas Redux* (New York: Oxford, 1983), bk. 2, p. 266; all future references to this work (abbreviated *Redux*) will appear in the text.

[14] Tania Modleski, *Feminism without Women: Culture and Criticism in a "Postfeminist" Age* (New York: Routledge, 1991), 46, 48. All future references to this book (abbreviated *Feminism*) will appear in the text.

[15] Anthony Trollope, *The Warden* (New York: Penguin, 1984), 114; all future references to this work will appear in the text.

It makes sense to turn to the works of Anthony Trollope when exploring such an impossibly infinite critical method because he has been avoided to some degree by literary criticism just for the reason that he also seems so infinite, so impossible to write about. The difficulty lies in great part in his predilection for the seemingly endless series. His famous chronicles—the Barsetshire and Palliser series—are simply symptoms of an even larger formal preoccupation. In a sense, what Trollope was attempting with these chronicles was an infinite series of series. "Trollope explained," his biographer tells us, "that the two series 'are by no means distinct, lapping in under each other occasionally.'"[16] Henry James, in fact, found that all of Trollope's prodigious production became one "huge 'serial'";[17] for J. Hillis Miller, Trollope's "motto as a writer, *nulla dies sine lineâ*, defines the writing of novels as the continuous production of a line or thread of words flowing day by day out of the pen onto the paper and leading by an unbroken sequence from beginning to end."[18] This endless sequence, this attempt to do more than just produce a distinct and separate series about the clergy and one about Parliament (already enormous undertakings), this emphasis on exhaustive interconnections almost beyond our capacity to comprehend, made Trollope worry in his autobiography that "I have had to spread my picture over so wide a canvas that I cannot expect that any lover of such art should trouble himself to look at it as a whole" (*Autobiography*, 184). And the question of just when that whole ends—if it ever does—may be the central one for Trollope's fiction. Nathaniel Hawthorne famously saw Trollope's work as a microcosm of everything trapped in a belljar. Trollope liked this description so much, he quoted it in his autobiography: Trollope's novels, Hawthorne wrote "are just as real as if some giant had hewn a great lump out of the earth and put it under a glass case, with all its inhabitants going about their daily business" (*Autobiography*, 144). This image suggests a substitution of part for whole that begins to put the whole into question (if the lump of earth is so comprehensive, what must the entire globe itself be?).

R. H. Hutton, one of Trollope's most sensitive contemporary readers (as Trollope himself felt), realized that the sheer weight of Trollope's writing was

---

[16] N. John Hall, *Trollope: A Biography* (New York: Oxford University Press, 1993), 468–69.

[17] Henry James, "Partial Portraits," in *Trollope: The Critical Heritage*, ed. Donald Smalley (New York: Barnes & Noble, 1969), 525–45; 537; all future references to this work (abbreviated "Partial") will appear in the text. James R. Kincaid agrees: "in a sense all of Trollope's writing is together a chronicle": *The Novels of Anthony Trollope* (Oxford: Oxford University Press, 1977), 44; all future references to this book (abbreviated *Novels*) will appear in the text.

[18] J. Hillis Miller, "Self Reading Self: Trollope," in his *Ethics of Reading: Kant, de Man, Eliot, Trollope, James, and Benjamin* (New York: Columbia University Press, 1987), 81–99; 93. The motto is from Trollope's autobiography, and is intended "for the benefit of those who may read these pages when young and who may intend to follow the same career. *Nulla dies sine lineâ* [Pliny the Elder's "No day without a line"]. Let that be their motto": Anthony Trollope, *An Autobiography* (New York: Oxford, 1980), 364–65; all future references to this work will appear in the text.

an attempt to capture—almost item by item—the way we live now: Trollope's serial impulse was mimetic of culture itself. His books "contain a larger mass of evidence as to the character and aspects of English Society . . . than any other writer of his day has left behind him. . . . [To later eras, Trollope's books] will picture the society of our day with a fidelity with which society has never been pictured before in the history of the world." [19] William Dean Howells found "the British life and character present in [Trollope's work] in the whole length and breadth of its expansive commonplaceness." [20] For Henry James too, the mass and expansiveness of Trollope's serial impulse are meant "to make a general portrait of society" ("Partial," 544). And our own contemporaries turn to Trollope's fiction as a simulacrum of English culture, asserting that "a more convincing impression of what everyday life was like in England in the middle Victorian years can be gathered from their pages than from any other source." [21] For Ruth apRoberts, Trollope's series impulse is the natural consequence of a Victorian interest in culture, an attempt to reflect society's panorama: "Trollope's novels are plentiful and various because . . . man conceived socially is plentiful and various. Everyman is single and once for all. Darwinian, historicist man is multiform, infinitely variable, infinite in potential." [22] Trollope's famous emphasis on mixed motives, his inability to tell just one side of the story (which he felt organized a book like *The Warden*), can be seen as symptoms of the same multiform and variable impulse. His attempt to reproduce culture meant an obligation to include everything. It is not for nothing that his ideal character becomes the Duke of Omnium.

J. Hillis Miller argues that such attempts at ubiquitous, or at least neverending, creation are "speech acts, they imitate God's autonomous performatives not by copying their results but by renewing their mode of generation." [23] In his attempt to reproduce everything, Trollope is concerned with the how, not the what, with the form, not the material, of the world. In reproducing the formal impulse of culture specifically in the impulse to interrelate everything, Trollope also reproduces the effects of cultural ideology, as we experience it in our inability to experience it *as* ideology, to arrest or grab hold of it. "The system of continuing the story indefinitely to a certain extent baffles criticism," the *Saturday Review* wrote about Trollope's series. "You can never say that the whole displeases you, because you can never be

[19] R. H. Hutton, unsigned obituary essay, *Spectator*, Dec. 9, 1882, 4:1573–74, in Smalley, *Trollope*, 504–8; 505, 508.

[20] Quoted in N. John Hall, "Introduction," *The Trollope Critics*, ed. N. John Hall (Totowa, N.J.: Barnes & Noble, 1981), vii–xxix; xviii.

[21] Asa Briggs, quoted by J. A. Banks in "The Way They Lived Then: Anthony Trollope and the 1870s," *Victorian Studies* 12 (1968): 177–200; 178.

[22] Ruth apRoberts, "Trollope and the *Zeitgeist*," *Nineteenth-Century Fiction* 37 (1982–1983): 259–71; 271.

[23] J. Hillis Miller, "Beguin, Balzac, Trollope and the Double Double Analogy," in his *Victorian Subjects* (Durham: Duke University Press, 1991), 213–28; 226; all future references to this essay (abbreviated "Beguin") will appear in the text.

sure that you have got the whole. If the plan is pushed much further, clever novels bid fair to become as ephemeral as the daily papers."[24] What Trollope's series perform is the ephemerality of a totalizing impulse whose sheer ambition ensures its failure; his series never rest at a whole because they are always striving for something larger.

And, as the references by these critics to the "day by day," "everyday life," "commonplaceness," and "the daily papers" suggests, Trollope's fiction stages that performance on the level of the everyday. Trollope's contemporaries remarked what George Eliot told him was "the skill with which you have organized thoroughly natural everyday incidents," and Trollope agreed. In his fiction, to varying degrees, he said "I have attempted to confine myself absolutely to the commonest details of commonplace life among the most ordinary people, allowing myself no incident that would be even remarkable in everyday life."[25] For Henry James, Trollope's "great, his inestimable merit was a complete appreciation of the usual" ("Partial," 527).

For D. A. Miller, when it comes to Trollope, this is "the usual appreciation of his appreciation of the usual"[26]—a phrase that implies that appreciation of Trollope's treatment of the everyday is as banal as the everyday itself. Many of Trollope's contemporaries shared this attitude and made similar reproaches. For Carlyle, Trollope was "irredeemably imbedded in commonplace, and grown fat upon it, and prosperous to an unwholesome degree."[27] As Carlyle's criticism of Trollope's prosperity suggests, however, the denigration of the everyday can grow out of unconscious assumptions about class—ones held by James as well: "Literally, then, Mr. Trollope accomplishes his purpose of being true to common life. . . . Life is vulgar, but we know not how vulgar it is till we see it set down in his pages."[28] Leslie Stephen's question—"We begin to ask whether it can be worth while to read a novel which is a mere reflection of the commonplace?"[29]—simply translates a criticism made by his brother's journal, the *Saturday Review* (extremely valuable for its open declaration of attitudes about which other Victorians knew enough to be uneasy—and only imply, not state): "it may be an accurate picture of the life led in the class which Mr. Trollope undertakes to paint, but the picture is scarcely worth painting."[30] For these critics, in emphasizing the ordinary, Trollope's fiction must unfortunately include too

[24] Unsigned notice of *Phineas Finn*, *Saturday Review*, March 27, 1869, 431–32, in Smalley, *Trollope*, 314–18; 318.

[25] Hall, *Trollope: A Biography*, 255.

[26] D. A. Miller, "The Novel as Usual: Trollope's *Barchester Towers*," in his *Novel and the Police* (Berkeley: University of California Press, 1988), 107–45; 107.

[27] Hall, *Trollope: A Biography*, 274.

[28] *Nation*, July 13, 1865, 1, 51–52, in Smalley, *Trollope*, 233–37; 234–35.

[29] Sir Leslie Stephen, "Sacrifice to the Duty of Fidelity," in *Trollope: The Barsetshire Novels*, ed. T. Bareham (London: Macmillan, 1983), 71–75; 72; all future references to this work (abbreviated "Sacrifice") will appear in the text.

[30] Unsigned notice of *The Small House at Allington*, *Saturday Review*, May 14, 1864, 595–96, in Smalley, *Trollope*, 205–10; 208–9.

much. It is not only the "faithful picture of the daily life of the upper and middle classes," as Bernard Shaw describes it, but its assertion that such classes have an everyday, its location of them in a social and economic context, threatens their exclusivity by connecting them to others, reveals them *as* classes.[31] The everyday doesn't allow Trollope's fiction to refuse what is common in the commonplace.

What may be most unsettling about the everyday for critics who wish unconsciously to enforce fixed and distinct stations of life is that, for Trollope, the everyday is precisely a matter not of fact but of style, located within language. Trollope's emphasis on form seems unsettling because it is so impossibly contradictory: critics are uncertain how to respond to an author whose attention to the everyday makes his work seem lifelike, photographic, real, and yet who—at one and the same time—repeatedly and insistently calls attention to his fiction as a construction.[32] Faced with this paradox, such critics assert the reality of the everyday by denying Trollope any style whatsoever. James tells us that Trollope's writing "has no more pretensions to style than if it were cut out of yesterday's newspaper" ("Partial," 532); Stephen that "we must not ask for exquisite polish of style. We must be content with good homespun phrases which give up all their meaning on the first reading" ("Sacrifice," 71). To such critics, Trollope's language becomes equivalent to the everyday; the editor of the *Critical Heritage* on Trollope recounts how "the *Westminster Review* (July 1869) deplored Trollope's doling out 'the ordinary daily conversation of commonplace people.'"[33] For the *Saturday Review* as well, all of Trollope's characters "are ordinary men and women, and their sayings and doings are neither above nor below the level of what we see in common and everyday life."[34] To these contemporaries, "the sketches of character on which [Trollope's stories] depend for their value are the result of shrewd observation cleverly expressed in every-day phrase."[35] As a more recent critic has put it, Trollope's style "has the impromptu quality, the looseness and artlessness, of ordinary speech."[36] As an exercise in ordinary language, Trollope's novels define the everyday not as the real, however, but as a medium, a formal quality. The everyday is not so

---

[31] Hall, *Trollope: A Biography*, 507.

[32] As Trollope's narrator famously does when he refuses to keep secrets from his readers, and tells them in the first volume of *Barchester Towers* that Eleanor won't marry Slope or Bertie; Anthony Trollope, *Barchester Towers* (New York: Penguin, 1983), 126–28; all future references to this work (abbreviated *Barchester*) will appear in the text. The form of such disclosures is actually much more the point than their content, since Trollope does of course continue to keep secrets from his readers, neglecting to tell them here that Eleanor will marry Arabin.

[33] "Introductory Notes to *He Knew He Was Right*," in Smalley, *Trollope*, 322.

[34] Unsigned notice of *Framley Parsonage*, *Saturday Review*, May 4, 1861, 451–52; in Smalley, *Trollope*, 121–25; 122.

[35] Unsigned review of *Phineas Finn*, *Examiner*, April 20, 1861, 244–45; in Smalley, *Trollope*, 118–20; 118.

[36] David Aitken, "'A Kind of Felicity': Some Notes about Trollope's Style," *Nineteenth-Century Fiction* 20 (1966): 337–53; 340; all future references to this article (abbreviated "Kind") will appear in the text.

much the province of a certain social position or class, but the culture that fosters them, the glue that holds them all together.

Ordinary language for Trollope—what he calls "everyday expressive modes of speech" (*Warden*, 39; the example he gives here is the archdeacon's figure "cut the ground from under us")—is loosely proverbial in being a mixture of colloquialisms, mottoes, maxims, platitudes, clichés, and tag lines.[37] The "downright honest figures" Lady Glencora prefers are a mixture of these types: "Two and two make four; idleness is the root of all evil; love your neighbour like yourself, and the rest of it" (*Redux*, 2.327). "Trollope's narrator loves proverbs," one of his editors declares, and follows A. O. J. Cockshut in calling Trollope's method "'the subtilising of . . . literary platitude[s]."[38] To such critics, Trollope's narrator and characters don't just express themselves in everyday phrases; Trollope also constructs his plots and forms his series around such proverbs. The proverb in this loose sense— for the OED it is "a short pithy saying in common and recognized use"— becomes for Trollope in its pith and commonness a symbol of the everyday *as* form—especially of the everyday as everything.

Trollope seems attracted to the proverb because it is a matter of style: what makes something proverbial is not so much what but how it is said. As a book of wisdom, the biblical book of Proverbs suggests the form's pretensions to truth as sayings expressive in all times and places, but the formal characteristics of the proverb transform just what kind of truth that is. Although proverbs are an instance of the way "ideology is inscribed in ordinary language," as Catherine Belsey puts it, this inscription comes about not solely by supporting what she has called "the authority of the concept of common sense itself, the collective and timeless wisdom whose unquestioned

[37] Students of proverbs have a horror of such loose associations. "I can conceive of no greater mental punishment," one of them writes, "than to be compelled to wade through a collection of so-called proverbs which almost invariably consists of a heterogeneous conglomeration of sayings, colloquialisms, idioms, slang, bon mots, rhymes, riddles, and a mass of stupid, silly, commonplace proverbs, producing in my unfortunate translators and myself a boredom verging on tears": Selwyn Gurney Champion, "Introduction," to his *Racial Proverbs: A Selection of the World's Proverbs Arranged Linguistically* (New York: Macmillan, 1938), xiii–xxxiii; xiii. Here, these heterogeneous connections get dismissed by being located in the commonplace or everyday (even more intriguing, Champion thinks that proverbs lend themselves to "racial" divisions).

This mixture is what makes Trollope's style ordinary for his critics; Aitken writes: "Trollope's conspicuous fondness for such clichés . . . is of a piece with his fondness for the commonplace words and colloquial phrasing which so often makes his writing resemble ordinary talk" ("Kind," 351). Ruth apRoberts: "Many of his images are repeated so often, and are so commonplace anyway . . . that they simply do not function as images; the world is one's oyster, the beautiful woman is the candle to the moth, people row in the same boat, and so on. . . . Such images are hardly what we are used to calling poetic, as all they do is maintain an air of comfortable ordinariness between teller and reader": *The Moral Trollope* (Athens: Ohio University Press, 1971), 21.

[38] David Skilton and Peter Miles, "Introduction," to Anthony Trollope, *Framley Parsonage* (New York: Penguin, 1986), 7–28, 20–21; all future references to this work (abbreviated *Framley*) will appear in the text; David Skilton, "Introduction," to Anthony Trollope, *Doctor Thorne* (New York: Oxford, 1980), xi–xxii; xviii; all future references to this work (abbreviated *Thorne*) will appear in the text.

presence seems to be the source and guarantee of everything we take for granted,"[39] but also by exposing the workings of such ordinary language, showing as well how such sense gets made. Absolutely antithetical statements, for instance, can be given proverbial form, as Trollope has Phineas Finn ruefully realize when attempting to goad himself into action by reference to such everyday figures (he finds just as many to stay him).[40] The same adage can also mean different things in different situations (Trollope, for instance, can write very different novels as illustrations of the same old saw). An emphasis on such multivalence combined with an assertion of the importance of context suggest that the meaning of proverbs doesn't so much establish an immutable truth as provide a *form* of expression always there, already available for any occasion, any meaning.[41] In fact, according to recent scholars of it, the proverb is a kind of speech act that gestures to itself.[42] Like Barthes's reality effect (figures whose only purpose in a narrative is to assert its verisimilitude), the proverbial is important in fiction not for its content but its effect: it establishes the ordinary; it performs the everyday. Like the performative mode in general, it suggests that language is concerned not with the true and false, but with what ordinary language theorists call the "felicitous or infelicitous, successful or unsuccessful."[43] David Aitken, for instance, finds Trollope's ordinary language, his proverbial style, predicated on just such notions of felicity, of what works ("Kind," 353).

In emphasizing the formal, the proverb cuts the ground from under us by connecting categories traditionally seen as culturally distinct. Loaded as it is

[39] Catherine Belsey, *Critical Practice* (New York: Methuen, 1980) 43, 3.

[40] "We all know those arguments and quotations, antagonistic to prudence, with which a man fortifies himself in rashness. 'None but the brave deserve the fair.' 'Where there's a will there's a way.' 'Nothing venture nothing have.' . . . 'Fortune favours the bold.' But on the other side there is just as much to be said. 'A bird in the hand is worth two in the bush.' 'Look before you leap.' 'Thrust not out your hand further than you can draw it back again.' All of which maxims of life Phineas Finn revolved within his own heart" (*Redux*, 1.10).

[41] Wolfgang Mieder argues that "proverbs are *not* absolute or universal truths. This is abundantly clear from such opposing proverbs pairs as 'Absence makes the heart grow fonder' and 'Out of sight, out of mind.' Proverbs only make sense in a given situation or context": "Introduction" to his *Proverbs Are Never Out of Season: Popular Wisdom in the Modern Age* (New York: Oxford, 1993), ix–xviii; x.

[42] Kenneth Burke, for instance, argues that proverbs provide a kind of pragmatics; they are "*strategies* for dealing with *situations*": "Literature as Equipment for Living," in his *Philosophy of Literary Form: Studies in Symbolic Action* (Berkeley: University of California Press, 1973), 293–304; 296. Roland Barthes sees the proverb—at least originally—as "pav[ing] the way for actions, it inserts itself into a fabricating order: [in proverbial speech about the weather] the farmer does not speak *about* the weather, he 'acts it,' he draws it into his labour. All our popular proverbs thus represent active speech which has gradually solidified into reflexive speech": *Mythologies*, selected and trans. Annette Lavers (New York: Hill and Wang, 1972), 154. Natalie Zemon Davis argues that "to the villager, his common proverbs . . . were available for many different circumstances and for recommending different courses of action": "Proverbial Wisdom and Popular Errors," in her *Society and Culture in Early Modern France* (Stanford: Stanford University Press, 1975), 227–67; 243.

[43] See, for example, Shoshana Felman, *The Literary Speech Act: Don Juan with J. L. Austin, or Seduction in Two Languages*, trans. Catherine Porter (Ithaca: Cornell University Press, 1983), 27.

with commonplaces, Trollope's fiction provides a good example of the impossibility of distinguishing between tag phrases from the Eton grammar and old saws of English folk wisdom (what Lady Glencora remembers as a "proverb about going safely in the middle" is actually from Ovid's *Metamorphoses* [*Redux*, 2.262]). Scholars of the proverb argue that the form provides an important site where distinctions between the elite and the popular are impossible to maintain.[44] Given the breadth of such inclusiveness, Trollope, unlike Eliot, may have felt that "the mysterious complexity of our life *is* to be embraced by Maxims" (and the title of the first chapter of *Framley Parsonage* is exactly one of the maxims that Maggie Tulliver ponders in *A Mill on the Floss*: "*Omnes Omnia Bona Dicere*").[45] The everything that everybody says is for Trollope good because it provides a model of the complex web of culture: Trollope's ordinary language tends to the proverbial because of what Geoffrey Bennington calls the "cultural competence" necessary to recognize proverbs (*Sententiousness*, 16). Since the expression of the proverbial is always to some degree citational, the proverb is not only "part of a complex literary internal cross-reference system which assumes a comprehensive experience of Western literature," but the degree to which such everyday language has already been said before makes it a quotation of what Derrida calls "anonymous" societies, a reference to the social text, to the entire, unbounded, cultural context.[46] The cultural capital involved in recognizing ordinary language as such connects Trollope's readers and characters in what they wish to be a privileged site: they want to get to define just what is ordinary, to constitute the everyday, the real, and the natural in their own image.

৵৾

Since Saussure declared the sign arbitrary, language has become for critics a system not of truth but of meaning—not of ideal preexistent essences

[44] Archer Taylor writes that when it comes to the proverb "the distinction between 'learned' and 'popular' is meaningless": *The Proverb* (Cambridge: Harvard University Press, 1931), 5. Davis spends a large part of her argument demonstrating that the proverb contains "an everyday vernacular alongside a serious Latin" (241); the proverb made "clerical and literary languages" and "common rural speech" equivalent (231). Aitken registers the degree to which Trollope's language is proverbial by emphasizing that his style is at one and the same time both colloquial and latinate (341). For a further discussion of the proverb, see Geoffrey Bennington, *Sententiousness and the Novel: Laying Down the Law in Eighteenth-Century French Fiction* (New York: Cambridge University Press, 1985), 16–18; all future references to this book (abbreviated *Sententiousness*) will appear in the text.

[45] The sentence in Eliot's novel of course reads "is not to be embraced."

[46] The description of the proverbial as part of a cross-reference system is from Roger D. Abrahams and Barbara A. Babcock, "The Literary Use of Proverbs," in *Wise Words: Essays on the Proverb*, ed. Wolfgang Mieder (New York: Garland, 1994), 415–37; 431. Derrida writes: "At the 'origin' of every speech act, there can only be Societies which are (more or less) anonymous": "Limited Inc a b c," in *Limited INC*, trans. Samuel Weber and Jeffrey Mehlman (Evanston: Northwestern University Press, 1988), 29–110; 75. All future references to this work (abbreviated "Limited") will appear in the text.

but of shifting significances generated by their placement within the system. For literary criticism, the role of context in determining meaning has always been the crucial focus of formalist accounts. The whole point of New Criticism was that literary meaning got made this way: Cleanth Brooks quotes T. S. Eliot to indicate "'that perpetual slight alteration of language, words perpetually juxtaposed in new and sudden combinations' . . . . The terms are continually modifying each other" and it is through that interrelation, he asserts, that they take on sense.[47] For Brooks, such networks of contrast and contiguity are characteristic of poetic as opposed to ordinary language. The role of poetry, in fact, as Coleridge expresses it, is to revitalize the ordinary—to give "'the charm of novelty to things of everyday'" (*Urn*, 7). For the New Critics, the language of science or of the man on the street—what Brooks calls "our everyday logic" (*Urn*, 211)—is ordinary, deficient, because it doesn't recognize the importance of interrelation and context. Brooks directly opposes the poetic to such ordinary everyday language, constructing the latter as made up of commonplaces, proverbial: "Donne might have said directly, 'Love in a cottage is enough.' 'The Canonization' contains this admirable thesis, but it contains a great deal more" (*Urn*, 17). For the New Critics, poetry contains whole worlds, and the complex intricate network of people's experience can be reflected only through the interplay and contingency of this kind of language.[48]

When critics inspired by New Criticism (such as Mark Schorer, or Stuart Tave in *Some Words of Jane Austen*) try to extend this approach beyond poetry to the novel, they retain the basic distinction between the poetic and the ordinary. Yet this is a distinction that Trollope's novels—if not the novel form itself—put into question. It is because he refuses such a separation of registers that for a certain group of conservative critics—Henry James or Geoffrey Tillotson, Sir Leslie Stephen or Lord David Cecil—Trollope has no style at all.[49] One index of Trollope's banality for such critics was that he published his daily budget of writing largely unrevised: such workaday production must be by definition commonplace, they suggest, lacking the refinement and inspiration of true literary effusion (and Trollope recognized in his autobiography that "there does, I fear, exist a feeling that authors, because they are authors, are relieved from the necessity of paying attention to everyday rules" about industry and production [*Autobiography*, 329]). Conflating style with a literariness somehow distinguished from the everyday is

[47] Cleanth Brooks, *The Well Wrought Urn: Studies in the Structure of Poetry* (New York: Harcourt Brace & World, 1947), 9; all future references to this work (abbreviated *Urn*) appear in the text.

[48] Terry Eagleton argues that they want poetry to contain a very bounded world, the world as they see it; as an outgrowth of the conservative Agrarian movement, they want to fix the limits of what culture should be, arrest the movement of modernity, by excluding others; see his *Literary Theory: An Introduction* (Minneapolis: University of Minnesota Press, 1983), 46–53.

[49] For their views on this subject, see Geoffrey Tillotson, "Trollope's Style," in Geoffrey Tillotson and Kathleen Tillotson, *Mid-Victorian Studies* (London: Athelone Press, 1965), 56–61; Lord David Cecil, *Early Victorian Novelists* (Harmondsworth: Penguin, 1948) 199.

conservative in that it occludes economic forces. Distinguishing poetic—self-defining and self-modifying—language as a special case also still preserves a notion of (ordinary) language as fixed and certain, still conserves the everyday as a kind of bedrock.

Despite their similarities, it is in refusing the everyday as a kind of bedrock, and the poetic as a special case, that post-Saussurians diverge from formalists like New Critics. This refusal is, in a sense, the subtext of Derrida's debate with John Searle about ordinary language.[50] Derrida demonstrates that supposed special cases actually characterize, and transform from the inside, the very system that wishes to set them apart. "Signature Event Context" begins by implicitly defining "ordinary language" as making meaning through context; it works through dissemination, which undermines the sense of language as a transparent medium of some preexistent reality.[51] But Derrida makes this point only to make another: the idea of context must itself be put into question; "context is never absolutely determinable" (3). J. L. Austin can seem to ground ordinary language only by excluding from it as extraordinary examples that call its consistency and fullness into question. As Jonathan Culler puts it: "to set aside as parasitic certain uses of language in order to base one's theory on other, 'ordinary' uses of language, is to beg precisely those questions about the essential nature of language that a theory of language ought to answer."[52] For Derrida, such internal contradictions in Austin's argument simply testify to the paradoxes informing language itself as a system. Because the ordinary attempts to project outside certain contradictions in its midst, the boundaries of inside and outside, the limits of the system of meaning-making, get blurred. Since the network of significance is never closed, it is also never fully determinable.

Acknowledging this blurring is politically important, since, as Tania Modleski asserts, "claims to take into account 'the total context' in analyzing speech acts involve an illusory ideal of mastery" (*Feminism*, 50). Given Derrida's argument, the illimitibility of culture means in part the impossibility of closing off the formal from the political. For Derrida, a formalist account

[50] Ordinary language philosophy in general has been interested in the ordinary as part of an everyday that is predominantly formal, not material. For ordinary language theorists, we need nothing outside the language that we have, and Gilbert Ryle describes that language as the everyday: "'common,' 'current,' 'colloquial,' 'vernacular,' 'natural,' 'prosaic,' 'nonnotational,' 'on the tongue of Everyman.'" Benson Mates, a critic of ordinary language philosophy, sums up its major tenet: "in daily life words function well enough and lead to no great problems": Ryle, "Ordinary Language," in *Ordinary Language: Essays in Philosophical Method*, ed. V. C. Chappell (Englewood Cliffs: Prentice-Hall, 1964), 24–40; 25; Mates, "On the Verification of Statements about Ordinary Language," in Chappell, 64–74; 67.

[51] The word "communication," for instance, has various and contradictory meanings, which make it impossible to establish that one meaning of "communication' is the real, literal, one, and all the others somehow only secondary and subordinate: Jacques Derrida, "Signature Event Context," in his *Limited INC*, 1–23; 1–3; all future references to this work (abbreviated "Signature") will appear in the text.

[52] Jonathan Culler, *On Deconstruction: Theory and Criticism after Structuralism* (Ithaca: Cornell University Press, 1982), 118.

that doesn't recognize the indeterminacy of form repeats the same old politics, strives for mastery. By refusing to acknowledge that language generates meaning through reference to itself, that this is the way that form works, ordinary language philosophers such as Searle, Derrida argues, are still, by searching for an authorizing site, engaged in a bid for power. In considering the ordinary as a formal category, then, Derrida redefines the formal:

> I do not "concentrate" in my reading ... either exclusively or primarily on those points that appear to be the most "important," "central," "crucial." Rather, I deconcentrate, and it is the secondary, eccentric, lateral, marginal, parasitic, borderline cases which are "important" to me and are a source of many things, such as pleasure, but also insight into the general functioning of a textual system. And were there to be a center to this debate, we would have reached it already, in the form of this difference in styles of reading. But what is involved is more than a difference in style. ("Limited," 44–45)

"More than a difference in style" repeats and reworks what Searle had leveled as a criticism of Derrida: Derrida's mistaken understanding of Austin's theory, according to Searle, is so flawed it must be "more than simply a misreading" (a formulation that Derrida declares "deserves to become proverbial" because it exposes the arrogance of Searle's position while at the same time unconsciously articulating the logic of the Derridean supplement that undermines the supposed certainty of such a position ["Limited," 41]).

The excess already inherent in a form that doesn't recognize it is for Derrida what puts the notion of "mere" formalism into question. Such differences in style between himself and Searle, Derrida asserts, are actually "ideological":[53]

> It is not necessary to point to a flesh-and-blood example, or to write moralizing pamphlets demanding the exclusion of wicked parasites (those of language or of the *polis*, the effects of the unconscious, the *pharmakoi*, people on welfare, nonconformists or spies) in order to speak an ethical-political language. ... I am convinced that speech act theory is fundamentally and in its most fecund, most rigorous, and most interesting aspects ... a theory of right or law, of convention, of political ethics or of politics as ethics. ("Limited," 96–97)[54]

Derrida's argument suggests that, when considered in terms of ordinary language, the everyday may describe a formal category, a mode of expression, but we can understand the formal in terms of the very political arena that the real, the referential, the "flesh-and-blood example" has usually claimed.

[53] He asserts about his own style: "if I call this analysis 'ideological,' I do so [not] ... to appeal to the dogmatic—one might also say ideological—usage to which the term 'ideology' is often put" ("Signature," 6).
[54] Derrida suggests that deconstruction as a formal analysis is deeply political in refusing the basic assumptions of the system in which it must also operate; it offers "the performance of a text which, by raising in passing the question of truth ... does not *simply* succumb to its jurisdiction" ("Limited," 43) because "the notion of evidence, together with its entire system of associated values (presence, truth, immediate intuition, assured certainty, etc.) is precisely what" it calls into question ("Limited," 40).

That ordinary language involves political action is Derrida's major contention, and explains the otherwise untheorized connection in Austin between ordinary language and the speech act itself. In a sense, what Austin implies is that it is language's everyday character to be performative, not some specialized function of it. For Austin, speech acts reside in language (like a promise) that, rather than referring to something else, does something by itself alone, is important in and of itself. But Austin argues that this performative quality is not limited to special cases, but is a part of all language.[55] When we read Austin through Derrida, speech acts become the site where the attempt to distinguish the ordinary, to bracket it off from something special, breaks down. Ordinary language makes sense according to the rules and conventions of its context, the laws that govern its performance (whether or not we can ever completely chart that context). Nevertheless, to understand the workings of form, for Derrida, necessitates engaging head-on with the rule of law: to understand action as formal is not to exempt it from systems of power.

And specifically not to exempt it from culture as just such a system. In "Structure, Sign, and Play in the Discourse of the Human Sciences," Derrida locates an implicit poststructuralism precisely in a historical, cultural context: the rise of a critical method like Lévi-Strauss's structuralism that would ultimately come to emphasize poststructural contradiction and the decentering of reference depended in turn on the rise of the science of "ethnology. In fact one can assume that ethnology could have been born as a science only at the moment when a decentering had come about: at the moment when European culture—and, in consequence, the history of metaphysics and of its concepts—had been *dislocated*, driven from its locus, and forced to stop considering itself as the culture of reference."[56] The contradiction of ethnology, for Derrida, is that the study of culture comes into being in part as an attempt to deny this decentering—through asserting the primacy of cul-

---

[55] Jonathan Culler explains that Austin actually breaks down the distinction between the constantive and the performative as he has defined them: "An utterance such as 'I hereby affirm that the cat is on the mat' seems also to possess the crucial feature of accomplishing the act (of affirming) to which it refers, *I affirm X*, like *I promise X*, is neither true or false but performs the act it denotes. . . . [Austin also highlights] the possibility of deleting the explicit performative verb. Instead of saying 'I promise to pay you tomorrow' one can in appropriate circumstances perform the act of promising by saying 'I will pay you tomorrow'—a statement whose illocutionary force remains performative. . . . 'The cat is on the mat' may be seen as a shortened version of 'I hereby state that the cat is on the mat' and thus a performative. But, of course, 'The cat is on the mat' is a classic example of a constantive utterance" (*On Deconstruction*, 112–13).

Speech acts as pointing to language as a self-referential system become important for Baudrillard as well, specifically when it comes to seriality. He argues that in modern capitalism (but this would seem to me also to have to include the late nineteenth century) seriality is related to the lack of origins; since art can no longer represent or reproduce the world, it can only repeat itself—it becomes simply the act of this repetition, a speech act itself; see his *For a Critique of the Political Economy of the Sign*, trans. Charles Levin (St. Louis: Telos, 1981), 105–7. Baudrillard's theory, of course, retains a notion of a lost original, a nostalgia for a world in which signs once pointed neatly to fixed outside referents.

[56] "Structure, Sign, and Play in the Discourse of the Human Sciences," in his *Writing and Difference*, trans. Alan Bass (Chicago: University of Chicago Press, 1978), 278–93; 282.

ture as a category, European culture anachronistically asserts the primacy of what it wants to be its own transcendent dominance, precisely at the moment it is forced to recognize other cultures—to face its own contingency and hybridity.[57]

But what are the politics of such cultural indeterminacy? Trollope's own explicit politics, which stressed an almost paradoxical mixture of qualities— "I consider myself to be an advanced, but still a conservative Liberal," he wrote in his autobiography (*Autobiography*, 291)—seem to many of his critics to smack of relativism, if not quietism, charges also leveled against a poststructural emphasis on form that is for its critics at best apolitical. And, for Trollope, the permeability of boundaries, the mixture of motives so that a man can be antithetical things at one and the same time, can mean such pulls in opposite directions that he might fall to the ground between two stools (one of Trollope's favorite clichés—see, for example, *Barchester*, 178),[58] especially when it comes to politics: equal ties to the Whigs and Tories are what doom the parliamentary career of Frank Gresham's father: "So between the two stools he fell to the ground, and, as a politician, he never again rose to his feet" (*Thorne*, 5). As these various figures suggest, Trollope finds the notion of ground uncertain—so uncertain that, despite Lady Glencora's reference to the proverb about going safely in the middle, he cuts the ground from under that path.[59] Trollope's insistence on unresolved and irresolvable paradox, on qualities that both depend on and contradict each other, make his politics of form—like poststructuralism's—result in what James Kincaid, quoting apRoberts, calls a kind of "situation ethics": "Judgments must refer to people and particular circumstances and not to fixed principles" (*Novels*, 11).

Yet Trollope locates his judgments in the particular circumstances of *all* of English culture, in a context that is infinite and indescribable. Just what such

[57] Hence, Lévi-Strauss engages in "a European science employing traditional concepts, however much it may struggle against them. Consequently, whether he wants to or not—and this does not depend on a decision on his part—the ethnologist accepts into his discourse the premises of ethnocentrism at the very moment when he denounces them" (ibid., 282). But, Derrida goes on to argue, "if no one can escape this necessity, and if no one is therefore responsible for giving into it, however little he may do so, this does not mean that all the ways of giving into it are of equal pertinence" (282). The ways in which Lévi-Strauss operates in this double-bind—"to preserve as an instrument something whose truth value he criticizes" (284)—is crucial to Derrida; he later goes on to refer to attitudes that are "absolutely irreconcilable even if we live them simultaneously" (293)—which might be his description of the interconnections of culture.

[58] See also Anthony Trollope, *The Last Chronicle of Barset* (New York: Penguin, 1967), 359; all future references to this work (abbreviated *Last*) will appear in the text.

[59] As does Derrida in his reply to Searle: "finally . . . confronted by a *Reply* which exudes such confidence in the possibility of distinguishing 'standard' from 'non-standard,' 'serious' from 'non-serious,' 'normal' from 'abnormal,' 'citation' from 'non-citation,' 'void' from 'non-void,' 'literal' from 'metaphoric,' 'parasitical' from 'non-parasitical' etc.—faced with a *Reply* so serenely dogmatic in regard to the intention and the origin of an utterance or of a signature, I wanted, before all 'serious' argument, to suggest that the terrain is slippery and shifting, mined and undermined. And that this ground is, by essence, an underground" ("Limited," 34).

cultural relativism might mean has been a problem for cultural studies even when the outlines of culture are not in question. Part of what has made Edward Said influential as a cultural critic is his implication that cultural limits are fixed, knowable—or, at any rate, that an attempt to keep them open is at best problematic. We can see such problems reflected in our cultural studies, he argues:

> In the absence of an enclosing domain called literature with very clear outer boundaries, there is no longer an authorized or official position for the literary critic. But neither is there some new sovereign method, some new critical technology compelling allegiance and intellectual loyalty. Instead there is a babel of arguments for the limitlessness of all interpretation; for ideologies that proclaim the eternal, yet determinate value of literature or "the humanities"; for all systems that in asserting their capacity to perform essentially self-confirming tasks allow for no counter-factual evidence.[60]

Said offers his own theory as a reconciliation of the desire for authority and the fear of compulsion, as the counterfactual evidence that can show up other, threateningly open, theories. Although he agrees that, like the social text it considers, "theory, in short, can never be complete, just as one's interest in everyday life is never exhausted by simulacra, models, or theoretical abstracts of it," he tries to fix its boundaries nonetheless, and precisely through that category of the everyday he has acknowledged as similarly illimitable: for him the critic's job is to expose critical theory as the product of a social context ("theory has to be grasped in the place and (of course) the time it emerges"), as if, despite his own recognition of its heterogeneity and incoherence, that context were nevertheless somehow graspable. It is "concrete instances drawn from everyday reality"—in some way (but how?) supposedly free of theory—that provide this outside context ("Traveling," 58–59).

In trusting his own ability to fix a cultural limit which he concedes as dangerous when it is the work of others, Said is doing nothing new, especially in grounding that ability in a privileged access to the everyday as real. But what might a cultural studies be that was able to keep the notion of context open? What might it mean if the everyday were the site of this vast contingency rather than the ground of certainty? How might that help us to "find a vocabulary in which to examine the interdependence between multiple elements of race, gender, class, and so on, without recourse to an either/or logic," as Kobena Mercer wonders—a vocabulary that goes beyond "repeating the race, class, gender mantra as if the serial acknowledgment of the various sources of identity was sufficient for an understanding of how different identities get articulated into a common project"?[61]

[60] Edward Said, "Traveling Theory," *Raritan* 1 (1982): 41–67; 45; all future references to this article (abbreviated "Traveling") will appear in the text.

[61] Kobena Mercer, "'1968': Periodizing Politics and Identity," in Grossberg et al., *Cultural Studies*, 424–49; 444, 442.

An attention to what texts mean when they talk about ordinary language might offer one vocabulary—one that debates the complicated relation of the other to seriality in ways that emphasize an inescapable insufficiency within any fixed context or identity. In considering the ordinary in terms of seriality, Derrida argues that speech acts are possible only because of the notion of reiteration—the repeatability of an act governed by law or convention.[62] In this idea of doing something over and over again (a formal principle of series fiction too), Derrida is interested in the notion of difference in sameness: repetitions are, of necessity, both different and the same. The rule of iterability organizes our cognizance of speech acts, allows them to mean according to a general rule, but "iteration alters, something new takes place" ("Limited," 40): "Limiting the very thing it authorizes, transgressing the code or law it constitutes, the graphics of iterability inscribes alteration irreducibly in repetition" (62). This structure has to do with politics for Derrida because he sees it as governing the relation of self to other: "*iter* . . . probably comes from *itara, other* in Sanskrit, and everything that follows can be read as the working out of the logic that ties repetition to alterity" ("Signature," 7). A chain of repetitions, in which each element is similar to but distinct from its predecessor, "implies *both* identity *and* difference" and, hence, iterability "ruins . . . the very identity it renders possible" ("Limited," 53, 76). This is why, in questions of power, for Derrida "iterability is at once the condition and the limit of mastery" (107).[63] Such a reading suggests that in its very form the series contains an indissoluble and paradoxical relation to the other, a contradiction that the speech acts of ordinary language cannot help but perform.

It is crucial to Derrida that speech acts are formal constructions—that they make sense not because they are true or false, grounded in some transcendent presence, but because they conform to certain conventions (a constructedness that self-reflexive novels like Trollope's never let us forget). Their constructedness both organizes power and calls it into question: "if the police is always waiting in the wings, it is because conventions are by essence violable and precarious, *in themselves* and by the fictionality that constitutes them, even before there has been any overt transgression" (105). But, for Derrida, with this fictionality too "everything becomes possible against the language-police; for example, 'literatures' or 'revolutions' that as yet have no model. Everything is possible except for an exhaustive typology that would claim to limit the powers . . . of fiction" (100). What such fiction tells us is

[62] As Jonathan Culler writes, "something can be a signifying sequence only if it is iterable, only if it can be repeated in various serious and nonserious contexts, cited, and parodied" (*On Deconstruction,* 120).

[63] Derrida also writes: "iterability . . . renders possible *both* the 'normal' rule or convention *and* its transgression, transformation, simulation, or imitation" ("Limited," 98), making it impossible to locate in form either a conservative or a subversive impulse—it necessarily carries both, which operate according to context. The political efficacy that Derrida sees in formal operations is that context can never be fixed; it can always be changed.

that even the exhaustive repetitions of the everyday called for by someone like Said are not enough to limit context, to draw the outlines of culture. Whether or not the kind of revolutions implicit in that openness allow for the benevolent politics Derrida always seems to herald (his argument that iterability "limits" mastery seems his own wish to limit power) is another question; the complications of this question are what get played out in the endless interdependent series of others who introduce problems like race, class, and gender into Trollope's model of culture, as a novel like *Framley Parsonage* suggests.

⁂

Trollope's current editors suggest that *Framley Parsonage* was one of his most popular books because it foregrounded the everyday and the series: it emphasized "the intelligent absorption in the essentially everyday, the tolerant analysis of conduct in the commonplace business of life, . . . the comforting sense of life going on."[64] *Framley Parsonage* provides a useful testground for what kind of politics the indeterminacy of context betrayed by the series and the everyday could mean, since it also foregrounds the social panorama, the modeling of culture itself, implicit throughout Trollope's form. Fresh from his own foreign travels, out of which he had written the travel book *The West Indies and the Spanish Main* (1859), when the chance to serialize a novel in *Cornhill's* presented itself, Trollope was interested explicitly in the depiction of culture. He originally offered the magazine a collection of *Tales of All Countries*, then an Irish story, but the editor wanted "an English tale, on English life," and, Trollope writes, the resulting novel, *Framley Parsonage*, "was thoroughly English" (*Autobiography*, 142–43). Yet as this publishing history suggests, that Englishness was defined against almost everything it was not.

Trollope's contemporaries sometimes criticized him because he seemed such a distinctly English, distinctly culturally bound, storyteller. The reviewer in the *Nation* finds Trollope's provincialism almost proverbial:

> That it is a good thing to be well off, that it is well to act honorably, that it is about the best of all things to be a well-to-do English gentleman . . . are the sort of maxims which Mr. Trollope directly or indirectly presents for the acceptance of his admirers. . . . The source, in fact, of Mr. Trollope's success is to be found in the satisfaction which he gives to the almost universal liking for accurate sketches of everyday life, and to the equally universal admiration for the easy optimism which sees in English society, as it now exists, the best of all possible arrangements in the best of all possible worlds.[65]

[64] Quoted by Skilton and Miles, in their "Introduction" to *Framley Parsonage*, 12.

[65] Unsigned notice of *Phineas Redux*, *Nation*, March 12, 1874, 174–75; in Smalley, *Trollope*, 385. The reviewer, of course, attempts to exempt himself from such provincialism by his own references to a French text.

The *Dublin Review* agreed that Trollope's novels were so instinct with the "every-day" of dominant English culture that "a serious social revolution in England might render Mr. Trollope's books dull and difficult, if not unintelligible, to another generation of English people." [66] But the background to *Framley Parsonage* suggests that Trollope recognized that English culture was not the limit of his fiction; it was interdependent on its often occluded relation with other cultures (regardless of whether Trollope understood those other cultures, as he largely did, from a circumscribed—English—point of view). Although cultural context was what gave his books sense, made them intelligible, Trollope's attempts to venture outside of it periodically (always unpopular, like his Irish tales, or the foreign novellas he—desperate to write them—even published under a pseudonym) suggest that the form responsible for what to some critics seemed the most exhaustive picture of a particular culture worked by pushing the limits of that culture. For Trollope also acknowledged that *Framley Parsonage* was a "hodge-podge" (*Autobiography*, 142)—a somewhat incoherent mixture of a little bit of everything that put any cultural coherence into question.

Yet the poststructural idea of culture as an open and messy form does not necessarily guarantee a breakdown of dominance. The interrelations and hybridities of a new subject position that Derrida draws at the end of "Structure, Sign, and Play" still seem predicated on the dominance and exclusions of misogyny, as the language of birth throughout the essay suggests: Derrida writes that the "common ground [of] irreducible difference" (293) implied for the breakdown of self and other within "the *seminal* adventure of the trace" (292)

> is a kind of question, let us call it historical, whose *conception, formation, gestation*, and *labor* we are only catching a glimpse of today. I employ these words, I admit, with a glance toward the operations of childbearing—but also with a glance toward those who, in a society from which I do not exclude myself, turn their eyes when faced by the as yet unnamable which is proclaiming itself and which can do so, as is necessary whenever a birth is in the offing, only under the species of the nonspecies, in the formless, mute, infant, and the terrifying form of monstrosity (293).

By accusing himself along with others who can read a hybridity that unsettles form and category only as monstrous, Derrida means to critique as well as to enact this attitude. But the invisible woman as conduit here, left out as she performs the very (speech) act of giving birth to the unnamable, suggests that even the most careful self-critical play must found its very depiction of excess and the double-bind on other unquestioned relations and exclusions.

Similar implicit assumptions of power underwrite J. Hillis Miller's depic-

[66] "The Novels of Mr. Anthony Trollope," *Dublin Review* 71 (October 1872): 393–430; in Smalley, *Trollope*, 361–70; 363, 361.

tion of Trollope's open seriality. Trollope's attempt to mimic the form of creation imitates what Miller calls "the divine mode of production": "It is an imitation of the divine creativity rather in renewing in its own way the divine mode of production than in being a slavish copy of something already existing" ("Beguin," 223). In this way, for Miller, Trollope takes over the Christian God's "infinite paternal power," which is "power as performative language" (222, 224). Such power, based on speech acts, is like that God's "exercise of a generative power based on nothing but his own say-so"—language (the logos) that in and of itself calls something into being (223). Miller charts this in Trollope as "an act of auto-affection and auto-fecundation in which Trollope, pen in hand, impregnates himself with his own creations." [67] The endless repetitions of Trollope's series allow for a self-contained patrilinearity that also funds literary criticism, for Miller argues that the proper critical attitude to Trollope would be to imitate his form: "it would thereby see the work as an inexhaustible resource of further acts of production rather than as something that can be worked through only once, imitated as exactly as possible, and then dismissed" ("Beguin," 224). What's remarkable about the performance of Miller's own language here is the profusion of various kinds of ideological maxims. They rest, first of all, on implicit gender assumptions (the unquestioning celebration of patrilineal filiations which, for him, though not for Derrida, replace the need for *any* female generation whatsoever).[68] They also depend on assumptions of class (that God's order is economic, based on a "divine mode of production"), and even the logic of empire (the compulsion to find "inexhaustible resources," to be a divine original, and not a "slavish copy"). If Miller's speech acts here reiterate Trollope's (as he suggests they should), they reveal that the endlessness of the series and the openness of form can allow various political registers to echo, rather than necessarily and only reject, a system of inequity and segregation.

If Miller's criticism replays Trollope's novels in its hodgepodge of dominance, it follows a dynamic articulated and performed by Trollope's close

[67] Miller, "Self Reading Self," 94. As I argue in my Holmes chapter, this wish for male completeness and immortality is based in the everyday. Miller writes elsewhere; "Trollope had to have his daily ration of novel writing, his daily period of inhabitation within the minds of a group of imaginary persons. . . . The daily writing served a deep existential need for him. It was a main principle of continuity in his sense of himself. . . . The continuity of the self is for Trollope the highest value, that to which everything else must, if need be, be sacrificed. In Trollope's own case the writing of novels was the diurnally renewed act of will which assured his own persistence as himself. The writing of novels made him and kept him what he was. It even gave him a proleptic experience of his persistence beyond the grave, as in that ruefully ironic passage in *An Autobiography* in which he imagines his posthumously published works appearing in parts for an indefinite period after his death": "The Values of Obduracy in Trollope's Lady Anna," in *Victorian Subjects*, 263–69; 264.

[68] The issue of gender here also puts the progressive politics of the Derridean supplement into question, for the translation of masturbation into birth in Miller's reading—"Trollope, pen in hand, impregnates himself"—however playful, suggests that underlying the supplement's conflation of excess and lack is a male wish for authorizing completeness and exclusion.

contemporaries: Trollope "stimulated the taste for which he catered. He created the demand which he supplied," wrote Herbert Paul in 1897.[69] *Framley Parsonage* also performs as well as documents cultural ideology, and, for Trollope's contemporaries, does so directly through its form. As one in a series, *Framley Parsonage* seems to them to bespeak a system in which "novels may be manufactured like Manchester goods." [70] What *Framley Parsonage* shows is how culture can assert a system of inequity through a network of interdependencies. The point of Trollope's Barsetshire series might in fact be to show that God, at least as represented by the Church of England, is involved in economics: the clergyman Mark Robarts's descent into debt opens onto a whole world of commerce and speculation—a system in *Framley Parsonage* as in other Trollope novels financed by the empire of "Mother England" (as Trollope calls it elsewhere).[71] The vortex of promissory notes and bill-discounting which Robarts can never really comprehend points to the bubble logic of an empty capitalism, which Trollope recognizes is kept going by the necessarily temporary infusions of colonial plunder: the logic of empire is to seize and mine the resources of a new culture until they are exhausted, then move on.[72] Trollope makes this connection in *Framley Parsonge* by the famous missionary meeting Robarts attends. Robarts's host Sowerby has actually invited him to give a sermon on the topic only as the occasion to entangle him in debt (Sowerby has become so bankrupt that only a respectable clergyman's name on a promissory note can buy him credit). Fanny Robarts's disbelieving exclamation " 'A charity sermon at Chaldicotes!' " (*Framley*, 41) becomes doubly ironic: the heavily mortgaged estate

[69] Herbert Paul in "The Apotheosis of the Novel under Queen Victoria," in *Nineteenth-Century* 41 (May 1897): 783–84; quoted in Hall, *The Trollope Critics*, xiv.

[70] Unsigned notice of *Framley Parsonage*, *Westminster Review* 71 (July 1861), 282–84; in Smalley, *Trollope*, 133–34; 134.

[71] He calls England the "mother country," for instance, in his discussion of its ultimate need to allow its colonies to develop and break free—"Introduction," *Australia and New Zealand* (London: n.p., 1873; rpt. London: Dawsons, 1968), 1–22; 10. For critics who argue that Trollope is anti-imperial, see C. A. Bodelsen, *Studies in Mid-Victorian Imperialism* (New York: Fertig, 1968), 50–52; his argument that Trollope was a Separatist oversimplifies what this chapter aims to show is a more complex attitude in Trollope's writing.

[72] Trollope makes his understanding of this bubble-logic plain again and again. In *The West Indies and the Spanish Main*, he argues that it explains Jamaica's current plight. "That Jamaica was a land of wealth, rivaling the East in its means of riches, nay, excelling it as a market for capital, as a place in which money might be turned; and that it now is a spot on the earth almost more poverty-stricken than any other" is a function of this logic; Jamaica was floated for a time only through the ungrounded productivity of the slave system; Anthony Trollope, *The West Indies and the Spanish Main*, (London: n.p., 1859; rpt. New York: Hippocrene Books, 1985), 77; all future references to this work (abbreviated *West*) will appear in the text. The overproduction of sugarcane in Barbados based on a short-lived system of overfertilization with guano, which ultimately exhausts the soil, provides a neat metaphor for the workings of slavery (200–201); guano is also one of the commodities Lopez trades in *The Prime Minister*, as he speculates increasingly in unstable if not nonexistent colonial exports. It is also not surprising that, in *Framley Parsonage*, Trollope has one of his impecunious aristocrats who is vying for the hand of the incredibly rich quack-medicine (Ointment of Lebanon) heiress, Miss Dunstable, teach her "to blow soap-bubbles on scientific principles" (119).

is actually the perfect site from which to assert the ideology of Empire through missionary work, since both are motivated by the same greed and ungrounded omnivorous speculation, while Mark Robarts, in his desire for class mobility, becomes the one upon whose charity that estate is allowed to function. Imperialism and capitalism, the inequities of racism and of the class system, depend on one another.

Trollope criticizes this interdependence of capitalism and imperialism, but does so only through other, less consciously criticized, interconnections: those speculators like Lopez in *The Prime Minister* or Melmotte in *The Way We Live Now* who, as "hollow vulgar fraud[s,]" expose the emptiness of such systems do so by recourse not just to class but also to race.[73] Lopez's vaguely Latin background hides what is also Melmotte's open secret: a Jewish heritage. The anti-Semitism of Trollope's culture was meant to be so ordinary and seem so natural that it could allow Lady Chiltern, for example, to unravel simply the intractable murder mystery that for a time puts Phineas Finn in peril of the gallows: " 'It was the Jew who did it, Oswald, surely,' " she says to her husband (*Redux*, 2.94)—as, indeed, it turns out, it was. That Jewish wealth is questionable—whether that of foreign murderers and adventurers like Melius, foreign speculators like Melmotte or Lopez, or simply foreign women like Madame Max Goesler (who turns the novel's prejudice from herself by exposing Melius)—does not indict capitalism (or imperialism, or racism), but provides them all with a convenient scapegoat to blame and punish. The indissoluble mix of capitalism, imperialism, and racism is reiterated again and again in Trollope's novels through such channels: Melmotte's exposure and disgrace (he has grown so enormous in England's mercantile and social worlds that he is himself a symbol of the—doomed—attempt to charter and control an exhaustive context) comes at his party for the Emperor of China. John Halperin makes a similar connection between money and empire (this time India) in *The Eustace Diamonds*: "A House of Commons forced to spend its time debating the penny and the Sawab of Mygawb can hardly be taken seriously," he writes, which draws the relation, but, it seems to me, misses the point.[74] Though it may ridicule Jewish speculators and Eastern potentates, Trollope's fiction, in spite of itself, through the interconnectedness of his series shows that the connection suggested by such figures is very serious indeed. Trollope's series, itself an empty structure spun out of control, scapegoats exotic others for what is an internal threat: the collapse of an ungrounded system that operates by taking its foundation precisely from its denial of any sameness or relation to the others that it traduces and helps to oppress. Although themselves inextricably interconnected, capitalism and imperialism operate by denying connections—such as the necessary connections between self and other.

[73] Anthony Trollope, *The Way We Live Now* (New York: Oxford, 1982), bk. 2, p. 44.
[74] John Halperin, "*The Eustace Diamonds* and Politics," in *Anthony Trollope*, ed. Tony Bareham (Totowa, N.J.: Barnes and Noble, 1980), 138–60; 155.

The interconnections of capitalism and imperialism come about through a web spun of language, what Trollope calls elsewhere the "gossamer" reels of literature, the ordinary language of his everyday.[75] In a chapter full of proverbs, Harold Smith's lecture at the missionary meeting in *Framley Parsonage* establishes the maxim as the proper tool of colonialism: "he ran on from platitude to truism, and from truism back to platitude" (96).[76] One of the authorities to whom Smith appeals in his talk seems important only to demonstrate the role of such language in enforcing cultural ideology, someone whose politics rest only on the kind of tag phrases learned in school—"Mr. Green Walker, a young gentleman who had lately been returned by his uncle's interest for the borough of Crewe Junction, and had immediately made his entrance into public life by giving a lecture on the grammarians of the Latin language as exemplified at Eton school" (95). And ordinary language not only guarantees the connection of capitalism, imperialism, and racism; its allows for another kind of dizzying identification that furthers the interests of such dominance. Harold Smith's maxims glorify an empty and abstract "Civilization." When connected to Christianity, that idea of civilization allows for the slippages by which, in Trollope's books and to his culture, all the various victims of imperialism can seem one and the same—savages without any culture of their own—no matter whether such people are European Jews, South Sea Islanders, freed black slaves in Jamaica, actual slaves in the southern United States, Australian or New Zealand aborigines, or the original inhabitants of South Africa.[77]

Trollope's critics praise him as "the only English novelist since Jane Austen to 'fathom the resources of the entirely commonplace'" and the commonplace becomes precisely one of the resources subsidizing imperialism.[78] The

[75] He, in fact, makes a direct (and highly questionable) connection between work, slavery, and language (including fiction writing): "If I have the means to lie in the sun and meditate idly, why, O my worthy taskmaster! should you expect me to pull out at thy behest long reels of cotton, long reels of law jargon, long reels of official verbosity, long reels of gossamer literature—Why, indeed? Not having means so to lie, I do pull out the reels, taking such wages as I can get, and am thankful. But my friend and brother over there, my skin-polished, shining, oil-fat negro, is a richer man than I. He lies under his mango-tree, and eats the luscious fruit in the sun; he sends his black urchin up for a breadfruit, and behold the family table is spread. He pierces a coca-nut, and, lo! there is his beverage. He lies on the grass surrounded by oranges, bananas, and pineapples. Oh my hard taskmaster of the sugar-mill, is he not better off than thou? Why should he work at thy order?" (*West*, 106).

[76] Trollope's platitudes in this chapter include "Those who live in glass houses shouldn't throw stones" (91), "Still waters run deepest," "It's all fair in love and war" (92), and "When he pays his money, then he takes his choice" (94).

[77] Although Trollope does actually at times attempt to make distinctions between such groups. What distinguishes the South Sea Islanders enough for them to appear in one of his novels is that he thinks that "unlike the Australian aboriginal, or even the African negro" for example, they are not "ineradicably savage"—but only because "Civilization is within their reach," the very "Civilization" Trollope puts into question in *Framley Parsonage*; see *Trollope's Australia: A Selection from the Australian Passages in "Australia and New Zealand,"* ed. Hume Dow (Melbourne: Thomas Nelson, 1966), 149–50, 150, 149 (my emphasis); all future references to this work (abbreviated *Australia*) will appear in the text.

[78] Introductory notes to *The Prime Minister*, in Smalley, *Trollope*, 417–19, 419. It bears remembering that the estate in *Mansfield Park* too is founded on plantations in the West Indies,

assumptions of racism hold sway *because* they have become commonplaces, so ordinary that they are beyond question. According to this logic, in his travel narrative about the West Indies, Trollope can write "it seems natural to us that white men should hold ascendency over those who are black or coloured" (*West*, 68). And he resorts to the proverbial expressly to debar such questioning: "it pains me to write words which may seem to be opposed to humanity and a wide philanthropy; but a spade is a spade, and it is worse than useless to say that it is something else" (*West*, 93). Harold Smith's (admittedly self-interested) attempts to keep the others from ridiculing the South Sea Islanders is similarly countered in *Framley Parsonage*: "Those who live in glass houses shouldn't throw stones" (*Framley*, 91) What the editors see as the organizing proverb of Trollope's plot in the novel—"Mark Robarts' mistake had been mainly this,—he had thought to touch pitch and not to be defiled" (494)—already points to a subtext of images of blackness and the hidden notions of race that underlie *Framley Parsonage*. In the midst of the entertainment and dalliance the missionary meeting provides, Robarts attempts to excuse his company to his wife by explaining that the somewhat questionable Bishop Proudie countenances their frivolity: as regards the Bishop, he tells his wife, "as well as regarding another great personage, the colour has been laid on perhaps a little too thickly" (74). Trollope unravels this proverb when writing in his travel books with some sympathy about the white former slave owner in Jamaica: "in his heart of hearts there dwells a feeling that after all slavery was not so vile an institution—that that devil as well as some others has been painted too black" (*West*, 91). Two of Trollope's major arguments in this travel book—that the ex-slave's monopoly on the labor market in Jamaica ought to be destroyed by the importation of workers from China and India, and that the "colored" (as in biracial; specifically black and white) race will ultimately take over the colonies—may explain how slavery (which specifically in Jamaica had been the ownership of black Africans by white Europeans) gets identified with what Homi Bhabha might call a "not-white, not-quite" devil here. But that this proverbial language about color and identity is also not quite logical in its application suggests the ways that an alternative logic of drift and contamination in poststructuralism can support, as well as question, cultural hegemony and dominance—it easily appropriates images of hybridity.

The relation established by the proverbial between the Bishop and slavery is meant to work in this novel because the readers of the Barsetshire series are already aware of the Bishop's submission to what Trollope wants to set up as another kind of slavery; his authority is imperiled (and therefore in a backhanded way asserted unquestionably as something he ought to have) by a woman's power. The Bishop's submission to his domestic slavery has al-

---

an echoing the editor to *Framley Parsonage* makes unconsciously when he directly compares that novel to Austen's earlier work as "another novel which shows the moderation of genteel country life invaded by the corruption of capital" ("Introduction," *Framley*, 19).

ready been played out in *Barchester Towers*, so that by the time of *Framley Parsonage* the reader just needs be told "he in all things now supported his wife's rule" (101). In the neat apotropaic turns of misogyny, the middle-class English women's powerlessness under patriarchy gets transformed into the threat of her dominance; in the neat turns of racism, the white man is accorded the absolute powerlessness of the black slavery he has actually enforced.[79] The connection between women and slaves follows a similar logic, which makes equivalent the very different relations each stands in to power and to each other. Mrs. Proudie's insistent takeover of the missionary meeting demonstrates the ways that women in her position could respond to their own oppression by colluding actively in the more vehement oppression of others. But that Trollope needs Mrs. Proudie to be so spectacularly to blame also suggests that it might be in the interest of the status quo still operating quite effectively in the hands of the meek little Bishop to deny any connection between gender and race. If they are refused any connection, the uneven violence done to both positions can continue to be enforced.

Such violence is managed characteristically at the level of form. Recourse to Trollope's endless series not only already makes known to us the Bishop's domination by Mrs. Proudie; it also secures the proper attitude to it. In explaining the workings of *in medias res*—arguably, the narrative stance of each of Trollope's novels in their relation to the series they make up—Trollope writes: "This rushing 'in media res' has doubtless the charm of ease. 'Certainly, when I threw her from the garret window to the stony pavement below, I did not anticipate that she would fall so far without injury to life or limb.'"[80] Trollope's form is predicated on a violence easily perpetrated on women; as his reviewers at the time wrote about *The Duke's Children* (the novel in which he makes this claim, without drawing its connection to his own work) "The death of the Duchess so early in the tale will be a great shock to many worthy people, but even duchesses must die that novels may be written."[81] Critics may point out that John Bold and Mary Flood Jones

[79] Marx argues that slavery is indissolubly related to gender, through a division of labor (and it is out of this connection, having to do, as it does, with private property as well, that his whole system of history grows)—"where wife and children are the slaves of the husband. This latent slavery in the family, though still very crude, is the first property, but even at this early stage it corresponds perfectly to the definition of modern economists who call it the power of disposing of the labour-power of others. Division of labour and private property are, moreover, identical expressions": *The German Ideology*, in *The Marx-Engels Reader*, ed. Robert C. Tucker (New York: Norton, 1978), 146–200; 159–60. The connection between women and slavery might provide one place to begin to investigate interrelated cultural notions of sexuality as well, since, Engels, at any rate, wants to show (through the example of classical Athens) how sex with slaves (and those otherwise enslaved as prostitutes) leads to homosexuality and pederasty: "But the degradation of the women recoiled on the men themselves and degraded them too, until they sank into the perversion of boy-love, degrading both themselves and their gods by the myth of Ganymede": *The Origin of the Family, Private Property, and the State*, in Tucker, 734–59; 738–39.

[80] Anthony Trollope, *The Duke's Children* (New York: Oxford University Press, 1983), 69. All future references to this work (abbreviated *Duke's*) will appear in the text.

[81] Unsigned notice of *The Duke's Children*, *Westminster Review* 114 (October 1880): 574; in Smalley, *Trollope*, 474.

(both supernumerary spouses, killed off in *Barchester Towers* and *Phineas Redux* respectively) perish "so that a series can proceed," but throughout Trollope's work woman is more pointedly the victim propelling the series.[82] Although Mr. Harding also dies in *The Last Chronicle of Barset*, Mrs. Proudie is the one who becomes the symbol for its his series's formal impulse. Trollope writes:

> It was with many misgivings that I killed my old friend Mrs. Proudie. I could not, I think, have done it, but for a resolution taken and declared under circumstances of great momentary pressure. . . .
>
> Two clergymen, each with a magazine in his hand, seated themselves, one on one side of the fire and one on the other, close to me. They soon began to abuse what they were reading, and each was reading some part of some novel of mine. The gravamen of their complaint lay in the fact that I reintroduced the same characters so often! "Here," said one, "is that archdeacon whom we have had in every novel he has ever written." "And here," said the other, "is the old duke whom he has talked about till everybody is tired of him. If I could not invent new characters, I would not write novels at all." Then one of them fell foul of Mrs. Proudie. It was impossible for me not to hear their words, and almost impossible to hear them and be quiet. I got up, and standing between them, I acknowledged myself to be the culprit. "As to Mrs. Proudie," I said, "I will go home and kill her before the week is over." And so I did. (*Autobiography*, 275)

The Barsetshire series ends with this novel in which Trollope kills Mrs. Proudie; yet, although she is so crucial to that series that her death seems to arrest its impulse, at one and the same time, compared to the archdeacon and the duke (who, like other characters, appear in the next series), she is also dispensable. In this way, her death marks an inexhaustibility of context that in her case is far from benign.

Violence to women is necessary to keep Trollope's series running straight. Trollope, whose autobiography recounts almost dispassionately the way he was brutally (because also dispassionately, routinely) whipped throughout his school years, makes such violence a routine part of his fictional world (perhaps because, as his autobiography also attests, violence was the one thing he learned at school: he tells us that when finally pushed to it, he was a dogged and brutal fighter himself).[83] Frank Gresham and Johnny Eames both thrash to narrative acclaim the different men who are jilters in their novels, and through their example Trollope suggests that a little judicious beating can often be in order—even (perhaps especially) when it comes to women. When the woman *he* has been accused of jilting finally finds a husband, Eames says "If he does beat her, I hope he will do it tenderly. It may be that a little of it will suit her fevered temperament" (*Last*, 859). Both Lady

[82] Philip Collins, "Business and Bosoms: Some Trollopian Concerns," *Nineteenth-Century Fiction* 37 (1982–1983): 293–315; 310. The title here perhaps says all about the hegemonic interconnections within this article that needs to be said.

[83] For his discussions of his "daily" thrashings, see *Autobiography*, 4, 8, and 18; for his own ultimate prowess as a fighter, see 13 and 19.

Glencora and Lady Laura Kennedy wish to be beaten, as preferable to the coldness they receive from their husbands.[84] Lady Glencora has been married to the future Duke of Omnium as one way of keeping her in order, and her husband is sure that women must be kept in order at all costs, for "if every foolish girl were indulged, all restraint would be lost, and there would be an end to those rules as to birth and position by which he thought his world was kept straight" (*Duke's*, 398). Although Lady Glencora is kept straight, the Duke's daughter is not—which turns out not put an end to the rules of his world (although this novel does put an end to Trollope's Palliser series): the Duke of Omnium's control is not total, but the things outside his control don't necessarily undo it either.

The everyday unequal relations between husband and wife that turn on the fulcrum of violence become the metaphor for the (uneven but indissoluble) connection of wives and slavery in Trollope's notion of culture. Trollope, who recognized slavery as the cause of the American civil war, employed just such a metaphor for it:

> It is disagreeable, that having to live with a wife who is always rebuking one for some special fault; but the outside world will not grant a divorce on that account, especially if the outside world is well aware that the fault so rebuked is of daily occurrence. "If you do not choose to be called a drunkard by your wife," the outside world will say, "it will be well that you should cease to drink." . . . The South has been the husband drunk with slavery, and the North has been the ill-used wife.[85]

Although Trollope's explicit sympathies are with the North, his conflation of secession with a divorce he rejects suggests that it is part of a wife's proper role patiently to bear her husband's ill-treatment rather than drive him away (and his treatment of women who separate from their husbands in *Phineas Redux* and *He Knew He Was Right* also suggests this). And making the violence of civil war part of what daily occurs in a relation so familiar as marriage seems to allow Trollope to deny violence altogether when it comes to the daily fact of slavery itself. Whenever he recounts his direct encounter with slavery as an institution (either the historical vestiges of it in the West

---

[84] Lady Glencora dreams of her old lover: "The Marquis of Auld Reekie had gone so far as to suggest that Burgo might probably beat her. But what hard treatment, even what beating, could be so unendurable as this total want of sympathy, as this deadness in life, which her present lot entailed upon her? . . . Would it not be even better to be beaten by him than to have politics explained to her at one o'clock at night by such a husband as Plantagenet Palliser?": Anthony Trollope, *Can You Forgive Her?* (New York: Penguin, 1982), 457; all future references to this book (abbreviated *Forgive*) will appear in the text. Lady Laura Kennedy says to her brother: "Never be a tyrant, Oswald; or at any rate, not a cold tyrant. And remember this, there is no tyranny to a woman like telling her of her duty. Talk of beating a woman! Beating might often be a mercy": Anthony Trollope, *Phineas Finn* (New York: Oxford, 1982), bk. 2, p. 158; all future references to this work (abbreviated *Finn*) will appear in the text.

[85] Anthony Trollope, *North America*, ed. Donald Smalley and Bradford Booth (New York: Knopf, 1951), 350; all future references to this book (abbreviated *America*) will appear in the text.

Indies or its actual practice in the United States), he takes care to stress how well the slave is treated, how he never sees any signs of ill treatment within slavery.[86] By turning violence against women, eroticizing it so that it is something that husbands may do tenderly and wives long for, Trollope also ultimately denies it, makes it disappear, in the relations of slavery which without this element seem merely, like marriage, "picturesquely patriarchal," as Trollope calls it (*America*, 381). Through their cultural interdependence, the violence of racism and imperialism gets hidden and naturalized by its perhaps more socially acceptable presence in misogyny.

Trollope is aware that the relations of colonizer and colonized are inescapably violent. In *Framley Parsonage* he shows himself keenly aware of the ruthlessness of imperialism. When asked by a critic to explain just how English empire will work in the South Sea Islands, Harold Smith replies:

> "We'll begin by explaining to them the benefits of civilization."
> "Capital plan!. . . . But how do you set about it, Smith?"
> "How do we set about it? How did we set about it with Australia and America? It is very easy to criticize; but in such matters the great thing is to put one's shoulder to the wheel."
> "We sent our felons to Australia . . . and they began the work for us. And as to America, we exterminated the people instead of civilizing them." (*Framley*, 62–63)

But Trollope's own fatalism about such ruthlessness explains his sanitation of the violence of race relations, since he argues elsewhere that making such violence palatable is the best response to it. Trollope (as if in the name of humaneness) writes: "Of the Australian black man we may say certainly that he has to go. That he should perish without unnecessary suffering should be the aim of all who are concerned in the matter. . . . Their doom is to be exterminated; and the sooner their doom be accomplished—so that there be no cruelty—the better it will be for civilization" (*Australia*, 138, 141). The matter-of-factness of such astonishing declarations is diffused throughout the interstices of culture via the route of gender—making violence to women usual, natural, everyday, is the first step in its dissemination.[87]

---

[86] In *North America*, for instance, Trollope writes that he finds slave cottages preferable "to the dwellings of most of our own agricultural labourers. Any comparison between the comfort of a Kentucky slave and an English ditcher and delver would be preposterous. The Kentucky slave never wants for clothing fitted to the weather. He eats meat twice a day, and has three good meals; he knows no limit but his own appetite; his work is light; he has many varieties of amusement; he has instant medical assistance at all periods of necessity for himself, his wife, and his children. Of course he pays no rent, fears no baker, and knows no hunger. I would not have it supposed that I conceive slavery with all these comforts to be equal to freedom without them; nor do I conceive that the negro can be made equal to the white man. But in discussing the conditions of the negro, it is necessary that we should understand what are the advantages of which abolition would deprive him, and in what condition he has been placed by the daily receipt of such advantages. . . . Such a state of things has its picturesquely patriarchal side; but what would be the state of such a man if he were emancipated to-morrow?" (380–81).

[87] To attempt to make sense of such shocking statements, we must understand them in context in Trollope's thought. He certainly recognized the injustices of imperialism. He argues, for

Yet Trollope himself is caught within this kind of circulation of cultural truisms; it bears remembering that Henry James's assessment of Trollope's appreciation of the usual is itself also gendered, for after the phrase usually quoted, James goes on to compare Trollope to women writers:

> This gift is not rare in the annals of English fiction; it would naturally be found in a walk of literature in which the feminine mind has laboured so fruitfully. Women are delicate and patient observers; they hold their noses close, as

---

example, against the wholesale condemnation in Britain of any violence committed by black people against white, emphasizing the way such violence might be justifiable defense and retaliation against imperial incursions: "Here, at home, all of us believe that we were doing a good deed in opening up these lands to the industry and civilization of white men. I at any rate so believe. But, if so, we can surely afford to tell the truth about the matter. These black savages were savage warriors, and not murderers; and we too, after a fashion, were warriors, . . . not calm administrators of impartial laws" (*Australia*, 140). But Trollope does not argue against imperialism per se, which he sees as inevitable: "It has been only natural, only human, that efforts should be made . . . to ameliorate the condition of these people, and—to use the word most common in our mouths—to civilize them. We have taken away their land, have destroyed their food, have made them subject to our laws, which are antagonistic to their habits and traditions, have endeavoured to make them subject to our tastes, which they hate, have massacred them when they defended themselves and their possessions after their own fashion, and have taught them by hard warfare to acknowledge us to be their masters. We have done the work perhaps with as little cruelty as was compatible with such a job. No one I think will say that the English should have abstained from taking possession of Australia because such possession could not be secured without injury to the blacks. Had the English abstained, the Dutch or the French would have come, and certainly would not have come with lighter hands" (*Australia*, 135). His making imperial dominance into a historical necessity suggests the ways in which Trollope's views represent a Victorian attitude that explains the sinister underside of Marx's notions of historical teleology (in "The British Rule in India," or "The Future Results of the British Rule in India," for example [in Tucker, *Marx-Engels Reader*, 653–58 and 659–64]). But to move from acknowledging the inevitability of an imperial desire on the part of world powers to an acceptance of genocide represents a kind of slide that is almost numbing in its logic.

We need not only to recognize the force of such slippages, but also to understand their logic—especially to understand how we too operate inescapably within it. To retain the shock that it seems to me absolutely and morally crucial that we continue to feel about genocide in order to be anything worth calling human (the problem with Trollope is that he is no longer shocked by this crime, and hence can begin to share the attitude that leads to it), we cannot, I think, too strongly indict such dizzying slides as Trollope's for the way they further cultural power and violence. Some kinds of cultural studies, in focusing on the concrete, want to refuse structural connections as amorphous abstractions—to oppose the practices of wife-beating and genocide, say, as different cultural actions that need to be understood in their specificity. But there's a problem in refusing structural connections—one I never realized more clearly than when I came across the enormity of Trollope's cultural racism in the passages I've just quoted. It would be a relief simply to separate the novels and the travel books through the concreteness of their form, say—to argue that the complications of the fiction are in excess of and begin to undo the simpler declarations of the travel narratives. But that would only have the charm of ease. To say that by enjoying Trollope's novels I am to some degree admitting cultural attitudes that are violently and inhumanly racist seems to me important and necessary, however, precisely because it is so counterintuitive (and so unpleasant to do). To deny any connection between them would be to refuse a notion of structural racism—and my own implication in it—that is difficult to keep hold of because it requires us to admit interconnections that are not only hidden at the level of the concrete and local, but even belied by that level. It is here particularly that I think that the refusal by some strands of cultural studies of what they see as the grand sweeps of theory is pernicious—unwittingly in service of the very systems of dominance they want to contest.

it were, to the texture of life. . . . Trollope, therefore, with his eyes comfortably fixed on the familiar, the actual, was far from having invented a new category; his great distinction is that in resting there his vision took in so much of the field. ("Partial," 527)

Trollope's attention to the everyday and the series made other critics too see him as "almost womanly"—"another Scheherazade."[88] Women's relation to the texture of everyday life is reiterated in responses to Trollope: "A Dublin lady friend of Trollope said that his 'close looking into the commonest objects of daily life always reminded her of a woman in a shop examining the materials for a new dress.'"[89] Scheherazade, a woman in a shop—gender, connected with race and class—all become part of the endless network of Trollope's cultural depiction in which he himself gets entangled.

Trollope's defenders attempt to exempt him from this grid, to project its dangers onto gender alone, precisely by recourse to this same network. Just as for Henry James, Trollope is distinguished by how much he takes in; for other critics as well it is his extensiveness that marks him. "Thinking of Barsetshire," W. P. Ker writes, "I do not forget Mrs. Oliphant and Carlingford, and I am not competent to choose between Salem Chapel and Barchester Cathedral. But Trollope's scene is immensely larger."[90] The banal performance of reproduction traced in the series by women writers like Oliphant becomes larger than life for these critics when performed by a male writer— as J. Hillis Miller contends, Trollope's dilation represents omnipresence and omniscience, a divine fiat, the reassuring authority of an act of god himself. In fact, references to legitimate female series writers in any century are rare; for Trollope and most of his critics, any practitioners in this form are male: Scott, Thackeray, Balzac, even Bulwer-Lytton, Percy Fitzgerald, and Thomas Arnold. After recounting a toast by Trollope to this fraternity, his biographer reminds us that Trollope's inheritance is a little closer to home: "Trollope's own mother had featured the widow Martha Barnaby in three novels, 1839– 43."[91] Occluding his own position in a complex web of relations, collapsing the network of inheritance to the patrilinial alone, gives Trollope the illusion that he is in control of his own repeating chain, the single and precise line that Miller lauds.

Michael Riffaterre investigates how Trollope's style proceeds by way of "stereotype, cliché, or proverb already established in usage"—proverbs that as "the first step or rung in a repetitive series" weave a network densely intertextual.[92] Riffaterre wants to highlight the banalities of Trollope's style

---

[88] Bradford A. Booth, "The Chaos of Criticism," in Hall, *The Trollope Critics*, 95–98; 98; unsigned notice of *The Last Chronicle of Barset*, *Athenaeum*, August 3, 1867, 141; in Smalley, *Trollope*, 301–2; 301.

[89] Hall, *Trollope: A Biography*, 112.

[90] W. Ker, "Anthony Trollope," in Hall, *The Trollope Critics*, 26–33; 33.

[91] Hall, *Trollope: A Biography*, 302–3.

[92] Michael Riffaterre, "Trollope's Metonymies," *Nineteenth-Century Fiction* 37 (1982– 1983): 272–92; 288, 279.

to prove that such commonplaces are not what he calls "handmaiden" to narrative, but "the *mater narrationis*, the womb of narrative."[93] His interest is ultimately in origins, in mapping the absolute limits of the network of narrative. He means to argue that the proverbial has "the authority of usage" because it refers to an "intertext" that has "the authority that stems from having been first, of being already said, the already there."[94] Like other critics, he co-opts for male authority a seriality he fears is an essentially female reproductive and relational impulse (perhaps the whole point for these men of references to a Christian God in grounding authority is to prove that their own gender and culture are primary, original, uncontingent). Yet his discussion of Trollope's stereotypes has ultimately nothing to do with women (except to disparage Mrs. Proudie); it comes to rest on Trollope's designation of Quiverful as father and patriarch, with all the resonances of paternity and male potency that name implies.[95]

When considering proverbs, Riffaterre intimates that he knows exactly what such ordinary language means and where it leads, a sentiment shared by another of Trollope's patriarchs, the Reverend Mr. Crawley: "When I hear jocose proverbs spoken as to men, such as that in this house the grey mare is the better horse, or that in that house the wife wears that garment which is supposed to denote virile command, knowing that the joke is easy, and that meekness in a man is more truly noble than a habit of stern authority, I do not allow them to go far with me in influencing my judgment" (*Last*, 724). Trollope too attempts to supersede the authority of usage to which he also refers, telling us in *Can You Forgive Her?*, for instance, of the proverbial wisdom that "she who doubts is lost" that "women doubt every day who solve their doubts at last on the right side" (*Forgive*, 534). But although the wish to control the disseminations of ordinary language (to ground it in an everyday, Trollope's view of it, that is somehow right) reveals a hidden unease about women's powers, that doesn't mean that the expansiveness of seriality necessarily benefits women either. Mr. Fothergill's urbane "One does not like partridge every day" in *Framley Parsonage* (117) refers to an old story in which Henry IV attempts to convince his confessor of the necessity for adultery, the need to enliven a monogamy that (he thinks) must ultimately become banal. The sameness of repetition here points to an illusion of difference in which all women are actually only similar and interchangeable. The everyday becomes a vast network which can swamp rather than liberate the other by reducing everything to its level, which is the point of the lesson that that great politician, Plantagenet Palliser, gives to his sons: "Such comforts will cease to be joys when they become matters of course. That a boy who does not see a pudding once a year should enjoy a pudding

[93] Michael Riffaterre, "On the Diagetic Functions of the Descriptive," *Style* 20 (1986): 281–94; 293.
[94] Ibid., 286.
[95] Ibid., 287–88; for the disparagement of Mrs. Proudie, see p. 290.

when it comes I can understand; but the daily pudding, or the pudding twice a day, is soon no more than simple daily bread" (*Duke's*, 197–98). Although the danger of the everyday seems here to be one of leveling—it can reduce the pleasures of the sons of dukes to the stark needs of the daily laborer—the interconnections that Trollope draws between radically different groups are not always so progressive, as we have seen. The fretwork of cultural interconnections in Trollope's series can never be stayed, but just what that means politically is also never fixed or certain. Just like the Duke of Omnium's own coalition government, the mix of connections also makes for mixed results.

The messiness of such uncertainty may explain the desire of critics and characters alike to fall foul of Mrs. Proudie. The postmortem of the missionary meeting becomes an attack on her, which unites the otherwise disparate company: "and then they all went to work and picked Mrs. Proudie to pieces, from the top ribbon of her cap down to the sole of her slipper" (*Framley*, 108). *Framley Parsonage* becomes by its end a novel about the evil of female dominance; in liking too much to rule, Lady Lufton is similar to her antagonist Mrs. Proudie, and she too must be humbled. The subtext in the novel about the South Sea Islanders might suggest the usual political reading of the connection between gender and race—that Trollope is displacing what is essentially a serious political consideration of the relation of Mother England to her colonies onto a domestic love story he can easily manage—that the dangers of revolution get tamed when they only refer to sons like Lord Lufton, who can win over his mother anyway.[96] Hence Lady Glencora's reference to herself as a "slave" and a "savage"—"rough, thick, and monstrously commonplace."[97] Although the rabidly conservative Lord Tulla's later analogy connecting "radical peer[s]" to "nigger[s]" (*Finn*, 103) through the violence of his language makes clear how uneven any connection like this must be, the almost sacrificial violence done to Mrs. Proudie (and to Lady Glencora, for that matter) still suggests the dangers of fragmentation, of rending into pieces. It poses as a challenge instead the need to keep trying to draw the web of interconnections between various political divisions, rather than establish another hierarchy in which questions of race become more political than those of gender, or vice versa. This is not to say that privileged aristocratic women and impoverished freedmen of Jamaica are equal—but only that the cultural network that entraps them both differently does so through a similar logic of filiation.

But what perhaps exposes the logic of this connection best is the figure that seems to get left out of these interconnections altogether—for if domi-

[96] This actually seems an attitude Trollope is ridiculing when he has Phineas Finn think "as for the colonies, he did not care if they revolted to-morrow. He would have parted with every colony belonging to Great Britain to have gotten the hand of Violet Effingham for himself" (*Finn*, 2.130–31).
[97] Anthony Trollope, *The Prime Minister* (New York: Oxford, 1983), bk. 1, pp. 28, 70; bk. 2, p. 22. All future references to this book (abbreviated *Prime*) will appear in the text.

nant ideology justifies imperialism through a network of misogyny and racism that connects white women and black men (and that needs to be confronted and addressed in terms of these connections), is there any space in all these interdependences (either dominant or dissident) for the figure of the black *woman*? Her occlusion in Trollope's text also follows a dominant strain of cultural logic: Hortense Spillers writes of the black woman's invisibility in historical accounts of slavery. She argues that this figure is occluded because patriarchal definitions of categories like gender become impoverished and flattened, make little sense, when subsumed under racism. Spillers suggests, for instance, that black African women transformed into slaves during the middle passage (including those who were pregnant or gave birth on board) don't even seem like women to culture because they partake of little of the "picturesquely patriarchal" necessary to conventional images of gender: such women enjoyed "few of the benefits of a *patriarchalized* female gender, which, from one point of view, is the *only* female gender there is." [98]

Spillers argues that the invisibility of the black woman exposes the imbrications of racism and misogyny and the workings of dominance through massive diffusiveness. The captive body of the slave marks a "point of convergence [where] biological, sexual, social, cultural, linguistic, ritualistic, and psychological fortunes join"; it becomes a symbol which "embodies sheer physical powerlessness that slides into a more general 'powerlessness' resonating through various centers of human and social meaning" ("Mama's," 67). The irony that marks this proliferation of connections is that with the captive body we also "lose any hint or suggestion of a dimension of ethics, of relatedness between one human personality and another, between human personality and cultural institutions" (68). The slave marks cultural interconnections precisely because he or she is used as a token to deny them (and one of the things that Spillers honors in the black community is its ability to preserve the relations of its members in the face of violent social forces that work deliberately to prevent black people from having any connection with one another [75]). For Spillers, it is the captive *female* body that "locates precisely a moment of converging political and social vectors" (75). The black woman refused by dominant culture not just as woman but as mother becomes the symbol of social interrelation because "if the child's humanity is mirrored in the eyes of its mother, or the maternal function, then we might be able to guess that the social subject grasps the whole dynamic of resemblance and kinship by way of the same source" (76). The black woman that gets left out of dominant culture both attests to its ideological infiltrations and (Spillers suggests) offers a way to rework them. [99] And that Trollope too

[98] Hortense Spillers, "Mama's Baby, Papa's Maybe: An American Grammar Book," *diacritics* 17 (1987): 65–81; 73. All future references to this essay (hereafter abbreviated "Mama's") will appear in the text.

[99] Although for just how troubled such reworkings might be, see what some critics have considered Henry Louis Gates's appropriation of this symbol of the African American mother in "The Master's Pieces: On Canon Formation and the African-American Tradition," *South Atlantic Quarterly* 89 (1990): 89–111; Michelle Wallace provides one critique of this appropriation

sees the black mother as some kind of symbol for but also challenge to slavery is shown by his suggestion that the best way to end that system is to free only black girls and all the children that they will later bear (*America*, 362).

Trollope's language makes occasional reference to some women of color: he mentions the Indian practice of suttee so often in parodying Victorian mourning and widowhood that it almost becomes proverbial. But such references actually close off any presence for women of color (the Western representation of suttee is, in fact, Gayatri Spivak's example of the way the identity of such oppressed women can operate only as an unrepresentable trace).[100] The closest that we get in his series fiction to any direct consideration that such women might have a narrative comes only very tangentially in the story of Madame Max Goesler; as she says to the Duke of Omnium, "in this country a woman with a foreign name, with means derived from foreign sources, with a foreign history, is specially suspected" (*Finn*, 2.219). In one of the precipitous conflations of Trollope's culture, nationality and race get coded together, in the familiar Victorian equation in which foreign equals Jewish equals black. Such racism in the Palliser novels is enforced by the very woman they also elsewhere identify with slavery: it is Lady Glencora who, frantic that Madame Goesler might marry the old duke and keep her husband and son from inheriting the title, anathematizes her: "The widow of a Jew banker! He, the Duke of Omnium. . . . And to do this for a thin, black-browed, yellow-visaged woman with ringlets and devil's eyes, and a beard on her upper lip,—a Jewess" (*Finn*, 2.216). But, even as she is denounced, the figure of a woman who might also suggest blackness once again disappears. The object of culture's racism and its anxieties is not so much Madame Max Goesler herself; she is only a conduit for the heir that she might present to Omnium, and to England: "Heavens, what a blow it would be, should some little wizen-cheeked half-monkey baby, with black brows, and yellow skin, be brought forward and shown to her some day as heir! What a blow to herself;—and what a blow to all England!" (*Finn*, 2.176).

As Lady Glencora's later fast friendship with Madame Goesler suggests, Trollope means for his reader to be critical of these views—or at least of Lady Glencora's expression of them. Trollope uses her as a scapegoat for English racism: the novel suggests that the ugliness of such attitudes arise from women's fevered temperaments. It is Glencora's articulation of them, her manner (as her husband later tells her regarding her behavior in general),[101] that is meant to be vulgar. But Trollope sees fit ultimately to bestow Madame

in "Negative Images: Towards a Black Feminist Cultural Criticism," in Grossberg et al., *Cultural Studies*, , 654–64; 661; Barbara Johnson, another in "Response," in *Afro-American Literary Study in the 1990s*, ed. Houston A. Baker, Jr. and Patricia Redmond (Chicago: University of Chicago Press, 1989), 39–44.

[100] Gayatri Spivak, "Can the Subaltern Speak?" in *Marxism and the Interpretation of Culture*, ed. Cary Nelson and Lawrence Grossberg (Urbana: University of Illinois Press, 1988), 271–313; see also Benita Parry's critique of this argument, in "Problems of Current Theories of Colonial Discourse," *Oxford Literary Review* 9 (1987): 27–58.

[101] For his complaints of her vulgarity, see *The Prime Minister*, 177.

Goesler on the Irish adventurer Phineas Finn (a character made to assert his own foreignness in the heart of Empire—to resign his appointment at the Colonial Office and return to Ireland)—a man to whom she herself proposes. As Trollope tells his readers elsewhere about such an act by a woman: "The offer of herself by a woman to a man is, to us all, a thing so distasteful that we at once declare that the woman must be abominable. There shall be no whitewashing of" it.[102] By this use of "whitewashing," Trollope is at least to some extent referring to the proverbial expression he uses elsewhere throughout his series: "To wash a blackamoor white."[103] His own proverbial language also ultimately connects Madame Goesler to blackness (and denounces her), suggesting the degree to which Trollope himself holds the attitudes he has Lady Glencora voice.

In his travel book *Australia and New Zealand*, Trollope writes of adolescent girls of "mixed breed" who, no matter how well treated they are as domestic servants, always wind up ultimately "vanish[ing] into the bush" (*Australia*, 135). His narrative makes clear black people's very pressing need to vanish before white eyes, since Trollope suggests that in the bush black men are killed as perfunctorily as white men shoot tigers or snakes. They are not seen as people precisely because of their color. When a black man "disappears" in this sense—when he has been shot down like an animal—"he cannot be traced. The very hue of his face prevents evidence as to his identity" (*Australia*, 136). Black people are fleeting figures in stories like Trollope's— ones who appear only to vanish—because his culture cannot imagine them as people. For Trollope's audience, such people simply can never be fully formed, solidified into identity, but flicker in and out around that category.

As Spivak has suggested, the very business of imperialism—of civilizing the savage—is that of "soul-making."[104] But the persons given souls by such cultural interference are not those of the conquered race, seen as animals, but the conquerors, who are made to feel their identity as human in comparison. Certainly the missionary meeting in *Framley Parsonage* works to assure its heartless participants, through their philanthropy, of their humaneness— and even Trollope's exposure of this works to the same end, for it is part of his larger definition of just what the human is (not the idealized, polarized, good and bad of authors like Mr. Popular Sentiment, as he calls Dickens in *The Warden*, but the mixed morality of Trollope's own realism). Trollope's most extended treatment of a black woman's story in his travel narratives makes clear this figure's usefulness in soul-making; in *The West Indies*, he gives his readers the short tale of a beautiful young woman "of the coloured race" named Josephine (25). By directly associating his encounter with her

---

[102] Anthony Trollope, *The Eustace Diamonds* (New York: Oxford, 1983), 321.
[103] The first is from Anthony Trollope, *The Small House at Allington* (New York: Oxford, 1980), 439; the second is from *The Prime Minister*, bk. 2, p. 205.
[104] Spivak, "Three Women's Texts and a Critique of Imperialism," *Critical Inquiry* 12 (1985): 43–61.

with Sterne's encounter with Maria, Trollope situates it within the context of the production of his own soul.[105] In *A Sentimental Journey*, Sterne's Yorick tells the reader as he goes off to search for the woman that Tristram Shandy has described: " 'Tis going, I own, like the Knight of the Woeful Countenance, in quest of melancholy adventures—but I know not how it is, but I am never so perfectly conscious of the existence of a soul within me, as when I am entangled in them." [106] An encounter with Maria not only assures him of his humanity but, as Eve Sedgwick has argued, bestows on him the sense of "universal consciousness" so necessary to Empire.[107]

Josephine is just one in a series of touristic encounters (including Sterne's with Cervantes) made to buttress English culture as a transcendent ideal—not a cultural construction but the way things are supposed to be. And this underlying impulse to transform the cultural into the transcendent and universal may help explain why Trollope fills Josephine's story with an excess of religious hatred and hierarchization (in addition to those of race, class, and gender). Josephine's tale of woe is that she has been jilted by a Jewish sea-captain, whom she has come to "hate . . . worse dan poison" (*West*, 26). And Josephine is herself a Baptist, about whom Trollope tells his reader "Now I hate Baptists—as she did her lover—like poison" (28). By repeating this woman's commonplace of ordinary language, but with a difference, Trollope performs the everyday politics of self and other involved in the iterations underlying the speech acts which attempt to distinguish hierarchies and cultures. Trollope's different repetition ironizes Josephine's language, translates it out of the dialect by which he codes for race into what is meant to be the universal idiom of his own prose style. By so doing, Trollope suggests that it is at the level of ordinary language and the everyday that souls get made: what may distinguish humanity within Trollope's fiction is the ability to have, and take for granted, its own everydayness. The "civilized" get to define what's ordinary language (for them) and what's extraordinary enough to be dialect.

One kind of racism is displaced onto another in this vignette: Trollope and Josephine both hate Jews (and it is important that even though she doesn't say she hates them, Trollope is careful to have Josephine distinguish herself from people who are "completely" black: "I teaches the nigger children," she tells Trollope [28]). Such displacements seem necessary to allow gender to operate: by preserving a racial scapegoat, Trollope's and Josephine's relations can seem, at least temporarily, free of race. Abdul JanMohamed has

---

[105] Trollope writes: "There was not about my Josephine all the pathos of Maria; nor can I tell my story as Sterne told his. But Josephine in her sorrow was I think truer to human nature than Maria. It may perhaps be possible that Sterne embellished his facts. I, at any rate, have not done that" (*West*, 29).

[106] Laurence Sterne, *A Sentimental Journey through France and Italy* (New York: Penguin, 1968), 137.

[107] Eve Sedgwick, *Between Men: English Literature and Male Homosocial Desire* (New York: Columbia University Press, 1982), 80.

argued that "the ideological function of . . . colonialist literature is to artic-
ulate and justify the moral authority of the colonizer and—by positing the
inferiority of the native as a metaphysical fact—to mask the pleasure the
colonizer derives from that authority."[108] But, just as in the earlier example
of wife-beating, when that authority gets coded for gender, it no longer needs
to mask its pleasures. The obvious erotic charge for Trollope in his encounter
with this woman makes pleasure in cultural dominance seem as ordinary as
the socially sanctioned male dominance of heterosexual relations.

If the black woman seems for a moment to get a story here, that's because
the story isn't really hers (and Trollope admits about Josephine that "whence
she came or who she was I did not know, and never learnt" [*West*, 25]). She
serves her ideological purpose and—like the young girls in the bush—she
vanishes ("I pressed her hand, and so she went, and I neither saw nor heard
more of her" [29]). But Trollope's record of the elusiveness of such figures
(even if that elusiveness serves a purpose for dominant culture), also points
to the ever-retreating cultural horizon that his series can only gesture to,
never get beyond. Trollope's series gestures to a figure it can never recognize;
its inability to realize the figure of the black woman, rather than *just* suggesting racist blindness (as it also very much does), might also suggest something useful about the limits of cultural imagination. The iterations and displacements of various kinds of privilege may reinforce one another, knit
themselves into an interlocking web of dominance; yet, although in its mas-
siveness that network may dream of totalization, it keeps growing, proliferating, precisely because it isn't (and can't be) complete. In this sense, it
doesn't just choose not to tell Josephine's real story; it never really can. And
that absence must call into question any pretension to completeness.

Taking the figure of the black woman as a sign for the incompleteness in
Trollope's cultural depictions that allows my argument to proceed carries
with it its own theoretical dangers: Deborah McDowell charts the way that
white feminists often use the figure of the black woman as a synecdoche for
practice, politics—everything that is resistant to theory, which then (supposedly) remains the white feminist's own province, yet gets her off the hook
for not including women of color in it.[109] I know I cannot elude these dangers; quoting Ralph Ellison, McDowell powerfully argues that, using anyone
or anything as a figure commits "the crime of reducing the humanity of others to that of a mere convenience, a counter in a banal game which involves
no apparent risk to ourselves."[110] Yet I hope that my recourse to the figure

[108] Abdul JanMohamed, "The Economy of Manichean Allegory: The Functions of Racial Difference in Colonialist Literature," in *"Race," Writing, and Difference*, ed. Henry Louis Gates, Jr.
(Chicago: University of Chicago Press, 1986), 78–106; 103.

[109] Deborah McDowell, *"The Changing Same": Black Women's Literature, Criticism, and
Theory* (Bloomington: Indiana University Press, 1995), 156–75.

[110] Ibid., 174. My chapter has been implying in part that the constitution of identity within
language means that to some degree we can relate to others only *as* figures—and necessarily dehumanize them in doing so. But seeing this very crime as *constituting* our humanness doesn't
mean that we should stop working always and unceasingly to lessen its effects.

of the black woman in exploring the very complexity of the banal might also
do something more. Rather than denying women of color a connection to theory, I hope instead it shows up the incompleteness of my own theory, which
needs precisely to be connected to, contested by, theories generated from the
place of that subjectivity. And the black woman is not the only monitor of
the insufficiency of my reading; even more hidden within my text—in the
references to Trollope's floggings in school, the note to Engels's view of homosexuality—remains the figure of the gay man (and the relations between
Slope and Mr. Proudie, as well as those unarticulated but perhaps desired by
Lilly Dale, demand a reading that takes sexuality into account). Judith Butler's work transforms the terrain of the performative to suggest that the series and the everyday are crucial for such an investigation: she argues that
drag illuminates the everyday iterations of heterosexuality that allow it to
pass as real; the performances of drag expose "the understated, taken-for-
granted quality of heterosexual performativity," that resides in "hyperbolic
norms [that] are dissimulated as the heterosexual mundane."[111] The insufficiency of my own reading of Trollope's political registers, I hope, suggests
that the difficulty in unraveling the tangled skein of connections in his works
keeps any one view of them from being definitive.

In treating the commonplaces of Trollope's style, Riffaterre maintains that
Trollope's repetitions call attention to themselves; they become significant in
their own right. For Riffaterre the choices they represent are either "comforting continuity or the rut of boredom."[112] I've been arguing that the recurrences of Trollope's seriality go beyond this either/or logic to carry another burden of significance: they perform the everyday logic of a cultural
totality that can never be wholly grasped. Critics have attempted to fix Trollope's fiction—to argue that it either subverts (J. Hillis Miller) or accom-
modates (D. A. Miller) cultural maxims. But in suggesting that the politics
of form are indissolubly mixed, Trollope's fiction seems to make such choices
beside the point. In presenting the everyday as everything, and that everything as more than we can ever take in, Trollope's series shows us the site
and mode of our engagement with the social system—its performance, not
its end. Although its critics have often accused it of accommodation, Trollope's fiction suggests that an emphasis on process is more than something
secondary, superfluous, to which we must reconcile ourselves. Trollope complicates the easy dismissal of formalism—makes it impossible to regard it
simply as a kind of conservatism masquerading behind the apolitical—but
he also makes it impossible to find a subversiveness inherent in its workings.
The trend of the series for Trollope is that in spite of itself it refuses the
charm of ease, it pushes the limits of the ordinary.

[111] Judith Butler, "Critically Queer," in her *Bodies That Matter: On the Discursive Limits of
"Sex"* (New York: Routledge, 1993), 223–84; 237.
[112] Riffaterre, "Metonymies," 281.

*Once again morning in the same streets. Once again the fatigue of so
many similarly passed nights. It is a walk that has lasted a long time.*

— Guy Debord, "On the Passage of a Few Persons through
a Rather Brief Period of Time"

3   The City, the Everyday,
and Boredom
The Case of Sherlock Holmes

This chapter is concerned with what happens when theorists attempt to represent the everyday with a particular figure, something they see as concrete.
One way to assert the everyday as the site of the real is to use language that
seems literally to embody it in one particular place: the city. Doing so may not
necessarily arrest the elusiveness and confusion of the everyday, however. Instead, the everyday's resistance to clear-cut reference gets transferred to the
feelings we have about the supposedly substantial and palpable reality before
us. "We are bored in the city," the theorists who directly connect the everyday with the city tell us.[1] The feeling of boredom as a visceral tedium that
can only be endured, never relayed second-hand, may seem itself to reach for
the literal. Yet of all sensations boredom is perhaps also the most diffuse. It
carries with it a burden of seriality, as we locate our tedium in massive repetitions we cannot seem to situate completely or arrest. The city too may
have become for some theorists a paramount figure for everyday life because
it similarly seems concrete and yet at the same time hopelessly confusing, unknowable, obscure.

Perhaps nowhere has the city been more of a central focus than in the writing of the Continental theorists of the everyday. For the philosopher and so-
ciologist Henri Lefebvre, the writer Maurice Blanchot, the cultural anthro-
pologist and social historian Michel de Certeau, and that disparate group of
1950s and '60s avant-garde intellectuals and artists who called themselves
the situationists international, the modern city (as opposed, perhaps, to what
we might now call the postmodern one) has been the crucial site putting into
play the category of the everyday.[2] As Blanchot writes: "We need these ad-

[1] Ivan Chtcheglov, "Formulary for a New Urbanism, " in *Situationist International Anthology*, trans. and ed. Ken Knabb (Berkeley, Calif.: Bureau of Public Secrets, 1981), 1–4; 1.
[2] For a discussion placing this theory of the everyday in its philosophical and social background, see Alice Kaplan and Kristin Ross's "Introduction" to *Everyday Life*, a special edition
of *Yale French Studies* 73 (1987): 1–4, and Michael Trebitsch's "Preface" to Henri Lefebvre's

mirable deserts that are the world's cities for the experience of the everyday
to begin to overtake us" (17). In its embodiment of both the poverty and the
rich potential of industrialization, mass production, and commodification,
the city for Lefebvre creates and symbolizes the everyday, that category he
uses to capture the alienation and banality of people's ordinary lives as well
as the potential already inhering within those lives for social change radical
enough to be truly revolutionary. As modern philosophical categories, the
city and the everyday depend on each other.

One of the modes tracing and cementing the interconnection of the city
and the everyday for these theorists is fiction;[3] it is the attitude connecting
these two categories that fiction particularly documents. Lefebvre notes "the
momentous eruption of everyday life into literature": James Joyce's *Ulysses*,
a novel, he writes, "encompassed by the City" (*Everyday*, 2–3). But, as Lefebvre insists whenever he turns to it, beyond its focus on the city and the
everyday, what stands out about *Ulysses* is that its "endless pages" (*Everyday*, 6) demonstrate that "a great novel can be boring" (*Critique*, 27). It is

---

Critique of Everyday Life: Volume 1, Introduction, trans. John Moore (New York: Verso, 1991),
ix–xxviii; all future references to this book (abbreviated *Critique*) will appear in the text. The
special edition of *Yale French Studies* that Kaplan and Ross edited collects some important
texts, including Maurice Blanchot's "Everyday Speech" (12–20; all future references to this essay will appear in the text). Edward Ball's article on the situationists in that journal ("The Great
Sideshow of the Situationist International," 21–37), as well as Peter Wollen's various articles
elsewhere ("Bitter Victory—The Situationist International," in *An Endless Adventure . . . ,*
ed. Iwona Blazwick [London: Verso, 1989], 9–15, and "The Situationist International," *New
Left Review* 174 [1989]: 67–95), and Sadie Plant's book on them—*The Most Radical Gesture:
The Situationist International in a Postmodern Age* (New York: Routledge, 1992)—are especially useful in introducing them to an American audience. The 1989–90 exhibition of situationist materials in Paris, London, and Boston, commemorating in part their role in the
May 1968 uprisings in France, helped trace this avant-garde group's roots back to the Futurists
and Surrealists as well as to less familiar radical groups, such as the Movement for an Imagist
Bauhaus, Cobra, and the Lettrist International. Like these groups, situationists were concerned
with making cultural interventions in the arenas of art, philosophy, and everyday life to effect
social change. They were enormously influential ("Our ideas are in everybody's minds," was
one of their slogans) but remained deliberately unestablished—although they proclaimed themselves *as* situationists (and fought quite bitterly over who was and was not included in their
group), for instance, anyone referring to such a thing as "situationism," which they were
adamant didn't exist, earned their immediate scorn. With Lefebvre, who was working from
Lukács and Heidegger, they are largely responsible for introducing "the everyday" into philosophical and popular discourse and, through this attention to it, changing the nature of what
was seen as the political arena.

[3] It is interesting for my argument that these theorists not only ascribe our recognition of the
very concept of the everyday in part to its appearance in literature, but trace that appearance
specifically to nineteenth-century fiction. Lefebvre, for instance, emphasizes the presence of the
everyday as an important organizing category in modernist novels like *Ulysses*, but asks as well:
"Was this revelation as sensational then as it seems now . . . ? And was it not foreshadowed already in Balzac, Flaubert, Zola and perhaps others?" (*Everyday Life in the Modern World*,
trans. Sach Rabinovitch [New Brunswick, N.J.: Transaction, 1984], 2; all future references to
this book [abbreviated *Everyday*] will appear in the text). Similarly, in discussing the novel as
"the zoo of everyday practices," de Certeau writes: "As indexes of particulars—the poetic or
tragic murmurings of the everyday—ways of operating enter massively into the novel or the
short story, most notably into the nineteenth-century realist novel": *The Practice of Everyday
Life*, trans. Steven Rendall (Berkeley: University of California Press, 1984), 78, 70. All future
references to this work will appear in the text.

this complex of the everyday and boredom, found in endless and "modern"—nineteenth- and twentieth-century—novels, and staged necessarily again and again in the city, that I will investigate in this chapter. And I want to stress that the idea of the "modern" here is indeed a temporal construction: to those of us nearing the end of this century, the city described by these theorists—one that can be boring rather than inescapably terrifying—may expressly bespeak a "modernism" much closer to the later nineteenth century than to any reality we think we experience now.

Those literary critics interested in boredom have treated it as an apotropaic response: they see it as the way the individual subject denies or manages the threat to his individuality from encompassing systems that swamp it, systems symbolized by the city, for instance.[4] I write "his" advisedly here, for I would like to show that while such a response has been the traditional—masculine—valence of boredom, it is not its only valence. As Roland Barthes suggests, "boredom is not simple" ("Women," 201). Neither is the city, nor the everyday, and the kind of give produced in their association might provide overlooked possibilities and practices for the modern subject produced by the very systems he (or she) wishes also to escape. Or, at any rate, theorists like de Certeau have found such give in the very structures of the ruling order: "Carried to its limit, this order would be the equivalent of the rules of meter and rhyme for poets of earlier times: a body of constraints stimulating new discoveries, a set of rules with which improvisation plays" (xxii). Such improvisation suggests the subject's paradoxical relation to the constitutive system—that cluster of structures and attitudes the subject can in no way simply shed because they are its very fiber. That cluster has most recently been designated as "power," more generally as "ideology," and the latter term

---

[4] D. A. Miller, in his excellent treatment of boredom in the novel, finds that boredom "binds" anxiety: "Far from the simple reflex-response to banality, boredom hysterically converts into yawning affectlessness what would otherwise be outright panic": *The Novel and the Police* (Berkeley: University of California Press, 1988), 145. Boredom for him both screens and does the work of the subject's constitution (its normalization) within englobing power. For Patricia Spacks, focusing on "the threat of boredom" can be a way of screening "larger, vaguer threats," especially people's powerlessness and insignificance within existing social structures: "The Necessity of Boredom," *Virginia Quarterly Review* 65 (1989): 581–99; 594; all future references to this essay (abbreviated "Necessity") will appear in the text. Spacks implicitly suggests that the city might be one locus of such structures when she argues that boredom "figures important ways in which human beings impinge on one another in crowded, anxiety-ridden societies" (592). Spacks attempts to imagine some "necessity," some utility, for boredom when it comes to women, although boredom continues mainly in her argument to be "life-destroying" for them: "Women and Boredom: The Two Emmas," *Yale Journal of Criticism* 2 (1989): 191–205; 200; all future references to this essay (abbreviated "Women") will appear in the text. But her suggestion that "we must posit two distinct versions of boredom . . . 'fructifying' and 'stultifying' boredom" ("Necessity," 591) in the larger gender context she introduces seems to leave room for the kind of position I take here—that there is a traditional masculinist posture of boredom that comes indeed in response to a perceived "life-destroying" threat, but also a feminist stance that seizes boredom to expose and explode such male anxiety and its subsequent scapegoating of women, a stance that makes clear the politics that inhere in the act of being bored. For her fuller discussion of boredom, which extends and revises these essays, see her *Boredom: The Literary History of a State of Mind* (Chicago: University of Chicago Press, 1995).

still seems to me appropriate as long as it is carefully distinguished from false consciousness.[5] In considering how the recent theoretical investigation of the city, the everyday, and boredom becomes a discussion of this more englobing notion of ideology, what I hope to do is open up that discussion to a critique of gender.[6]

The everyday life that is so palpable in the city to its theorists—and so boring—seems that way to them because of a particular characteristic. For these theorists, the dailiness of urban life reflects the subject's placement in the senseless replication and endless monotony of commodity capitalism. The boredom of everyday city life is the boredom of the assembly line, of one thing after another, of pieces locked in an infinite series that never really progresses: the more it changes, the more it remains the same. Blanchot states that the tedium of the everyday comes from its identity as "the inexhaustible, irrecusable, always unfinished daily" (13). Lefebvre too argues that "the everyday imposes its monotony" through its unremitting succession:[7] "The quotidian is what is humble and solid, what is taken for granted and that of which all the parts follow each other in such a regular, unvarying succession that those concerned have no call to question their sequence" (*Everyday*, 24).[8] What characterizes the everyday's tedium is its seriality.

This is a peculiarly urban tedium because—once again, in people's modern(ist) *fictions* about the city—seriality is central to depictions of it. In dis-

---

[5] The term "power" seems less useful because so directly associated with the theory of Michel Foucault. "Ideology," on the other hand, has a long history of association with a range of poststructural oppositional groups—feminists and lesbian theorists, deconstructive and Lacanian critics, those engaged in an antiracist critique. It seems more useful to me precisely because through its association with these disparate groups there is more give in it.

[6] And let me emphasize from the beginning that my use of terms like "masculine" and "feminist" is intended in no way to confuse those positions with biological gender—although the masculine posture of boredom, for instance, is most often assumed by a subject defined as biologically male (and even such a category is far from transparent and open to a great deal of drift), there is no transcendent principle (only the most refractory social pressures) demanding that association. I will sometimes use the shorthand of "men" and "women" in discussing the subject positions I chart here, because subjects assume to some degree the postures associated with the gender society imposes on them. But this chapter is precisely about resistance to these postures—mostly about "feminist" resistance, since that is what I know. But, as my reading of *The Picture of Dorian Gray* suggests, I recognize that there are important male resistances as well, the most signal the struggle undertaken by gay men. Certainly not all men are easily or happily "masculine" in the traditional sense of the term (thank God), nor are all women either "feminine" or (unfortunately) "feminist."

[7] "The Everyday and Everydayness," trans. Christine Levich, Alice Kaplan, and Kristin Ross, in Kaplan and Ross, *Everyday Life*, 7–11; 10; all future references to this essay (abbreviated "Everyday") will appear in the text.

[8] Lefebvre does recognize that people's construction of the everyday—and especially their boredom with it—comes directly out of their attempt to overlook the progression underlying that seeming succession: the everyday gets registered as tedium because "the days follow one after another and resemble one another, and yet—here lies the contradiction at the heart of everydayness—everything changes" ("Everyday," 10). For Lefebvre, however, the hidden progression people deny and avoid (and which he implies becomes available through the *critique* of everyday life) is not the decay and dissolution of human mortality and individual death, but the Marxist teleology that transfigures such a process.

cussing the mid- to late-Victorian representations of the city underlying its modern delineation, however, the literary critic Carol Bernstein suggests that that very seriality can defeat those depictions:

> The assumption is that the city is a collection of objects and rituals . . . [but] to assume that each object and each action must be represented by a specific word is to put oneself in the power of an endless cascade of language. Even if one were to posit some sort of closure by the representation of a segment of the city, more or less homogeneous and ordered, there remains the possibility of a continuing series of segments, limited only by the totality of objects and actions, of further conceivable series, in the city itself.[9]

As *Ulysses*'s "endless pages" already suggest, representations of the city seem to generate endless proliferation; taken to its ultimate extension, such ongoingness, as Bernstein suggests here, would ultimately produce an infinite series of series. It is perhaps for this reason that cities are "deserts" for Blanchot—almost sublime tracts of empty vastness stretching in all directions, built over by the works of humankind that actually only exaggerate, rather than fill in, that enormous vacuity.

Representations of the city seek (unsuccessfully) to manage the threat implicit in its endlessness by breaking it down, into seemingly more manageable parts; the supposed concreteness of the city is forced to seek even more concrete and material representation. The city gets figured metonymically in fictions about it as the street or the museum, but each figure in its own way retains that sense of endless replication. The street that stretches in all directions (the pavement that seems to ground a construction without a visible center) is perhaps a familiar and obvious metonym for the city (Charles Dickens's essays on walking the streets of mid-Victorian London are some of the most effective uses of this metonym).[10] But the museum too, with its seriality of collections attempting to account for the various histories of natural or artificial production, is a product and symbol of the city in nineteenth- and twentieth-century literature (as attested by the essays of Paul Valéry, and more famously, Walter Benjamin, which directly connect the museum and its collections to the street and the city).[11] Leslie Fiedler argues that the museum

---

[9] "Nineteenth-Century Urban Sketches: Thresholds of Fiction," *Prose Studies: History, Theory, Criticism* 3 (1980): 217–40; 224.

[10] "The Streets—Morning" and "The Streets—Night," in his *Sketches by Boz: Illustrative of Every-Day Life and Every-Day People*, vol. 12 (1957) of *The New Oxford Illustrated Dickens*, 21 vols. (Oxford: Oxford University Press, 1948-58), 47–52, 53–58.

[11] For Paul Valéry, "the glorious chaos of the museum follows me out and blends with the living activities of the street": "The Problems of Museums," in his *Degas, Manet, Morisot*, trans. David Paul (New York: Pantheon, 1960), 202–6; 205. For Benjamin, see "A Berlin Chronicle," and "One-Way Street [Selection]" in his *Reflections: Essays, Aphorisms, Autobiographical Writings*, trans. Edmund Jephcott, ed. Peter Demetz (New York: Harcourt, 1978), 3–60, 61–94, and *Charles Baudelaire: A Lyric Poet of High Capitalism*, trans. Harry Zohn (London: New Left, 1973). Also see Naomi Schor's discussion of Benjamin's collecting and his streetwalking in "Cartes Postales: Representing Paris 1900," *Critical Inquiry* 18 (1992): 188–244; all future references to this essay will appear in the text.

is one of those "institutions for which the city was a necessary pre-condition," especially because, as Philip Fisher suggests, "museums became more and more central exactly in cultures touched most deeply by the factory system." [12] Lefebvre and de Certeau both use the museum as a symbol for the reification and alienation of everyday life.[13] In theory and in fiction, the tedium of the street and the museum attests to the supposed rootlessness, commodification, and senseless teeming of modern urban capitalism.

To argue that the everyday refers to an essential reality of monotonous tedium, or that the city is a material manifestation of one kind of economic reality that creates such monotony, however useful such claims may be in some cases, is to overlook what may be the most important aspect of the city and the everyday. Categories like "the everyday" and "the city" seem to me just that—categories, constructions, objects created through critical attempts to define and explain them, and not essential phenomena. As the infinite proliferation associated with the city suggests, categories like "the everyday" and "the city" remain especially vague and amorphous, resist definition. I'm interested in why they nevertheless get defined as they do in different contexts: why do these theorists associate these constructions in this way? This is where the role of fiction is crucial. The Marxist-influenced association of the everyday and the city is one *story* people can tell about them, as these theorists do, and it may well be an important fiction enabling certain progressive politics: to associate modern urban life with a banalized and dreary ongoing sameness might expose and help to change current economic relations. But, when seen as a fiction (not as truth), and looked at it from another point of view—when, as I will contend, you add gender to it—this story turns out to enable other (rather destructive) politics. Rather than being just a stark tale of alienation, the endless succession of urban tedium can also be a compensatory fantasy of privilege, the kind of boredom that, as Patricia Spacks

[12] Leslie Fiedler, "Mythicizing the City," in *Literature and the Urban Experience: Essays on the City and Literature*, ed. Michael C. Jaye and Ann Chalmer Watts (New Brunswick: Rutgers University Press, 1981), 113–21; 113; Philip Fisher, *Making and Effacing Art: Modern American Art in a Culture of Museums* (New York: Oxford University Press, 1991), 165.

[13] That the museum represents the site of alienation for Lefebvre is indicated, for instance, by his suggestion that the lost beauty of "everyday man" has been "congealed into so many museum pieces floating on the muddy ocean of destitution" (*Critique*, 44). Although de Certeau also uses "museum" as a term for stagnation and alienation, for him the street and the museum are also similar because they can provide a counterpractice; they can both allow for travel stories, ways to traverse, link, organize, and make relations within existing parameters (xviii). This is an identity of the museum that Philip Fisher also emphasizes. He writes: "It is essential to see that the 'subject' of the museum is not the individual work of art but the relations between works of art. . . . That we walk through a museum, walk past the art, recapitulates in our act the motion of art history itself, its restlessness, its forward motion, its power to link" (8–9). Carol Bernstein argues that the city and the museum are antipathetic, the attempt to "turn the city into a museum containing collections of objects which are neatly classifiable" (235) doomed. But, as Douglas Crimp implies, in its seriality the museum is actually a good symbol for the city, as disparate and proliferating as the city: "The history of museology is a history of all the various [doomed] attempts to deny the heterogeneity of the museum, to reduce it to a homogeneous system or series": "On the Museum's Ruins," in *The Anti-Aesthetic: Essays on Post-Modern Culture*, ed. Hal Foster (Port Townsend, Wash.: Bay, 1983), 43–56; 49.

puts it, declares "the sufferer's specialness" ("Necessity," 592). In the context of the city, to imagine modern daily life as a tediously unchanging succession screens and denies the appalling decay and sudden violent death that the cultural imagination even in the later nineteenth century certainly already located in the city; that recent theorists continue to want to define the city this way is nostalgic, conservative—an attempt to conserve a vulnerable male privilege. Urban boredom can be seen as an apotropaic denial of the threat of mortality and the disintegration of the very body that seems to ground and give materiality to the individual self.

Although the fantasy of immortality and an integral self seems common enough to humankind, it has been strong-armed by culture into a *masculine* fantasy because woman has been made the vehicle enabling it. Whether, as in the famous case of Emma Bovary, she is the locus of boredom herself, or, as in the case of Sherlock Holmes, she is what causes boredom in others— either way she becomes a useful scapegoat who sacrificially purges the threat behind such boredom. The graphic description of Emma Bovary's rotting corpse suggests how intimately boredom is tied to the threat of mortality; the narrator's continuing existence, his control and dominance of the story, seems to come about precisely because Emma Bovary's provincial boredom destroys her. Her sacrifice seems to allow him to escape such threat, to purge and exculpate his more urbane ennui. Similarly, by taking woman as one cause of Holmes's boredom, Arthur Conan Doyle's stories suggest that by dispensing with women (as the neat society of Holmes and Watson continually tries to do—witness the death of Watson's wife or wives), a man can dispense with the threats that underlie boredom.[14]

The seriality of Doyle's stories (the way Sherlock Holmes, in seemingly endless story after story, each somehow always the same, has continued to live past his own death, and—through spin-offs, remakes, sequels—even the death of his creator) enacts the fantasy of existence without end and figures the way that, as Susan Stewart has put it, to "to play with series is to play with the fire of infinity."[15] Yet such fire can be dangerous; such fictions also expose how the power of infinity is one men feel they must wrest from women—their figure of maternity as the source for the generation of the series attests as much. It is an old and perhaps tedious story that mothers get

[14] Part of the tongue-in-cheek analysis of Watson's biography by such groups as the Baker Street Irregulars is their attempt to account for just how many wives Watson runs through. Doyle is not at all clear on this point—it might be one, it might be two, and it is uncertain just how or when she/they die, or whose forgetfulness (Doyle's? Watson's?) obscures the account. Interestingly, a similar obscurity in Watson's biography has to do with the status of his wound: did the Jezael bullet he took in the Afghan campaign disable him in the shoulder? the leg? or both (the single bullet theory)? The connection here between women and wounding goes without saying, but what's worth comment is the uncertainty that attends it: through it, Doyle seems to be at least acknowledging that such misogyny (even as he practices it) is actually an unsuccessful attempt to pin down and contain vague threats, to ground amorphous categories.

[15] Susan Stewart, *On Longing: Narratives of the Miniature, the Gigantic, the Souvenir, the Collection* (Baltimore: Johns Hopkins University Press, 1984), 159; all future references to this book will appear in the text.

blamed for bringing man forth again and again into a world of death; what I'd like to consider here are some counterpractices associated with women and boredom. As Spacks quote Kierkegaard: "Strange that boredom, in itself so staid and solid, should have such power to set in motion" ("Women," 193). The boredom in Doyle's stories suggests one way the feminist reader might seize and transform women's traditional relation to it, and through that to the city and the everyday—to ideology itself. Boredom in these stories (written by a doctor already bored by his profession, bored by the body?) might not just deny the decay of the body and the dissolution of the self (although it does that quite well); it might also provide a means to explode the fiction of the self, to exploit the anonymity traditionally bewailed by the banalized urban subject.

The complex of the city, the everyday, and boredom in Doyle's fiction suggests that one relation to ideology might be to work within it by accepting boredom, by giving up some of the privileges for which its (male) subjects strive. One of those privileges may be satisfaction (if that is the opposite of boredom); another is the very concept of the integral self founded on such satisfactions. A feminist reevaluation of such seemingly homosocial fiction as the Holmes stories can trace within them women's identification with a bankrupt dailiness—a marginalization that renders women so far outside of the fears and fantasies still available to men that they become indifferent to them. Seen in this way, such boredom or indifference can open a space within ideology's overwhelming constraints.[16] The story "A Scandal in Bohemia" provides one example of women's tactical use of everyday boredom. "The Adventure of the Illustrious Client" suggests specifically how everyday seriality can do more than simply project onto women the traditionally masculine denial of human mortality. Read against the grain in this fashion, such theoretical fictions (whether by the theorists of the everyday or by Doyle) suggest that the categories of the city and the everyday are less impoverished— and monotonous—than they traditionally appear. Before turning to these

[16] And I am thinking here of the powerful force accorded indifference within feminist lesbian criticism. Adrienne Rich suggests, for example, that instead of "some primal male 'fear of women' and of women's sexual insatiability . . . [i]t seems more probable that men really fear . . . that women could be indifferent to them altogether, that men could be allowed sexual and emotional—therefore economic—access to women *only* on women's terms, otherwise being left on the periphery of the matrix": "Compulsory Heterosexuality and Lesbian Experience," in her *Blood, Bread, and Poetry* (New York: Norton, 1986), 23–75; 43. Rich's (utopian/feminist) lesbian indifference here is in sharp contrast to the other equally powerful cultural refraction of indifference that Teresa de Lauretis draws from the work of Luce Irigaray. Writing of Irigaray's pun on "hom(m)o-sexuality" as opposed to homosexuality (a distinction we might now make between the homosocial and the homosexual), de Lauretis notes: "I want to remark the conceptual difference between the . . . term, homosexuality, by which I mean lesbian (or gay) sexuality, and the diacritically marked hommo-sexuality, which is the term of sexual indifference, the term (in fact) of heterosexuality": "Sexual Indifference and Lesbian Representation," *Theatre Journal* 40 (1988): 155–77; 156. What I might call a "masculine" boredom de Lauretis wants to describe as a heterosexual compulsion that is largely indifferent to distinctions of masculine and feminine, but as pernicious and leveling in its cultural force as the dominant tendency I am charting.

stories, however, I will first consider the theoretical connections I have outlined—among boredom, the city, and the everyday.

⁂

The problem with the everyday is trying to get anyone interested in it. Certainly Henri Lefebvre, to whom we now attribute the importance of the concept, found this to be the case. In his "Foreword to the Second Edition" (1957) of *Critique of Everyday Life, Vol. 1, Introduction* (1947), he recounts "the way the book was received when it was first published. What was the official, academic response? Utter silence" (5). He ascribes that reaction mainly to the historical moment: postliberation France assumed too optimistically that the world was about to change: "Socialism was on the march. . . . [T]he rumble of revolution could already be heard. . . . Therefore many Marxists saw criticism of everyday life as useless and antiquated; they perceived it as a reworking of an old-fashioned, exhausted critique of bourgeois society, little more than a critique of triviality—therefore a trivial critique" (6).[17] But was this apparent boredom with the topic an effect of history only? Guy Debord, premier situationist and Lefebvre's student, encountered the same reaction (and in Lefebvre's own "Group for Research on Everyday Life") in 1961: "The most striking feature of the present 'Group' . . . is obviously not the fact that it has not yet discovered anything, but the fact that the very existence of everyday life has been disputed from its very inception. . . . Most of the talks we have heard so far have been by people who are not at all convinced that everyday life exists, since they haven't encountered it anywhere."[18] For such people, he explains, "everyday life is always elsewhere. Among others" ("Perspectives," 69). Debord also ventures a reason for this:

> If people censor the question of their own everyday life, it is both because they are aware of its unbearable misery and because sooner or later they sense—whether they admit it or not—that all the real possibilities, all the desires that have been frustrated by the functioning of social life, were focused there. . . . That is, awareness of the profound richness and energy abandoned in everyday life is inseparable from awareness of the poverty of the dominant organization of this life. ("Perspectives," 71)

People's indifference to the everyday marks resistance to it, Debord explains: they don't want to know what that boredom screens. Through a reaction so natural that it seems invisible, such boredom veils and furthers what the sit-

---

[17] It may be worth noting that, although Lefebvre attempts late in his career to make a distinction between "everyday life" and "the everyday" in order to designate more precisely what he sees as the double poles of that concept, he is by no means consistent in this differentiation, and I have (as Lefebvre himself largely does) ignored this distinction in terms.

[18] Guy Debord, "Perspectives for Conscious Alterations in Everyday Life," in Knabb, *Situationist International Anthology*, 68–75; 68; all future references to this essay (abbreviated "Perspectives") will appear in the text.

uationists called "conditioning," what I have been calling the ideological. Perhaps the simplest definition of the ideological is that it is whatever seems natural; the subjects constituted by it can't see it (without great effort, and then never totally). We take it as given, without question. The everyday, that part of life—the majority of it—that people don't recognize or they ignore, becomes for these theorists the symbol and site of such conditioning.

Boredom with the everyday points to it as the site of the ideological; this explains why the situationists were so vehemently against boredom. "*Boredom is counterrevolutionary*," they wrote in their journal. "In every way." [19] This complete denunciation of boredom implies an injunction to escape it (which was, if anything, the doctrine connecting the otherwise heterodox group). Such an injunction carries with it the wish that one might also escape from ideology, implying that ideology simply conditions; it doesn't necessarily determine.[20] But the continued association of the everyday with ideology in these theories, part of their dogged attention to an object they acknowledge resists consideration, can't help but emphasize the persistence and inescapability of the everyday, of ideology.

Lefebvre's and Debord's own relentless attentions to the vague and elusive category of the everyday reveal that hand in hand with the everyday's continued resistance goes an increasing insistence upon it. Alice Kaplan and

[19] Situationist International, "The Bad Days Will End," in Knabb, *Situationist International Anthology*, 82–87; 86. The situationists had, however, a Gallic awareness of the power of exercising boredom on others; see, for example, their own exercise of it in their strategy of *détournement* (making over, by wresting partly out of context, past works—such as giving *Birth of a Nation* a sound track denouncing the KKK): "far from aiming at arousing indignation or laughter by alluding to some original work, [*détournement*] will express our indifference toward a meaningless and forgotten original" (Situationist International, "*Détournement* as Negation and Prelude," in Knabb, 55–56; 56). Debord was initially influenced by Lefebvre's early work on the everyday and sat in on his seminar. Yet, even though one of the situationists' slogans was "Plagiarism is necessary—progress implies it," Lefebvre and the situationists ultimately split precisely over who owned this topic, amid mutual accusations of plagiarism.

[20] Debord gets his sense of everyday life as "both infinitely rich (potentially at least) and infinitely poor, bare, alienated" from Lefebvre (*Critique*, 31) and inherits from him as well this wish to see ideology as simply false consciousness. Although Debord's own notion of the society of spectacle comes close to defining the subject as created by an ungrounded and inescapable system of signs, the emphasis he takes from Lefebvre on people's alienation within the reified consumer culture of the everyday carries with it another burden. As Michael Trebitsch writes in his "Preface" to Lefebvre's *Critique*, "for Lefebvre everyday life is not reduced to the inauthenticity of *Alltäglichkeit*, as in Heidegger or Lukács. . . . [For Lefebvre] It is both a parody of lost plenitude and the last remaining vestige of that plenitude. . . . His critique of everyday life is a dual reading, at once a rejection of the inauthentic and the alienated, and an unearthing of the human which still lies buried therein" (xxiii–xxiv). Such doubleness implies a shedding of false consciousness to uncover an essentially human (Marxist) reality. This doubleness links the everyday for Lefebvre with his method of dialectical reasoning: the site of people's worst alienation, he writes, is also the only possible site for the revolution that will transform that alienation. "The one in the other. The one via the other" (*Critique*, 58), the everyday exemplifies the "*double movement*" of Hegel's *aufgehoben*, which "means *at the same time* to abolish something (as it was) and to raise it to a higher level" (*Critique*, 177). Such a method can be very useful in uncovering irresolvable contradictions, but it continues to promise that its teleology will ultimately somehow resolve them; the everyday represents for Lefebvre an ideological blind spot he knows people cannot see, and yet he suggests that attention to it will somehow miraculously reveal its mystery in the fullness of time.

Kristin Ross, in their "Introduction" to the 1987 *Yale French Studies* special issue *Everyday Life* (itself an insistence upon work that it claims "remains underacknowledged and little translated in this country" [1]), write that nonetheless everyday life "has, of course, become in our own time the urgent issue on a host of political and cultural agendas" (2–3). By focusing on the very category they know escapes them, these theorists point to the paradoxes inhabiting that category. Boredom begins to suggest more than just the subject's resistance to the knowledge of its ideological constitution; it also marks the impossible task of contemplating that state. Blanchot writes: "boredom is the everyday become manifest: as a consequence of having lost its essential—constitutive—trait of being *unperceived*" (16). For him, the attempt to arrest the everyday in order to make it fit a system, the attempt to elevate its insignificance into meaning (even as he himself tries), can only fail. Its tediousness marks its ongoing passage beyond such transfigurations.[21] Lefebvre too sees the monotony of the everyday as a marker that it "evades the grip of forms" (*Everyday*, 182).[22] The ambiguity of the everyday thus marks the paradox of the subject's relation to his or her conditioning: that one must work to recognize a state that is unrecognizable, to elude an ideology that is constitutive and inescapable.

It was precisely through this vexed struggle, to escape the tedium of the everyday through a system founded on a relentless attention to it, that another theoretician involves himself in such paradoxes: Sherlock Holmes becomes a consulting detective because he finds himself so bored with what Conan Doyle calls the "humdrum routine of everyday life":[23] "My life is spent in one long effort to escape from the commonplaces of existence," Holmes says (*Complete*, 190): "My mind . . . rebels at stagnation. Give me problems, give me work. . . . I abhor the dull routine of existence. I crave for mental exaltation. That is why I have chosen my own particular profession, or rather created it" (89–90). Rather than having lifted himself above the commonplace and created himself anew as he seems to imply here, however, Holmes is actually practicing an almost obsessive attention to the very every-

---

[21] For Blanchot, this implies a deconstructive principle that undoes the very constraining and constitutive system in which it must still operate, by playing upon its contradictions (rather, than as for Lefebvre, resolving them); for Blanchot, the everyday represents not the dialectical, but the aporia. It is aporetic in Blanchot's theory because "to experience everydayness is to be tested by the radical nihilism that is as if its essence, and by which, in the void that animates it, it does not cease to hold the principle of its own critique" (19) or (no less oracularly) "the everyday is the inaccessible to which we have always already had access" (20). The everyday may not escape the system, but it calls it into question. Blanchot writes: "the everyday breaks down structures and undoes forms, even while ceaselessly regathering itself behind the form whose ruin it has insensibly brought about" (17).

[22] He emphasizes in this later book that the everyday represents "the system of non-systems, [a] cohesion of incoherence" (142). "Everyday insignificance can only become meaningful when transformed into something other than everyday life; in other words, it is not possible to construct a theoretical and practical system such that the details of everyday life will become meaningful in and by this system" (98).

[23] Arthur Conan Doyle, *The Complete Sherlock Holmes* (London: Penguin, 1981), 176; all future references to this book (abbreviated *Complete*) will appear in the text.

day that Doyle has his characters find so constraining: Holmes's "extraordinary genius for minutiae" (91), especially his success at reconstructing a person's history from studying "any object in daily use" (92), suggest how his methods build on the same everyday routines that have also exasperated him. His analyses are meant to transform what was previously, when he simply experienced it, unbearable.

The success of his analyses in doing so might seem to obey the situationists' injunction and confirm the implications of Lefebvre's dialectical reasoning: that critical consciousness provides a route out of false consciousness, that analysis can abolish ideology, that the *critique* of everyday life is exactly what will renew it. Such success might seem to confirm this if Holmes ever experienced it. But repeatedly and insistently throughout the stories, Doyle has Holmes make clear that, rather than being the bedrock for his system, everyday life is precisely the mystery that continues to elude him. In their first adventure together, *A Study in Scarlet*, he tells Watson: "It is a mistake to confound strangeness with mystery. The most commonplace crime is often the most mysterious, because it presents no new or special features from which deductions may be drawn" (*Complete*, 50).[24] His detection succeeds when he can make use of a method of reasoning different from that applied "in the everyday affairs of life," one that recognizes "that what is out of the common is usually a guide rather than a hindrance" in solving mysteries (83). Rather than mystery offering an escape from Holmes's boredom, the tedious everyday becomes that mystery he cannot escape; in fact, Holmes himself comes to embody it. In the mystery that introduces him, *A Study in Scarlet*, in an endless slippage in which the detective becomes that which he seeks to dispel, *Holmes* is the real mystery. It is Watson who is bored with "the monotony of . . . daily existence" (20) and happy enough to spend his time trying to figure out just what it is his new roommate does. Precisely out of his desire to escape from the mystery of the everyday Holmes becomes the enigma that baffles poor old Watson. Because the mystery of the everyday remains insoluble, contaminating, Holmes never escapes his boredom, and the stories begin and end repetitively with him lapsing out of or into ennui.

This ineluctable resistance of the everyday suggests that ideology is something more than simple false consciousness, that seeming solutions to it keep getting "appropriated" (something theorists of the everyday keep coming up against though they wish otherwise—the term "appropriated," in fact, was put into use by the situationists, who in spite of their desire to escape ideology suspected just such a problem within the everyday).[25] It suggests too that the mystery at the heart of the detective form is the mystery of the workings

---

[24] Or: "'As a rule,' said Holmes, 'the more bizarre a thing is the less mysterious it proves to be. It is your commonplace, featureless crimes which are really puzzling, just as a commonplace face is the most difficult to identify'" (*Complete*, 183). Or: "'The more featureless and commonplace a crime is, the more difficult it is to bring it home'" (*Complete*, 202).

[25] It is this part of their thought that has made them such a strong influence on Baudrillard and Foucault; see Sadie Plant's *Most Radical Gesture* for a discussion of their effect on later theorists, as well as for the claim about their use of "appropriation."

of ideology—like all possible explanations of a mystery, a bit of an anticlimax, since the notion that the detective novel is the exemplum of the ideological has been a commonplace of recent criticism, in poststructuralist readings as various as Catherine Belsey's deconstructive materialist approach (the contradictions of the ideological help us to resist or undo it) or Mark Seltzer's and D. A. Miller's new historicist accounts (the contradictions of the ideological keep us oscillating within it).[26] What the everyday adds to this old debate about ideology is an emphasis on a new kind of profession or practice (one that, like Holmes's, is predicated on old structures) within it.

The idea that the everyday might represent a kind of practice marks Michel de Certeau's contribution to the theory of the everyday, a characterization of everyday life inextricably connected to the city.[27] De Certeau takes as the symbol of the practice of the everyday, of the relentlessly pedestrian, simply that: what he calls the enunciatory practice of walking in the city. De Certeau builds on past theorists' concentration on the city and the street—Blanchot writes that the everyday "is in the street—if it is anywhere" (17)—but emphasizes not so much the streets themselves as some ground for the everyday, as what people do in them.[28] *The Practice of Everyday Life*, a book dedicated to the man on the street, makes negotiating the intricate succession of the city's streets a shorthand for the practice of the everyday. Such practices are meant to make the range of the subject's relations to ideology—if only provisionally, fleetingly—clear.

The response of the man in the street to this practice ("We are bored in the city" the situationists tell us) suggests something different (different even perhaps from de Certeau's view of it) about the subject's relation to ideology. Far from being the empty and anonymous entity he appears to these theorists, the man on the street seems a privileged individual to those of "us" who can't aspire to his privileges, most notably his boredom: walking the streets is a much different activity for women, or for those racial groups increasingly defined as the urban underclass.[29] Boredom can be a privilege and even a power: this much is clear in Lefebvre's complaint about the academic silence that greeted his work on the everyday; that institution's continued in-

---

[26] Catherine Belsey, "Deconstructing the Text," in her *Critical Practice* (New York: Methuen, 1980), 103–24; Mark Seltzer, *Henry James and the Art of Power* (Ithaca: Cornell University Press, 1984); D. A. Miller, *The Novel and the Police*.

[27] De Certeau writes that the everyday recounts "moves, not truths" (23): "As one explores the terrain of these practices, something is constantly slipping away, something that can be neither said nor 'taught' but must be 'practiced'" (77).

[28] His concentration on the city echoes the theorists of the everyday that precede him—it is an understanding of the everyday that is so prevalent and central that de Certeau, like these other theorists, almost simply assumes it. Blanchot as well seems to expect that we understand that the everyday is a symbol of the arenas that concentrate it and call it forth, "the dense presence of great urban centers" (17), a view of it, he tells us without citation (perhaps because it is throughout it), that he takes from Lefebvre's work.

[29] These groups may take their revenge in the current popular (white male) imagination precisely by figuring those sexual or violent encounters that might shatter his boredom in the city (but, he must ask himself, at what price?).

difference would have effectively silenced him, for, as women well know, what does it matter how much you talk about something if nobody listens? Part of the attraction of Sherlock Holmes is that his boredom with the everyday allows him to seem to rise above it, and this makes him extraordinary: he doesn't care a bit about all those ordinary things—even eating or sex— that most people have to care about. But the everyday continues to foil Holmes; it is more powerful even than this master policeman, which suggests one way for critics to make use of it. As de Certeau notes, "the ingenious ways in which the weak make use of the strong" within the everyday can "lend a political dimension to everyday practices" (xvii). One of those practices, especially for subject positions even more marginalized, more anonymous, than the man on the street, can in fact be boredom—destroying it, and the privilege it connotes, in others by assuming it tactically one's self.

For the situationists, walking the street is a flight from boredom.[30] But this practice can also be related to the tactical use of boredom. Although de Certeau does not himself emphasize boredom, his description of walking in the city shows how it can create its own "discourse . . . [that] eludes urbanistic systematicity" (105) precisely through a kind of apathy. People's overfamiliarity with and indifference to the symbolic markers administering them, such as street signs, allows them to give those markers other meanings: "These words . . . slowly lose, like worn coins, the value engraved on them. . . . [T]hese names make themselves available to the diverse meanings given them by passers-by" (104). Through an "emptying-out and wearing-away of their primary role," they "become liberated spaces that can be occupied" (105). Even as people must work within the networks of power, must use the streets the city provides to get from one place to another, they can chart a different meaning and trajectory in them—dreamily tracing in the names of the streets narratives like the tales of parapraxis in Freud's *Psychopathology of Everyday Life* (stories made up out of "relics of meaning, and sometimes by their waste products" [de Certeau, 105]).

De Certeau tells of a man who, when he goes to Paris to visit his mother, finds himself delaying, straying onto streets that first carry the name of the (holy) father (Rue des Saints-*Pères*) and then of his new home in a town away from his mother (*rue de sèvres*).[31] The story he tells by choosing this path, for de Certeau, weans this man away from his mother, who comes to stand for the englobing system that creates subjects. For de Certeau, everyday practices like walking in the city are "ultimately . . . the repetition" of the process of detachment, of differentiation from/indifference to the mother's body, the "joyful manipulation that can make the maternal object 'go

---

[30] The situationists called this practice the *dérive*—exemplified, for instance, by taking a walk around Berlin while using a map of London—and, along with their ideas of psychogeography and unitary urbanism, it was part of their tactics of social transformation to put play and adventure back into the city's everyday.

[31] The town's name carries similar connotations: "sevreuse" means dry-nurse, one who weans children away from their mothers.

away'" (109).[32] The desire to escape from restraint is imagined as the desire to escape from the mother. While this man will ultimately have to visit his mother, de Certeau's account suggests, the story he tells by his desire not to—his boredom with her—is already potentially transformative.

This potential may be because of the lesson the mother supposedly encodes. De Certeau writes: "In reproduction through sexuality, individuals have to die" (197). As a scapegoat for man's mortality, the mother needs to be deprived of her power, made worn out, insignificant, stale.[33] Differentiation from her may be joyful because it allows the subject to tell himself that he has created himself anew. Walking is so central in de Certeau's theory because it is also an attempt to keep ahead of death: "writing repeats [death's] lack in each of its graphs, the relics of a walk through language" (195). To engage with death's presence he asserts has been part of his own practice: "To write (this book), then, is to be forced to march through enemy territory, in the very area where loss prevails, beyond the protected domain that had been delimited by the act of localizing death elsewhere" (198). Yet, in implicitly localizing death as the mother, de Certeau attempts to avoid mortality; the story he tells hopes for immortality: "The writer is also a dying man

---

[32] In positing that the subject's understanding of its possibilities in this space are symbolized by and can be traced to "the child's differentiation from the mother's body" (109), de Certeau at least provisionally recognizes that such possibilities are determined by gender; he takes the subject's potential for counterpractices making do and making over the system in which it operates as far back "as the naming that separates the foetus identified as masculine from his mother—but how about the female foetus," he asks, "who is from this very moment introduced into another relation to space?" (109). He may answer his own question implicitly with the story he suggests that a woman traces as *she* walks through the city; streetwalking does not seem available to women as a counterpractice in his description of it. He tells of a woman who unconsciously walks only on streets which have no proper names, trying to elude the identities they would impose on her. But de Certeau points out that she doesn't really escape them; they just control her negatively (104).

[33] The association of sex and death, and the mother's responsibility for them, are part of de Certeau's philosophical heritage (he in fact quotes François Jacob's *Logique du vivant* for the connection of reproduction and death). He is perhaps more familiarly following in the footsteps taken by that theorist of the everyday who most influenced him, Sigmund Freud. In *The Psychopathology of Everyday Life*, Freud begins directly with this connection. In the first parapraxis he describes, the famous *Signorelli* incident, the repressed content is the connection of sex and death. Characteristically, in his account Freud accords the power of the connection to men, not women—he tells us that what he keeps from his memory is how certain male Turks place such a high premium on sexual enjoyment that they think that life is not worth living without it, how a patient of his own has killed himself because of an incurable sexual disorder: Sigmund Freud, *The Psychopathology of Everyday Life*, 1901, vol. 7 (1960) of *The Standard Edition of the Complete Psychological Works of Sigmund Freud*, trans. and ed. James Strachey. 24 vols. (London: Hogarth, 1953–74). We might push Freud's reading further to argue that the overly emphatic masculine meaning of his parapraxis—it turns on the words *Signor* and *Herr*—is actually consoling. The power of these words to assert themselves may hide a threat to masculine power that seems instead to come from women—what James Swann has argued is the power Freud's mother seemed to him to have over death, the way, rubbing her hands together one day she produced flecks of dirt to show her son that we all come from and will return to death, a fact Freud continually associated with and blamed on women and, Swann argues, continually wanted to forget: James Swann, "Mater and Nannie: Freud's Two Mothers and the Discovery of the Oedipal Complex," *American Imago* 31 (1974): 1–64.

who is trying to speak. But in the death that his footsteps inscribe on [the] page, he . . . expects from the other the marvellous and ephemeral excess of surviving through an attention that it alters" (198). The attention the child expects from that other, the mother, who gives it ongoing life but to whom it wants to give no thought, provides the model for this relation of writer and reader; the mother's complete subjection to the infant's needs, the tedium when she asks for attention, seem meant magically and conversely to ensure the subject's endless importance.

This mother can fulfill this function partly because she remains always a symbol, never a subject: we never hear what bores *her*. Perhaps (although de Certeau and male culture seem unable to think this way) her son's visits do. What stories other than these male fantasies of containment and escape does *she* trace out of her boredom? Feminists, like other marginalized groups, have long recognized that anger has been a strategic practice. But what about boredom? How much of the feminist enterprise has come about simply because women have been so bored with the limited positions that the masculine has given them, with the timeworn topics that obsess men and dominate culture? The tedium of the stories that reflect only a limited and unceasing male point of view have driven women to tune out, daydream, read against the grain. What is the tradition of female letters except an attempt by women writers to make over the "waste products" of a dominant system that bores them?

Women have been especially marginalized through those cultural practices that theorists tend to characterize as belonging to the everyday—domestic maintenance, the repetitive production of food and children. Even Henri Lefebvre recognizes that everyday life "weighs more heavily on women, who are sentenced to everyday life" ("Everyday," 10).[34] He almost recognizes as well that they have been especially inventive in response. He at any rate quotes a passage from *A Room of One's Own* to show this "famous and talented English woman writer['s] . . . acute sensitivity to . . . the subtle richness of the everyday" (Critique, 28).[35] Part of the richness of the everyday might be that it offers women room within it that (masculine) theorists ignore.

In considering the "masculinist" theory of the everyday, Naomi Schor regrets that it has been simplified to confirm a view of ideology as totally con-

[34] See also his claim in *Everyday Life in the Modern World*: "the *misery of everyday life*, its tedious tasks, humiliations [are] reflected in the lives of the working classes and especially of women, upon whom the conditions of everyday life bear heaviest—child-bearing and child-rearing, basic preoccupations with bare necessities, money, tradesmen, provisions, the realm of numbers, a sort of intimate knowledge of things outside the sphere of material reality: health, desire, spontaneity, vitality; recurrence, the survival of poverty and the endlessness of want, a climate of economy, abstinence, hardship, repressed desires, meanness and avarice" (35).

[35] He also associates woman with the very ambiguity that is for him the hallmark of the possibilities of the everyday (although he can see her ambiguity, see *her*, only in terms of man: "woman plays the traditional female role—a role which is certainly still a real one—of an ambiguous figure who excites [man's] contradictory actions and thoughts" [*Critique*, 25–26]).

taining: "this grim, unrelenting disciplinary locus of daily activity has in recent years come to dominate our views of representations of everyday life, as
though . . . the street had been overtaken by the prison" (190). What bothers
Schor about this explanation of the workings of ideology is that it "leaves no
residue, no excess, no waste, no detail, no small everyday gesture, however
small and apparently insignificant, unaccounted for, unsaturated with dire
meaning" (192). This description of the prevailing theoretical refraction of
the everyday could on the face of it also be a description of Sherlock Holmes's
method. The Holmes stories do—patently, obviously—work in this way.
Holmes's method is to try to account for every everyday gesture. But the
boredom in the stories (as well as their readers' overfamiliarity *with* them,
which, as the endless and ongoing proliferation of the Holmes stories, in
books and movies and on TV, suggests, in no way detracts from their attraction and popularity) suggests to me that there is something more going on in
them as well, something that addresses the impatience Schor feels with an inherent "masculinism" within the current theoretical debate over ideology.

The "masculinist" aspect of this debate may be the way it continues to be
caught up in the dilemma of whether we are completely contained in ideology, or whether we escape it. This debate has so consumed critical attention
in recent years that we may have forgotten that this is just one way, and
maybe by this time a rather tedious way, of posing the problem. As not quite
an alternative to this debate, but as a position almost oblivious to it, Schor
identifies a view of the everyday "we might call the feminine or feminist,
though it is not necessarily held by women or self-described feminists." Such
a view, she writes, takes women off the streets and out of the city, "links the
everyday with the daily rituals of private life carried out within the domestic
sphere traditionally presided over by women" (188). This view is indeed held
by self-described feminists (such as Bettina Aptheker in her book *Tapestries
of Life: Women's Work, Women's Consciousness, and the Meaning of Daily
Experience*);[36] Alice Echols in fact gives this kind of feminism a name: cultural feminism, which takes this sphere as the site of a women's countercul-
ture.[37] Even when feminists hold this view, however, it does indeed seem
symptomatic of precisely the kind of appropriation feminism has most to
fear: the idea that women should be associated with and take their strength
from the dailiness of a (nurturing) home is held at the same time, though out
of a much different set of goals, by many men (such as the theorists of the
everyday) and also antifeminists. But that this doesn't much bother these
feminists, and that cultural feminism *does* bother the men and antifeminists
who to some degree share its assumptions suggest that, although its assumptions and (lack of) theory are still highly problematic, there may be something in its practice.

[36] Amherst: University of Massachusetts Press, 1989.
[37] Alice Echols, *Daring to Be Bad: Radical Feminism in America, 1967–1975* (Minneapolis:
University of Minnesota Press, 1989), 5.

If the focus of this kind of practice is on the home, that may be a symbol for the way it makes itself at home in the waste and margins of the dominant system.[38] But it seems to me that this kind of feminism provides not some content or essential locus, but once again an important form or practice, a kind of indifference that works as well in the city as it does in the domestic sphere (a false opposition anyway meant to devalue women's traditional sphere *and* occlude her contributions outside it). My impatience for years with what seemed to me cultural feminism's ignorance of the subtleties of theory now seems to me partly misguided: it might be that such feminists know all about theory, but simply don't care. They may be engaged in a feminist practice that seizes boredom and exercises it as critical consciousness— a very different strategy from the boredom masculine culture just unthinkingly assumes and employs against women. Highlighting and revising the powers of such heedlessness has the potential to politicize boredom, to realize the everyday counterpractices that de Certeau outlines.

This revision tends to ignore the debate about ideology—perhaps the only way right now out of the theoretical impasse that debate has become. Far from being a cavalier or wishful denial of an insoluble dilemma, such indifference may be an appropriate response to a debate that has been posed from the beginning in terms of false absolutes. Escape or containment is an ideal end—not unimportant but of more burning interest to those with the privilege and position to worry about it. As a notation for something both inside and outside systems, more ambiguous, vague, or just dull than those systems can reckon, the everyday seems to point to a daily practice of getting on with things even when our understanding of what that practice ultimately means is impossible—something that can perhaps happen only at the margins of our consciousness, that we experience as boredom, almost a kind of Zen that we take for granted. This may be why the mystery of the everyday remains the hardest to solve. The critique of boredom has been useful in denaturalizing and exposing the ideological, but boredom itself may have a political function. It helps not so much to circumvent the ideological (the old dream

---

[38] In this it is like French feminism, but while French feminism hopes to transform culture by troping and camping up its truisms, this feminism attempts to transform by simply ignoring those truisms, even as it operates within them.

The everyday also concerns some other kinds of feminists, such as Schor. Patricia Williams needs recourse to the everyday, elusive and jumbled as it remains in her account of it (precisely because it is elusive and jumbled), to negotiate the complex intersection of a feminist and antiracist critique: "everything I have ever learned is running around in my head; little bits of law and pieces of everyday life . . . in weird combinations." "Everyday life is a confusing bit of business," she writes, but "that life is complicated is a fact of great analytic importance": *The Alchemy of Race and Rights: Diary of a Law Professor* (Cambridge: Harvard University Press, 1991), 14, 10. Toril Moi is drawn *as* a feminist to theories of everyday practice (like Pierre Bourdieu's) because "for a feminist, [a] great advantage of Bourdieu's microtheoretical approach is that it allows us to incorporate the most mundane details of everyday life in our analyses," finding social significance in "much of what patriarchal minds like to trivialize": "Appropriating Bourdieu: Feminist Theory and Pierre Bourdieu's Sociology of Culture," *New Literary History* 22 (1991): 1017–49; 1019, 1020.

of false consciousness) or to embrace its constraints (the fantasy of totalization) but to inhabit it differently through an in-difference to constraints,
which don't simply vanish but may become beside the point in those sites
where we can for a time ignore them.[39] Here might lie the importance and
efficacy of the tedium theorists find in the everyday.

The central figure of the everyday, the man on the street, has a literary heritage, that points to the function of gender within this practice. The theorists
of the everyday inherit their concentration on, and ambiguous relation to,
this figure from the *flâneur*, that musing and distracted stroller found in
Baudelaire (and Poe) and emphasized by the surrealists and Walter Benjamin. At the same time, certain situationist texts make clear that their sense
of walking in the city also has a distinctly English literary background: de
Quincey's aimless search in *Confessions of an English Opium-Eater* for his
lost Ann through "the mighty labyrinths of London."[40] Woman, excluded
from this practice, continues to some degree to inform it.

Raymond Williams sees the urban experience of the man on the street as
underlying the detective form, particularly the stories of Sherlock Holmes,
who, for the literary critic John Rignall, is the direct descendent of the *flâneur*.[41] Holmes, similar to de Quincey in his neurasthenia, his use of stimu-
lants—both drugs and mystery—as a response to a commonplace world, is
also at home in the labyrinths of London: one of the first things Watson no-

[39] This is the logic of the everyday practice de Certeau calls *la perruque* (25–28).

[40] Guy Debord, *Mémoires*, quoted in Greil Marcus, "Guy Debord's *Mémoires*: A Situationist
Primer," in *On the Passage of a Few People through a Rather Brief Moment in Time: The Situationist International, 1957–72*, ed. Elisabeth Sussman (Cambridge: MIT Press, 1989), 124–
31; 131. See also Debord's "Unitary Urbanism in the 1950s," which repeats this reference to de
Quincey and claims that "London was the first urban result of the industrial revolution and the
English literature of the nineteenth century bears witness to an increasing awareness of the
problems of the atmosphere and of the qualitatively different possibilities in a large urban
area. . . . Towards the end of the century this sensation [the unmapped adventures of the *dérive*]
is so frequently expressed in novelistic writing that [Robert Louis] Stevenson presents a character who, in London at night, is astonished 'to walk for such a long time in such a complex
decor without encountering even the slightest shadow of an adventure'": "Unitary Urbanism in
the 1950s," trans. Thomas Y. Levin, *On the Passage of a Few People*, 143–47; 147.

[41] Williams notes it in "the new figure of the urban detective. In Conan Doyle's Sherlock
Holmes stories there is a recurrent image of the penetration by an isolated rational intelligence
of a dark area of crime which is to be found in the otherwise (for specific physical reasons, as
in London fogs, but also for social reasons, in that teeming, mazelike, often alien area) impen-
etrable city. This figure has persisted in the urban 'private eye' (as it happens, an exact idiom
for the basic position in consciousness) in cities without fogs": "The Metropolis and the Emergence of Modernism," in *Unreal City: Urban Experience in Modern European Literature and
Art*, ed. Edward Timms and David Kelley (New York: St. Martin's Press, 1985), 13–24, 17–18.

Rignall writes that the *flâneur*'s posture "is taken over late in the nineteenth century by the
subgenre of the detective novel, whose archetypal hero, the amateur detective Sherlock Holmes,
penetrates the obscurity of the great city," in his *Realist Fiction and the Strolling Spectator*
(New York: Routledge, 1992), 7–8.

tices about him is that he takes long walks through the city (*Complete*, 20), and he tells Watson during one case "It is a hobby of mine to have an exact knowledge of London" (185).[42] Like the theorists of the everyday, Doyle also defines the city as the site of the everyday; he has Watson associate London with "the routine of life" (218) and the mystery of the everyday that escapes his detection:

> My dear fellow, [Holmes says to Watson] . . . life is infinitely stranger than anything which the mind of man could invent. We could not dare to conceive the things which are really mere commonplaces of existence. If we could fly out that window hand in hand, hover over this great city, gently remove the roofs, and peep in at the queer things which are going on . . . the wonderful chain of events, working through generations and leading to the most *outré* results, it would make all fiction with its conventionalities and foreseen conclusions most stale and unprofitable. (190–91)

The city is the site of the mystery of everyday, yet the mystery that sparks Holmes's compensatory dreams of omniscience seems different from what motivates de Quincey. The serial chain that draws Holmes through London seems not to be forged by woman: Watson repeats throughout the stories that Holmes (like Hamlet) has no interest in the sex. Holmes's exclusive maculinism is reinforced by the tradition of the *flâneur* behind him; as Janet Wolff has argued, the *flâneur* is by definition male, the *flâneuse* "non-existent. . . . Women could not stroll alone in the city."[43]

Yet woman continues to inform Doyle's urban fictions as well. Holmes's relation to the street and the everyday depends in a complicated way exactly on his relation to women. At the beginning of one story, out of boredom Watson joins Holmes on one of his city walks: "'What do you say to a ramble through London?' [Holmes asks.] I was weary of our little sitting-room and gladly acquiesced. For three hours we strolled about together, watching the ever-changing kaleidoscope of life as it ebbs and flows through Fleet Street and the Strand" (*Complete*, 424). The Strand is a common reference in

[42] According to Watson, "Holmes's knowledge of the byways of London was extraordinary" (*Complete*, 489). In another case, when driving in a closed cab, Watson tells us "I lost my bearings and knew nothing save that we seemed to be going a very long way. Sherlock Holmes was never at fault, however, and he muttered the names as the cab rattled through squares and in and out by tortuous by-streets" (*Complete*, 99). In repeated references throughout the stories Doyle makes clear that it is an important part of Holmes's character that he is "well up in [his] London" (*Complete*, 234).

[43] Janet Wolff, "The Invisible *Flaneuse*: Women and the Literature of Modernism," in her *Feminine Sentences: Essays on Women and Culture* (Berkeley: University of California Press, 1990), 34–50; 41. This is, of course, only one story of women's relation to the street: the Holmes stories actually show lower-class women (and middle-class women who had to make their own living, such as the plucky governess in "The Adventure of the Copper Beeches"—interestingly, another woman Holmes singles out for admiration) moving around the city quite well. Such comparative freedom comes in part because the class snobbery that underwrites Victorian ideology (and our own contemporary constructions of it) isn't much interested in such women— it is one of the benefits of indifference.

Holmes's wanderings, but it figures in the canon as more than just one of the arteries on which he and Watson conduct their tourism of the everyday; *The Strand* was also the periodical that established Holmes in the popular imagination. The first two Holmes novels had only limited success; it was not until Doyle began publishing short stories about the detective in that magazine that his career really took off. And "A Scandal in Bohemia," the story that launched that success, shows Holmes's relation to women—and their relation to the everyday—as more complex than it seems on the surface.

"A Scandal in Bohemia" tells the story of Holmes's defeat at the hands of Irene Adler; he is "beaten by a woman's wit" (*Complete*, 175). The King of Bohemia has engaged Holmes because he has been threatened by Adler, a strikingly intelligent and beautiful diva, of "dubious and questionable" reputation (161). Once the King's mistress, Adler has promised to disrupt his upcoming marriage; she has an compromising photograph of herself and the King that she means to send his royal fiancée. The King's attempts to recover the photograph through waylaying and searching Adler and burglarizing her home have all been unsuccessful: the photograph is nowhere to be found. Holmes (a reader of Dupin, and in a scenario strongly evocative of "The Purloined Letter") arranges to locate the photograph by having Adler show him where it is. Disguised as a clergyman, he stages some violence to himself on the street outside Adler's home; she takes him in and, tricked into thinking her house is about to go up in flames, reveals the photo's hiding place. Holmes retreats, confident in his ruse, but when he returns with the King to take possession of the photograph, both it and Adler are gone. She had seen through Holmes and, disguised as a man, followed him home through the streets of London to be sure of his identity. Partly out of the pride of having defeated the great detective, and because she has tired of the King anyway (and has married someone else herself), Adler leaves a promise to let the King marry in peace, and a photograph of herself that Holmes accepts in lieu of his fee and (presumably) cherishes throughout his career.

"A Scandal in Bohemia" established the Holmes canon, and it also establishes the paradoxical importance of women to it. Catherine Belsey has maintained that, although women seem insignificant in and ignored by these stories, they are really the mystery that draws Holmes, the mystery that short-circuits his method. This reading, although infinitely helpful, is not a revelation; rather than being some hidden and subversive deconstructive principle, the power of women's inexplicableness is part of what made these stories so popular. This is the relation to women that Doyle explicitly thematizes in the enormously successful "Scandal," when he has Irene Adler—"*the* woman," as Holmes calls her—best him early in his career, and it continues throughout the stories. "'Woman's heart and mind are insoluble puzzles to the male,'" Holmes tells Watson elsewhere (*Complete*, 988), and he complains that "'the motives of women are so inscrutable. . . . How can you build on such a quicksand? Their most trivial action may mean volumes, or their most extraordinary conduct may depend upon a hairpin or a curling tongs' " (657). The open secret of these stories, the logic of the purloined letter that structures Doyle's depiction of Irene Adler, is that women, like the everyday, provide only a quicksand on which to build a system, and yet (for Holmes and for later theorists of the everyday) remain the ground of that system. The ambiguities women introduce into Holmes's system may indeed point out the contradictions of Victorian ideology (in Belsey's reading they reveal a division over female sexuality). But in going out of its way to trumpet these contradiction, the Holmes canon suggests (as Audrey Jaffe might argue) that simply exposing such inconsistencies doesn't undo ideology; they may in fact be one of its lures.[44] Adler's besting of Holmes doesn't undo the system he represents, but actually seems to help enormously in establishing it.

The success of "A Scandal in Bohemia" may have to do with the way it appropriates (by itself staging) such threats as the one posed by Adler. In this reading, Holmes's stagecraft may not be successful—Adler's beats his—but *Doyle's* reassuringly directs them both, suggesting still some omniscient and englobing (masculine) power. More positively in my view, however, Holmes's career may have taken off with this story *not* because readers were hungry for a neat and total system (Doyle's first two Holmes novels had concentrated on laying out and detailing Holmes's positivist assumptions, to no great popular effect) or duped into thinking that Adler's reactions spelled revolution: more interesting than the ideological universe in which Doyle's characters operated was what they did in it, how they made do within it. Their skill in operating within circumstances that in "A Scandal in Bohemia" become a little more ordinary than in the preceding novels, far from ideal (both Holmes and Adler are constrained by limitations here, and find ways to work within and around them), is part of this story's attraction. Woman is the mystery that both obsesses and bores Holmes, just as the everyday does, because he knows she is what disregards his theory; he must engage with her skillfully in what de Certeau would recognize as the constant tacti-

---

[44] Audrey Jaffe, "Detecting the Beggar: Arthur Conan Doyle, Henry Mayhew, and 'The Man with the Twisted Lip,' " *Representations* 31 (1990): 96–117. Teresa de Lauretis sees women in a similarly double relation to the city, one that underscores her role in attempts by englobing systems of cultural meaning to manage their own structure and divisions; see her "From a Dream of Women," in *Cinema and Language*, ed. Stephen Heath and Patricia Mellencamp (Los Angeles: American Film Institute, 1983), 21–34. Taking Italo Calvino's *Invisible Cities* as a model, she notes specifically: "Zobeide, a city continually built from a dream of woman, built to keep women captive—the city a representation of woman, woman the ground of that representation. In complex circularity ('streets wound about themselves as in a skein'), 'woman' is at once the dream's object of desire and the reason for its objectification, the source of the drive to represent and its ultimate, unattainable, aim" (21–22). The circularity of this depiction means for de Lauretis that woman is trapped in its double-binds: "on the one hand, sexual difference is supposed to be a meaning-effect produced in representation; on the other, paradoxically, it turns out to be the very support of representation" (26). Yet at the same time "the city . . . cannot disengage itself from the trouble caused by 'woman,' the problems she poses in *its* discursive operations" (24).

cal skirmishes, without end or point, that represent the logic of the everyday. Similarly, Adler learns that she too is engaged in an ongoing battle (she tells Holmes that she retains the incriminating photograph "only to safeguard myself, and to preserve a weapon which will always secure me from any steps which [the King] might take in the future" [*Complete*, 175]). She confronts a patriarchal power symbolized by a "King" whose appointees, like Holmes or the men who waylay her, are everywhere. Rather than attempting impossibly to remain outside that power, or to overthrow it by confronting it directly, Adler temporarily bollixes and eludes it by working within it. She can confound it in part by doing what it least expects—joining it through her marriage to the respectable "English lawyer named Norton" (174). In capturing this endless and skillful engagement within a city that seems little different whether it is run by ministers or thieves (hence Holmes's identity as both and the double meaning—kingdom and demimonde—of the title's "Bohemia"), Doyle captivated his first readers, drawing *them* through the seemingly interminable series of Holmes mysteries begun in the pages of *The Strand*.

The serial logic of the everyday that informs the Holmes canon is at odds with a content within them that (perhaps too) vehemently exclaims their— and Holmes's—extraordinariness. Although what seems to make these stories popular is obviously their escapism—Lefebvre defines "escapism [as] the desire to get away from everyday life" (*Everyday*, 85)—their attraction is actually more complex. Rather than escape from what they define as the everyday, these stories continue to perform it in their very structure (hence the importance in them of the inexhaustibly ordinary Watson). In fact, readers may even be drawn to these stories in part by their very familiarity with this practice. Part of the attraction of "A Scandal" is finding that Holmes can be just like everybody else. This story animates the Holmes series perhaps because it reveals what de Certeau argues is the radical attraction of the everyday within any theoretical system, that "the trivial is no longer the other (which is supposed to ground the exemption of the one who dramatizes it); it is the productive experience of the text" (5). Like the stories in the popular women's press that Lefebvre cites showing celebrities driving cars or taking baths (*Everyday*, 175), part of what seems attractive to readers (women readers, anyway) is that such extraordinary figures have an everyday life too.

This association of the productive experience of the everyday with gender is especially clear in the Holmes's stories. "A Scandal in Bohemia" asserts Holmes's ordinariness: the scandal is also in *Holmes's* "Bohemian soul" (*Complete*, 161)—that he can (but just once) fall prey to commonplace emotions, be attracted to a woman, and hence be defeated by her.[45] Such a con-

---

[45] Bohemianism is directly connected to (threatened) masculinity in these stories: a "Bohemian intermediary" (*Complete*, 1079) supplies the monkey-gland serum that is meant to boost the virility of Professor Presbury, nervous about marrying a younger woman, in "The Ad-

tent asserts one of the commonplaces of misogyny: how dangerous women are and how vigilant and powerful Holmes must be to avoid them, a commonplace the story buttresses with other truisms about women (Holmes learns where Adler hides the incriminating photograph of the King of Bohemia by relying on the Freudian cliché that, instinctively when in danger, "'a married woman grabs at her baby; an unmarried one reaches for her jewel-box'" [173]). But while Holmes knows everything about Irene Adler as a woman, he also completely underestimates her. Irene Adler is also a skillful practitioner of what has traditionally been seen as the everyday. Just as she finds a way to inhabit the male province of walking in the city by taking advantage of what that province ignores, this story is a space inhabited differently by two views of women; condemned in the male imagination as "dubious and questionable" (161), the next thing to a streetwalker, Adler complicates that characterization by donning male clothes, "'my walking-clothes, as I call them'" (175).[46] Holmes never knows that she is following him because he doesn't pay attention to the men on the street around him. Adler tells Holmes "'Male costume is nothing new to me. I often take advantage of the freedom which it gives'" (174–75), in a slippage that emphasizes the prerogatives of male boredom by assuming them. Adler's masquerade doesn't transform the masculine character of the *flâneur*, or women's exclusion from that identity; as Wolff argues (42–43), women can partake in his activities only by becoming masculinized themselves (the King of Bohemia says about Adler, "she has the face of the most beautiful of women, and the mind of the most resolute of men" [166]). But her performance not only points up how such identities are performed, it also suggests the different practices that can operate within a space that seems already settled. Like the (feminized) Grimpen Mire at the end of *The Hound of the Baskervilles*, whose "soft undulations" and "obscene depths" (760) hide the criminal and the traces of his crime below its placid surface, the quicksand of woman and the boredom of the everyday conspire to hide from the detective what is right under his eyes, and allows something else or something more to go on at the same time.

※

The detective as *flâneur* seems to carry into the everyday what Schor calls "the all-seeing perspective of the taxonomist" (216). Certainly for Jaffe and Rosemary Jann this perspective is the attraction of the Holmes stories, al-

---

venture of Creeping Man." Holmes's worries about the degradation of the race at the end of this story suggest as well the complicated racism that goes hand in hand with such misogyny.

[46] As students of cross-dressing know, of course, this act is ambiguous; while complicating women's relation to street walking it also confirms in male eyes Adler's identity as the usual kind of female streetwalker because it suggests a kind of sexual looseness and knowledge.

though (for Jann as for Belsey) woman's mystery is supposed to put it into question.[47] But the theory of the everyday suggests instead that it isn't so much that Holmes's system of meaning breaks down when confronted by the ambiguity of woman and the everyday; it is simply that (everyday) life is so complicated that his system sometimes nods. Because Holmes finds Adler "'a lovely woman, with a face that a man might die for'" (*Complete*, 169), he forgets to pay attention to her resolute mind. He locates her threat in her body, her face, which draws off his gaze. He can see her only as (what he defines as) a woman. As this story shows Holmes and his readers, it is the intermittent obliviousness of systems to other things working within them that allows for the tactics of the everyday (as de Certeau argues) to do more than the "collectors, describers, analysts" administering those systems bother to look out for (67). Even in fiction, especially fictions of the city, no taxonomist is so perfect as to keep his collection completely ordered.

The Holmes stories are a collection too (as they tell us repeatedly: hardly one goes by in which Watson doesn't refer to his collection of tales, Holmes to his collection of cases, which he chronicles in the "commonplace books" [*Complete*, 284, 623, 1034, 1096] he keeps in his Baker Street "museum" [255]). When collections and collecting appear in the Holmes stories, they outline a connection between the urban everyday and seriality that suggests not only why the masculine might need museums to police that connection, but also how woman's indifference might work within such policing. *The Strand*, as the site of these stories as a collection, asserts the connection of the street and the museum. One of Holmes and Watson's wanderings on the Strand makes this connection explicit. In "The Adventure of the Illustrious Client," they dine there twice (at that cliché, Simpson's), "looking down at the rushing stream of life in the Strand" (988), each time to discuss the case of the evil Baron Gruner.

The Baron, a man of enormous wealth and urbanity, a collector and connoisseur, is also a man of tremendous evil—among other things, he has murdered his wife. Yet, despite all the hints of his depravity, nothing has been made to stick to him, and he has been able to come to England and entangle himself with the innocent and beautiful Violet de Merville. Holmes is engaged by an intermediary from an anonymous but illustrious client to prevent their marriage. He finds Violet mesmerized by the Baron, however, and indifferent to any intervention on her behalf. Yet Holmes learns from a past mistress of the Baron's of the existence of a certain book, in which the Baron chronicles his relations with women. He knows that if he can show that book to the pure-minded Violet, he can effect her break from him. Holmes enlists the help of Watson, who poses as a purveyor of Chinese ceramics, to play upon the Baron's collecting mania. Watson distracts the Baron just long enough to gain Holmes access to his house; Holmes is able to make off with

---

[47] Jann, "Sherlock Holmes Codes the Social Body," *ELH* 57 (1990): 685–708.

the Baron's diary, however, only because the Baron's past mistress, Kitty Winter, appears unexpectedly at a critical moment, and blinds the Baron with vitriolic acid.

This story of the Baron lays bare the threats supposedly implicit against men in the ongoingness of the everyday. The Baron has met that ongoingness by seeming to appropriate it: he has become a collector, and a collector of women. The Baron is specifically a wife-murderer as well as a collector; the connection between the two activities becomes even closer through his diary. Not only does he collect "books and pictures" (*Complete*, 987), he has himself a book of pictures that reveals that "this man collects women, and takes a pride in his collection, as some men collect moths or butterflies. He had it all in that book. Snapshot photographs, names, details, everything about them. It was a beastly book" (990)—a "lust diary," Holmes calls it (998). The elimination of one wife allows the Baron to take another in the same logic with which he takes up and discards the mistresses/streetwalkers he chronicles serially in his book. The Baron's collection of women, however, actually reflects their threat. Emily Apter traces the connection between collectomania and erotomania in fin-de-siècle cabinet literature, of which the Baron's diary is a specimen. "The quasi-literary medical cabinet," Apter writes, is a kind of lust diary—"a mixture of doctor's memoir, nosological *observation*, and *roman à tiroir* . . . [bearing] a striking affinity to bedroom dramas or alcove pornography . . . [and] the prostitution novel." [48] This is a subgenre she sees developing unsurprisingly out of a time when the psychopathology of everyday life transformed every interior into a museum of the psychological and ideological symptoms of the sexual order [49]—an Austrian from the same milieu that gave rise to Freud's theories, the Baron in his diary records a sexual order in which sexual relations have become alienated, commodified. Yet, for Apter, the women collected in such chronicles are not merely objectified. Apter also sees such women invested with an unorthodox power. [50] What "empowers the female collectible," she argues, is the effect she has on the collector: the possession of her metonymically infects and possesses "the very master-collector whose aloofness and control were believed to be impregnable" (9): [51] she has the power, that is (and often through her own indifference to him), to dispel his privilege of indifference.

---

[48] Apter, "Cabinet Secrets: Fetishism, Prostitution, and the Fin de Siècle Interior," *Assemblage* 9 (1989): 7–19; 8; all future references to this essay will appear in the text.

[49] It flourished "toward the end of the nineteenth century, when the bourgeois interior became increasingly like a museum" (7), she writes, and some of the most extreme versions provide in the flourishes of their domestic interiors a companion lexicon to Freud's contemporary "theorizing (as verbal parapraxis) the lapses, double-entendres, and unintended puns that erupted into normal speech" (17).

[50] For Apter, the woman collected by such male connoisseurs becomes a kind of female fetish, and, in light of the notorious doubleness of the fetish both to reassure and to threaten (men), she gains this power.

[51] In the popular imagination, "cast in the role of brothel client and/or depraved medical man, [the collector] loses his professional cover, and becomes prey to the basest instincts, little

With the inclusion of the Baron's diary, the Holmes story both refers to and aligns itself with this tradition.[52] Holmes knows just what "would drive a real connoisseur wild"; his knowledge confirms (what his neurasthenia and ennui already suggest) that this is a tradition with which he, too, is familiar. He explains to Watson about the Baron: "He has the collection mania in its most acute form—and especially on this subject, on which he is an acknowledged authority" (*Complete*, 995). Holmes's tacit identification with the Baron which allows Holmes to recognize a collector's mastery as his greatest weakness suggests how the complacency of mastery can become its own undoing, how vulnerable and apotropaic is Holmes's fatigue with his own genius, how much mastery has to lose. Part of the effect of this story when read in this way is to destroy the prerogatives of such mastery, especially the security that grants it the privilege of boredom.

Dull and pedestrian Watson recognizes so well the power of indifference (not just perhaps because Holmes exercises it on him throughout the stories, but also because his very averageness aligns him with the indifferent everyday) that he tries to assume it in his encounter with the Baron, hoping in that way to goad the Baron out of his own boredom.[53] But although Holmes's and Watson's plan succeeds momentarily in driving "the languor . . . from [the Baron's] eyes" (*Complete*, 997), what ultimately arouses and defeats him is an "intensity of hatred . . . such as woman seldom and man never can attain" (990): it is Kitty Winter, one of the women the Baron has ruined and discarded, who returns to throw vitriol in his face. Looking at the Baron in his frenzy of pain, Watson tells the reader: "The features which I had admired a few minutes before were now like some beautiful painting over which the artist has passed a wet and foul sponge" (998). The collector has become the collectible, the Baron like Kitty Winter, a ruined version of the objects he collects.[54]

---

better than the lust-stricken women of easy virtue whose species he collects. The implicit equivalence between collector and prostitute . . . represents a significant dislocation of the male collector/female collectible opposition" (15).

[52] And calls into question just how extraordinary and *foreign* a tradition it really is (the Continental background of Baron Gruner aside): like any psychopathology, it inheres in everyday life, a suggestion underscored when Doyle, himself a medical man, has his Dr. Watson impersonate a collector. Doyle makes quite a point that this is a false identity for the innocently ordinary Watson—he fails miserably in his attempt to convince the Baron of his connoisseurship—but the connection between the knowledge of doctors and sexual pathology, between Doyle's work and cabinet literature, gets established nonetheless.

[53] He assumes it correspondingly as the Baron begins to see through his disguise; as the Baron starts to press him, " 'You can do business or not,' said I with indifference" (*Complete*, 997). Watson had learned in *The Hound of the Baskervilles* that "incredulity and indifference were evidently my strongest cards" (*Complete*, 737), a disclosure that complicates the cheerful obtuseness that Holmes so takes for granted in his companion.

[54] This mutation is a staple in the Holmes stories. The villain in *The Hound* who collects moths is "not unlike some huge moth himself" (*Complete*, 709), and Holmes says to Watson: "he will be fluttering in our net as helpless as one of his own butterflies. A pin, a cork, and a card, and we add him to the Baker Street collection" (*Complete*, 750). The collector of antiquities in "The Adventure of the Three Garridebs" is an old "fossil" (*Complete*, 1051); in "The Adventure of the Veiled Lodger," Holmes and Watson meet a woman who "from keeping

Donna Haraway has argued that one of the impulses driving collecting has to do specifically with the fear of such transformations: The "public activities of the Museum were dedicated to preserving a threatened manhood," she writes. For Haraway, as for other theorists of collecting, the activity represents "a practice to produce permanence, to arrest decay." [55] What is especially masculine about this practice, Haraway contends, citing *The Second Sex*, is that it grows out of a male anxiety over death, an anxiety displaced and scapegoated onto the woman that gave him birth. The "truth" of the museum, which is "the effective truth of manhood," the illusion upon which the ideology of masculinity is founded in our culture, is that "the body can be transcended. . . . It is in the craft of killing that life is constructed, not in the accident of personal, material birth" (28–29).[56] Susan Stewart too recognizes in the cultural symbolic an association of women's power with seriality in "maternity's generation of the series" (xi). In an attempt to deny women such power and wrest from them the secret of creation (somehow cleansed of the mortality disrupting seriality and causing the ellipsis of death), Haraway argues, men kill women (among other living things) into art; such a practice of "preservation" transfers immortality metonymically to man.

Doyle shares this response at least in part. In "The Curse of Eve" (one of his stories not about Holmes), he tries to use the indifference of the everyday to diminish the threat of maternity by depicting a frantic husband's attempt to bring a doctor to his wife's maternity bed: "He had not imagination enough to realize that the experience which seemed so appallingly important to him, was the merest everyday matter of business to the medical man." [57] Here the doctor, rather than the woman, is in control of the everyday, overfamiliar and bored with what still seems to the husband his wife's extraordinary achievement. While the motive for such cultural responses need not be grounded in the supposedly "material" fact of female maternity (that it is a fact that women give birth seems to me, as Apter argues in another context, "uncontestable . . . [but] hardly exhaustive" [12]), the ideology of mas-

---

beasts in a cage . . . seemed, by some retribution of fate, to have become herself a beast in a cage" (*Complete*, 1099). Holmes, the collector of mysteries, is himself a mystery; the collector of criminals is himself a very good criminal. Although Jaffe has an excellent discussion of such oscillations, I think there is more going on here than she accounts for with her schema of containment.

[55] Haraway, "Teddy Bear Patriarchy: Taxidermy in the Garden of Eden, New York City, 1908–36," in her *Primate Visions: Gender, Race, and Nature in the World of Modern Science* (New York: Routledge, 1989), 26–58; 55; all future references to this essay will appear in the text. Amy Boesky, for example, similarly writes: "Undermined by the frightening souvenirs of decomposition and decay . . . the collection asks its audience to discriminate, to see what is preserved against all that threatens such preservation": "'Outlandish Fruits': Commissioning Nature for the Museum of Man," *ELH* 58 (1991): 305–30; 323.

[56] Haraway sees these attitudes encoded into the museum as a response to an urban dilemma: "the Museum's task of regeneration [meant to work for and on] a miscellaneous, incoherent urban public threatened with genetic and social decadence, threatened with the prolific bodies of the new immigrants, threatened with the failure of manhood" (29).

[57] Doyle, "The Curse of Eve," *Round the Red Lamp* (London: Methuen, 1894), 89–108; 99.

culinity does seem to depend on a bid for creation and mastery fought out on the site of the body. By claiming dominion over the everyday, what masculinity hopes to do with that (male) body is to arrest its everyday incremental change.

Or so "The Adventure of the Illustrious Client" suggests. Watson's simile comparing the Baron's ruined features to a painting points to one of the sources motivating this story, a novel directly about masculine reification of the body: *The Picture of Dorian Gray*. At a dinner party with the American publisher of *Lippincott's*, both Doyle and Wilde agreed to serialize novels in that magazine: Wilde wrote *Dorian Gray*.[58] The Holmes story alludes to this novel that Doyle knew well precisely because it makes the process of collecting and its relation to seriality so explicit. In displacing his process of degeneration onto his portrait, Dorian Gray tries to preserve himself. What takes Wilde's story out of the realm of homosocial cabinet literature (to which, like Doyle's, it also belongs) and into the homosexual, out of the conservation of dominant ideology into its disruption, is that the body Dorian Gray kills into art (along with that of Sybil Vane, among others) is his own. The monstrous and unnatural exposed in *Dorian Gray* is not so much the product of Wilde's own internalized homophobia (although that is there enough) as it is of the destructiveness of cultural definitions of masculinity. Dorian Gray attempts to base himself and his sexuality on a (masculine) fantasy of the control of the everyday, on the attempt to co-opt its featureless interminability for his own private and unchanging immortality.

This desire is implicit in the tedium of the everyday, which bespeaks human resistance to each day's intimations of mortality. De Certeau writes:

> Its message is seen in the faces that are slowly decaying, but they have only lies with which to say what they presage (be quiet, you stories of getting old told by my eyes, my wrinkles, and so many forms of dullness), and we are careful not to let them speak (don't tell us, faces, what we don't want to know). (194)

And Susan Stewart adds:

> The temporality of everyday life is marked by an irony which is its own creation, for this temporality is held to be ongoing and nonreversible and, at the same time, characterized by repetition and predictability. The pages falling off the calendar, the notches marked in a tree that no longer stands—these are the signs of the everyday, the effort to articulate difference through counting. Yet it is precisely this counting that reduces differences to similarities, that is designed

[58] Doyle produced *The Sign of the Four*, the novel he wrote right before "A Scandal in Bohemia." The "Illustrious Client" depends throughout on *Dorian Gray*; many of its details don't make much sense without this reference (such as Watson's reference to the Baron's age: "In age I should have put him at little over thirty, though his record afterwards showed that he was forty-two" [*Complete*, 996]). Its close relation to Wilde's novel may explain why this story opens with Holmes and Watson sharing a Turkish Bath.

to be "lost track of." Such "counting," such signifying, is drowned out by the silence of the ordinary. (14)

Human mortality bars people from the infinite continuance that they wish seriality to promise. This explains why the tedium of the everyday is so often associated with longing and dissatisfaction: Stewart titles her book *On Longing*; Lefebvre writes that "the secret of the everyday [is] dissatisfaction" (*Critique*, 35). Out of an unrelenting boredom, Dorian Gray (like Holmes with his cases) longs for new experiences that only become stale. Such boredom may also mark Wilde's own ennui with conventions, such as masculinity, that may be absolutely necessary to make meaning in traditional contexts, but that don't make a lot of sense when seen from other contexts (heterosexual masculinity as it defines but is also made over by homosexuality; patriarchy producing women who find ways to make do in it). Wilde's novel makes the tantalizing quality of this tedium absolutely clear: that of continually transforming without ever being able to produce anything radically new.

Doyle's stories also thematize the efficacy of such boredom, the tedium within which those who make do in dominant structures must operate. Although it seems at first that boredom remains a male prerogative—the Baron is as good at it as Holmes is—"The Illustrious Client" also explores boredom as something the weak can use against the strong. Kitty Winter does seem to be the stereotypical passionate woman, to incarnate the banality that hell hath no fury like a woman scorned.[59] The Baron's rejection has filled her with a fury that eats at her like the very acid with which she transforms him ("one read the terrible years which had left their leprous mark upon her" [*Complete*, 989]). Yet Kitty's passion is just one of the various women's responses in this story, and perhaps emphasized by it because it is actually the most familiar and reassuring. The difficulty confronting Holmes in this story is not Kitty's fury (in the end, her anger is what delivers Holmes out of his dilemma): it is how to separate the Baron from the woman he has chosen to be his new wife, Violet de Merville.

The difficulty with Violet is how cool she is. It does no good to tell this woman of her fiancé's criminal past, for example; she simply doesn't care. Although the story does everything possible to contrast Kitty and Violet ("if ever you saw flame and ice face to face," Holmes tells Watson, "it was those two women" [*Complete*, 992]), the coolness of Kitty Winter's last name suggests a connection between them as well (and Kitty is motivated not so much by passion as by bleak desperation; she attacks the Baron because she personally has nothing left to lose). In her cool disregard, both of Holmes's heroics and the Baron's villainy, Violet may be as much of a threat to men as

---

[59] She is a "brand . . . [a] flame-like young woman" (*Complete*, 989), and she tells Holmes "'I'm easy to find. . . . Hell, London, gets me every time'" (*Complete*, 989).

Kitty is in her anger. And what's maddening about Violet herself is that although she outwardly obeys the men who try to advise her, she is really indifferent to their advice (these men include not only her father, but also Holmes's illustrious client, who, the story broadly hints, may be Edward VII; this may be *his* adventure because it reveals to ultimate power the way obedience can be ambiguous). Her attitude bespeaks not real obedience but a disturbing tenacity; she has "a will of iron" (*Complete*, 986), the same quality that Doyle gave to the formidable Irene Adler, with her "resolute" mind. "*Tenacity*" is, according to de Certeau, one of the tactics of the everyday, one of "countless ways of refusing to accord the established order the status of a law, a meaning, or a fatality" (26) by acceding to but also ignoring that order. Violet's attitude bothers the normally cool Holmes—"there was something indescribably annoying in the calm aloofness and supreme self-complaisance of the woman whom we were trying to save" (*Complete*, 992–93)—who sees it as diminishing himself and other men: "'If your head is inclined to swell, my dear Watson, take a course of Miss Violet de Merville,'" he says (991).

The story tries to soften the threatening possibility of women's unconcern by suggesting that it is ultimately a male device. The Baron suggests that Violet's coolness is really just a post-hypnotic suggestion of his own, and even fiery Kitty confesses that under his spell she was indifferent: "'I took little notice—you see, I loved him myself at the time'" (*Complete*, 990);[60] Violet's indifference is characterized not as an ennui like the Baron's own, but as an apathy produced by her obsession with him. Her cure also dramatically denies her any connection to other women which might suggest similar feelings within them. Recognizing that she will be unmoved even by the Baron's disfigurement, Holmes insists they must show Violet the Baron's book. "No self-respecting woman could stand" to be part of such a collection (*Complete*, 998), he tells Watson. In order to respect her self, Holmes implies, she must abstract that self out of seriality, break the ongoing chain of substitutable women the Baron has constructed.

But Doyle's fiction denies a seriality to women like Violet (setting it up as a trap in which her anonymity in it becomes like her sexual objectification by men) in order to preserve seriality for itself. Not only are the Holmes stories an ongoing series, Holmes himself is more than just a collector. Even though the stories emphasize the "commonplace books" in which he records the "names, details, everything about" his criminals, and although he compares his mind frequently to a "lumber-room," a museum in which he stores arcane information, Holmes is also, as far as Doyle's stories are concerned,

---

[60] Holmes too shares this hypnotic power over women, one that relies on their association with the commonplace: "He had an almost hypnotic power of soothing when he wished. The scared look faded from her eyes, and her agitated features smoothed into their usual commonplace" (*Complete*, 902).

the most important exhibit in the collection, for what are these stories if not
their own kind of commonplace book recording everything about Holmes?
In fact, Sherlock Holmes is perhaps the best example of a subject of sheer
seriality, a proliferating cultural icon, a literary simulacrum without origin
or end (letters addressed to number 221B Baker Street still find their way
through the London mail).

Doyle himself emphasizes this aspect of Holmes and suggests that one attraction of his kind of seriality is that it seems to promise an escape from the
trap in which masculine ideology constructs the self—it promises the escape
of immortality. After attempting to kill off Holmes (in "The Final Problem"
which, like "His Last Bow" after it, was anything but last or final), Doyle
brings him back precisely as a kind of copy, a substitution of himself.[61] Although Holmes initially reappears to Dr. Watson in the guise of a collector
in "The Adventure of the Empty House," he leads Watson through the maze
of London to gaze at another version of himself as a collectible instead: in
the museum-like setting of the Baker Street rooms that Holmes's brother has
preserved after his (supposed) death, Holmes has literally installed a facsimile of himself, a model in wax. " 'I trust that age doth not wither nor custom
stale my infinite variety,' " he says to Watson as they look at his copy, "and
I recognized in his voice the joy and pride which the artist takes in his own
creation" (*Complete*, 489). The (male) apotropaic fantasy of seriality, of control of the everyday, is revealed here: a kind of self-propagating cloning or
parthenogenesis, an infinite proliferation that specifically preserves the self,
one that magically dispels the tedium of age and custom, that transforms
the everyday. The endlessness of the series this is meant to set up gets emphasized when Doyle copies his own device. When Doyle turned to Spiritualism near the end of his career, writing Holmes stories in order to support
that interest, he shamelessly plagiarized himself, resurrecting the facsimile
of Holmes in a late story—"The Adventure of the Mazarin Stone"—almost
as if to call attention to the kind of wish (for the endless existence of the
self) that Spiritualism represents; he even has Watson make a point of such
flagrant copying (" 'We used something of the sort once before,' " he says
[1013]).[62]

[61] Watson's fear at the beginning of "The Adventure of the Empty House" that he is at "risk
of telling a twice-told tale" (*Complete*, 483), which is, by (Shakespeare's) definition, tedious,
emphasizes that this kind of repetition takes place on the familiar terrain of boredom and the
everyday.

[62] Philip Fisher has argued that images like this facsimile of Holmes—busts of statesmen, for
instance—are conjured by systems nervous about their authority and trying to claim some referential ground; these images work "as an act of replacement in which those who were important to society are claimed to be symbolically present. . . . [I]f there were no fear that the institution itself would become vulnerable if the visible presence did not continue to preside over it,
then the statue or portrait itself would cease to function": *Making and Effacing Art: Modern
American Art in a Culture of Museums* (New York: Oxford University Press, 1991), 14. In "The
Adventure of the Six Napoleons," in which it appears a monomaniac is smashing busts of

Although Patricia Mellencamp argues that one "negative view of the city [sees it] as a dingy museum of copies and forgeries," the Holmes stories suggest that such a view may actually be productive—of the longings, fantasies, and stories that make the city the site and symbol of the masculine attempt to dominate and control what it defines as the powers of nature.[63] It is the site of that attempt because it is also, in these stories, the very site of mortality: in another of his expeditions on "the Strand," in gazing at "the great city," Watson—who tells us he is not usually given "to impressions"—makes clear what impression the city should leave with us; as he watches people move from shop window to shop window: "there was, to my mind, something eerie and ghostlike in the endless procession of faces which flitted across these narrow bars of light—sad faces and glad, haggard and merry. Like all humankind, they flitted from the gloom into the light and so back into the gloom once more" (*Complete*, 98). The ghostliness of this present existence may actually seem to promise that there are such things as ghosts (also the promise of Spiritualism), and so to dispel that later gloom a little. But the city, as site of this worldly existence, also suggests the threatening possibility that there may be nothing beyond it.

"The Illustrious Client" also make clear that Doyle's wish through Holmes for an endlessly self-perpetuating self—the male cultural wish that Holmes represents—may be founded on nothing. It does so by founding that wish on that quicksand, a woman. The line Holmes quotes as he gazes lovingly on his own self-creation is, of course, originally about Cleopatra: Shakespeare's play demonstrates that Cleopatra will neither wither nor stale in the male imagination; she can rise above the everyday precisely because she dies in it (and for a man). Doyle's stories make clear that woman is a paradoxical means to dispel the tedium of everyday life since woman is actually what Holmes insists bores him most. Yet the infinite variety these stories yearn for may have precisely to do with the ambiguity that undercuts the wish for self: the ambiguity, I have been arguing, of the everyday.

In spite of their explicit wish to break from tedium, the Holmes stories always return Holmes to his essential boredom because of what that state suggests: the tedium of the everyday seems endless, the promise of the everyday's boredom is that it will go on forever. In understanding the everyday as a political practice, what matters is how one reads this promise. The boredom that is part of the rhetoric of mastery represents a paradoxical attempt to harness the everyday's endlessness in order to preserve (the illusion of) individual importance; the tactics of the weak (like Kitty's—she makes the Baron

Napoleon all over London, Doyle seems to be directly exploring the relations between referentiality and seriality. The importance of those proliferating images of Napoleon turns out to have nothing to do with any historical "truth." Yet, although these images proliferate and call reference into question, they do so in a closed series: only six Napoleons are important.

[63] Mellencamp, "Last Seen in the Streets of Modernism," *East-West Film Journal* 3 (1988): 45–67; 58.

as faceless as herself) instead give themselves up to and play upon the everyday's very anonymity. The political force of the everyday is that it enables a practice of persistence, of continuing on in impossible circumstances, an endless practice that continues past the very point of personal mortality. Much recent criticism can see the political force of boredom only as sinister, terroristic, what conditions the self into the meshes of ideology.[64] Yet such an argument could conversely suggest that boredom is terrifying only when seen from the perspective of the self.

What makes the Holmes stories infinitely variable for me is precisely the way they give themselves over to staleness; Doyle also recognizes that more things can happen in the terrain of the everyday than he can control. Critics have suggested that Doyle created Sherlock Holmes as an attempt to escape the tedium of his faltering medical practice. Yet he carried that tedium with him—long after he was tired of Holmes, Doyle was unable to kill him off. In representing an infinite seriality, Holmes does figure his creator's desire for the extraordinary, for personal immortality; but Doyle's boredom with Holmes suggests something more: at the end of "The Red-headed League" (a story that more than any other gives itself over to and celebrates the very staleness of its conventions), Holmes tells Watson " *'L'homme c'est rien— l'oeuvre c'est tout'* as Gustave Flaubert wrote to George Sand" (*Complete*, 190). Doyle's recognition of the insignificance of the individual also explains the most explosive posthumous scandal of his biography, one that revolved around the remarks he made in an address to a Spiritualist luncheon: "I wound up by saying, very solemnly, that I was something greater than Governments and the master of Cabinet Ministers. By the time I had finished my tremendous claims I am convinced that they expected some extravagant occult pretension, whereas I actually wound up with the words, 'for I am the man in the street.' "[65] Doyle's amusement at confounding his fellow spiritualists by ascribing (political) strength to a figure of the very anonymity their movement wished to deny, and assuming that (lack of) identity himself, suggest Doyle's own attraction to the oblivion of everyday practices. The recognition of the importance of work, of practice, over individual identity, and the reference to one of the most famous female practitioners of walking in

---

[64] See D. A. Miller's discussion of boredom, for instance, for the best expression of this view.

[65] Doyle, *The Wanderings of a Spiritualist* (London: Hodder and Stoughton, n.d.), 97–98. A writer named Hesketh Pearson quoted Doyle's claim to be the man in the street as the epigraph to his biography of Doyle, and used that idea as the book's organizing theme. This characterization so outraged Doyle's son, Adrian, that he wrote his own biography of his father to refute it; Doyle's daughter and his other biographers have continued to deny it—one biographer, for instance, claiming that "no 'man in the street' could have created Sherlock Holmes": James Bliss Austin, "The Family's Counter-Attack," in *The Quest for Sir Arthur Conan Doyle: Thirteen Biographers in Search of a Life*, ed. John L. Lellenberg (Carbondale: Southern Illinois University Press, 1987), 105–10; 108; see his summary of this controversy. The family's objections seem to come from obvious class bias: Dame Jean Conan Doyle couldn't agree that her father, who had after all been given a title, was in any way an "ordinary" man; see her "Foreword" to *The Quest for Sir Arthur Conan Doyle*, xi–xv; xiii.

the city, George Sand, suggest that one might even begin to found a politics on those practices in Doyle's work, stories that have as their central subject not the certain knowledge with which the detective winds up each case but the repeated mystery that keeps the series going on.

The mystery of woman, of the everyday, of the infinite variety of the city and its streets, is the mystery of going on, of survival in the face of what would collect and transform those mysteries into something ordered or known. This survival may be something different from the fantasies of escape or fears of containment that have so occupied criticism in recent years: something less heroic than one, less horrific than the other—something less dramatic, more ordinary. The alternative to the debate about ideology may come in the recognition that, from the position of those without the luxury to argue over such ideals as freedom or its opposite, that debate has never really begun; it is already over. The mystery of everyday life lies in its power to continue as if those debates had never been.

It seems to be her first book, I said to myself, but one must read it as if it were the last volume in a fairly long series. . . . For books continue each other.

—Virginia Woolf, *A Room of One's Own*

4   *Unbegun and Unfinished*

Race, Modernism, and the Series as Tradition

When does the series become an outmoded form? Or, rather, when—no matter what its continued perseverance—do writers begin to make that case against it? And why? As I pointed out in my introduction, one way we can retroactively define Victorian literature is through its association with the series. But that doesn't mean that series fiction ends when that period does. Dorothy Richardson's *Pilgrimage* may be a lesser-known work of modernism because it is a twentieth-century text that keeps the series central. At any rate, Richardson's contemporaries may have defined Victorian fiction as outmoded by defining the series (and Richardson) as archaic. I'm concerned in this chapter mainly with Virginia Woolf, the writer whom current feminism finds most useful to contrast with Richardson. The claim that writers shunned the series in no way holds true for all of modernism. D. H. Lawrence, for instance, never abandoned that form. My argument in this chapter, however, is that Woolf never really did, either, although she might have wanted to seem to claim to. The question is: why?

At the beginning of *Pilgrimage*, its heroine Miriam Henderson feels herself about to take leave of "a world which would go on without her, taking no heed . . . There would be no more silent sunny mornings with all the day ahead and nothing to do and no end anywhere to anything."[1] In part, Richardson means to signal to her readers that she is about to take her character from the protected, patriarchal world of her Victorian childhood where she is chaperoned and occupationless, and simply waits to marry (the stability of which world has always been an illusion anyway, as her father's bankruptcy shows) to a modern world in which she gets a job, pushes her way alone in London, has affairs—where stability and constriction get trans-

---

[1] *Pointed Roofs*, in *Pilgrimage*, vol. 1 (*Pointed Roofs, Backwater, Honeycomb*) (London: Dent, 1967), 4 vols. (1967), pp. 13–185; chap. 1, p. 16; all future references to this novel (abbreviated *Roofs*) will appear in the text.

formed into flux and possibility. This change, of course, heralds the change
in form between Victorian realism and Richardson's own more experimental novel. But the change between these worlds may not be as radical as it
seems, since "go[ing] on . . . taking no heed . . . with no end anywhere to
anything" refers as much to the method of Richardson's novel as it does to
a Victorian past it is meant to leave behind.

As May Sinclair wrote in a famous characterization of Richardson's form
that provided one defining term for modernism itself: "In this series there is
no drama, no situation, no set scene. Nothing happens. It is just life going
on and on. It is Miriam Henderson's stream of consciousness going on and
on."[2] Despite Sinclair's application of William James's notion of "stream of
consciousness" to characterize Richardson as modernist, other contemporaries of Richardson recognized in the ongoing series form of her novels the
burden of the past. Rachel DuPlessis has implied that, for Virginia Woolf,
Richardson represented the nineteenth century (just as Gertrude Stein did
the twentieth).[3] Woolf found in Richardson "the shapeliness of the old accepted forms."[4] This past may seem so much like a burden precisely because
one cannot break away from it; the past is always part of, experienced only
through, the present (part of the point, it seems too, of the relentless emphasis on present impressions—what Avrom Fleishman calls Richardson's "eternal autobiographical moment"[5]—within Richardson's formal method).

[2] Sinclair, "The Novels of Dorothy Richardson," *The Little Review* 4 (1918): 3–11; 5–6.
Richardson does attempt to distinguish her work from an outdated past specifically by distinguishing her books from a male writing that she characterizes in terms of the sequentiality of the
series impulse. In *The Tunnel* and in *Dawn's Left Hand*, she defines men's writing as "rows and
rows of 'fine' books": "bang, bang, bang, on they go, these men's books, like an L.C.C. tram":
The Tunnel in *Pilgrimage*, vol. 2 (*The Tunnel, Interum*) (London: Dent, 1967), pp. 9–287,
chap. 6, p. 130; all future references to this novel will appear in the text; *Dawn's Left Hand*, in
Pilgrimage, vol. 4 (*Oberland, Dawn's Left Hand, Clear Horizon, Dimple Hill, March Moonlight*) (London: Dent, 1967), pp. 129–267, chap. 9, p. 239; all future references to this book
(abbreviated *Dawn*) will appear in the text. But she can imagine countering such a tradition
only in its own terms. Rachel Blau DuPlessis argues that Richardson's narrative is so "wayward
and prolix" in order to counter misogyny in its own image, to displace its very mass: "The monumental—really excessive—length of *Pilgrimage* may be attributable to Richardson's desire for
vengeance on culture, for a female alternative to the cultural bulk of 'the finest literature,' and
for a massive mountain of narrative to be placed between the main character and the hegemonic
stories and opinion that haunted her": *Writing beyond the Ending: Narrative Strategies of
Twentieth-Century Women Writers* (Bloomington: Indiana University Press, 1985), 143, 145.
[3] She writes: "As early and middle Woolf was challenged by Dorothy Richardson's *Pilgrimage*
and its critique of narrative, one might equally attempt the notion that later Woolf . . . was challenged by the formal designs, the repetitions, the grids, the critiques of the center, the other otherness of the work of Gertrude Stein. Woolf's subsequent remarks . . . show that vital and fruitful
tension in her work between—baldly—the nineteenth and twentieth centuries": Rachel Blau
DuPlessis, "Woolfenstein," in *Breaking the Sequence: Women's Experimental Fiction*, ed. Ellen
G. Friedman and Miriam Fuchs (Princeton: Princeton University Press, 1989), 99–114; 101.
[4] Virginia Woolf, "The Tunnel," in *The Essays of Virginia Woolf*, vol. 3, 1919–1924, ed.
Andrew McNeillie (London: Hogarth, 1988), 6 vols. projected, 4 vols. to date (1986–94), 10–
12; 12.
[5] Fleishman, *Figures of Autobiography: The Language of Self-Writing in Victorian and Modern England* (Berkeley: University of California Press, 1983), 428.

In asserting its series form, *Pilgrimage* insists also on the everyday. At the beginning of her series, Richardson implicitly cautions her readers not to be like Miriam's family, who are not interested in "the little real everyday things that give you an idea of anything, but only the startling things that are not important."[6] *Pilgrimage* demonstrates instead that it is in "perfectly 'ordinary and commonplace' things, [that] life is embodied."[7] *Pilgrimage's* form demystifies the extraordinary into the everyday.[8]

And *Pilgrimage* means for the everyday to be a property of form, not content, to capture a sense of dailiness through its own pace and length. In that sense, *Pilgrimage's* realism is not so much a reflection of some preexistent reality, as it is a performance meant to produce that reality. For Richardson in particular, the everyday *is* the series. The ongoingness of the everyday in *Pilgrimage* actually provides the means to arrest the present moment. Of all the series this book has treated, Richardson's is the most expansive, and not just in sheer page numbers. It also takes the longest to tell over the shortest span of time — enacting the everyday as series by almost (but not quite) stalling its reading time to the clock time of Miriam's daily life. Miriam's relation to the translation that forms her first serious written work characterizes Richardson's own (and the reader's) relation to *Pilgrimage* as a daily record: "Coming between her and the immediate grasp of the text were stirring memories; the history of her labour was written between the lines; and strangely, moving within the whole, was the record of the months since Christmas. On every page a day or group of days. It was a diary" (*Deadlock*, 5.143). Any separation between the series and the everyday (almost) vanishes.

Miriam remains deeply interested in this temporal sense that she also sees

---

[6] *Backwater*, in *Pilgrimage*, 1: 187–346, chap. 5, p. 265; all future references to this book will appear in the text.

[7] *Clear Horizon*, in *Pilgrimage*, 4: 269–400, chap. 6, p. 368; all future references to this book (abbreviated *Clear*) will appear in the text. Richardson means to distinguish herself from "people who are . . . in the midst of their bland security, depressed about life in general, and have 'a poor opinion of humanity.'. . . They are the people who talk about 'ordinary everyday life' and approve of 'far horizons' and desert islands and the other side of the moon, as if they were real and wonderful and life was not": *Deadlock*, in *Pilgrimage*, vol. 3 (*Deadlock, Revolving Lights, The Trap*) (London: Dent, 1967), 9–229, chap. 1, p. 19; all future references to this book will appear in the text. Richardson's own form is definitely not meant to be "fantasy . . . that implies a belief in the dullness of everyday life": *Dimple Hill*, in *Pilgrimage*, 4: 401–552, chap. 5, p. 454; all future references to this book (abbreviated *Dimple*) will appear in the text.

[8] Which seems to be the entire point of the novels in the series devoted to travel. In *Oberland*, Miriam meets a Swiss woman "on her way home to a place with a tripping gentle name, a fairy keep agleam on a lakeside amidst mountains. To her it was dailiness, life as now she knew it, a hemmed-in loneliness. Visitors came from afar. Found it full of poetry. Saw her perhaps as a part of it, a figure of romance": *Oberland*, in *Pilgrimage*, 4: 9–127, chap. 1, p. 19; all future references to this book will appear in the text. In *March Moonlight*, Richardson has a character tell a similar story: "In *Madeira*, as a stranger, deeply impressed, *day* after *day*, by the continuous sunshine and blue sky, I met, when remarking at breakfast upon the fineness of the day, with what seemed to me a singular lack of *response*, and was *puzzled*, if not somewhat *embarrassed*, until I discovered that in Madeira *every* day is a fine day": *March Moonlight*, in *Pilgrimage*, 4: 553–658, chap. 1, p. 571; all future references to this book (abbreviated *March*) will appear in the text.

as somehow distinctly narrative: the winding off of her days makes her life seem like a book to her. She explicitly calls it "the novel going on."[9] But Miriam is also deeply disturbed by such ongoingness: "Going on. People went . . . mad" (*Honeycomb*, 10.475). This kind of seriality is for Miriam a form of death: "Life went on and on, a great oblivious awfulness, sliding over everything. Every moment things went on that could never be recovered . . . on and on, and it was always too late, there was always some new thing obliterating everything . . . grinning with its sameness in an awful blank where one tried to remember the killed things" (*Tunnel*, 30.249–50) What the series kills in *Pilgrimage* is any sense of stable self. The joy of the everyday feels transfiguring to Miriam because it intensifies the very self it swamps, but the seriatim stream of the everyday seems to annihilate her identity:

> The walls of her room . . . they had seen her endless evening hours of waiting for the next day to entangle her in its odious revolution. They had watched her, in bleak daylight, listening to life going on obliviously all round her . . . [they had seen] her vain prayer that life should not pass her by . . . waiting indifferent, serene with the years they knew before she came, for those that would follow her meaningless impermanence. When she lost the sense of herself in moments of gladness . . . they were all round her, waiting, ready to remind her, undeceived by her daily busy passing in and out. (*Deadlock*, 3.86)

The walls of Miriam's room represent the shell of identity emptied out by the everyday's adamant, indifferent stream. Dailiness ticks off the slow death of the self. *Pilgrimage* sees mortality as a wasting sickness: "the relentless slow progress of every kind of incurable disease" (*March*, 1.568). The everyday's narrative of identity ultimately means "always alone, and just cancer coming" (*Roofs*, 12.172).

Perhaps for this reason, Virginia Woolf seems determined to dispense with the series as a possible form for her own writing. That writing, as it tries to "cop[y] the order of the day, observ[e] the sequence of ordinary things" (which Woolf argues is "the novelist's aim"), seems to refuse the very series impulse so entangled with the sequential and the ordinary.[10] For Woolf, work

---

[9] *Honeycomb*, in *Pilgrimage*, 1: 345–490, chap. 10, p. 451; all future references to this book will appear in the text. In its emphatic stress on Miriam's present impressions, *Pilgrimage* seems (even pathologically at times) to be about what Richardson calls a "deep everyday joy" (*Dawn's*, 8.209). For Richardson, the daily instant offers a kind of existential ecstasy; in the collapse of her identity into the usually unrecognized daily moments of life around her, Miriam feels "there, in the midst of joy and wonder, not surprise but an everyday steadiness and clarity beyond anything she had yet experienced" (*Clear*, 1.282). Her allegiance to this steadiness, her drive to experience it, is at odds with rationality (it makes Miriam act in otherwise inexplicable ways: rejecting suitors, severing friendships, quitting jobs) and at odds with narrative itself (its dwelling in each present moment to the exclusion of all else makes *Pilgrimage*'s chronology practically unreadable).

But the everyday is also ongoing, and that ongoingness seems sinister to Miriam; *Pilgrimage* is also expressly about the equation of sequentialness and pain, what Miriam calls "the everyday sense of the winding off of days in an elaborate unchanging circle of toil" (*Deadlock*, 5.140).

[10] "Phases of Fiction," *Collected Essays*, 4 vols. (New York: Harcourt, 1967), 2:56–102; 99.

which still preserves that impulse comes out of an outdated mode of serial production. She does not mean to "go on perseveringly, conscientiously, constructing our thirty-two chapters after a design which more and more ceases to resemble the vision in our minds."[11] Because (as she outrageously asserts) "on or about December 1910 human character changed," Woolf demands new forms to reflect a new sense of identity.[12] Quoting Walter de la Mare, she implies that "an endless war twixt contraries," which she sees forming her contemporaries' sense of the world—and the self—since before the war, just may not be able to be captured in a serial form that smacks of the "'empty track of leaden day by day."[13] Yet Woolf's work, through repeated characters like the Dalloways in *The Voyage Out*, *Mrs. Dalloway*, and *Mrs. Dalloway's Party*, retains a trace of the series precisely around the category of identity.[14]

For Woolf, as for Richardson, the identity produced by the series and the everyday is radically, crucially, gendered. Richardson locates the differences between their everydays as the defining difference between the sexes: "Far worse than the normal incompatibility of man and woman is the absence in their daily life of a common heritage" (*March*, 3.605). Culture, however, (as Lefebvre and de Certeau have argued too) bleeds off the everyday onto woman, trying to make her alone into "the compendium of dailiness" (*Dimple*, 10.534) in the hope of letting man rise above the toil and contradictions of the everyday. It is a reaction against this fraudulent skewing that catapults Miriam Henderson into a gender politics she refuses to call feminism: in a scene that Woolf read before sending her own narrator in *A Room of One's Own* to contemplate the volumes of misogyny in the British Museum, Miriam comes upon an ugly tract of gender superiority. Its male author argues with what Richardson elsewhere calls "peevish facetiousness" (*Deadlock*, 2.50) that "woman is undeveloped man." Reading it poisons Miriam's everyday existence; it causes her "sleeplessness, and everyday a worse feeling of illness. Everyday the new torture" (*Tunnel*, 24.221).

Modern critics have wanted to call feminist Miriam's (and Richardson's) political identity forged through such splits in the everyday. Yet, despite being thrown with a lurch into an inescapable gender consciousness, Miriam identifies as "her best most liberating words" precisely a rejection of "feminism," as "'an insult to womanhood . . . [and] a libel on the universe'" (*Deadlock*, 12.219). What Miriam rejects in feminism is its picture of woman as in need of some kind of ontological unshackling: "You think I

[11] "Modern Novels," ibid., 3: 30–33; 33.

[12] "Character in Fiction," ibid., 3: 420–38; 421.

[13] "Dreams and Realities," *The Essays of Virginia Woolf*, vol. 2, 1912–1918, ed. Andrew McNeillie (London: Hogarth, 1987), 252–55; 254.

[14] The Dalloways are not the only characters that Woolf carries over from book to book, just the ones she dwells on most extensively. Crosby from *The Years* reappears in *Three Guineas*, Lady Hibbert of "Phyllis and Rosamond" reappears in *Jacob's Room*, Mr. Bowley of *Jacob's Room* shows up in *Mrs. Dalloway*, as does Rose Shaw in *Mrs. Dalloway's Party*—and I am sure I have not here noted all the recurrences.

can cheerfully regard myself as an emancipated slave, with traditions of slavery for memory and the form of a slave as an everlasting heritage?" (*Deadlock*, 12.219) she asks. Whether or not her rejection of the term "feminism" ultimately adds up to an acceptance of its meaning anyway (as some feminists claim), Richardson insists in *Pilgrimage* that the identity of woman she constructs there is a formal category that explores and contests the different forms of connection that make up the series.

It is crucial that when contesting this form Miriam specifically refuses it as "the form of a slave." Critics have long been conscious of the element of class in Richardson's gender critique—both its conscious analysis of classism and its unconscious repetitions of it. There is perhaps no better text to represent the inequity within the middle class along the faultline of gender: Miriam's numbed fingers, her daily gnawing hunger, palpably demonstrate the price women pay for independence from men. Although Miriam for a time (as teacher and governess) explicitly trades on the cultural capital she has inherited from her middle-class background, that still never buys her out of want and privation. Although Richardson out of her own class bias wishes to refuse Miriam's connection to the working class, she cannot help but demonstrate it through her poverty. Yet one thing modern critics have overlooked in *Pilgrimage*—overlooked specifically in their attempt to make sense of the role of gender in Miriam's coming to identity in the complicated scene in which she explicitly rejects feminism—is the role of race within it too. Miriam breaks with her lover, Shatov, and her past at this moment by coming to a radical gender consciousness that she insists nonetheless on calling antifeminist. Yet what she thinks enables her epiphany are "the blind unconscious outlines" of "the presence of a negro" (*Deadlock*, 12.219, 217) sitting at the back of the restaurant in which she stages this drama:

> He sat near by, huge, bent, snorting and devouring, with a huge black bottle at his side. Mr. Shatov's [Jewish] presence was shorn of its alien quality. He was an Englishman in the fact that he and she could *not* sit eating in the neighbourhood of this marshy jungle. But they were, they had. They would have. Once away from this awful place she would never think of it again. Yet the man had hands and needs and feelings. Perhaps he could sing. He was at a disadvantage an outcast. There was something that ought to be said to him. She could not think what it was. In his oppressive presence it was impossible to think at all. Every time she sipped her bitter tea, it seemed that before she should have replaced her cup, vengeance would have sprung from the dark corner. . . . There was no *time* to shake off the sense of contamination. It *was* contamination. The man's presence was an outrage on something of which he was not aware. It would be possible to make him aware. (*Deadlock*, 12.217)

Miriam's coming to consciousness of her own gender politics is an attempt to deny her connection to this man—unlike "negroes," she argues, (white) women have never been enslaved—to make him aware of what she thinks he outrages, and to ward off his vengeance. His presence enables the articulation of her political identity; she becomes aware of that identity by countering it against him and against feminism. Richardson makes his presence that threat to the self around which it forms. In Woolf's writing too, gender identity, in its attempt to break with the very series it actually continues, relies on the scapegoating of class—a well-recognized but still highly contested issue in Woolf criticism—but also of race, a less discussed but crucial element in her work.

Those are the elements in Woolf's work that I will examine in this chapter. But I don't want to consider Woolf's classism and racism in order to single her out in a way that makes my own position seem somehow free of those internalized cultural attitudes. What I want to do is analyze her work in order to make a point about the impossibility of just such political maneuvering—the impossibility of political purity. Woolf's handling of the paradoxes of the series and the everyday—especially her continued use of a form like the series with which she wants to break—demonstrates the political utility of foregrounding an important law of the unconscious: our replication of the behaviors and patterns we most desperately deny (perhaps one compulsion behind the repetitions of the series form). In this respect, our work of analysis (like the self that has internalized—been produced by— such structures) must remain "unbegun and unfinished," as Woolf writes of Richardson's heroine in *Pilgrimage*.[15]

Character has always been a central issue in Virginia Woolf's fiction, but precisely because, to her contemporary critics, it seemed so *absent* from her novels (in Richardson, character is central because of her obsessive focus on Miriam). Current poststructuralist critics see that absence as exemplary of postmodern, decentered identity, but critics of the time claimed such a model of the self was unreadable. Arnold Bennett complained that Woolf simply couldn't create character.[16] Thinking about Bennett's charge, Woolf wrote in her diary "My answer is—but . . . it's only the old argument that character is dissipated into shreds now."[17] Yet Woolf's contention "that we're splinters

---

[15] "The Tunnel," 10.

[16] A remark that inaugurated a curious obsession between Bennett and Woolf and sparked Woolf's manifesto as a writer, known variously as "Character in Fiction" or "Mr. Bennett and Mrs. Brown." See Samuel Hynes, "The Whole Contention between Mr. Bennett and Mrs. Woolf," in his *Edwardian Occasions: Essays on English Writing in the Early Twentieth Century* (New York: Oxford, 1972), 24–38; Edward L. Bishop suggests that Bennett was willfully blind to Woolf's model of the subject because he didn't want to admit all it implied: "Arnold Bennett felt that characters need to 'clash' with one another and complained that the younger generation is 'so busy with states of society as to half forget that any society consists of individuals.' . . . Bennett *has* seen what is there, he just doesn't want to; [Woolf's work] is about society and the individual's relationship to it, about ideology, in Althusser's sense of the word": "The Subject in *Jacob's Room*," *Modern Fiction Studies* 38 (1992): 147–75; 153.

[17] "Tuesday 19 June 1923," *The Diary of Virginia Woolf*, vol. 2, 1920–1924, ed. Anne Olivier Bell (New York: Harcourt Brace, 1978), 248.

& mosaics, not, as they used to hold, immaculate, monolithic, consistent wholes" has by no means had an easy or untroubled critical reception.[18] A critic of modernism such as George Lukács, for instance, would argue that such a definition of the self reveals not just a problem with character but everything wrong with the very ideology of modernism itself.

For Lukács, the problem with modernism has to do with the defining importance of form within it. Even when modernism and earlier nineteenth-century realism employ the same formal techniques, Lukács notes a crucial difference: in modernism, "technique . . . is absolute," he argues, while, in the best earlier narrative form, style "is rooted in content."[19] That content provides "a carefully plotted sequence" that reveals a larger "pattern of the whole" ("Ideology," 18). According to this schema, Walter Scott's use of the series would involve for Lukács a narrative pattern that is properly "dynamic and developmental" ("Ideology," 19); modernism, on the other hand, is "aimless and directionless" (18).

For Lukács, the void of modernism's form is revealed through the hollowness of its characters. Modernism's desperate injunction to "only connect!" Lukács implies comes from its inability to integrate its subjects within themselves or with each other.[20] For Lukács, the breakdown of stable and consistent personality marks the breakdown of a stable and consistent world into a degraded seriality: "Attenuation of reality and dissolution of personality are thus interdependent: the stronger the one, the stronger the other. Underlying both is the lack of a consistent view of human nature. Man is reduced to a sequence of unrelated experiential fragments. . . . In Eliot's *Cocktail Party*, the psychiatrist . . . describes the phenomenon: 'Ah, but we die to each other daily. . . .'" ("Ideology," 26). No longer seen as a product of a social context or collective, "man as animal," rather than "man as social being . . . leads straight to a glorification of the abnormal and to an undisguised

---

[18] "Monday 15 September 1924," in Woolf, *Diary*, 2: 314.

[19] See George Lukács, "The Ideology of Modernism," in his *Meaning of Contemporary Realism*, trans. John Mander and Necke Mander (London: Merlin Press, 1963), 17–46; 18, 19; all future references to this text (abbreviated "Ideology") will appear in the text.

[20] Compared to realism, which he argues locates its subjects within their social world, Lukács writes, "The ontological view governing the image of man in the work of leading modernist writers is the exact opposite of this. Man, for these writers, is by nature solitary, asocial, unable to enter into relationships with other human beings" (ibid., 20). Modernism's notions of the problems of identity makes for a focus on individuality per se that obscures man's (supposedly true) place as social animal within the social totality, a place realism instead (according to Lukács) properly captures, as it focuses on the "unity of the world . . . a living whole inseparable from man himself" (39). What bothers Lukács about the fractures of modernism is what he calls "an ideological problem, deriving from the ontological dogma of the solitariness of man" (30) (the implication is that realism in comparison reflects not ideology but scientific truth): what bothers Lukács about modernism is that "man is constitutionally unable to establish relationships with things or persons outside himself; but also that it is impossible to determine theoretically the origin and goal of human existence" (20–21)—that is, that once you begin to question the assumptions of the social "totality," you must also start to question the assumptions of (his kind of) Marxism, the theory that purports to give a total picture of "the origin and goal of human existence" (21).

anti-humanism" (32), Lukács argues. And Lukács is absolutely clear about where he wants to locate such madness—"we die to each other daily" because we situate our selves in the series and the everyday—in the sequence of unrelated experiential fragments of everyday life rather than in the abstract social totality theorized by Marxism. Modernism's view of identity creates what Lukács sees as a kind of psychopathology, an abnormality that Freud rightly locates, he thinks, in the "dreariness" of everyday life "under capitalism" (29).[21] The theory of the subject's dissolution provides it with an "incognito" which divorces being from deeds and which, Lukács insists, quite directly leads to fascism (27), which, he implies, as have other critics after him, is a direct outgrowth of the banality of modern everyday life.[22]

But what happens when we consider the split, decentered subject presented in Woolf's work in its relation to the series and the everyday and *also* in relation to what Lukács calls the resulting "incognito"? This model of the subject also has poststructural theorists, and they are less disparaging of it: Jacques Lacan gets his notion of ego identity as a kind of prosthesis we strap on around a lack in part from a contemporary of Woolf's and a member of her circle, Joan Riviere, in her classic psychoanalytic essay "Womanliness as Masquerade."[23] For Lukács, the "incognito" is a false alter ego obscuring

[21] He thinks Freud goes wrong, however, in tracing any connection between such psychopathology and what Lukács sees as truly normal life (ibid., 30). Lukács's insistence on "morbidity" as a special condition resulting from a distorted social context and not a dynamic inherent in or constitutive of subjectivity per se suggests one reason for the mutual preoccupation linking Bennett and Woolf. For Lukács, unlike realism, both naturalism *and* modernism have a morbid fascination with everyday life—or at least with the morbidity that defines the character of the everyday under capitalism—as well as a bankrupt serial connection. For Lukács, oppositions like Bennett's and Woolf's are just two sides of the same coin, simply different expressions of capitalism's same old currency (29, 43). Although I would agree that, however much they deny it, naturalism and modernism are linked, and linked in seeing subjectivity as a kind of pathology, the Lacanian-influenced model of identity I will be tracing through Woolf in this chapter assumes that such pathology cannot simply be shed to reveal some essential normal self beneath. It is inscribed within subjectivity and ensures its insoluble contradictions; we put it on when we put on selfhood (a topic obviously of great interest to a writer like Woolf, intermittently defined as mad). Freud's recognition that the normal and the pathological are themselves two sides of the same coin seems crucial in exposing wishful fantasies of some pure ground outside this currency. Whether or not it is our social conditions that determine such inescapably conflicted identity (and I'm willing to believe they have a great deal to do with it, which is why we work to change them, even though we do so on faith), analysis of those conditions (scientific Marxism) is in no way escape from them, just as bringing some things to consciousness doesn't banish the effects of the unconscious. These are questions of faith, not science (hence, I think, the Christian teleology still underlying most Marxism, even as it denies it)—and even the heavens or utopias we try to imagine, including Marxist ones, are constructed with the tools and modes of thought of the system that has created us—that is, they too are still within its constraints.

[22] See Lukács, "The Metaphysics of Tragedy," in his *Soul and Form*, trans. Anna Bostock (Cambridge: MIT Press, 1974), 152–74, for more on everyday life. For the connection between everyday life and fascism, see also Alice Yaeger Kaplan, *Reproductions of Banality: Fascism, Literature, and French Intellectual Life* (Minneapolis: University of Minnesota Press, 1986).

[23] According to Lacan, during the mirror stage, the imago in the mirror manufactures for the subject an "orthopaedic" fantasy of its own totality (i.e., manufactures the fantasy of the subject itself), an image of self-sufficiency and self-completeness it will always try and never be able

the true self; for Lacan, the "masquerade" is all the self there is. Yet I'm intrigued by Lukács's reference to this version of identity (even though I disagree with his valorization of a prior, unified, undissociated self). I find useful his recognition that identity as disguise, masquerade, identity as the incognito, is inextricably tied to the political realm. It seems to me, however, that Woolf's model of the self and its placement in the series and the everyday redefines the political and makes much more complex some questions about it that Lukács—and critics today—still take for granted.

Woolf, as much as Lukács, is a pointed and resolute critic of fascism; as Woolf scholars know, *Three Guineas* and *Between the Acts* were written directly in response to it. The contradictions and artificiality of the self seem meant in her work not as the precondition for fascism but the refusal of it. Unlike Lukács, she is reluctant confidently to offer another kind of social totality as a buttress against fascism's totalitarianism. And this may be precisely because she suspects the limits of her own refusal of the total, suspects that even in its most frenzied of contradictions, identity is as much haunted by the specter of a baleful politics as it is in the smug assumption of its "immaculate, monolithic, consistent" universality. I say "may be" here because I am actually not sure just how much Woolf's work is in control of all this—the argument I venture in this chapter comes as much from that work's seemingly unconscious performance as it does from the careful analysis undertaken in it. But in saying that Woolf is not exempt from implication in a system even when she quite explicitly critiques it herself, I recognize that that insight is, in fact, part of Woolf's own redefinition of politics that makes politics so complicated.

In following up the political ramifications of seeing identity as a disguise that we put on, I also want to follow up Lukács's other notions: the dangerous effects of the dissolution of identity on the social organism, which I will consider in Woolf's treatment of class, and the destructiveness implicit in the notion of man as animal, which I see exposed in Woolf's treatment of race. While considering these issues in light of the politics of the series and the everyday, Woolf's work still shifts Lukács's terms and comes to different conclusions. The most radical difference may be that Woolf's work remains contradictory, ambivalent, and forces us directly to engage with that ambivalence (including our own as critics) as part of the political.

---

to match, hence "the assumption of the armour of an alienating identity, which will mark with its rigid structure the subject's entire mental development"; see Jacques Lacan, "The Mirror Stage," in his *Ecrits: A Selection*, trans. Alan Sheridan (New York: Norton, 1977), 1–7; 4. For his discussion of women in particular in relation to masking and masquerade, see "The Signification of the Phallus," *Ecrits*, 281–91; 290, or "The Meaning of the Phallus," in *Feminine Sexuality: Jacques Lacan and the école freudienne*, ed. Juliet Mitchell and Jacqueline Rose, trans. Jacqueline Rose (New York: Norton, 1982), 74–85; 84. Joan Riviere's "Womanliness as Masquerade" was originally published in *The International Journal of Psychoanalysis* 10 (1929): 303–13; it has been republished in *Formations of Fantasy*, ed. Victor Burgin, James Donald, and Cora Kaplan (London: Methuen, 1986), 35–44.

In considering these kinds of politics in Woolf's work one has to consider the ways that Woolf herself provides an incognito; Woolf's image itself has become a mask behind which group different political interests.[24] In this response to Woolf, which waves her as the standard authorizing *them*, opposed approaches—materialist critics of Woolf and poststructuralist apologists—are actually more similar than we think. For Lukács, part of what gives modernism its false view of identity is its very emphasis *on* identity, on the individual in and of itself; modernism's pathos about the individual's isolation simply reflects its bourgeois position within class relations. Yet materialist critics (Queenie Leavis, Mary Childers) still single out Virginia Woolf as somehow *individually* responsible for such attitudes in her work, rather than locating them in the very structures and tradition that formed that work. By stabilizing Woolf as a sovereign individual, they lose what is arguably Marxism's strongest force, its large-scale structural critique. At the same time, poststructuralist feminists wind up stabilizing Woolf too. In her well-known attention to Woolf as the symbol of poststructuralism, Toril Moi directly critiques the ideological assumptions underlying Lukács's notion of identity. His emphasis on "the totality of human life" and "the complete human personality," Moi argues, is "part of patriarchal ideology. At its centre is the seemingly unified self—either individual or collective—which is commonly called 'Man.' . . . this integrated self is in fact a phallic self, constructed on the model of the self-contained, powerful phallus. Gloriously autonomous, it banishes from itself all conflict, contradiction and ambiguity."[25] Yet in her own attempts to emphasize "the radically deconstructed character of Woolf's

[24] In part, that image exemplifies the commodification and reproduction of contemporary consumer culture that put easy politics into question. Referring to the ubiquitous pictures of Woolf herself (on T-shirts, graphics, posters) currently associated with everything from various kinds of feminism to the highbrow reviews that still scout at feminists, Brenda Silver writes: "Woolf, it is clear, sells, and not just to one audience"—to audiences, in fact, at political odds with each other: "What's Woolf Got to Do with It? or, The Perils of Popularity," *Modern Fiction Studies* 38 (1992): 21–60; 22. Feminist critics from various and often opposed positions (Rachel Bowlby, Mary Childers, indeed almost any feminist critic who has written on Woolf recently) all argue that she has become an icon for something else; discussions of her work really code "the shape and direction of literary history itself" or of literary theory—or whatever (Bette London, "Guerrilla in Petticoats or Sans-Culotte? Virginia Woolf and the Future of Feminist Criticism," *diacritics* 21 [1991]: 11–29; 12). But Woolf's own treatment of identity as masquerade suggests that it is a mistake to try to locate some true identity, some prior essence, behind the disguise, rather than to question how that representation functions, what it serves. Woolf as icon points to a political dynamic within contemporary criticism. In an apotropaic gesture, she becomes elevated as a celebrity just as critics began to examine the implications of the breakdown of identity in her work. In a rebound against one implication of politics of identity were we to consider identity's breakdown—that the self is significant not as an essence, but as a construction, the site of the play of larger determining forces—identity politics gets redefined into its more familiar and insidious form: the self remains central, causal, the supposed author of experience rather than the product of it. Virginia Woolf tautologically becomes an exemplary identity precisely because she is defined as a celebrity, cast as outside of everyday concerns and larger forces: unique, individual, so little a part of the world that she can choose to leave it through suicide.

[25] Moi, *Sexual/Textual Politics: Feminist Literary Theory* (New York: Methuen, 1985), 5, 8.

texts," Moi, like other poststructuralist feminists after her (Rachel Bowlby, Bette London) loses sight too of the conflict, contradiction, and ambiguity of that work. Her celebration of Woolf as a "progressive, feminist writer of genius" makes Woolf a bit too positive, recuperates her as a political revolutionary on the level of representation—a position not so different from that assigned by her detractors, in that it maintains the illusion of a pure politics.[26] The Woolf encoded in her own writings, however, refuses to be either feminism's heroine or (notwithstanding the ugly classism and racism expressed there) its scapegoat. This is the perspective offered in that writing, at any rate, when Woolf tries herself to see fellow writers not with "the arrogance of a judge" but with "the more valuable insight of a fellow sinner."[27]

The manipulation of Woolf's own image brings into focus the way the politics of unified identity are always in hidden service to some larger theory or system, which obscures its own self-interest precisely by manufacturing an image of the self as free and autonomous, outside of its control. And such a model of identity relies on the categories of the series and the everyday. The appeal identity politics makes to lived experience—to the "daily"—especially attempts to shore up the supposed transparency and authority of the self by grounding it in an everyday it offers as "a prediscursive, direct, and unmediated apprehension of social truth."[28] In order to redefine the model of the self, then, Woolf's work also needs to redefine the category of the everyday. And her dispute with Arnold Bennett over character rested precisely in recasting the everyday; she recognized her task was to transform Bennett's understanding of that category with her own: "I mean how give ordinary waking Arnold Bennett life the form of art?" she asks.[29] When Woolf exhorts her readers to "examine for a moment an ordinary mind on an ordinary day" in "Modern Fiction," she meant specifically to question how what she called "materialists" like Bennett had impoverished the representation of the material world, not to dispense with it. This famous passage goes on to make an implicit connection between the everyday and identity: "Life is not a series of gig-lamps symmetrically arranged; life is a luminous halo, a semi-transparent envelope surrounding us from the beginning of consciousness to

[26] Ibid., 18. It isn't that Moi lets Woolf off from criticism, but she does let her own deconstructive method off from it, so that the Woolf she finally remakes in its image—Woolf the radical deconstructor—becomes almost politically flawless, reflecting back Moi's (wish for her) method's completeness (even though the point of that method is to undermine supposed completeness). Bowlby and London are more aware of this problem. Bowlby seems to me to do the most subtle and sophisticated job of understanding and working within this complexity: *Virginia Woolf: Feminist Destinations* (New York: Basil Blackwell, 1988).

[27] Virginia Woolf, "A Positivist," in *Essays*, 3: 64–67; 65.

[28] The connection of identity politics and the daily is in Diana Fuss, "Essentialism in the Classroom," in her *Essentially Speaking* (New York: Routledge, 1989), 113–19; 113. The second phrase is from Joan Scott, "Multiculturalism and the Politics of Identity," *October* 61 (1992): 12–19; 17.

[29] "Wednesday 31 May 1933," in *The Diary of Virginia Woolf*, vol. 4, 1931–35, ed. Anne Olivier Bell (New York: Harcourt Brace Jovanovich, 1982), 161.

the end."[30] Ordinary life reveals to us that consciousness takes place within a kind of envelope; in everyday life, we take up, we conduct, our identity as a kind of screen or mask.

The implicit connection between identity and the everyday relies on the refusal of another connection: life is *not* a series of gig-lamps symmetrically arranged. The notion of series as inevitable progression is a model of genealogy—and a particular genealogy for herself—that Woolf refuses along with what she sees as male notions of history. Woolf associates specific series—*Tom Brown's School Days* and "that long line of red backs" that made up the Waverly Novels—with memories of her father.[31] In Woolf's own self-construction, his death seems meant to free her from the trap of such lines; if, as she tells us in *A Room of One's Own*, "a woman writing thinks back through her mothers," those connections imply not a line but the luminous amniotic halo; identity becomes something that we shouldn't think of as a stream but (as Richardson suggests) a deep pool.[32] This may be the understanding that organizes Woolf's depiction of Mrs. Dalloway, which prompted her to write of that novel that "I think the design is more remarkable than in any of my books."[33] What might be remarkable is the way Clarissa Dalloway as a character gestures both backward (to *The Voyage Out*) and onward—to the series of stories about her party that Woolf had yet to write, and about which their editor claims: "It is particularly uncharacteristic of Virginia Woolf's normal writing habits that she should have allowed her completed novel's central concern to retain the hold on her imagination that it obviously then had. . . . usually when she had finally revised a novel, Virginia Woolf was only too anxious . . . to shut it out of her mind."[34] Mrs. Dalloway's haunting presence in Woolf's work suggests a notion of series as immanence and not as development, a thinking through a maternal envelope that continues to surround us and give us life.

But this passage suggests more as well: it gives us the political outlines of Woolf's definition of the series and the everyday. That the consciousness in-

[30] Virginia Woolf, "Modern Fiction," *Collected Essays*, 2: 103–10; 106. For her reference to such writers as materialists, see p. 104.

[31] In "Impressions of Sir Leslie Stephen," she writes: "I cannot remember any book before *Tom Brown's School Days* and *Treasure Island*; but it must have been very soon that we attacked the first of that long line of red backs—the thirty-two volumes of the Waverly Novels, which provided reading for many years of evenings, because when we had finished the last he was ready to begin the first over again": *The Essays of Virginia Woolf*, vol. 1, 1904–1912, ed. Andrew McNeillie (New York: Harcourt, 1986), 127–30; 127–28.

[32] Virginia Woolf, *A Room of One's Own* (New York: Harcourt, 1989), 97; all future references to this book (abbreviated *Room*) will appear in the text. Richardson's preference for consciousness as a deep pool is quoted in Vincent Brome, "A Last Meeting with Dorothy Richardson," *The London Magazine*, June 1959, 29; quoted in Lynette Felber, "A Manifesto for Feminine Modernism: Dorothy Richardson's *Pilgrimage*," in *Rereading Modernism: New Directions in Feminist Criticism*, ed. Lisa Rado (New York: Garland, 1994), 24–39; 25.

[33] "Monday 15 October 1923," *Diary*, 2: 272.

[34] Stella McNichol, "Introduction," to *Mrs. Dalloway's Party* (New York: Harcourt, 1975), 1–12; 10.

forming us as subjects is given its shape within these categories through gender is a crucial theme of Woolf's work. But encoded within *this* passage are racial and class aspects of the connection between identity and such determinants. Woolf, for instance, sets up the passage in her essay by declaring her notion of self and fiction an act of revolution, relying on what is at least in part a racial metaphor to support her case: "the accent falls differently from of old . . . so that, if a writer were a free man and not a slave . . . there would be no plot, no comedy, no tragedy, no love interest or catastrophe in the accepted style." [35] Class informs the passage too, for as one critic suggests, the symmetrical gig-lamps Woolf is criticizing there may conjure up for her the gatherings of the upper classes in Mayfair she attended unwillingly as a girl: "dinners and dances, . . . the evening appearance of a horse-drawn vehicle, or an oncoming line of them, . . . artificially lit and arranged." [36] Woolf, however subtly, associates her fiction with an attack on class elitism and implies that it will even burst the shackles of slavery.

As the moments of class elitism and racism in her own work will suggest, however, there is no pure ground, no authentic, unmediated everyday, in which Woolf can base the politics of that fiction. Part of what her fiction may offer instead is the recognition that the oppression of class and race, the everyday in which this is naturalized, and the series in which it is arranged are not authorized by some truth, but ideological, constructed. At the same time, however, so is the critique of this oppression, and the critique is constructed within the same social system that gives rise to the oppression in the first place, so that its distinction from it will always be to some degree partial, uncomfortably inhabited by it.

And perhaps this sense of equivocalness and complicity is what distinguishes Woolf's everyday from Lukács's. Lukács complains that "the disintegration of personality is matched by a disintegration of the outer world" ("Ideology," 25); as an outgrowth of the corrupt tendencies of capitalism, modernism has "emptied everyday life of meaning" (45). Many of Woolf's materialist critics make just this criticism of Woolf: her fiction ignores the everyday; she simply doesn't attend to the material world.[37] Yet Woolf's writing actually proclaims the connection of identity and the everyday: in her re-

[35] Woolf, "Modern Fiction," in *Collected Essays*, 2: 106.

[36] Tony Davenport, "The Life of Monday or Tuesday," in *Virginia Woolf: New Critical Essays*, ed. Patricia Clements and Isobel Grundy (Totowa, N.J.: Barnes & Noble, 1983), 157–75; 157. He also finds a hint of racism here, connecting these lines to "the slang sense of 'spectacles,' as used, for example, in answer to a question from Dr. Thorndyke about the appearance of one Schonberg: '"Like?" interrupted the resident. "He's like a blooming Sheeny with a carroty beard and gold giglamps"'" (in R. Austin Freeman's 1909 detective work, *The Moabite Cipher*) (157–58).

[37] See, for example, "[Personality] manifests itself to a great extent through externals— through the houses we live in and the clothes we wear and our life day to day with our intimates and with our acquaintance. Surely one of the 'essential principles' on which Dr. Johnson insists must be, that human existence is inexorably welded with the surroundings it lives with": Elizabeth A. Drew, "A Note on Technique," extracted in *Clarissa Dalloway*, ed. Harold Bloom (New York: Chelsea House, 1990), 12–16; 14.

sponse to Bennett, "Character in Fiction," for example, she states that an understanding of identity is so crucial that "every day questions arise which can only be solved by its help."[38] And one of Woolf's early critics suggests that, in a novel like *Mrs. Dalloway*, identity and the everyday are indissoluble: "In *Mrs. Dalloway* [the chief thing] is [the characters'] intimate daily life with all the things which make it up and have reference only to themselves, but which are nevertheless more certainly their being than their actions are."[39] Just as she redefines the series, Woolf doesn't take for granted the very *meaning* of the everyday life she is accused of ignoring; her materialist critics cannot recognize her interest in it, because for her (though not for them) that category doesn't have certain or stable meaning. Her writing is concerned instead with what one recent critic calls "the contradictory universes contained in the everyday world."[40]

The everyday is not, in Woolf's work, a ground that (under the proper economic system) would unify or integrate the self (as it would for Lukács—just as, for him, under capitalism it tears the self apart). For Lukács and for Henri Lefebvre, that popularizer of the concept in modern philosophy (whose *Everyday Life in the Modern World*, among his other texts, perhaps took its understanding from Lukács), the everyday is a perfect example of the Marxist dialectic, at one and the same time an impoverished category that contains its own transcendence, both the locus of capitalism's dreariness and the only site on which to revolutionize and change it. Yet Woolf's use of the term actually exposes the very paradoxical *modernism* of the category as it is formulated by these materialist critics of modernism and the modern world: while in their schema, the everyday is able to transcend the conditions that create it—it promises its own epiphany in the midst of confusions— Woolf's version of it finds in its contradictions no such recuperative or saving grace. In Woolf's work the everyday represents instead precisely that site where transcendence or integration is impossible. Erich Auerbach, in considering modernism (and Woolf in particular), rather than seeing the category of the everyday as what leads to fascism, as Lukács does, suggests instead that it is what escapes its domination: "It is precisely the random moment which is comparatively independent of the controversial and unstable orders over which men fight and despair; it passes unaffected by them, as daily life."[41] Like Lukács's view of the everyday which it supposedly coun-

---

[38] Virginia Woolf, "Character in Fiction," *Essays*, 3: 420–38; 421.

[39] Edwin Muir, "Virginia Woolf," *Nation and Athenaeum*, April 17, 1926, 70–72, excerpted in *Virginia Woolf: The Critical Heritage*, ed. Robin Majumdar and Allen McLauren (Boston: Routledge & Kegan Paul, 1975), 178–85; 184.

[40] Ann Marie Hebert, "What Does It Mean? How Do You Explain It All? Virginia Woolf: A Postmodern Modernist," in *Virginia Woolf Miscellanies*. Proceedings of the First Annual Convention on Virginia Woolf, Pace University, New York, June 7–9, 1991, ed. Mark Hussey and Vara Neverow-Turk (New York: Pace University Press, 1992), 10–19; 13.

[41] Auerbach, "The Brown Stocking," in his *Mimesis: The Representation of Reality in Western Literature*, trans. Willard R. Trask (Princeton: Princeton University Press, 1953), 525–53; 552.

ters, however, Auerbach's offers another illusion of it as a pure position. Woolf's everyday occupies neither one nor the other of these political poles, but calls into question the opposition between them. The contradictions of the everyday are unresolvable in Woolf's work, and operate like the remnant of the series that work also disavows while depending upon it. The alignment of the everyday and the series provides a useful site on which to examine not just the model of contradictory identity in Woolf's work but the construction of her own paradoxical political identity—a thoughtful and self-aware critic of class and empire who was also classist and racist in her own right— as a way of rethinking our definition of politics.

The Dalloways mark the trace or the recasting of the series impulse within Woolf's fiction, and Woolf herself, as well as her critics, felt Clarissa Dalloway to be her most contradictory heroine.[42] *Mrs. Dalloway* too has also been considered one of her most problematic political statements: "I want to criticise the social system," Woolf wrote about it in her diary, "& to show it at work, at its most intense—But here I may be posing."[43] This novel meant to be a social critique that focuses on a party suggests the most stereotypical responses to Woolf's politics: the materialist critique of its elitist content; the poststructuralist celebration of its ludic form. Woolf's own emphasis on the possibility of *posing*, however, offers another way to consider these politics. How does the notion of identity as a pose, a construction, a mask, negotiate these stereotypes, and reflect on the very notion of stereotype itself? Let me turn now to consider such questions in terms of the complicated politics of class and race in Woolf's work, drawing on critics who themselves attempt to negotiate between the supposedly radical divide of materialism and poststructuralism: Slavoj Žižek, Donna Haraway, Frantz Fanon, Homi Bhabha.

---

[42] Woolf found, for instance, that Lytton Strachey's criticism of Clarissa Dalloway echoed what had been her earlier despair about a discrepancy within the character: "What he says is that there is a discordancy between the ornament (extremely beautiful) & what happens (rather ordinary—or unimportant). This is caused he thinks by some discrepancy in Clarissa herself; he thinks she is disagreeable & limited, but that I alternately laugh at her, & cover her, very remarkably, with myself": "Thursday 18 June 1925," *Diary*, 3: 32. Both materialist and poststructuralist critics of Woolf agree. In an early analysis, Dorothy M. Hoare writes: "*Mrs. Dalloway* is not Virginia Woolf's highest accomplishment nor her most important work. The reason for this is that there is in it (unconsciously as far as the author is concerned) an unresolved contradiction in values": "Virginia Woolf," excerpted in Bloom, *Clarissa Dalloway*, 22–23; Blanche Gelphant locates this "inherent aesthetic proble[m] of the novel: that the middle-class Mrs. Dalloway does not seem an appropriate character to reflect and to reflect upon the theme of rebellion": "Love and Conversion in *Mrs. Dalloway*" (ibid., 86–98; 96–97). Makiko Minow-Pinckney sees the contradiction differently; Clarissa Dalloway " is a decentered subject of flows and part-objects, like Septimus, but she is also the cool, composed hostess of the evening party. . . . Women have to constitute themselves as split subjects in order to enter the symbolic and play a man's game": "The Problem of the Subject in *Mrs. Dalloway*" (ibid., 183–92; 191). For Rachel Bowlby, "Whereas Septimus Smith is the extreme 'case' of someone who has lost all contact with the external, common orders of daily life and daily time, Clarissa is questionably situated like St. Margaret's, neither within nor without" (Bowlby, *Virginia Woolf*, 92).

[43] "Tuesday 19 June 1923," *Diary*, 2: 248.

In examining the everyday to argue against the fixed position and pure ground of politics, especially identity politics, however, I also want to think about just what that critique entails. Although poststructural feminism has made the deconstructive breakdown of gender and sexuality a useful political tool, are there different stakes involved when we unsettle class and race? Woolf's *Orlando* is a classic literary expression of the breakdown of identity and gender: Orlando's move between genders and object choices is mirrored by a kaleidoscope of myriad and shifting identities; Woolf ends her novel, in fact, with Orlando calling upon a "great variety of selves"—"(of which there may be more than two thousand)" Woolf wryly tells us.[44] But she also singles out the first of those selves, the selves with whom she opens the novel: "the boy who cut the nigger's head down; the boy who strung it up again" (*Orlando*, 309).[45] The book's opening images of the young Orlando, slashing and slicing with his cutlass at the Moor's head hanging in his attic, suggests that the radical fragmentation and division within the category of race may be problematic, and involve a violent scapegoating that redounds on those subjects we identify with that category—suggested already by how comfortable Woolf is in her writing with calling such subjects "niggers." Making more fragments of what is already fragmented, cutting the Moor's head to pieces, inaugurates Orlando's own adventures in deconstructing, while bleeding off any threat to Orlando of the breakdown of his or her self. In a relative economy, Orlando retains some ground and privilege because they are denied to others. Whatever changes happen to it, Orlando's body remains intact (the preservation of that body over time, in fact, is as remarkable in this book as its sex change), reflecting that so, pretty much, does Orlando's economic and social position: because of that position, there is a place in the world for Orlando's complete imago, no matter how false that completeness may be, while the shrunken fragment that represents the Moor suggests that there is no subject position (however illusory) in this world at all for him—any Moors we meet in the rest of the text are shadowy figures whose stories remain more splintered than Orlando's—remain untold.[46]

[44] Virginia Woolf, *Orlando: A Biography* (New York: Harcourt, 1928), 309, 314; all future references to this text will appear in the body of the text.

[45] Jane Marcus writes: "*Orlando* writes the history of English literature based on a founding gesture of violence and conquest, Orlando slicing at the shrunken head of a Moor, the trophy of a violent British adventure against African blacks": "Britannia Rules *The Waves*," in *Decolonizing Tradition: New Views of Twentieth-Century "British" Literary Canons*, ed. Karen R. Lawrence (Urbana: University of Illinois Press, 1992), 136–62; 144. My reading of this novel sees Woolf participating in as well as analyzing such gestures.

[46] There is, for example, "the story of his adventure with a Moor in Venice of whom he bought (but only at sword's point) his lacquered cabinet, [which] might, in other hands, prove worth telling" (110), but the Moor's own story cannot be articulated in this novel or this economy. As this passage suggests, all the allusions to Moors in this novel are also allusions to *Othello*; Woolf makes that explicit when she has Orlando unknowingly watch Shakespeare's play (56–57). The Moor in that scene may be completely enough constituted to act and move about on the stage, however, because Orlando for a moment identifies with him and gives him shape. He notices the play only because it seems so like his own experience: "The frenzy of the Moor

While the refusal by many antiracist theorists of a poststructuralist notion of identity—in "The Race for Theory," Barbara Christian articulates a common objection: why does the self break down just when members of oppressed minorities begin to assume it?—does retain the illusion of essential identity often at odds with those very theorists' recognition of the way ideology and economics determine subject position, poststructuralism itself, it seems to me, isn't exempt from a similar critique.[47] For in refusing to consider how its method at one and the same time may do material violence, even as it strives to create a more flexible politics, poststructuralism seems at odds with its own recognition of our implication within the insoluble contradictions of the systems we analyze. In the sections that follow, I try to keep sight of such contradictions as I analyze them in Woolf's treatment of class and race.

꽃

The poststructural insistence on identity as masquerade is meant to counter its understanding as innate, prediscursive, essential. Identity is seen instead to be a position taken up within a system, one that determines experience materially and ideologically, rather than vice versa. What is perhaps most ideological about identity formation is that this process is largely unconscious: experience becomes identical with an everyday life we take for granted and assume as the locus of the real. As subjects, we act as if our experience is natural, if not universal, rather than itself the production of the various gender, class, and racial structures—among others—that form us. But, for a theorist like Lacan, the notion of identity as masquerade means more than this counterintuitive critique of experience as a real presence and a true ground, more than the understanding of identity as construction. It also lays bare the paradox at the heart of that construction: that its very lack of essence is what gives it form. Lacan borrows this paradox from Joan Riviere's "Womanliness as Masquerade," in which she appeals to everyday experience to define femininity as a kind of impersonation adopted by women to obscure their adeptness at supposedly masculine behaviors: "Womanliness therefore could be assumed and worn as a mask, both to hide the pos-

---

seemed to him his own frenzy" (57) (all this is related, of course, to Woolf's own identification and rivalry with Shakespeare as a writer, and if I had time I might want to compare the dead Moor's head with the dead Judith Shakespeare, who seems, however, to be able to take up her whole body when she returns as the living dead from her grave at the crossroads to stalk the end of *A Room of One's Own*). Woolf makes clear that the rent and fractured Moor is in fact meant to be important not in itself but as a symbol for Orlando's own split self: "Orlando was strangely compounded of many humours—of melancholy, of indolence, of passion, of love of solitude, to say nothing of all those contortions and subtleties of temper which were indicated on the first page, when he slashed at the dead nigger's head; cut it down; hung it chivalrously out of his reach again" (73).

[47] Barbara Christian, "The Race for Theory," *Feminist Studies* 14 (1988): 67–79; especially 71–72.

session of masculinity and to avert the reprisals if she was found to possess it. . . . The reader may now ask how I define womanliness or where I draw the line between genuine womanliness and the 'masquerade.' My suggestion is not, however, that there is any such difference: whether radical or superficial, they are the same thing." [48] Lacan picks up the notion that we are not to expect to find true (sexual) identity hidden behind some mask; called into being by its very nonexistence, identity *is* the masquerade, constituted by the very gap or absence that calls it into question. When Riviere goes on to suggest that "in everyday life one may observe the mask of femininity taking curious forms" the effect is in part to defamiliarize the everyday, to make curious that site we take for granted in naturalizing full and essential identity, to see it too as the form that *is* identity.[49]

The notion of masquerade in the psychoanalytic work of Riviere and Lacan—and in a host of critics who used that work as a basis, including Stephen Heath, Mary Anne Doane, and Judith Butler—has been useful in calling into question the hidden assumptions of gender and sexuality encoded into our understanding of everyday experience. Such an analysis is often considered at odds with a materialist or class critique: Diana Fuss, for instance, criticizes "the tendency to psychologize and to personalize questions of oppression *at the expense of* strong materialist analyses of the structural and institutional bases of exploitation." [50] Yet the notion of identity as an empty mask is not at all new to an economic analysis. Marx, for instance, sees identity under capitalism as the outgrowth of class relations: labor *produces* the worker as a commodity; the proletariat, estranged from their species being, take their identity solely from their (estranged) labor, which stamps on their tortured bodies its own visage.[51] "The capitalist" too, Marx writes, "is merely capital personified and functions in the process of production solely as the agent of capital." [52] Lukács's criticism that form is all there is in modernism overlooks the way Marx too emphasizes the primacy of form. Marx may seem to imply some natural, essential identity beyond capitalism, one undistorted by its obscenities, but it is too simple to suggest that everyday experience for him can ever exist outside of determining structures. There is no unmediated experience; people's very *senses*, he writes, are "theoreticians." [53] They perceive everyday reality itself according to the structures of thought implicit in the economic system that forms the subject. Subjects will literally see, hear, touch differently—will be different subjects, ones whose identities

---

[48] Riviere, "Womanliness as Masquerade," *Formations of Fantasy*, 38.

[49] Ibid., 39.

[50] Fuss, "Essentialism in the Classroom," 117. Fuss isn't indicting psychoanalysis per se here so much as some of the worst excesses of identity politics, but her critique borrows from conventional wisdom that places the psychological and material in radical opposition.

[51] Karl Marx, "Economic and Philosophic Manuscripts of 1844," in *The Marx-Engels Reader*, ed. Robert C. Tucker (New York: Norton, 1978), 66–125; 70–74.

[52] Karl Marx, *Capital*, vol. 3, in ibid., 439–42; 440.

[53] Marx, "Economic and Philosophic Manuscripts," in ibid., 87.

are no longer seen to be "essential," individual, but *social*, created by the aggregate—after the "transcendence of private property" than they do under capitalism, but only because they will do so not naturally but according to a new set of rules, a new (and for Marx a much better) determining structure.[54] In fact, what Slavoj Žižek calls "the 'religion of everyday life'" that Marx wishes to explode refers to people's tendency to act as if the everyday objects and things they experience are expressions of some universal or ideal outside economic relations, rather than the products of the social system.[55]

Žižek, in fact, directly connects Marx and Lacan around the issue of masquerade: Marx's analysis of the commodity form, according to Žižek, anticipates, among other things, Lacan's mirror stage and the breakdown of "the transcendental subject."[56] For Žižek, Marx emphasizes, as does Lacan, the way the subject is identical to its lack, its empty form: *"the failure of its representation is its positive condition,"* he writes (*Sublime*, 175). Positing identity as a kind of incognito or masquerade points not to some essential reality behind it but to the ways it is constituted by the very breaches and failures of the system that gives it meaning; they are productive. For this reason, Žižek warns, "we must avoid the simple metaphors of demasking, of throwing away the veils which are supposed to hide the naked reality" (28–29). In Žižek's reading of him, what Marx teaches is that political structure grows out of no essential content, no a priori reality, but *establishes* that reality through its workings. Žižek connects Marx and Lacan because Lacan credits Marx with the notion of the symptom, when symptoms are defined as "meaningless traces; their meaning is not discovered, excavated from the hidden depth of the past, but constructed retroactively—the analysis produces the truth; that is, the signifying frame which gives the symptoms their symbolic place and meaning" (56). Such a circular and self-perpetuating dynamic explains why subjects cannot refute ideological illusion—the artificiality of the signifying system—with supposedly actual everyday reality that seems to contradict it; on the contrary, Žižek argues, ideology instead "determin[es] the mode of our everyday experience of reality itself" (49), so much so that we learn to say of those others who don't conform to our stereotypical notions of their identity: "You see how dangerous they really are? It is difficult to recognize their real nature. They hide it behind the mask of everyday appearance" (49).

And in making this argument, Žižek connects the traces of lack with the series impulse. He quotes Jacques-Alain Miller, who writes that "in every structure there is a lure, a place-holder of the lack, comprised by what is per-

[54] Ibid., 87–89.
[55] Žižek, *The Sublime Object of Ideology* (New York: Verso, 1989), 32; all future references to this book (abbreviated *Sublime*) will appear in the text.
[56] Ibid., 24, 17. Žižek writes that Marx's analysis "presents us with a pure—distilled, so to speak—version of a mechanism offering us a key to the theoretical understanding of phenomena which, at first sight, have nothing whatsoever to do with the field of political economy" (16).

ceived, but at the same time the weakest link in a given series. . . . This element is *irrational* in reality, and by being included in it, it indicates the place of lack in it." [57] Thought of in these terms, the series simply plays out more obviously a tendency within all narrative: it is compelled to repeat by its inability ever to represent that which must be excluded from representation and yet is constitutive of it.

In this schema, the weakest link in the given series that makes up Virginia Woolf's modernism is the series itself. The lack constituting identity, which makes up Woolf's representations of character, corresponds to the irrationality of the series in her fiction—fiction which refuses but nonetheless preserves the vestige of that supposedly outdated form. Clarissa Dalloway in particular figures the irrational element in Woolf's treatment of form that lays bare the collapse of its seeming integrity (as "modernist fiction," for instance); the unconscious of Woolf's text cannot lay her to rest. She is the living dead stalking across Woolf's work (like Judith Shakespeare in *A Room of One's Own*), the specter whose shadow connects those unwilling texts into the pattern of the series they wish to reject as over and done with, as past: "The return of the dead signifies that they cannot find their proper place in the text of tradition," Žižek writes (*Looking*, 23). Such specters will continue to haunt us, he suggests, "until we give them a decent burial, until we integrate the trauma of their death into our historical memory" (23). To some degree the very breakdown of identity in Woolf's work necessitates the living on too long of characters like the Dalloways. The traces of the serial impulse are carried by such undead in Woolf's work because she has been unable to rewrite the literary and cultural history which determines her relations to (supposedly, retroactively) past forms. The classism and racism clustering around such figures as the Dalloways operate as expressions of the (denial of) this wound, the obsessive and doomed attempts to refuse the "unpaid symbolic debt" of culture that Žižek also locates in anti-Semitism and genocide (23).[58]

The everyday as much as the series is the site on which this trauma is denied and perpetuated. Although Virginia Woolf's materialist critics had difficulty in recognizing in her work any reference to the everyday at all, Woolf

---

[57] Slavoj Žižek, *Looking Awry: An Introduction to Jacques Lacan through Popular Culture* (Cambridge: MIT Press, 1992), 53; all future references to this book (abbreviated *Looking*) will appear in the text. Žižek explains: "The basic presupposition of psychoanalytic interpretation, its methodological a priori, is, however, that every final product of the dream work, every manifest dream content, contains *at least one* ingredient that functions as a stopgap, as a filler holding the place of what is necessarily *lacking* in it. This is an element that at first sight fits perfectly into the organic whole of the manifest imaginary scene, but which effectively holds within it the place of what this imaginary scene must 'repress,' exclude, force out, in order to constitute itself" (52).

[58] To read the Dalloways as the undead isn't as excessive as it might seem; at any rate, J. Hillis Miller has already made a move in that direction in his essay "*Mrs. Dalloway*: Repetition as the Raising of the Dead," in Bloom, *Clarissa Dalloway*, 169–90.

used the category of the everyday precisely to consider the construction of identity in relation to class, as a function of the economic. Woolf's contemporary critics—Queenie Leavis, Frank Swinnerton, even Arnold Bennett, who called her "the queen of the highbrows" [59]—proclaimed Woolf's elitism by denying any interest she had in the everyday. R. D. Charques speaks for this view in arguing that Woolf "skims as lightly as a bird—as lightly as Clarissa Dalloway with her touch of the jay about her—over the ordinary preoccupations of men and women. . . . There is no place in [Woolf's "serene and lovely" novels] for commonplace reality, for the crude strife of material desires, for the harshness and bitterness of class struggle. . . . When all praises have been sung, Mrs. Woolf's art remains the art of a governing class in English society." [60] Even Elaine Showalter, who might quarrel with Charques's gender assumptions about Woolf's fragility and grace, continues Leavis's attack on Woolf's elitism to argue that she "was cut off from an understanding of the day-to-day life of the women whom she wished to inspire" (294).

Yet dailiness is a formal as well as a thematic feature of Woolf's fiction, for like Joyce she organizes the events of her fiction around the events of one day. She does this not just once, however, but several times: *Mrs. Dalloway* is her most celebrated attempt, but *Between the Acts* too takes place on a single day, and it continues, as do the opening sections of *The Waves*, the attempt to connect that structure symbolically to individual life and the sweep of human history. The suggestion in these works is that the importance of identity and history lies in dailiness, not transcendence, but that we cannot by its very nature signify this: "Indeed," Woolf writes, "most of life escapes, now I come to think of it: the texture of an ordinary day." [61] She emphasized such dailiness from the beginning of her career: "As a painter," she wrote to her sister very early on, "I believe you are much less conscious of the drone of daily life than I am, as a writer." [62] It is the handling of the everyday that she thinks distinguishes the novel, and the best novelists; it captures for her what she defines as the most important part of writing, character, identity. Throughout her career she praises Jane Austen for her ability "to bring before us one of those perfectly normal and simple incidents of average human life," noting with approval Macaulay's claim that Austen "has given us a multitude of characters, all, in a certain sense, commonplace, all such as we meet every day." [63] Similarly, of Henry James she writes: "It needs the skill of

[59] Bennett, "Queen of the High-Brows," *Evening Standard*, Nov. 28, 1929, 9, in Majumdar and McLaurin, 258–60; 258.

[60] Charques, "The Bourgeois Novel," in his *Contemporary Literature and Social Revolution*, 1933, 108–14, in Majumdar and McLaurin, 342–50; 343, 345.

[61] "Saturday 5 April 1924," *Diary*, 2: 298.

[62] "To Vanessa Bell," Tuesday [22? August 1911], Letter 581 of Virginia Stephen (Woolf), *The Flight of the Mind*, vol. 1, 1888–1912, of *The Letters of Virginia Woolf*, ed. Nigel Nicolson (London: Hogarth, 1975), 475.

[63] The first line is from Virginia Woolf, "Jane Austen," in *Essays*, 2: 9–16; 14; the second is from the editor's gloss to "Jane Austen Practising," *Essays*, 3: 331–35; 335 n2.

the very highest to make novels out of such everyday material. Mr. James is one of the few who attempt to picture people as they are." [64]

For Woolf, picturing people as they really are means defining identity in terms of its economic determinants—"the daily drop of the daily bill" as she calls it in *Between the Acts*.[65] Her more conventional novels *Night and Day* and *The Years* may have seemed to Woolf the failures they did because they were attempts to capture an everydayness from which she felt disqualified by lack of experience—the dailiness of going to work, of holding a job, the very experiences Richardson could write about in *Pilgrimage*. Richardson's definition of the everyday in terms of the series—and in terms of the series as a particular round of toil—provided an unarticulated model against which Woolf measured herself: "Every day includes much more non-being than being" Woolf writes. "The real novelists can somehow convey both sorts of being. . . . I have never been able to do both. I tried—in *Night and Day*; and in *The Years*." [66] But the very terms of her failure—her inability to represent identity as the "non-being" revealed in the drudgery of the everyday—already puts into question a definition of identity politics that demands personal experience as a guarantor.

It is in fact women's nonbeing within the economic system that establishes for Woolf their political identity. *Three Guineas* is in part an early argument insisting that it is women's unpaid (and unrecognized) domestic labor that supports patriarchy and capitalism. Because the everyday is for most women a realm of labor enforced by a system unwilling to recognize its existence or necessity, "often nothing tangible remains of a woman's day," Woolf writes.[67] She defines women as "wives and mothers and daughters who work all day and every day, without whose work the State would collapse and fall to pieces, without whose work your sons, Sir, would cease to exist," arguing that the recognition of women's nonbeing in the system would threaten the fullness and stability of men's being within it.[68] Woolf implies in *Three Guineas* that it is precisely because women have gotten along with so few of capitalism's rewards, because they are so accustomed to being invisible within capitalism every day, to having no subjecthood in a system that depends on them, that they may be able to resist those rewards and explode the system that offers them.

In so implying, Woolf may herself well ignore that the domestic labor of upper middle-class and working-class women is still widely unequal—

[64] Virginia Woolf, "Mr. Henry James's Latest Novel," in *Essays*, 1: 22–24; 22.

[65] Virginia Woolf, *Between the Acts* (New York: Harcourt, 1941), 197; all future references to this book (abbreviated *Between*) will appear in the text.

[66] These are what Woolf calls "moments of non-being . . . a kind of nondescript cotton wool. . . . A great part of every day is not lived consciously": Virginia Woolf, *Moments of Being: Unpublished Autobiographical Writings*, ed. Jeanne Schulkind (New York: Harcourt, 1976), 70; all future references to this work (abbreviated *Moments*) will appear in the text.

[67] Virginia Woolf, "Women and Fiction," in *Collected Essays*, 2: 141–48; 146.

[68] Virginia Woolf, *Three Guineas* (New York: Harcourt, 1938), 54; all future references to this book (abbreviated *Three*) will appear in the text.

although in part *Mrs. Dalloway* acknowledges that the everyday life that women like Clarissa Dalloway and Lady Bruton take for granted rests on the invisible work of their servants[69]—but Woolf does suggest that such positions are not essential. We cannot begin to change them until we begin to change the representational system in which they take their meaning. Hence, although Woolf outlines clearly in *The Years* the unthinking daily brutality of the Pargiters to their old family servant Crosby (the very Crosby who returns for a moment in *Three Guineas*), she indicts Crosby too for clinging much more tenaciously than they to a dying social system that has legitimated a ruling and a governed class in the first place. This is something more than—although it is also—blaming the victim: it also begins to elaborate a social analysis in which clear oppositions and pure positions, so that we always know at every moment just exactly how someone is made the victim, become increasingly impossible.

The debate about Woolf's own politics in materialist feminism may be interminable precisely because it continues to be cast in terms of pure and stable class positions. The question in those terms is whether Woolf can be truly political—that is, a committed socialist—given her own supposedly clear-cut identity, her privileged background and unconscious prejudices. What could an aesthete living in Bloomsbury say about politics? How could someone whose background was upper middle class, professional, elite, know anything about class? The tacit assumptions of these questions make them seem very simple ones: that there exists a position (Woolf simply doesn't occupy it) where class allegiances are clear, conscious, undivided, where the prejudices of the system that creates us are something we can learn to cast off, not something that constitutes us, whatever our class position. Yet although Woolf's work contains some unmistakable and disturbing class prejudice, which, I think, critics need to discuss, that does not, however, make the question of class politics any less complex or more stable; it is the recognition of those uncertainties that Woolf's work offers to the debate.

In fact recent problems in feminism suggest that the attempt to hold onto a system in which the identity of those in power and those oppressed are

---

[69] Alex Zwerdling writes: "Service is assumed to be part of the natural order by the governing class, dependable in its regular rhythms, creating an environment of basic security by maintaining a predictable daily routine": *Virginia Woolf and the Real World* (Berkeley: University of California Press, 1986), 126. Certainly Woolf ironizes Mrs. Dalloway's recognition of this by having her think "but all the more, she thought, taking up the pad, must one repay in daily life to servants, yes, to dogs and canaries, above all to Richard her husband, who was the foundation of it": *Mrs. Dalloway* (New York: Harcourt, 1925), 29; all future references to this book will appear in the text. Just how unrelenting Woolf is in having Mrs. Dalloway connect domestics and domesticated animals in providing her life with its foundation, and then giving credit for everything to her husband, can be seen in the musings of the Mrs. Dalloway who appeared in the earlier novel, *The Voyage Out*: "I often wonder . . . whether it is really good for a women to live with a man who is morally her superior, as Richard is mine [Richard is about to kiss the novel's young heroine adulterously]. I suppose I feel for him what my mother and women of her generation felt for Christ": *The Voyage Out* (New York: Harcourt, 1920), 52; all future references to this book (abbreviated *Voyage*) will appear in the text.

fixed and unchanging has itself been in service of a certain kind of power. Academic feminism's claims that all women have been victimized have overlooked how different kinds of women in different contexts have had power over other *women*, that oppression is relative, and that we all, as functions and expressions of the system in which we operate, engage in power—our new role as feminist critics might very well be to chart the different contexts in which this happens, the different degrees to which people exploit each other. Such careful comparisons remain important—I think criticism can usefully expose the differences of wealth and power between Richard and Clarissa Dalloway, but also the differences between Mrs. Dalloway and her servant Lucy (as well as their similarities as women). It makes sense to me to note Woolf's own class assumptions; it makes sense too to note Woolf's own recognition of this problem—even more, to note the way her example shows that such recognition doesn't exempt us from repeating it in our own kind of serial replication. Perhaps our vigilance should be directed at reducing the degree we too have internalized the corruption of the system that produces us. That seems to me the only consolation when the belief that we can somehow escape it has vanished. If I say that Woolf is politically valuable in pointing out this dynamic, that doesn't exempt her from criticism under it, though it may prevent those tones of moral certainty in which it would be comforting to conduct this critique.

It is precisely the contradictoriness of Woolf's definitions of identity, the series, and the everyday—and of her tone—that for some of her materialist critics call her politics into question: complaining that Woolf's slippery irony has supposedly shielded her from criticism of her elitism, Mary Childers maintains that poststructural critics use "Woolf's very style of writing . . . to suppress any political reading of it as always too simple and too polemical compared to the multivocality of her writing."[70] Yet the assumption connecting multivocality, complexity, and contradiction with the apolitical impoverishes the definition of the political itself. In support of her argument for Woolf's lack of politics, Childers quotes passages from Woolf's writing that actually seem to me expressly to reject as too simple and dangerous a definition of politics as fixed and pure truth: "My difficulty always was the political attitude to human beings—that some were always right, others always wrong. I did hate that. And do still," Woolf writes.[71] "All I ever said was that I hate all forms of principle. Whats the good of saying This is true, when nothing is true, except that some sounds are nicer than others and some shapes? No views are true."[72] This radical skepticism, however, doesn't

---

[70] Mary M. Childers, "Virginia Woolf on the Outside Looking Down: Reflections on the Class of Women," *Modern Fiction Studies* 38 (1992): 61–79; 70.

[71] "To Margaret Llewelyn Davies," 25 July 1930, Letter 2210 of *A Reflection of the Other Person*, vol. 4, 1929–1931, of *The Letters of Virginia Woolf*, ed. Nigel Nicolson (London: Hogarth, 1978), 191; quoted in part in Childers, 69.

[72] "To Ethyl Smith," 7th April [1931], Letter 2343 of *Letters*, 4: 304; quoted in Childers, 78. Childers responds: "it is tempting to conclude that the repetition and historical irresponsibility

make for some essentially better politics than Childers's, say; what is different about Woolf's skeptical politics is that they directly put the assumptions of such essences into question. Woolf writes elsewhere: "some politics are beginning to interest me, as I suppose they interest City men—like a football match." [73] Edward Bishop argues that Woolf "was searching for a way of dealing with [politics] that would not be like a football match—where the teams change but the game remains the same." [74] On the contrary, I think Woolf was interested in politics precisely for the way it is a game, an arbitrary (not true) system, although one (as she notes about football matches, male games, uniforms, and costumes in *Three Guineas*) with very high stakes indeed. [75]

For J. Hillis Miller, *Mrs. Dalloway* is Woolf's attempt to represent the radical uncertainty encoded within the everyday: "'Nothing matters'—compared to this reality, which is only defaced, corrupted, covered over by all the everyday activities of life, everything else is emptiness and vanity: 'there is nothing,' wrote Woolf during one of her periods of depression, '—nothing for any of us. Work, reading, writing, are all disguises.'" [76] In *Mrs. Dalloway*, as in Woolf's other writing, what the everyday disguises is that reality is nothing, is nothing but a disguise. This is Slavoj Žižek's reading of the everyday: unlike other materialist theorists who assert it as the locus of the real, Žižek insists on the everyday as imaginary. "This is the image of everyday reality offered by psychoanalysis," he writes, "a fragile equilibrium that can be destroyed at any moment, if, in a quite contingent and unpredictable way, trauma erupts" (*Looking*, 17). Yet, although the everyday is imaginary, this does not mean for Žižek that reality is simply an illusion: "the Real cannot be inscribed, but we can inscribe this impossibility itself, we can locate its place" (*Sublime*, 172–73). This very impossibility of

---

of Woolf's writing is directly related to the beauty of her language, that in order to put ideas on the backs of rhythms, Woolf has to show more respect for music than for the truth of others' lives" (78). Although I agree with many of Childers's criticisms of Woolf in this essay, and sympathize with her materialist and feminist goals, any assumption of the "truth" seems to me to make for much more chilling politics than any contradictions in Woolf. Childers claims that "my own position is that contemporary feminists might make Woolf a more vital figure by addressing the political contradictions of her texts at least as much as their reputedly coherent feminist theory" (71)—an approach to Woolf I laud. Childers may be unconsciously drawn into what she sees as the need to redress a balance, instead of inaugurating the new critique to which she usefully gestures, because the economic pressures of the institution on feminists—and Childers's essay poignantly charts her own personal experience of these pressures—force us to reduce identity politics, and personal experience, into divisions among feminists where we see each other as antagonists. The politics of contradiction, if we could forge them, might actually provide a way for feminism to see its contradictions and differences as something more than failures or radical divides—perhaps even as connections.

[73] "Wednesday 16 November 1921," *Diary*, 2: 143.

[74] Bishop, "The Subject in *Jacob's Room*," 156 n13.

[75] In his article "Joan Riviere and the Masquerade," Stephen Heath directly connects Woolf's discussion of male display in *Three Guineas* to this notion of identity as masquerade (56); in Burgin et al., *Formations of Fantasy*, 45–61.

[76] Miller, "*Mrs. Dalloway*," 186.

its inscription operates like "a hard kernel, a leftover which persists and cannot be reduced" (*Sublime*, 47). The symbolic order itself is in fact created in response to this impossibility, is called into play around it.[77] For Žižek, the subject is expressly a function of this productive nothingness within the heart of the everyday—"We can inscribe, encircle the void place of the subject through the failure of his symbolization, because the subject is nothing but the failure point of the process of his symbolic representation" (*Sublime*, 173).

This is the view of the subject produced within Woolf's everyday as well. In the trauma of his madness, Septimus Smith comes to see humankind as a smiling facade, to see that human beings "are plastered over with grimaces" (*Mrs. Dalloway*, 89), to recognize that there is nothing behind this disguise. Woolf's novel concurs in this judgment, as it indicts the idols of social conformity and forceful conversion which "stamp indelibly" (102) their features on "the face of the populace" (100)—a face Woolf exposes as a malleable form created in whatever image molds it. Hence the importance in the opening of *Mrs. Dalloway* of the ironically faceless image of power that drives by in the motor car. The crowd keeps trying to invest that image with a face in order to reflect it back, to define itself as the English populace through that image's reflected glory. In refusing to give power any fixed face,

---

[77] Žižek writes: "In other words, the Real cannot be inscribed, but we can inscribe this impossibility itself, we can locate its place: a traumatic place which causes a series of failures. And Lacan's whole point is that the Real is *nothing but* this impossibility of its inscription: the Real is not a transcendent positive entity, persisting somewhere beyond the symbolic order like a hard kernel inaccessible to it . . . in itself it is nothing at all, just a void, an emptiness in a symbolic structure marking some central impossibility" (*Sublime*, 172–73). Although this passage provides what seems to me Žižek's best reading of Lacan's notion of the real and its relation to the symbolic, it is a reading at odds with the rest of Žižek's work, which actually (as the passage I just quoted in the text demonstrates) insists on the metaphor of the real as a hard and resistant kernel everywhere else throughout. This insistently repeated metaphor provides the very hallmark of Žižek's readings, around which they obsessively circulate—everything (the sublime object of ideology, the *objet petite a*, the subject) gets reduced to it sooner or later. His emphasis on that hard kernel transforms his understanding of the real ultimately into a "transcendent positive entity"—precisely Derrida's critique of Lacan (see Derrida, "The Purveyor of Truth," *Yale French Studies* 52 [1975]: 96–177), and—despite Žižek's dismissal of this critique and of Derrida—a continued problem in Žižek's work too (see *Sublime*, 153–55, and also Slavoj Žižek, *For They Know Not What They Do: Enjoyment as a Political Factor* [New York: Verso, 1991], 73–79; all future references to this book [abbreviated *They Know*] will appear in the text). He keeps wanting to make these nothings into something (as implied by the logic of "the impossibility unearthed by Derrida through the hard work of deconstructive reading supposed to subvert identity constitutes the very definition of identity" [*They Know*, 37]), so that when he argues about a Patricia Highsmith story that "the gaze of the men in the saloon, capable of discerning the fascinating contours of the object of desire where a normal view sees nothing but a trivial everyday object, is literally a gaze capable of seeing nothingness" (*Looking*, 9), he is to all extents and purposes describing his fantasy of his own critical gaze. As far as I'm concerned, the implicit gesture throughout Žižek's work to this ultimately authorizing truth or transcendence—*he* knows what the real is—has everything to do with gender assumptions; his notion that the everyday is a fragile equilibrium (*Looking*, 17), for instance, comes from a reading of J. B. Priestley's play *The Dangerous Game*, where the trauma organizing the symbolic has to do with the father's repressed secrets and his resulting death.

Woolf highlights the dynamic by which that face—and, through it, power—
is nevertheless relentlessly and inexorably constructed and naturalized.

Mrs. Dalloway is an attempt in part to analyze the self-perpetuation of
power through class. Clarissa Dalloway, aware of the smiling facades people
put on for each other, quite consciously constructs her own face in the mirror: "She pursed her lips when she looked in the glass. It was to give her face
point. That was her self—pointed; dartlike; definite. That was her self when
some effort, some call on her to be her self, drew the parts together, she alone
knew how different, how incompatible and composed so for the world only
into one centre, one diamond, one woman" (*Mrs. Dalloway*, 37). As Perry
Meisel suggests, Woolf's image for Clarissa Dalloway's masquerade subtly
places it within an economic and political context: "'diamond' resonates
with the novel's seemingly unrelated tropology of finance, empire, and the
material resources of colonialism 'where only the spice winds blow,' a tropology into whose range 'diamond' may vibrate so as to make it signify a
specific type of imperial wealth, and that suggests Clarissa's personal wholeness to be dependent in turn upon the stability of her husband's money."[78]
Although Woolf may here imbricate Clarissa Dalloway's identity in a cluster
of class, racial, and gender influences, she also maintains that the understanding of identity—especially of her own—resists such analyses. In her
memoir, *Moments of Being*, Woolf contends that "this influence, by which I
mean the consciousness of other groups impinging upon ourselves" is crucial to the construction of the self, but ignored or scanted by most autobiography (*Moments*, 80). But, although she acknowledges that she too is implicated every day in such social structures, she also knows that she cannot
really recognize such influences as she tries to sketch her identity: "It is by
such invisible presences that the 'subject of this memoir' is tugged this way
and that every day of his life; it is they that keep him in position. Consider
what immense forces society brings to play upon each of us, how that society changes from decade to decade; and also from class to class. . . . I see myself as a fish in a stream; deflected; held in place; but cannot describe the
stream" (*Moments*, 80). Part of the disguise of the self in the everyday is to
make subjects blind to the ways their own identities get built up, even when
(and this is Woolf's point with Clarissa Dalloway too, what makes her such
a contradictory character) they realize they construct them.

Yet, in *Mrs. Dalloway*, Woolf emphasizes the importance of recognizing
the masquerade by damning Miss Kilman through her inability to see even
that. Ill favored, ugly, and poor herself, Miss Kilman hates Mrs. Dalloway
for her class privilege, her poise, her beautiful things: "There rose in her an
overmastering desire to overcome her; to unmask her" (125). But although
Woolf gives Miss Kilman her own moment of defamiliarization in front of a
mirror—"saw herself thus lurching with her hat askew, very red in the face,

---

[78] Meisel, *The Myth of the Modern*, excerpted in Bloom, *Clarissa Dalloway*, 63–65; 64.

full length in a looking-glass" (133)—Miss Kilman, unlike Clarissa Dalloway, cannot really recognize or long keep hold of the fact that her identity too is a mask; she cannot see herself as the book presents her, her mackintosh a perfect objective correlative for the defensive facade that is all she is (she is "some prehistoric monster armoured for primeval warfare," Mrs. Dalloway thinks [126]). Paradoxically, however, Miss Kilman's is perhaps the most feeling and tragic example of identity as masquerade in the book. Although she thinks "it was this egotism that was her undoing" (132), she actually so rails against the class position she has been allocated because of her lack of faith in the ego; she secretly suspects the impossibility of divorcing any true ego, any complete and inner self, from the outer husk of clumsiness, cheapness, and envy that makes her what she is. Her desperate unhappiness comes from a felt awareness that her identity is restricted by the limits of this facade, *is* this facade. Miss Kilman seeks refuge in the cathedral as an attempt to escape this shell, to be "divested of social rank, almost of sex" (133). But with the loss of this shell she loses her identity, which returns to the penitents in the church as soon as their prayers are done; once they uncover their faces, they become instantly again "middle class, English men and women, some of them desirous of seeing the wax works" (133). Woolf's wry aside about the wax works suggests the fundamental equivalence between those identities and such empty busts; yet it is what animates them nonetheless.

In musing on people's compulsion to insist on the truth of their imagoes, Woolf writes: "Circumstances compel unity; for convenience sake a man must be a whole." [79] It seems part of Clarissa Dalloway's class privilege that she is less hampered by such compelling circumstances, that she has the latitude to seem to put on and take off the self, that she can even recognize identity as a social convention. Woolf's implicit class assumptions come out in her scapegoating of Miss Kilman's blindness to such conventions. Her treatment of Miss Kilman seems a reflex of the prejudice with which she denigrates Joyce's *Ulysses*, the book she was reading while she wrote *Mrs. Dalloway* (and one, like *Pilgrimage*, that she worried had scooped her theory of the everyday). "An illiterate, underbred book it seems to me: the book of a self taught working man, & we all know how distressing they are, how egotistic, insistent, raw, striking, & ultimately nauseating." [80] Although Woolf acknowledges Miss Kilman's and Joyce's "egoism" as the expression of class determinants, in a classic double-bind she still blames them for it, dismissing them, as she does Charlotte Brontë in *A Room of One's Own*, because they express a social grievance, even one she finds justified. When Mrs. Dalloway counters her daughter's defection to Miss Kilman by calling out after her over the banister "Remember our party to-night!" (*Mrs. Dalloway*,

[79] Virginia Woolf, "Street Haunting: A London Adventure," in *Collected Essays*, vol. 4 (London: Hogarth, 1967), 155–66; 161.
[80] "Wednesday 16 August 1922," *Diary*, 2: 189.

126), when Miss Kilman complains to Elizabeth that "I never go to parties. . . . People don't ask me to parties. . . . Why should they ask me? . . . I'm plain. I'm unhappy" (132), both are acknowledging that, though the social game of the governing class is presented as true and natural, that class actually governs because it knows that it is a game, and knows its rules. The upper middle classes are at ease with social conventions. They have the training necessary to move naturally among them, and they use that knowledge to enforce class difference. The lower classes, supposedly true to the station to which they've been called, always have to *work* at seeming natural within a game they rarely get to play.

The ease of the upper classes with convention allows them to recognize the social system's artificiality, and deftly to manipulate it. The party becomes Woolf's central symbol for the artificiality of identity. "My present reflection," she writes, as she considers continuing *Mrs. Dalloway* into *Mrs. Dalloway's Party*, "is that people have any number of states of consciousness: & I should like to investigate the party consciousness, the frock consciousness & c. . . . where people secrete an envelope which connects them & protects them from others, like myself, who am outside the envelope, foreign bodies." [81] The recognition of the party consciousness as a construction, an envelope, signifies for Woolf "a kind of liberation caused by wearing a mask." [82] The liberation is the exposure of the artificiality of the entire system, but the privilege to recognize the system as artificial may be reserved for those who can take it for granted.

Yet Woolf also shows in *Mrs. Dalloway* that such matters remain life and death ones even for characters like Clarissa Dalloway. Peter Walsh's criticism of Clarissa Dalloway, which stings her, is precisely that she plays the game too well. In Septimus Smith's death, she recognizes that really to put off the mask of self, to opt out of the system, means a kind of death she is not willing to risk: "She had once thrown a shilling into the Serpentine, never anything more. But he had flung it away. . . . A thing was that mattered; a thing, wreathed about with chatter, defaced, obscured in her own life, let drop every day in corruption, lies, chatter" (*Mrs. Dalloway*, 184). Although Woolf's writing acknowledges the stark defacement of this vision of radical nothingness, her works also defend against it. Her autobiography records the longing for "a deeply hidden and inarticulate desire for something beyond the daily life" (*Moments*, 141), a desire for moments of transcendence or connection ("We—I mean all human beings—are connected with this" [*Moments*, 72]). Borrowing from fellow modernists such as Hardy and Conrad, who find such moments hidden in the "commonplace," she calls them "moments of being." [83]

[81] "Monday 27 April 1925," *Diary*, 3: 12–13.
[82] "Monday 30 January 1939," *The Diary of Virginia Woolf*, vol. 5, 1936–1941, ed. Anne Olivier Bell (New York: Harcourt, 1984), 203.
[83] Woolf, for instance, quotes Conrad's Marlow: " 'Nothing could have been more commonplace than this remark; but its utterance coincided for me with a moment of vision. It's extraor-

Such a longing for transcendence seems to connect her to the modernist project of Lukács's and Lefebvre's dialectic as well. But unlike those theorists, Woolf also implicitly concedes that the desires for such moments are wishful, a response to a threat:

> I hazard the explanation that a shock is at once in my case followed by the desire to explain it. I feel that I have had a blow; but it is not, as I thought as a child, simply a blow from an enemy hidden behind the cotton wool of daily life; it is or will become a revelation of some order; it is a token of some real thing behind appearances; and I make it real by putting it into words. It is only by putting it into words that I make it whole; this wholeness means that it has lost its power to hurt me; it gives me, perhaps because by doing so I take away the pain, a great delight to put the severed parts together. . . . And this conception affects me every day. (*Moments*, 72, 73)

The desire for wholeness and pattern covers over and denies the very threat of the void that prompts it in the first place. Woolf writes elsewhere that "through the tremor and vibration of daily custom one discerns bone and form." [84] The reality one imagines underlying the everyday turns out to be that of *vanitas*.

Although throughout her work Woolf gestures to this structure and wholeness, at one and the same time she also sees it as a desperate imposition, even an attempt to meet violence with violence; in her fiction, it is characters like the conservative and domineering politician Richard Dalloway in *The Voyage Out* whom Woolf ironically connects with such a vision of "Unity" (*Voyage*, 64). (It is a mark of Woolf's growing recognition of the way we are all inscribed in the political system that by the time she writes *Mrs. Dalloway* she can no longer keep Richard Dalloway simply a bully or blame him completely for everything that is wrong in his—and her—world.) For him, what he sees behind the everyday is "in one word—Unity. Unity of aim, of dominion, of progress. The dispersion of the best ideas over the greatest area. . . . [In achieving this,] I grant that the English seem, on the

---

dinary how we go through life with eyes half shut, with dull ears, with dormant thoughts. . . . Nevertheless, there can be but few of us who had never known one of these rare moments of awakening, when we see, hear, understand, ever so much—everything—in a flash' ": "Joseph Conrad," *Collected Essays*, vol. 1 (London: Hogarth, 1966), 302–8; 305. She also refers to Hardy's *Moments of Vision* in her diary; "[Saturday 31 July]" *Diary*, 3: 105. These epiphanies are similar to Marx's transfigured senses. Though Woolf does gesture to them, like Marx she also recognizes that they remain imaginary, utopic. Woolf's modernism is obviously still built on the gesture to the very epiphanies that she also finds bankrupt; hence the contradictoriness of her work. She is perhaps attempting to work through this paradox when she has Lily Briscoe distinguish between "Truth" and "little daily miracles" in *To the Lighthouse*, relocating (to a degree at least) transcendence and universality to context-bound everydayness: "What is the meaning of life? The great revelation had never come. The great revelation perhaps never did come. Instead there were little daily miracles, illuminations, matches struck unexpectedly in the dark": *To The Lighthouse* (New York: Harcourt, 1927), 161; but see Bhabha's critique of Habermas's similar attempt, which I cite in the last paragraph of this section.

[84] "Reading," *Essays*, 3:141-61; 153.

whole, whiter than most men, their records cleaner" (*Voyage*, 64).[85] Yet this vision is part of what kills Rachel Vinrace in that book, showing that it is not just mistaken but also dangerous, part and parcel of a principle of death. As she dies, her lover thinks, echoing Richard Dalloway's language of unity and dispersion: "So . . . this was death. . . . They had now what they had always wanted to have, the union which had been impossible while they lived. . . . It seemed to him that their complete union and happiness filled the room with rings eddying more and more widely" (353). Even while eerily desiring Rachel's death, the novel reveals through it the irony of this view, the violent power of such visions of unity and their ultimate emptiness. As her lover comes to realize, if there is anything beyond the everyday, it is only this void: "Underneath the life of every day, pain lies, quiescent, but ready to devour" (344). Woolf suggests that the eddying rings of Richardson's and her own modernist series still carry fatal limitations in their desire for order and connection.

Woolf introduces Richard Dalloway specifically as part of a debate about whether we locate politics merely at the level of social change, or also at the level of representation. Richard Dalloway thinks he knows: artists simply "*leave* things in a mess" (*Voyage*, 45), while "commonplace" politicians (45) like himself see things clearly and act. Yet as Woolf writes in her diary: "It seems to me more & more clear that the only honest people are the artists, & that these social reformers & philanthropists get so out of hand, & harbour so many discreditable desires under the disguise of loving their kind, that in the end there's more to find fault with in them than in us. But if I were one of them?"[86] Richard Dalloway consoles himself that his notion of transcendence can be translated into political effectiveness on the everyday level: "Well, when I consider my life, there is one fact I admit that I'm proud of; owing to me some thousands of girls in Lancashire—and many thousands to come after them—can spend an hour every day in the open air which their mothers had to spend over their looms. I'm prouder of that, I own, than I should be of writing Keats and Shelley into the bargain!" (*Voyage*, 65).[87] Woolf's early portrait of Richard Dalloway's complaisance and blindness is such that she suggests that he is the exemplary figure of someone whose reforms support and authorize the very system of oppression they address—

---

[85] Even in her first novel, Woolf so complicates Richard Dalloway that he goes on to say "'But, good Lord, don't run away with the idea that I don't see the drawbacks—horrors—unmentionable things done in our very midst!'" (*Voyage*, 64).

[86] "Saturday 19 July 1919," *The Diary of Virginia Woolf*, vol. 1, 1915–1919, ed. Anne Olivier Bell (New York: Harcourt, 1977), 293.

[87] Yet Keats and Shelley are loaded terms for Woolf because she associates them with a radical kind of politics that calls into question the assumption of complacent politicians like Richard Dalloway that they even know what politics are. In *A Room of One's Own*, Keats represents the only working-class poet of genius, while Shelley, in Woolf's essay "'Not One of Us,'" redefines politics by showing that "alongside the public battle wages, from generation to generation, another fight which is as important as the other, though much less is said about it. Husband fights with wife and son with father. The poor fight the rich and the employer fights the employed" (*Collected Essays*, 4: 20–26; 25).

the extra hour of fresh air humanizes a monstrous system enough to allow it to continue every day. The problem with Richard Dalloway is not that he doesn't see the problems of empire and capitalism, but that he thinks he can ameliorate them while still retaining—and profiting from—those systems. This profit takes place under the "disguise of loving their kind," a pose someone like Richard Dalloway doesn't admit as such. The dangers committed under its name are so extreme that Woolf devotes a related short story in *Mrs. Dalloway's Party*, "The Man Who Loved His Kind," to considering them. A friend of Richard Dalloway's, a man supposedly on the opposite side of the political spectrum from him, is shown to have the same politics nonetheless; he takes on the same incognito as disinterested reformer, and the point of the story, Dean Baldwin maintains, is to show up such disinterestedness, to reveal that there is "no pristine purity that [such characters] can claim." [88]

But whether writers somehow best politicians, even when Woolf shows that the very problem of politics is located within its representation, is still open to question. For the distinction between the two groups is once again impossible to draw; as Woolf asks, "But if I were one of them?" Woolf herself recognized she was caught in what she tried to write against—political structures as much as narrative ones like the series; that recognition in fact marked her conscious difference (in one of her late and most consciously political essays, "The Leaning Tower") from fellow modernists who more explicitly proclaimed their politics, their socialism, their allegiance to the working classes. Woolf saw in this a kind of hypocrisy that "explains the violence of their attack upon bourgeois society and also its half-heartedness. They are profiting by a society which they abuse." [89] As she writes in *Three Guineas* "it would be interesting to know what the true-born working man or woman thinks of the playboys and playgirls of the educated class who adopt the working-class cause without sacrificing middle-class capital, or sharing working-class experience" (*Three*, 177 n12). Such writers refused to admit the ways their very critique might be useful to a system that rewarded them for it; Woolf saw that she was the product of a system she couldn't even escape in her abuse of it. (The recognition explains her attempts in *Three Guineas* to expose the fascism at the heart of English patriarchy and her convoluted—and desperate—attempts still to position women outside of it; by *Between the Acts*, she recognizes that the fascism in the heart of the English countryside has also poisoned the very relationship between Isabella and Giles Oliver—that even their exclusion by patriarchy doesn't save women from participating in its violence.[90]) But that recognition may also have killed her: barely a year after she wrote this essay she was dead.

[88] Dean R. Baldwin, *Virginia Woolf: A Study of the Short Fiction* (Boston: G. K. Hall, 1989), 45.

[89] "The Leaning Tower," *Collected Essays*, 2: 162–81; 175.

[90] Woolf suggests in fact that if women leave the system of capital and politics unchanged when they enter it, they will simply become like men: "You will have to leave the house at nine

196 | Novels of Everyday Life

Or, at any rate, this may be one we want to add to the competing legends that attempt to appropriate the symbolic resonance of Woolf's suicide, her making literal the death of the subject. But what is important to Woolf's politics is that, while Septimus's death, the death of the subject, and Woolf's own death may put the system into question, by doing so they still carry with them no essential political charge. In her later depiction of the Dalloways, it is *Mrs.* Dalloway who, perhaps profiting by the reading of *Antigone* she introduces in *The Voyage Out* to smooth over the blustering political views of her husband, has come to see that the entire system itself—its everyday-ness—must be put in question: "She always had the feeling that it was very, very dangerous to live even one day" (*Mrs. Dalloway*, 8). For Mrs. Dalloway too, however, the only way possible to shatter the system to achieve some vision "obscured in her own life, let drop every day in corruption" (184) is the empty transcendence of more corruption—death—and not even (yet) her own, but the convenient sacrifice of a shell-shocked soldier, one of the very lower-middle-class figures Woolf indicts imperialism and capitalism for sacrificing in their wars. His death marks both the connection of women and the working classes and the inescapable perpetuation of the system that continues to separate them.

In attempting to work through the symbolic effect of this kind of death on the representational register that determines our understanding of material reality, Slavoj Žižek follows Lacan to make Antigone the political exemplar of such an action, the very figure of the living dead. Her "striving for radical self-annihilation . . . [represents] what Lacan calls the 'second death' going beyond mere physical destruction, i. e., entailing the effacement of the very symbolic texture of generation and corruption" (*Looking*, 63–64). This act ultimately enables us "to break out of [the] ideological closure" that comes from maintaining the symbolic system as somehow real, precisely because it breaks with the very "everyday feelings and considerations" that are all we "pathetic everyday compassionate creatures" (*Sublime*, 117) can imagine.[91] It marks "a place which cannot be symbolized, although it is retroactively produced by the symbolization itself" (*Sublime*, 135). This effect, which is also and impossibly retroactively a cause, is the paradoxical mechanism that drives the entire political structure—of neocapitalism, postmodernism, the new world order—according to Žižek. Antigone is important because she not only participates in it, she exposes it, exposing "the site of *das Ding*, of the real-traumatic kernel in the midst of the symbolic order"

---

and come back to it at six. That leaves very little time for fathers to know their children. You will have to do this daily. . . . You will have to perform some duties that are very arduous, others that are very barbarous. You will have to wear certain uniforms and profess certain loyalties. If you succeed in those professions the words 'For God and Empire' will very likely be written, like the address on a dog-collar, round your neck" (*Three*, 70).

[91] The first phrase comes from Slavoj Žižek, *Enjoy Your Symptom: Jacques Lacan in Hollywood and Out* (New York: Routledge, 1992), 59; all future references to this book (abbreviated *Enjoy*) will appear in the text.

(*Sublime*, 135), the material and referential ground the symbolic cannot capture but without which it cannot function.

Antigone was also important to Woolf and figured throughout her writing—in *The Voyage Out*, *Three Guineas*, *The Years*; as much as the Dalloways she performs as a recurring character connecting Woolf's work into a series. I introduce Žižek here not in order to make Woolf into an Antigone of the sort who shatters the system by being immured in it, by sacrificing herself. I want to try instead to resist the ways my analysis falls into such a pattern (though it does). We can perhaps see the danger of making Woolf into such a sacrifice when we look at what Žižek himself explicitly does with Woolf, for his sacrifice of her is meant to allow his critical integrity. In a chapter titled "Why Does the *Phallus* Appear?" Žižek uses the image of Woolf as a kind of Antigone, a figure that "dissolves all traditional ('substantial') symbolic links" (*Enjoy*, 139). But, he insists, she does so unwittingly, as a kind of dumb "monster figure" (*Enjoy*, 139). Her noble sacrifice in fact rests on Žižek's ability to translate what he calls her "ethereal, sublime" beauty into a distortion, an anamorphotic projection that (he argues) impossibly intrudes the real into the symbolic, disrupting it. His (supposed) ability to make us see Woolf's face as ugly, "a grimace of reality," is actually the mechanism that is supposed to explode the system: "Have we not thus also delineated the contours of a *postmodern* critique of ideology which instructs us to assume such a foreign gaze upon one's own ideological field, whereby the ideological anamorphosis loses its power of fascination and changes into a disgusting protuberance?" (*Enjoy*, 140). Implicit in this claim is one about Žižek himself: his triumph as a critic in the American academy (he suggests) depends on the foreignness of his own gaze, as demonstrated in its ability to resist a culturally defined sense of beauty, to find in Woolf's face instead a ("real") disgust, which he implies clinches his ability somehow also to see through his own ideological position, to stake out a supposedly pure position. He makes Woolf into Antigone to create for himself as critic an illusion of political exemption.

To Woolf, *Antigone* was not that kind of political symbol:

> [Sophocles's play] could undoubtedly be made, if necessary, into anti-Fascist propaganda . . . [but] when the curtain falls we sympathize, it may be noted, even with Creon himself. This result, to the propagandist undesirable, would seem due to the fact that Sophocles . . . uses freely all the faculties that can be possessed by a writer; and suggests, therefore, that if we use art to propagate political opinions, we must force the artist to clip and cabin his gift to do us a cheap and passing service. Literature will suffer the same mutilation that the mule has suffered; and there will be no more horses. (*Three*, 169–70 n39)

This astonishing note that refuses any pure ground, that refuses politics for art altogether, has made Jane Marcus argue, perhaps out of desperation, that "there was a method in [Woolf's] madness, and we might call it Marxist-feminist."[92] I have been suggesting that, if we still want to find a politics in Woolf's art, it is one that not only puts such traditional definitions of politics into question; it is also one that, as in Woolf's note here, puts into question its own politics. Such a maddening endeavor indeed won't allow us to transport Woolf outside "the system of generation and corruption"; as the struggle in her own writing makes clear, it can only entail a careful attention to her workings *within* that system every day.

⁂

That identity in Woolf's writing is a construction formed around a hollow center is not just the emphasis of critics today; it is indeed the view on which Woolf herself always insisted. Clarissa Dalloway realizes that the thing "let drop every day" is precisely this recognition of "the impossibility of reaching the centre which, mystically, evade[s]" those who try (*Mrs. Dalloway*, 184). Only Septimus Smith embraces the impossibility by killing himself, revealing—but at a terrible price—that "'I' is only a convenient term for somebody who has no real being," as Woolf says in *A Room of One's Own* (4). Identity is *"nothing but* this confrontation of an entity with the void" (*They Know*, 36), Žižek writes, and in her own depiction of the mirror stage—a short story called "The Lady in the Looking-Glass: A Reflection"—Woolf has her narrator turn from all the possibilities captured in her reflection to the subject reflected: "Here was the woman herself. She stood naked in that pitiless light. And there was nothing. Isabella was perfectly empty."[93]

Yet although Woolf's work suggests that a full and integral essence of self is an illusion, it also suggests something more. The price Septimus pays for being an object lesson suggests that this view of self takes place on two different registers in Woolf's work. There are subjects like Clarissa Dalloway who see through, but can still assume, the illusion of wholeness; others, like Septimus Smith, are only torn apart by its impossibility. Woolf's fiction does explicitly indict the social system as what separates those registers. But what I want to consider here is the way nonetheless that Clarissa Dalloway's recognition—her reading of the system—rests on others' sacrifice.

In considering the Mrs. Brown of "Mr. Bennett and Mrs. Brown," who is Woolf's symbol for the dissolution of character amid "the confusion and 'complexity' of . . . 'daily life,'" Rachel Bowlby writes: "It is surely no accident that the encounter with Mrs. Brown takes place on a train. By this time, the imagery of public transport had become literally a commonplace for sug-

---

[92] Jane Marcus, "Tintinnabulations," in her *Art and Anger: Reading like a Woman* (Columbus: Ohio State University Press, 1988), 157–81; 178. Marcus's famous—and at the time (1974) highly controversial—essay "'No More Horses': Virginia Woolf on Art and Propaganda" (*Art and Anger*, 101–21) takes its title from this passage of Woolf's.

[93] *The Complete Shorter Fiction of Virginia Woolf*, ed. Susan Dick (New York: Harcourt, 1989), 221–25; 225.

gesting the repetitive and banal 'types' of realist fiction,' as with the standardized 'man on the Clapham omnibus.'"[94] Although Bowlby argues that Woolf means to alter the very terms of realism by adopting them, the "curiously ambivalent suspension half-way between two states" that the third-class railway carriage suggests to Bowlby suggests as well Woolf's own suspension between the status quo and her critique of it.[95] Certainly images of transport—capturing the wish perhaps to travel beyond such suspension—mark throughout Woolf's work the breakdown of character associated with the series and the everyday. It is while riding in a bus that Clarissa Dalloway expounds her theory of the decentered self to Peter Walsh:

> Clarissa once, going on the top of an omnibus with him somewhere . . . had a theory. . . . It was to explain the feeling they had of dissatisfaction; not knowing people; not being known. . . . You met every day; then not for six months, or years. It was unsatisfactory, they agreed, how little one knew people. But she said, sitting on the bus going up Shaftesbury Avenue, she felt herself everywhere; not "here, here, here"; and she tapped the back of the seat; but everywhere. (*Mrs. Dalloway*, 152)

Woolf's point may well be to transfigure such commonplaces into a different theory of the self's place in the everyday world. In her diary, she attempts to ground her own identity in the everyday, suggesting once again that the envelope of consciousness contains no hidden core but is significant in and of itself.

> The immense success of our life, is I think, that our treasure is hid away; or rather in such common things that nothing can touch it. That is, if one enjoys a bus ride to Richmond, sitting on the green smoking, taking the letters out of the box, airing the marmots, combing Grizzle, making an ice, opening a letter, sitting down after dinner, side by side. . . . well, what can trouble this happiness? And every day is necessarily full of it.[96]

But can such a model only alter the terms it uses, simply upset the old conventions without being affected by them? In what ways must it retain in spite of itself a "standardized" notion of the self rooted in the everyday?

While awaiting publication of *Mrs. Dalloway*—always a time of instability for Woolf's identity—Woolf goes along with Leonard for their own ride on an omnibus, after Leonard lectures—probably on some Labour issues—to the (probably working-class) students of an adult school; the school and the bus ride (they pass the seat of the Archbishop of Canterbury, the Houses of Parliament, a memorial to war dead) give Woolf the opportunity for some

[94] Bowlby, *Virginia Woolf*, 7, 3.
[95] Ibid., 4.
[96] "Sunday 14 June 1925," *Diary*, 3: 30.

standard humanist reflection: the similarity of people underneath the superficial differences of class, her own connection to the "standardized man on the omnibus." And yet the breakdown of distinctions and the supposed leveling of the bus ride abruptly end: "& so home," Woolf writes, "passing a nigger gentleman, perfectly fitted out in swallow tail & bowler & gold headed cane; & what were his thoughts? Of the degradation stamped on him, every time he raised his hand & saw it black as a monkeys outside, tinged with flesh colour within?"[97] The expansion of identity represented by the mixing of classes in third-class railway carriages and omnibuses comes up against a limit. Woolf's reference to the "nigger gentleman" (the racial epithet vying with the honorarium to reflect a supposed oxymoron) blends racism and classism in a way Patrick Brantlinger points out are distinctive to the ideology of the British empire: the supposedly fixed racist hierarchies of imperialism substitute for, and are meant to stabilize, an increasingly unstable class situation in England.[98] I would argue, however, that Woolf's work doesn't toy with a threatening breakdown of class identity that ultimately gets shored up by a reassuring fixity of race; on the contrary, it is the very irresolvable *contradictions* this image represents for Woolf's culture—"nigger"/gentleman, monkey/human, black/"flesh colour"—that must for us as critics put the supposedly essential revolutionary politics of the breakdown of (class) identity into question.

This image does indeed draw on other class-based fantasies in Woolf's writing. She records in her diary that "one thing Adrian said amused me—how it positively frightened him to see the people's faces on the Heath 'like gorillas, like orang-outangs—perfectly inhuman—frightful' & he poked his mouth out like an ape. He attributes this to the war. . . . Perhaps the horrible sense of community which the war produces, as if we all sat in a third class railway carriage together, draws one's attention to the animal human being more closely."[99] As Elsie Michie has shown, the simian has long been used to attempt to dehumanize people of those classes as well as races at odds with the status quo.[100] Part of how this image polices class is to racial-

[97] "Sunday 17 May 1925," *Diary*, 3: 23.

[98] Patrick Brantlinger, "Victorians and Africans: The Genealogy of the Myth of the Dark Continent," in *Race, Writing, and Difference*, ed. Henry Louis Gates Jr. (Chicago: University of Chicago Press, 1986) 185–222; 200.

[99] "Friday 7 June 1918," *Diary*, 1: 153. Woolf elsewhere continues this metaphoric chain when discussing the war: "I become steadily more feminist," she writes to Margaret Llewelyn Davies, founder of the Working Women's Guild (in the presence of whom Woolf was always especially conscious of the issues of class), "owing to the Times, which I read at breakfast and wonder how this preposterous masculine fiction [World War I] keeps going a day longer. . . Do you see any sense in it? I feel as if I were reading about some curious tribe in Central Africa": "To Margaret Llewelyn Davies," Sunday [23 January 1916], Letter 740 of *The Question of Things Happening*, vol. 2, 1912–1922 of *The Letters of Virginia Woolf*, ed. Nigel Nicolson (London: Hogarth, 1976), 76. Feminism here seems able to operate without a corresponding consciousness about race.

[100] Michie, "'The Yahoo, Not the Demon': Heathcliff, Rochester, and the Simianization of the Irish," in her *Outside the Pale: Cultural Exclusion, Gender Difference, and the Victorian Woman Writer* (Ithaca: Cornell University Press, 1993), 46–78. Anne McClintock also briefly

ize it—by insidiously suggesting that racial distinctions are actually taxo-
nomic ones, radical divides that mark humans from animals, men from
monkeys, or even from their closer primate cousins. Rather than the contradictions of class, there is the denial of any connection; the dissolution of
self becomes *degradation*, complete breakdown. One of Leonard Woolf's favorite tag lines from Kipling—which Woolf quotes with approval—suggests
that such questions for her are questions of identity: " 'There is too much ego
in your cosmos,' says the fat German to the enraged gorilla" in Kipling's
"Bertram and Bimi." [101] As the line suggests, for a gorilla to have ego would
be a threat; the breakdown of the gorilla as subject—the denial of its very
sentience—seems a way of depriving it of power. When seen in the context
of race, then, as people are transformed into gorillas, the politics of identity's
breakdown seem to turn on themselves.

In Woolf's image of the wealthy black man, the accoutrements of wealth
(coat, hat, cane) are shown to be a ludicrous costume—precisely her strategy of exposure in *Three Guineas*, when she considers men's academic gowns
or robes of state. But there the exposure seems meant to reflect on the system; here on the black man himself. Woolf holds up as a masquerade the traditional costume of a British gentleman, but here only as a means to call into
question this man's identity *as* a man. His identity is an incognito stamped
on him; the black skin on the back of his hand a frail integument stretched
over but barring him from the promise of (supposedly) true "flesh colour"
within—that is, from Woolf's own color, the color of dominance. As a political tool, the exposure of identity as masquerade has very different consequences in this image and in *Three Guineas*. What that helps us to see, I
think, is that, even for politics, the sign is arbitrary: context determines its
meaning. But it also may make us read less comfortably and in a new way
Woolf's politics in *Three Guineas*, where in fact she makes a connection between these two contexts when she writes: "That to express worth of any
kind, whether intellectual or moral, by wearing pieces of metal, or ribbon,
coloured hoods or gowns, is a barbarity which deserves the ridicule which
we bestow upon the rites of savages" (*Three*, 20).

Behind the "diamond" of Mrs. Dalloway's constructed self that Perry Meisel connects with the plunder of empire, or behind the "whiteness" of the
men of England that her husband Richard Dalloway more explicitly proffers,
seems to lie this image of race. If the self in Woolf's work is constituted in a
split, that split seems situated in what Homi Bhabha calls "the 'voyage out'
of the colonialist civilizing mission." [102] But I don't want to turn an attention
to such issues into the contention that questions of class in *Mrs. Dalloway*
actually *mask* questions of race. It seems to me that race no more provides

discusses the figure of the monkey in terms of British imperialism; see her *Imperial Leather: Race, Gender, and Sexuality in the Colonial Contest* (New York: Routledge, 1995), 214–17.

[101] As provided by the editor's gloss to "Tuesday 22 August 1922," *Diary*, 2: 191 n11.

[102] Bhabha, "Freedom's Basis in the Indeterminate," *October* 61 (1992): 46–57; 47.

the bedrock for or an essential answer to political questions than gender, sexuality, or class does.

Donna Haraway, in fact, traces the perniciousness of Western science's attempt to locate race as the bedrock for its own institutional endeavors; monkeys, primates, and so-called primitive human groups identified with them get made to stand for man's true nature hidden behind the mask of culture.[103] This is in part an attempt to ground an essential individual; Haraway writes that the "frameworks for watching monkeys and apes" frequently depend "on the structure of colonial discourse—that complex search for the primitive, authentic, and lost self, sought in the baroque dialectic between the wildly free and subordinated other."[104] Such work often aggrandizes itself into a affidavit of man's ultimate truth, as in Robert M. Yerkes's contention about the ultimate significance of his research on apes, that it was "an effective demonstration of the possibility of re-creating man himself in the image of a generally acceptable ideal."[105] This wish about identity is a wish about mastering the series: Frantz Fanon discusses racial stereotyping in terms of "the various theories that have tried to prove that the Negro is a stage in the slow evolution of monkey into man"; racism constructs a series that culminates in the white man.[106] It is also a wish about the everyday. Western science aligns monkeys and black people by placing them outside of culture so that they can point to a natural essence outside of ideology, an escape from the everyday into the ideal—Marx's "religion of the everyday."[107] Haraway insists, however, that none of the theories based on such a premise are ideal, none "can be seen as innocent, free of determination by historically specific social relations and daily practice in producing and reproducing daily life."[108]

The emphasis on racial contradictions can be disturbing to a system that wishes to resist its implication in such contradictions. In *Black Skin, White Masks*, Fanon argues that "the Negro is not. Any more than the white man" (231). In discussing Lacan's mirror stage, Fanon argues that within the so-

[103] Haraway, *Primate Visions: Gender, Race, and Nature in the World of Modern Science* (New York: Routledge, 1989), 246. For the fullest treatment of the monkey as figured in an alternative, African-influenced system of signs, a deconstruction of Western transcendence, see Henry Louis Gates Jr., *The Signifying Monkey: A Theory of African-American Literary Criticism* (New York: Oxford, 1988).

[104] Haraway, 245.

[105] Haraway, *Simians, Cyborgs, and Women: The Reinvention of Nature* (New York: Routledge, 1991), 13. As Haraway points out, "Yerkes is well known for helping design the intelligence tests for conscripts; these test results were frequently used for immigration restriction and other racist purposes during and after the war" (49).

[106] Frantz Fanon, *Black Skin, White Masks*, trans. Charles Lam Markmann (New York: Grove, 1967), 17; all future references to this book will appear in the text.

[107] Haraway, *Simians*, 14. Marx himself, however, also uses race as a bedrock. He asserts that "the profound hypocrisy and inherent barbarism of bourgeois civilization lies unveiled before our eyes, turning from its home, where it assumes respectable forms, to the colonies, where it goes naked": "On Imperialism in India," in Tucker, *Marx-Engels Reader*, 653–64; 663.

[108] Haraway, *Simians*, 106.

cial system the black man provides the white man's *radical* other. The full and complete imago the white subject sees in the mirror which shores up his sense of identity is white; the image of the black subject, on the other hand, is a reflection which horrifies white culture, and which it resists, because it provides a "guise" (154) of the other that exposes lack, calls the whole structure into question. Fanon writes: "When one has grasped the mechanism described by Lacan, one can have no further doubt that the real Other for the white man is and will continue to be the black man. And conversely. Only for the white man The Other is perceived on the level of the body image, absolutely as the not-self—that is, the unidentifiable, the unassimilable" (161 n25). In this way, the image of the black subject represents a "secret which is part of the ineffable," one that portends "the destruction, the dissolution" of being (171).[109] For Fanon, what is masked with racial stereotypes is this lack: it is not just that the stereotypes of black people need to be exposed as such, rather than as essences; it is the idea that identity itself is an essence, rather than a stereotype, that needs to be exposed. But in exploring that deconstruction of identity, I also intend something more: when it comes to race, such deconstruction isn't sufficient. The black subject's exposure of the constructedness of identity still places it in a double-bind because white culture finds a way to appropriate even that.

In Homi Bhabha's reading of Fanon, "the stereotype," Bhabha writes in terms similar to Žižek's "is, in fact, an impossible object": "As a form of splitting . . . the stereotype requires, for its successful signification, a continual and repetitive chain of other stereotypes. This is the process by which the metaphoric 'masking' is inscribed on a lack which *must* then be concealed . . . the same old stories of the negro's animality . . . which must be told (compulsively) again and afresh, and [are] differently gratifying and terrifying each time."[110] Bhabha suggests "it is difficult to agree entirely with Fanon that the psychic choice is to 'turn white or disappear.' There is the more ambivalent, third choice: camouflage, mimicry, black skins/white masks."[111] By hiding the fact that they are constructed, not natural, stereotypes are

---

[109] Fanon makes these claims in recounting the story of a white prostitute who "hunt[s] for Negroes" as clients after learning of a fellow prostitute who went mad after sleeping with a black man (171). That Fanon places on a sexual level this aspect of what black people represent can be seen as an aspect of his claim that white culture sexualizes blackness, partly in response to its appearing a corporeal property to begin with. But it seems to me it is also connected with the unfortunate tendency in his book to scapegoat women, to blame gender for the very contradictions and double-binds he uncovers in his analysis of race.

[110] "The Other Question: Difference, Discrimination and the Discourse of Colonialism" in *Literature, Politics, and Theory: Papers from the Essex Conference, 1976–84*, ed. Francis Barker, Peter Hulme, Margaret Iversen, and Diana Loxley (New York: Methuen, 1986), 149–72; 169, 164.

[111] Bhabha, "Signs Taken for Wonders: Questions of Ambivalence and Authority under a Tree outside Delhi, May 1817," in Gates, *Race*, 163–84; 181. This is an odd moment in Bhabha's reading of Fanon because it seems to take onto itself what is actually, as far as I can tell, Fanon's thesis; such ambivalence seems the *point* of Fanon's argument.

meant to consolidate and confirm dominant power relations—and are at least in the short term quite effective. But the element of camouflage or mimicry within the construction of the black subject works against that insistently, and cannot fully be repressed. In cycling through the slippery chain of stereotypes, "the white man's eyes break up the black man's body and in that act of epistemic violence its own frame of reference is transgressed, its field of vision disturbed":[112]

> The native wears his psychic wounds on the surface of his skin like an open sore—an eyesore to the colonizer. . . . It says: All these bits and pieces in which my history is fragmented, my culture piecemeal, my identifications fantasmic and displaced; these splittings of wounds of my body are also a form of revolt. And they speak a terrible truth. In their ellipses and silences they dismantle your authority. . . . My revolt is to face the Life of literature and history with the scraps and fragments that constitute its double.[113]

The black stereotype is meant to replicate—that is, shore up by also differing from—the white subject producing it; but in doing so it also connects that subject to the proliferating series that cannot be stayed. Its placement in this series gone out of control disturbs its supposed stability and certainty.

Racism has always been one of the supports that screen from culture its masquerade; yet, at the same time, that masquerade makes racism an open secret. In Joan Riviere's essay, the woman's masquerade depends upon a seemingly repressed scenario of race. Riviere describes how the analysand who performs her womanliness does so directly in response to racial fantasies about black men, whose threats of sexuality and aggression she defuses through her seductiveness, in a classic instance of having it both ways.[114] Yet this scenario isn't repressed in Riviere's essay; what's disturbing

---

[112] Bhabha, "Interrogating Identity: The Postcolonial Prerogative," in *Anatomy of Racism*, ed. David Theo Goldberg (Minneapolis: University of Minnesota Press, 1990), 183–209; 185. Bhabha argues that stereotypes are at least temporarily effective because "caught in the Imaginary as they are, these shifting positionalities will never seriously threaten the dominant power relations, for they exist to exercise them pleasurably and productively. They will always pose the problem of difference as that between the pre-constituted, 'natural' poles of black and white with all its historical and ideological ramifications. The *knowledge of the construction* of that 'opposition' will be denied the colonial subject" ("Other Question," 165). Bhabha sees the stereotype as a "limited form of otherness, [a] fixed form of difference" (ibid.) that stabilizes but also points to difference's more radical play, but he recognizes that "its symbolic meaning, however, is thoroughly ambivalent" (170).

[113] Bhabha, "Postcolonial Authority and Postmodern Guilt," and subsequent "Discussion" in *Cultural Studies*, ed. Lawrence Grossberg, Cary Nelson, and Paula A. Treichler (New York: Routledge, 1992), 56–66, 66–68; 65–66.

[114] "Obviously it was a step towards propitiating the avenger to endeavour to offer herself to him sexually. This phantasy, it then appeared, had been very common in her childhood and youth, which had been spent in the Southern States of America; if a negro came to attack her, she planned to defend herself by making him kiss her and make love to her (ultimately so that she could then deliver him over to justice). But there was a further determinant of the obsessive behaviour. In a dream which had a rather similar content to this childhood phantasy, she was

is not that it is hidden, but that it is so visible. It is generally ignored by the theory elaborated from it (neither Lacan, Heath, nor Butler makes any mention of it),[115] suggesting the ways too that the everyday's significance takes place on its surface, not in some hidden and obscure depths.

It is not surprising that one of the primary stereotypes for the black subject is the monkey, since monkeys in Western culture are synonymous with mimicry; yet such reflections are actually reciprocal. White culture's identification of its black other with the monkey actually rebounds on it, since the black subject's supposedly empty aping of the white subject's humanness and selfhood can swing back to incriminate that selfhood too as a masquerade. In fact, in Lacan's writing on the mirror stage, the monkey—he actually means other primates, chimpanzees in particular—may be precisely his symbol for a kind of symbolic enlightenment. The chimp, who outdoes the human child at this point in "instrumental intelligence," is unperturbed by the specular economy. His imago in the mirror "has been mastered and found empty,"—while the more pitiful and less savvy human infant is caught in the endless alienating oscillations of trying to live up to what seems a full and complete ideal.[116] In a curiously enigmatic allusion, Lacan refers his readers to Lévi-Strauss for examples of such imagoes—"veiled faces it is our privilege to see in outline in daily experience."[117] And perhaps one of these everyday imagoes is a figure that Lévi-Strauss records as taboo in many cultures—the practice of dressing a monkey up like a man and making fun of it.[118] Such practice, it seems, might make the element of mimicry and masquerade in humanness itself too apparent.

Woolf was herself a highly informed and serious critic of imperialism, partly because she had been able to see its oppressive and violent effects up close. Jane Marcus outlines Woolf's family lineage, her descent from "Anglo-Indian policymakers."[119] Educated on money earned in the West Indies, the Stephen men (her grandfather James Stephen was permanent undersecretary for the Colonies) shaped British policy about slavery and colonialism in a way that consolidated such policy with their patriarchal views: "Woolf's insistence in her work on the relation of patriarchy to imperialism and of both to class and fascism comes from careful study of her family's legacy," Marcus ar-

---

in terror alone in the house; then a negro came in and found her washing clothes, with her sleeves rolled up and arms exposed. She resisted him, with the secret intention of attracting him sexually, and he began to admire her arms and caress them and her breasts" (Riviere, 37).

[115] More and more work about the repressed subtext of race in psychoanalysis is starting to appear. For an excellent essay on this topic, see Jean Walton, "Re-placing Race in (White) Psychoanalytic Discourse: Founding Narratives of Feminism," *Critical Inquiry* 21(1995): 775–804.

[116] Lacan, "The Mirror Stage," in *Ecrits*, 1.

[117] Ibid., 3. Lacan's reference is to Lévi-Strauss's *Structural Anthropology*, chapter 10.

[118] Claude Lévi-Strauss, "Principles of Kinship," in his *Elementary Structures of Kinship*, trans. James Harle Bell et al. (Boston: Beacon Press, 1969), 478–97; 494–95.

[119] Marcus, "Britannia," 137.

gues.[120] She carefully and resolutely reads novels including *The Waves*, as well as *Mrs. Dalloway*, as anti-imperialist tracts, and locates their project as a critique of the quest for a "definition of the (white male) self against the racial or sexual Other." [121] And Woolf does explicitly argue in *Three Guineas* that a consciousness of gender or class identity, and an attention to their inequities, necessitates a similar treatment of race (*Three*, 60, 80, 102). But even Marcus, not much given to criticizing Woolf, admits that "Woolf had a double legacy regarding race," that she remains complicit in what she critiques.[122] And how could it be otherwise?—for, as Fanon suggests, the self constructed within culture—whether white or black—is a self born into racism. Patrick McGee, insisting on this doubleness, criticizes both Woolf and Marcus for downplaying it: "Perhaps the greatest lie of imperialism is the belief that self-criticism and self-knowledge lead to self-liberation and knowledge of the other." [123] The difficulty of Woolf's politics is that her writing exposes the violence and oppression of the wish for exemption even as that writing itself participates in that wish.

Woolf's fiction incorporates black identity not just in terms of its stereotypes but also in terms of their radical effect. In a short story titled "The Evening Party," a precursor to *Mrs. Dalloway* and *Mrs. Dalloway's Party*, an early investigation into the incognitos of party consciousness, Woolf records the indebtedness of such gatherings to social inequities—to racial exploitations—they must ignore and deny; the ideal of social perfection such parties assume, a professor tells one of the other guests, relies precisely on such exclusions:

> "let me whisper it, the conversation of these ladies, earnest and benevolent, with exalted views on the destiny of the negro who is at this moment toiling beneath the lash to procure rubber for some of our friends engaged in agreeable conversation here. To enjoy your perfection—"
> "I take your point. One must exclude."
> "The greater part of everything." [124]

Yet although Woolf's fiction questions this system of oppression, it still makes use of its terms, for those hypocritical ladies—also profiting from the very system they seem to question—are characterized as savages themselves, with "matted hair and yellow tinted skin." [125] In reflecting on them, and the professor's indictment of them, his interlocutor articulates how the image of the dark other functions within this representational system: "Don't you re-

[120] Ibid., 149.
[121] Ibid., 137.
[122] Ibid., 150.
[123] McGee, "The Politics of Modernist Form; Or, Who Rules *The Waves*?" *Modern Fiction Studies* 38 (1992): 631–50; 649.
[124] "The Evening Party," in *Complete Shorter Fiction*, 96–101; 98.
[125] Ibid.

member in early childhood, when, in play or talk, as one stepped across the puddle or reached the window on the landing, some imperceptible shock froze the universe to a solid ball of crystal which one held for a moment. . . . then we were absolute and entire; nothing then was excluded; that was certainty—happiness. But later these crystal globes dissolve as one holds them: some one talks of negroes."[126] The terms here—the solid ball of crystal that forms after an imperceptible shock—are similar to Woolf's apotropaic desire in *Moments of Being* for the integrity of the world revealed behind the cotton wool of daily life. But the possibility of that integrity is even more tenuous here—and the image of the "negro" is what undoes it.

And it undoes it in Woolf's writing specifically through the stereotype of the black subject as animal, as monkey, and through its relation to the everyday. In a very early fragment of a short story titled (by her editor at least) "[The Monkeys]," Woolf's lyrical description of monkeys playing in the jungle emphasizes that even within that seeming paradise a desperate battle for survival is taking place: "The monkeys knew of the great battle that was daily fought."[127] Woolf's dystopia here is, as Haraway suggests, an attempt to naturalize ideology, to find in the heart of darkness an image for supposed civilization. That this is a fragmentary and disturbing image for Woolf, and that white culture cannot entirely scapegoat its degradation onto its black other, is part of the message of *The Voyage Out*: after Richard Dalloway's adulterous kiss, Rachel Vinrace thinks that "she and Richard had seen something together which is hidden in ordinary life" (*Voyage*, 77). This secret masked by the everyday is supposed to be a kind of savagery at the heart of British society, and even within innocent Rachel herself, as revealed in her dream: she dreamed "of a little deformed man who squatted on the floor gibbering, with long nails. His face was pitted and like the face of an animal. . . . All night long barbarian men harassed the ship; they came scuffling down the passages, and stopped to snuffle at her door" (*Voyage*, 77). The black stereotype contaminates the white subject, reflects back to it its fantasy. But this very fantasy suggests that for Woolf, as for Conrad, the black subject remains only an other, simply a reflection or distortion of whiteness. Fanon and Bhabha analyze the utility of this image for white culture, show the way it is a counter circulating within and in service to the representational system, which it also unsettles. But although Woolf too points to that dynamic, she continues also to assume it. In retaining the fantasy that there is something hidden behind the very mask of the everyday that she has shown elsewhere to be empty, constitutive, Woolf participates in the contrivance by which, Bhabha writes, (white) "culture reaches out to create a symbolic textuality, to give the alienating everyday an 'aura' of selfhood."[128]

[126] Ibid., 98–99.
[127] "[The Monkeys]," in *Complete Shorter Fiction*, 324–25; 325.
[128] "Freedom's Basis," 47.

Woolf makes the disintegrating black subject into white culture's other partly because of how much she identifies with it, how much she has internalized what it represents. Although throughout her writings, the simian is her customary and unthinking metaphor for people of color, that metaphor is to some degree complicated by her own relation to it: Leonard, whom as prospective husband fresh from colonial service in Ceylon she had introduced to her friends as "a penniless Jew" who had "hung black men" (a complicated construction itself, since elsewhere Woolf associates the "swarthiness" of Jews with Africans), had a pet monkey from whom he was inseparable, acting out by metonymy his relation to Woolf herself, whose pet name was "Mandrill";[129] Vanessa as well called her a "poor little monkey."[130] Woolf even applies Leonard's critique of the gorilla ego to herself: "As L. very truly says there is too much ego in *my* cosmos."[131] And yet Leonard's worry, as well as Woolf's, was actually that there was not enough, that Woolf was unable even to maintain the most borderline illusion of identity. Woolf is attracted enough to the notion of black identity as masquerade to mention in her diary her attendance at a showing of sculpture from the Ivory Coast and the Congo at the Chelsea Book Club—"the Nigger's show," she called it, but her editor tells us it was actually "a pioneer exhibition which excited great interest and a revision of accepted ideas."[132] The revision of accepted ideas implied in the African masks for Woolf herself might have seemed extreme enough to explain her later fascination with a disturbing anecdote from the life of her friend Roger Fry. Woolf tells the story of the mad French peasant woman who shot herself for love of Fry: "This creature thought he laughed at her, seeing that he dyed vests yellow & sent them to her, telling her to turn to the East & put them on, as a cure for tuberculosis.

---

[129] Leonard figures as a penniless Jew in a couple of letters: "To Violet Dickinson," [4 June 1912], Letter 620 of *Letters*, 1: 500; "To Janet Case," [June 1912], Letter 622 of *Letters*, 1: 501. Woolf brags about him hanging black men in "To Lady Robert Cecil," [June 1912], Letter 629 of *Letters*, 1: 504. She associates Jews and Africans in her description of a visitor, on whom she exercises the same racism she notes that visitor exercising on others: "Oh to have a knapsack & go tramping! she said, being a swarthy hooknosed red cheeked racy Jewess. At least that phase lasted out lunch—We discussed races; she was born in South Africa. Natives smell she said. Native servants rooms smell very strong": "Thursday 8 February 1940," in *Diary*, 5: 264–65.

[130] Quoted in Mark Hussey, "Refractions of Desire: The Early Fiction of Virginia and Leonard Woolf," *Modern Fiction Studies*, 38 (1992): 127–46; 143.

[131] "Tuesday 22 August 1922," *Diary*, 2: 191; my emphasis.

[132] "Thursday 15 April 1920," *Diary*, 2: 30 n9. The fuller passage is interesting: "Rain has come—what I mind much more is the black sky: so ugly. Yesterday I think I was unhappy all day long. . . . The day before I went to the Nigger's show in Chelsea; very sad impressive figures; obscene, somehow monumental; figures of Frenchmen, I thought, sodden with civilization & cynicism; yet they were carved (perhaps) in the Congo 100's of years ago" (30). The connection of "ugly" (and "obscene") blackness with unhappiness continues Woolf's identification of her madness with the dangerous and decentered black subject. Woolf's confusion of this African sculpture with a product of France suggests the ways in which the black image gets appropriated as a reflection of the internal problems of a sodden and cynical white culture.

And sent her pictures of negro sculpture. For some reason, against my habit, I feel as if I should like to write a story of this."[133] Woolf's editor glosses this episode by telling us about Fry's lover; "She was obsessed by suspicious fancies which led to misunderstandings; these came to a climax when he sent her the photograph of a negro mask he had recently bought, which she interpreted as a cruel joke at her expense" and in response to which she took her life.[134] The mask of the self implied in the mimicry blackness represents can quite literally lead to madness and the death of the subject within the hysterical white culture of Woolf's world. Woolf's unglossed disclosure that at one social gathering she and her friends "laughed over the letter of the mad negress" seems in this context an attempt to displace and manage what she saw as an explicit threat.[135]

In *A Room of One's Own*, Woolf discusses women's ability to resist the lures of the integral self, which always imply a desire for mastery, appropriation:

> The desire to be veiled still possesses [women]. . . . [they can] pass a tombstone or a signpost without feeling an irresistible desire to cut their names on it, as Alf, Bert, or Chas, must do in obedience to their instinct, which murmurs if it sees a fine woman go by, or even a dog, Ce chien est à moi. And, of course, it may not be a dog. . . . It is one of the great advantages of being a woman that one can pass even a very fine negress without wishing to make an Englishwoman of her. (*Room*, 50)

The doubleness of Woolf's irony here (*pace* Childers) actually reflects the inescapable doubleness of her politics. Her tone is able to characterize the "very fine negress" as an object at the very same time she heralds her as what escapes the objectification of selfhood; that tone allows her to participate in the very system of oppression she also exposes.[136] Her own identification with such figures reflects the fine line she felt she also must toe in this economy: to expose as an illusion the very pose of identity which remained nonetheless necessary to function, and often impossible for her. I don't mean to be saying here that Woolf's identification with the exploited subjects she also disparages somehow rehabilitates or undoes her racism. Woolf's analysis of class is ambivalent as well and as implicated in its own critique, but her treatment of race may be more chilling because its unconsciousness may *perform*

---

[133] "Saturday 14 June 1924," *Diary*, 2: 303.

[134] Ibid., 303 n1.

[135] "Friday 25 November 1921," *Diary*, 2: 145. For a reading of the cultural stereotypes connecting madness and blackness, see Sander L. Gilman, "On the Nexus of Blackness and Madness," in his *Difference and Pathology: Stereotypes of Sexuality, Race, and Madness* (Ithaca: Cornell University Press, 1985), 131–49.

[136] It is in fact in response to this passage that Marcus admits the complicity of Woolf's writing with cultural racism: "Britannia," 149–50.

better the dubious and equivocal nature of political positions that Woolf works elsewhere to analyze.

For Fanon and Bhabha, as well as for Woolf, the ultimate effect of that inescapable ambivalence remains a product of the way we define the series and the everyday. Bhabha criticizes Habermas for the way his theory uses the category of the everyday simply to shift the locus of truth and authority: "The claim to knowledge shifts from the 'universal' to the domain of context-bound everyday practice." Bhabha writes, "Validity claims seek justification for their propositions in terms of the specificity of the 'everyday.'" [137] Fanon, Bhabha argues, exposes the everyday as a "grotesque psychodrama," a "constellation of delirium" in which racism is constructed, rather than as a natural ground.[138] Fanon insists that when seen any other way, the everyday becomes a conduit connecting all other political positions to fascism, the culmination of a great cultural series leading directly up to it; he quotes Aimé Césaire: "Yes, European civilization and its best representatives are responsible for colonial racism. . . . 'It is savagery, the supreme savagery, it crowns, it epitomizes the day-to-day savageries; yes, it is Nazism, but before they became its victims, they were its accomplices'" (90–91). Woolf connects Mussolini with the insidiousness of such a view of the everyday, which he knew furthered his political project: "he is the Coué of Italy: repeats every day & every way & c." [139] And this is the version of the everyday assumed as a religion. In *The Voyage Out*, Rachel Vinrace, who has never paid much attention to that theory of transcendence encoded within England's state religion, wakes up one day after her experiences of empire—both her recognition of, and her participation in, its horrors—to listen to the words of the service: "Be merciful unto me, O God . . . for man goeth about to devour me: he is daily fighting and troubling me. . . . They daily mistake my words: all that they imagine is to do me evil. . . Break their teeth, O God, in their mouths" (*Voyage*, 226–27). What's distinctive about the exposure of this religion of the everyday in Woolf's work is that it allows us to apply it not just to the social system that she criticizes, but to that writing's operations, as well as to our own relation to it as critics. "Be merciful unto *me*, O God"—the dream of transcendent exemption from violent everyday relations is shown to be itself a form of violence, the stance of innocence actually steeped in the system it decries: break the teeth, O God, of the man who goes about to devour me. Our fear as critics too is that our words will be, as we like to call it, "mistaken"; that all our good intentions will be unable to keep us from facing the

---

[137] "Freedom's Basis," 50.

[138] The first phrase is from "The Other Question," 149; the second is from "Interrogating Identity," 186.

[139] "Monday 26 November 1934," *Diary*, 4: 263. As the editor explains, "Dr. Emile Coué (1857–1926), French psychotherapist whose formula 'every day and in every way I am becoming better and better' became proverbial" (263 n13).

same charges that we make against others, which prompts us perhaps even more desperately to cry out against them, to stop their mouths with blood. Woolf's politics seem to me important because they don't attempt to hide these desperate paradoxes, but place them directly on the surface of her writing and insist we attend to that surface rather than to some consoling profundity always elsewhere. At the same time, those politics also don't obscure their own desire—disturbing but inescapable—for atonement.

❧

Homi Bhabha's notion of iteration, which he borrows from Derrida, underlies the reading of stereotypes in this chapter: reiteration both repeats and alters, and (as I explore in my chapter on Trollope) opens up the definition of the series. In my discussion in this chapter so far, the series has shifted from a rather strictly defined narrative form to a more diffuse pattern of repetition, revision, and connection that informs—provides the very possibility for—the construction of identity (Derrida and Bhabha suggest that the very illusion of the self is made up through its—imperfect—contrast with the others from which it differs). I want to extend the notion (and the usefulness) of the series impulse within literary history even further now by considering it as a general and constitutive principle of that history itself—if we take that history to mean what we ordinarily mean by it: a series of texts connected by repetition, revision, influence. Part of Woolf's major struggle as a writer was to claim for herself and other women a place in that series.

Woolf helps us to think of literary history as an ongoing series—unbegun and unfinished—because her own work complicates and appropriates for feminism an important insight about tradition: that the construction of whatever series of texts seems to make up the tradition is always in process, and each new text retroactively recasts the series that leads up to it, configuring it differently in order to connect with it. I say that Woolf *appropriates* this insight because it is usually asserted by a patriarchal tradition, voiced recently, say, by Harold Bloom. Rewriting the tradition involves deliberate "misreading," Bloom claims—that is, willful re-reading—to find in the past what the present needs. But the battle between waning fathers and potent sons that Bloom also sketches is only one way to imagine this series of connections; when women's texts are added to the set, the combinations and permutations of the series become almost infinite, and spill over in so many directions that the neat Oedipal symmetries between father and son are shown to be a desperate attempt to keep chaos in order. Woolf's most spectacular revision of this kind is the story of Judith Shakespeare (a character she doesn't actually invent, but borrows from the title of a popular novel of the time, written by a man),[140] whose very implausibility as a historical fig-

---

[140] William Black, *Judith Shakespeare: A Romance* (New York: Sampson Low, 1893).

ure, Tania Modleski suggests, exposes the constructedness of male history as well, recasting tradition as a series of forcible exclusions.[141] But what happens to the construction of literary history and the series when Woolf's own work gets repeated, revised, critiqued, by writers who follow her?

Given Woolf's own classism and racism, it might seem unlikely to imagine literary history as a series of works connecting Woolf's books with the writing of contemporary African American novelists. And yet many of those novelists imagine literary history precisely that way, writing themselves into the series of texts that make up tradition by drawing their connections to Woolf. These connections have to do as much with limits that must be transgressed as with possibilities. One of the most important of these marks of influence is Toni Morrison's M.A. thesis at Cornell, which is in part on *Mrs. Dalloway*; it's not surprising, moreover, that the subject of that thesis is suicide.[142] For some African American writers, claiming connection with Woolf is a way forcibly to seize the tradition. Yet—given the attitudes and assumptions in Woolf's work—to construct an alternative, feminist series of texts in direct descent from her may also be a form of suicide, still carrying for African American women writers the risk of writing themselves out of history.

Except that Woolf's work is also so much about reclaiming sites that seem lost to history. Its particular interest in the everyday as one of those sites may be what allows such unlikely allies as Woolf and African American writers to forge themselves into a series. And the everyday suggests the kind of attitude those later texts might take to such a predecessor; their differences from Woolf don't spell out a wishful emphasis on the essential liberation of contradiction, if only because the story told by the everyday is not one of freedom or autonomy but one in which its actors can only (as de Certeau might call it) "make do" within the series that gives shape to them. In connecting literary history through conflict, reworking, making-do, the everyday may help transform what has seemed to be a totalizing picture of feminism itself. The writing of the everyday can begin to uncover the differences between women that inform their connections. The everyday becomes a figure for how disparity and division, rather than harmony and integrity, make up the series. The resources of the everyday lie in its intransigence, the way its reduction to the bare minimum can still provide a literary heritage for writers

---

[141] Tania Modleski, *Feminism without Women: Culture and Criticism in a "Postfeminist" Age* (New York: Routledge, 1991), 55.

[142] Toni Morrison, "Virginia Woolf's and William Faulkner's Treatment of the Alienated," MA thesis, English Department, Cornell University, 1955. The connection between Woolf and Alice Walker was the main focus of the Third Annual Conference on Virginia Woolf at Lincoln University. See *Virginia Woolf: Emerging Perspectives*, Selected Papers from the Third Annual Conference on Virginia Woolf, Lincoln University, Jefferson City, Mo., June 10–13, 1991, ed. Mark Hussey and Vara Neverow (New York: Pace University Press, 1994), especially Barbara Christian, "Layered Rhythms: Virginia Woolf and Toni Morrison," pp. 164–77 in that volume.

such as Alice Walker and Paule Marshall, or critics such as Barbara Christian and Bernice Reagon, who find in the daily practice of ordinary black women a way to make do and make over the history that also constrains them. To these writers, the everyday, as the figure both for the hidden forces that shape us and for the energies that stray within, or make over, such forces, becomes also the representative figure for a kind of doubleness. And this understanding of the everyday provides a model to help make over approaches that ignore or repress doubleness. To insist on a fracture within literary history—finding resources within its strictures—is one way to counter a universalizing sweep that tends otherwise to deny such practices, exclude certain voices.

Which also means recognizing splits in categories such as "woman," "feminism," and "the everyday." Such recognition would begin to heed the call of black feminists like Hazel Carby, who writes: "Feminism has to be transformed if it is to address us. . . . In other words, of white feminists we must ask, what exactly do you mean when you say 'WE'??" [143] One way Carby suggests that white feminists (like myself) confront this question is to recognize the differences between the "day-to-day struggles" of white women and black women (and also the different struggles within these groups).[144] Their everydayness is not stable (part of what makes the everyday the normalizing vehicle of power that it seems to feminists influenced by Foucault might be the assumption that it is the same for everyone.[145] Hence the everydayness of the dominant—read white—group gets imposed on others as another form of power).

Standard literary feminism has taken for granted that Woolf's *Room of One's Own* is an important text, but perhaps what makes it an important influence on African American feminism too is the way it stresses the need to uncover differences within the category of the everyday (even when it ignores its own injunction). In taking the everyday as "the common life which is the real life" (*Room*, 113), Woolf's text tries in part to synthesize, homogenize, the everyday's pattern (think of the synthesizing force inherent in the climax of androgyny that ends Woolf's text). But "the crumpled skin of the day" (24) Woolf wishes to fling into the hedge is not so easily skimmed off; the supposedly deep commonalties between women are disturbed within that text by "puzzles that one notes in the margin of daily life" (35). For Woolf finds that there is something about the everyday that disturbs conventional ideas about it—unsettling her own desire "to feel the usual things

---

[143] Carby, "White Women Listen! Black Feminism and the Boundaries of Sisterhood," in *The Empire Strikes Back: Race and Racism in 70's Britain*, ed. Centre for Contemporary Cultural Studies (London: Hutchinson, 1982), 233.

[144] Ibid., 215, 219.

[145] For one reading of women's relation to the way power comes from the bottom up, in terms of daily normalizing practices, see Nancy Armstrong, *Desire and Domestic Fiction: A Political History of the Novel* (New York: Oxford, 1987).

in the usual places," making it "impossible for me to roll out my sonorous phrases about 'elemental feelings,' the 'common stuff of humanity'" (91). Woolf's shift of attention to the everyday, to "ordinary people in the street" (63), especially women's "infinitely obscure lives" (89) (obscure because so ordinary), opens up a vision of difference that goes beyond and disturbs the blanket conclusions about women and history she wishes to draw. That recognition of the differences that inhabit our own desire for unity has been useful to various feminists in helping to call into question the single vision of woman and culture that Woolf's text also propagates.

Of *A Room of One's Own*, Adrienne Rich writes: "Like Virginia Woolf, I am aware of the women who are not with us here because they are washing the dishes and looking after the children. Nearly fifty years after she spoke, that fact remains largely unchanged. And I am thinking also of women whom she left out of the picture altogether—women who are washing other people's dishes and caring for other people's children." [146] To include those women left out altogether not just by cultural history but, worse, by feminist revisions of it like Woolf's, Alice Walker (in "In Search of Our Mother's Gardens") quotes Woolf in order to revise her prose, to insert into and write over it the everyday reality of black women in America, silenced by dominant culture, yet for each of whom "being an artist has still been a daily part of her life"—for instance, the poet Phillis Wheatley, who, far from having a room and five hundred pounds of her own, "owned not even herself." [147] Walker's notion of the everyday involves not so much a specific content as it does a form, or an impulse, the series as open-ended and amorphous—unbegun and unfinished. It is not just these anonymous women's songs—for many of them remain unrecorded—but *"the notion of song"* ("In Search," 237), not just their stories—for many of them remain unfinished—but the urgency of them (240) that is the legacy Walker tells us their daily lives leave African American women writers like herself. "Torn by 'contrary instincts,'" Wheatley's "struggling, ambivalent lines" (236–37) record the difference of these women's struggles. And Walker too begins her own essay from a place of division to record the ongoing strain out of which she must still write: an epigraph (from Marilou Awiakta's poem "Abiding Appalachia") that reads: "Creation often / needs two hearts" (230).

[146] Rich, "When We Dead Awaken: Feminist Writing as Re-Vision," in her *On Lies, Secrets, and Silences* (New York: Norton, 1979), 38.
[147] Walker, "In Search of Our Mothers' Gardens," in her *In Search of Our Mothers' Gardens: Womanist Prose* (San Diego: Harcourt, 1983), 242, 235; all future references to this essay (abbreviated "In Search") will appear in the text. Walker says elsewhere that she taught Woolf's writing—especially *A Room of One's Own*—in her course on black women writers at Wellesley (along with Kate Chopin's work) "not because they were black, obviously, but because they were women and wrote, as the black women did, on the condition of humankind from the perspective of women": John O'Brien, "Interview with Alice Walker," in Alice Walker, *Everyday Use*, ed. Barbara Christian (New Brunswick, N.J.: Rutgers University Press, 1994), 55–81; 70.

Paule Marshall also sees the everyday as the medium in which such differences get registered. In her statement about literary heritage, "From the Poets in the Kitchen," she too brings to our attention "unknown bards" like Woolf's Judith Shakespeare. Her poets are not the sisters of great men, however, but, like Walker's, "a group of ordinary housewives and mothers" even more invisible.[148] Immigrants to Brooklyn from Barbados, negotiating the "strange customs and laws" of an alien culture (7), these women infuse an artistic practice Marshall will imitate in her writing with tactics learned from the struggles of their workaday lives: "Using everyday speech, the simple commonplace words—but always with imagination and skill—they gave voice to the most complex ideas. Flannery O'Connor would have approved of how they made ordinary language work, as she put it, 'double-time,' stretching, shading, deepening its meaning. Like Joseph Conrad they were always trying to infuse new life in the 'old old words worn thin . . . by . . . careless usage'" (9). Locating their art in all that is left to them, conserving, turning over, the used-up and worn-out, infusing new life by accepting the ordinary *as* ordinary distinguishes this everyday practice, just as "common speech and the plain, workaday words that make it up are . . . the stock in trade of some of the best fiction writers" (3). Marshall connects this heritage to standard literary culture, exemplified not by Woolf but by O'Connor and Conrad, but only to insist that what is best *there* is most like the "rich legacy of language and culture" that comes from the everyday life of these black women (12).

For Marshall, her coming to voice occurs when the gap in the series of texts she has been reading—as a child, she had "a special passion for the long, full-blown, richly detailed 18th- and 19th-century picaresque tales: 'Tom Jones,' 'Great Expectations,' 'Vanity Fair'" (10)—is filled when she finally comes across Paul Laurence Dunbar and a whole tradition of "Negro writers" (11) she hadn't known existed.[149] And although she admits that she is indebted to "the usual literary giants . . . white and black" (11), the tradition of which she is part and which takes shape around her is actually more defined by her training in the everyday, given to her by her mother's friends in the kitchen. The complexity of the everyday for Marshall, the way it works for her double-time, is to introduce a notion of "fundamental dualism" (9), of unresolvable opposition and contradiction into an otherwise closed language and culture. And "it wasn't only what the women talked about—the content—but the way they put things—their style," Marshall writes (7). For Marshall too, the everyday becomes less its content (the triv-

[148] Marshall, "From the Poets in the Kitchen," in her *Reena and Other Stories* (Old Westbury, N.Y.: Feminist Press, 1983), 4; all future references to this essay will appear in the text.
[149] That Marshall connects books such as *Great Expectations* and *Vanity Fair* to *Tom Jones* by defining them as picaresque (they're not usually put in that category) suggest the way in which not just they but the whole tradition becomes for her a *series*—an open-ended succession of connections (which, arguably, is what defines the picaresque).

ialized banalities of endless drudgery that black women especially are made to perform) than the styles and tactics derived from it.[150]

Barbara Christian seems to polarize the connections between African American writers and Woolf: in discussing Alice Walker's interest in Woolf, she rejects her as "an upper-class British white woman," hung up on high aesthetics rather than the folk traditions of everyday culture.[151] But Walker's continued interest in Woolf suggests the ways that—despite their very real divisions—both writers are interested in the everyday as a divided ground. And this is the importance of the everyday in Christian's writing as well. What Christian calls "the tone of the commonplace" informs black women's writing, she argues, as a way of "making space," of keeping that work from being "reduced to a stereotype."[152] Although the concentration on the ordinary she describes can be part of a realism fully as conventional as the heroic mode she sees black women writers refusing, her point is more complex than this qualification allows. In using the everyday to gesture toward a "space" outside the homogenizing structures of a history and culture that ignore them (whether or not this gesture can ever be successful), African American women writers interrogate the notion of culture as totalizing, the notion of the ordinary as single and common to us all. By "making space," the everyday undoes a monolithic idea of history and culture by suggesting how the same space can be inhabited simultaneously in different ways. What distinguishes "commonplaces" from "stereotypes" for these writers may be that the commonplace for them makes space within the supposedly unchanging patterns that give stereotypes their oppressive force.

One important version of feminist struggle—taken by Catherine Gallagher, say—has been to emphasize such patterns as determining, to show how the level of the everyday is exactly where dominant structure seems most entrenched and totalizing: "the women's liberation movement . . . forced us to see that the more 'personal' and 'mundane' the issues, the more resistance to change we encountered," she writes.[153] The version of the everyday theorized by these African American women writers, on the other hand, emphasizes the importance of conflict and difference instead; it supplies a notion of struggle that is itself in conflict with an understanding of the everyday as total and totalizing. This is the message that Bernice Johnson Reagon, in "Coalition Politics: Turning the Century," wants women to carry together into the next century as they continue to construct their—radically

[150] For more on the way the everyday gives voice to such complex and subtle ideas, see bell hooks's discussion of the phrase "Halfway, I'm just halfway" as an example of the theory and abstraction in everyday (African American) speech: "Feminist Theory: A Radical Agenda," in her *Talking Back: Thinking Feminist/ Thinking Black* (Boston: Southend Press, 1989), 39.
[151] Christian, "Introduction," *Everyday Use*," 3–17.
[152] Christian, "Ordinary Women: The Tone of the Commonplace," in her *Black Women Novelists: The Development of a Tradition* (Westport, Conn.: Greenwood Press, 1980), 71, 73, 71.
[153] Gallagher, "Marxism and the New Historicism," in *The New Historicism*, ed. H. Aram Veeser (New York: Routledge, 1989), 42.

multiple—histories. Reagon argues that we need to keep connecting uneasy and unlikely constituents into the kind of series we can also see as a coalition. Yet what's important about this connection is that it makes you "feel threatened to the core."[154] For Reagon, a sense of history that leads to social change means coming together with people who aren't like you, people you don't like, in order to work together for a world in which everybody can live. And that work happens on the level of the everyday: "It ain't that important what you do in a crisis. . . . In fact that's all you pay attention to: when that great day happen. You go wishing everyday was like that. Everyday ain't like that, and what really counts is not what you do [in a crisis, but] . . . Monday, Tuesday morning at work. . . . do it everyday you get up and find yourself alive" (368). It is perhaps Reagon's sense of the everyday as the ongoing place of guerrilla skirmishes that makes Hortense Spillers see her essay as the signal one in a book (the anthology, *Home Girls*, which it ends) that, she thinks, "could have *started* at any point and not *ended* at all."[155] And in doing so she sees this text "raise, by a slightly different route, the hint of an inquiry that Virginia Woolf approached in *A Room of One's Own*" (179). In forging their literary history through a coalition with Virginia Woolf, these African American women writers perform the risky politics (unbegun and unfinished) of the series and the everyday—a risk and a politics they tell us are necessary to our common survival: to reroute the standard series, to continue constructing and reconstructing a series of direct encounters with identities (within ourselves or "others") that we would rather avoid, ignore, wish away. As Reagon's essay makes clear, politics may simply be the attempt in our everyday struggles to recognize the uneasy coalition that makes up this "WE." Entering the political debate means giving our own meaning and shape to our past history, to the series of related elements that comes before and produces us, and that will follow after. Literary history becomes directly connected to politics here because the literary tradition constitutes the province in which we imagine possibilities: it gives shape to our dreams for (and in) the future. African American women writers may recognize their connection with a predecessor like Woolf by rewriting her to give her influence a different meaning—more complex, more messy. By casting the everyday as the site of such divisions, they suggest how a radical, shifting, open-ended notion of the series might just provide us with a model of history that could change the future—the very future to which, if the series shows us anything, it shows us that we are inescapably, but perhaps also fortunately, bound.

---

[154] Reagon, "Coalition Politics: Turning the Century," in *Home Girls: A Black Feminist Anthology*, ed. Barbara Smith (New York: Kitchen Table/Women of Color Press, 1983), 356–68; 356; all future references to this work will appear in the text.
[155] Spillers, "Review Essay: 'Turning the Century': Notes on Women and Difference," *Tulsa Studies in Women's Literature* 3 (1984): 178–85; 178; all future references to this work will appear in the text.

Afterword: "Enough!"

In his 1933 *New Introductory Lectures* (themselves the repetition of a series of *Introductory Lectures* he had published twenty years earlier), Sigmund Freud tells the story of an American psychiatrist. American practitioners of psychology, especially ego psychology—with its studied denial of the role of the unconscious so central to psychoanalysis—were often Freud's symbol for a certain kind of earnest and misdirected dullness. This particular American, in the face of Continental theory, had written a paper entitled "Enough!"— hence, Freud writes, giving "energetic expression to his boredom at [what bothered him most in it] the 'compulsion to repeat.'" [1] The compulsion to repeat as Freud described it has exactly to do with the contested issue of the unconscious. Within psychoanalysis, that compulsion, more than anything else, makes manifest, acts as the interface of, the unconscious—it comes in fact to *represent* the unconscious in psychoanalytic theory: "*the resistance of the unconscious*," Freud writes elsewhere, is "the compulsion to repeat." [2] Freud provided an etiology of that compulsion in *Beyond the Pleasure Principle*: it is ultimately fueled by the instinctual desire to restore the earliest stage of things, to regress to the inorganic quiescence before life, an impulse that Freud sometimes also called the death drive, and that he read in any series of repetitions, the form (of repetition) figuring more significantly than the content repeated. Yet the debate here is not as straightforward as it seems. What the American was actually objecting to was not *Freud's* and (psychoanalysis's) definition of the repetition compulsion, but its insidious appearance within ego psychology, the "Individual Psychology" of Freud's disciple turned rival, Alfred Adler.

[1] Sigmund Freud, *New Introductory Lectures on Psycho-analysis*, vol. 22 (1964) in *The Standard Edition of the Complete Psychological Works of Sigmund Freud*, ed. James Strachey, 24 vols. (London: Hogarth, 1953–74) 3–182; 143.
[2] Sigmund Freud, "Addenda" to "Inhibitions, Symptoms and Anxiety," in *Standard*, 20: 77–175; 159–60.

Boredom, as I've argued earlier, is a most effective rhetorical strategy. And, in this particular instance, Freud cites the American not just to dismiss but to *identify* with his boredom. Part of the point of the *New Introductory Lectures* is to assert psychoanalysis as an established field in the face of continued dismissal of it. Freud writes:

> There is a common saying that we should learn from our enemies. I confess I have never succeeded in doing so; but I thought all the same it might be instructive for you if I undertook a review of all the reproaches and objections which the opponents of psycho-analysis have raised against it, and if I went on to point out the injustices and offenses against logic which could so easily be revealed in them. But on second thought I told myself that it would not be at all interesting but would become tedious and distressing and would be precisely what I have been so carefully avoiding all these years.[3]

Freud's own feelings about what is "not at all interesting . . . tedious" when it comes to the theory of the psyche echoes the boredom of the American which he also charts. He uses this hapless psychiatrist in effect to turn to Adler and shout "Enough!" at a strategic moment in his own text.

Freud asserts here that psychoanalytic theory cannot address all its critics' objections, nor should it. That is simply not the way to advance an argument. It is a way that bores Freud, one that even distresses him, one that he has always tried to avoid. The American psychiatrist seems on the face of it to provide an example of the way most critics of psychoanalysis simply won't engage: they don't address psychoanalysis in its own terms; they stop listening; they break off rational discourse. But the American's example also allows Freud at the same time himself more insidiously (because through rhetoric and not supposedly rational discourse) to stand in the place of the American and say "enough" to Adler. Adler is a much more formidable critic with whom one might engage. He has, after all, been part of psychoanalysis's inner circle; he insists that he is evaluating psychoanalysis on its own terms, and has chosen to turn from it. Freud addresses Adler at this point in his argument precisely to confront such internal disagreements. But he never really does that. By wishfully dismissing Adler by proxy, rather than ever fully confront his objections directly, Freud repeats the very position he deplores in psychoanalysis's critics.

At the end of this project, I find myself in a similar dilemma. I want, like Freud (through identifying with Freud) to excuse my omissions and blind spots. I want to transform any serious critics into ones that are simply dismissive so that I can dismiss them in turn. But that is not all: I find my hand on this page tracing the word "Enough!" as not only a way to end, but also a way to continue. Here I am, at the conclusion, still writing. The compulsion to repeat, which in a sense I have been saying is what the everyday and the series are all about, describes the form as well as the content of my book.

[3] Sigmund Freud, *New Introductory Lectures*, 139.

So what do I say to critics real and imagined who might cry out to me "Enough!," who have already—in audiences and readers' reports—energetically cried it out? Such criticism seems to turn on the question of repetition: serious critics of the kind of poststructuralism I admire argue that it wants to have it both ways. Criticism of Derrida, of Freud through Lacan, especially of Foucault, argue that such theory supposedly uses its recognition that we can't help but repeat what we criticize as a spurious authorization for its own repetitions. My simple reaction is to want to dismiss this criticism as itself an instance of bad faith. Such critics, I want to say, by criticizing poststructuralism, hope indirectly to claim exemption from unwitting repetitions themselves, and hence from the unconscious. Such criticisms record a protest against, a flight from, what they see as the specter of determinism. To me, everything political—if not also ethical—about poststructuralism resides in its complicated attitudes about determinism. It *confronts* the risks that come along with the understanding of our inescapable complicity with what we observe. Unlike its critics, it does its best not to pretend to a position of objectivity and innocence outside the forces creating us. The practitioners of such Continental theory in an American context, such as Judith Butler and Homi Bhabha, emphasize that the point is to keep working within those structures to employ the infinitesimal changes within them (a Herculean task), to recognize that repetition is both the same and—a little bit—different. That little bit—never entire, never complete, never ultimately locatable—is still worth everything. At the same time, at is best, such criticism works hard not to convert its own inescapable complicity into self-legitimating cynicism or one-upmanship: Freud's understanding of the counter-transference translates into his compassion for Little Hans or the Wolf Man (notably missing in his dealings with Dora), his ability to learn from them. Derrida's constant evocation of the poignancy of human vulnerability and limitations—as in "Différance" (with is "Ozymandias"-like tombs of the pharaohs and kingdoms of death)—provides another instance of what makes this theory so evocative to me. My own practice strives to follow these models. Turning Freud's own critical insights upon his practice as I do here may almost embarrassingly reveal the desire to forge a connection with him through his shortcomings, but the desire *is* for connection: the goal is not to discredit or triumph over him.

But either this work has demonstrated that by now, or it has not. I feel that all I can do in conclusion is to repeat myself. Just how we deal with determinism—whether the shaping power of the unconscious or of narrative form—has been fundamental to this book. In fact, it seems to me that I never write about anything else. So maybe it's time to shift the focus of the debate. Rather than simply dismissing the critics who keep prompting such repetition, I will try one more time to think about repetition: what desires it serves, what work it does. Rather than shout down any opponents in the pretense of ending something that keeps on going anyway, perhaps I should recognize my debt to them for keeping it going. That ongoingness helps move us away from content—never so transparently what is really at issue, as I've been arguing about the everyday—and back to form: in this case, the compulsion to repeat that generates not only the series, but critical debate.

The Forsyte saga, that series in English fiction perhaps most familiar to us now, took shape as a series out of a similar context[4]—and afterword written by its author in response to his critics. John Galsworthy had published his novel *The Man of Property* in 1906. Its thinly veiled autobiography detailed the affair of Irene Heron Forsyte and the architect Philip Bosinney (paralleling Galsworthy's own ten-year illicit liaison with his cousin Arthur's wife, Ada Cooper Galsworthy). Finishing it just before he and Ada Galsworthy were finally able to marry, Galsworthy, out of frustration, submerged guilt, and the dictates of the naturalist mode he had taken for the novel, kept his own lovers from such union. Bosinney is killed; Irene, without money or will to live, returns to the husband Soames who had earlier raped her in hope of keeping her his property. Critics, such as the influential Edward Garnett, who had also closely edited the manuscripts of Joseph Conrad, Arnold Bennett, and D. H. Lawrence, were appalled by what they saw as the unremitting and brutal finality of the ending, its lack of hope.[5] A dozen years later, Galsworthy returned to that ending in the short story "Indian Summer of a Forsyte" (later always published as a coda to the novel called an "Interlude"). In it, he reversed the finality of his conclusion: Irene, it turns out, hasn't stayed with Soames—she leaves him immediately after the novel closes, earns her own living, and makes the connection with his cousin Jolyon that will ultimately lead to her happy marriage to him.

This return to and rewriting of his earlier novel inaugurated the trilogy Galsworthy would publish in 1922 as *The Forsyte Saga*, followed seven years later by another Forsyte trilogy, *A Modern Comedy*, and a collection of short stories, *On Forsyte 'Change* (1929), as well as a posthumous trilogy about related characters. Galsworthy subsequently wrote that he remembered Sunday, July 28, 1918, as the happiest day of his writing life, because it was then that he got the idea to extend *The Man of Property* into a series of novels.[6] Like many such public recollections, this one was in part a screen memory: to some extent, *The Man of Property* had already been a continu-

---

[4] I suggest that it is most familiar to us now because of the 1967 BBC production of it that engrossed American TV viewers in 1969 (and helped inaugurate the PBS series, "Masterpiece Theatre"). That enormously successful BBC production of the Forsyte saga bespeaks the force of the series impulse driving this narrative (as in the Holmes stories), spinning it out again and again to popular demand. The BBC in fact is already involved in yet another rehearsal of this series, a monumental remake of its first Forsyte saga, commemorating its thirtieth anniversary.

[5] For a detailed account of Garnett's objections, see James Gindin, *John Galsworthy's Life and Art: An Alien's Fortress* (London: Macmillan, 1987), 156–64. See also Florence Hardy's letter to Ada Galsworthy after publication of "Indian Summer of a Forsyte," which she reads aloud to her husband, Thomas Hardy: "Now I can read *The Man of Property* without a terrible feeling of despair," in Gindin, 411.

[6] Ibid., 413.

ation of Forsyte material. Before that novel, the name of Jolyon's father had already figured in an earlier one (*Villa Rubein*, 1901) and Galsworthy had written a short story about Jolyon's uncle ("Salvation of a Forsyte," 1901) and tried his hand at a play about the Forsytes that never came together (*The Civilized*, 1902). He had also had inklings about a series while writing *The Man of Property*: that novel's original title had actually been *The Forsyte Saga*, which he had scrapped most probably in order to reserve it for the series.[7] Galsworthy's unconscious editing of his own history was reflected within his series: his artist, young Jolyon Forsyte, only becomes a popular success once he too "made a regular series of his paintings."[8] The idea to connect his work this way, however, turns out not to be the brilliant inspiration with which Jolyon would like to credit himself. He realizes that long ago he had been advised to turn to the series by a critic whose emphasis on the main chance rather than art he had disliked and dismissed. It turns out that he has conveniently forgotten that advice in order to deny his own appreciation of economic success, his own similarities to the critic and the rest of the money-loving Forsytes.

Galsworthy's insistence on a discreet and happy anniversary for the Forsyte saga, just like the happy ending he rescripts for Irene, may also have been a defense against his critics: rather than allaying censure by converting *The Man of Property* into a series, Galsworthy's revisions had opened its floodgates. The next generation of modernist writers, including Virginia Woolf and D. H. Lawrence, charged Galsworthy with trying through his series to have things both ways.[9] *The Man of Property*, especially when read in the context of Galsworthy's contemporary thesis plays—*The Silver Box* (1906), about the inequities of class in the system of justice, and *Justice*

---

[7] Ibid., 156.

[8] John Galsworthy, *The Man of Property*, Book One of *The Forsyte Saga* (*The Man of Property, In Chancery, To Let*) (New York: Penguin, 1978), 1–364; part 3, chap. 3, p. 250; all future references to this book (abbreviated *Man*) will appear in the text.

[9] See Virginia Woolf, "Character in Fiction," in *The Essays of Virginia Woolf*, vol. 3, 1919–1924, ed. Andrew McNeillie (London: Hogarth, 1988), 6 vols. projected, 4 vols. to date (1986–94), 420–38. Woolf in fact critiques Galsworthy the author as himself a man of property. She writes ironically: "Here is the British public sitting by the writer's side and saying in its vast and unanimous way, 'Old women have houses. They have fathers. They have incomes. They have servants. They have hot water bottles. That is how we know that they are old women. Mr. Wells and Mr. Bennett and Mr. Galsworthy have always taught us that this is the way to recognise them. . . .' And old women of course ought to be made of freehold villas and copyhold estates, not of imagination" (433). Woolf implies that, like Soames, Galsworthy, as a "materialist," confuses people with property, with "freehold villas and copyhold estates" (Soames builds a house at Robin's Hill as a showplace to display, and a prison to control, Irene, who runs off with its architect instead). Woolf's dismissal of this kind of fiction—she writes: "I threw that ugly, that clumsy, that incongrous tool out of the window" (432)—is in part a dismissal of the series form. As she later records in her diary when searching for a title for the work she was calling "The Pargiters," she was looking for one that would distinguish her kind of fiction, one that did "not compete with the Herries Saga, the Forsyte Sage, & so on": "Saturday 2 September 1933," in *The Diary of Virginia Woolf*, vol. 4, ed. Annie Olivier Bell (London: Hogarth, 1982), 5 vols. (1977–1984), 176.

(1910), about the inhumanity of solitary confinement in prison—had initially appeared on the literary scene as scathing social critique: Soames, a man of property, was seen to stand only for the killing acquisitiveness underlying the English bourgeois character. His cousin Jolyon was taken for Soames's diametrical opposite; Jolyon's "Diagnosis of a Forsyte" (part 2, chap. 10), critiquing his family's acquisitive, mercantile, middle-class standards, became the moral of the artist's cry from the heart against society's smothering of authentic expression. In supposedly capitulating to those standards, in changing the ending of *The Man of Property*, in making Irene herself ultimately comfortable and happy, Galsworthy seemed to other aspiring iconoclasts—especially D. H. Lawrence—to "g[i]ve into the Forsytes." [10]

For Lawrence, once we get a "series of Galsworthian 'rebels,'" we find that they, "like all the rest of the modern middleclass rebels, [are] not in rebellion at all . . . They worship their own class, but they pretend to go one better and sneer at it" (67). [11] Lawrence finds the early satirical promise of *The Man of Property* reversed so spectacularly "that we wonder sometimes if Mr. Galsworthy is not treating his public in real bad faith, and [actually] being cynical" (70). [12] Although this reading might deplore that, over the course of the series, a man of property like Soames can become its central figure, Lawrence writes that, compared to Bosinney, "one cannot help preferring Soames Forsyte, in a choice of evils" (62). Soames's treatment of Irene (it seems) is at least honest. Lawrence does lament that the illicit passion of Bosinney and Irene heralding rebellion in the first novel is transformed by the end of the series into the censured affairs of the next generation: the series itself condemns the attraction between Jon (Jolyon's and Irene's son) and Fleur (Soames's daughter) as indulgent and self-serving. The hypocritical attitude the series displays to sexuality, as Lawrence sees it—pretending to promote what it actually finds "nasty," faking it, he writes (63)—reflects back on the earlier lovers. To Lawrence, Bosinney and Irene are "runaway dogs . . . running in the backgarden and furtively and ignominiously copulating" (61); Galsworthy's men are "property hounds [like Bosinney] . . . sniffing round property bitches"; his women are, like Irene,

[10] D. H. Lawrence, "John Galsworthy," in *Scrutinies by Various Writers*, ed. Edgell Rickword (London, Wishart, 1928), 52–72; 59. All future references to this essay will appear in the text.
[11] Lawrence's language throughout the essay bears out that this problem is for his particularly one of the series. The Forsytes, and middle-class moral bankruptcy, are marked for his precisely by what he sees as an empty seriality, a monumental ongoingness: "They have no life, and so they live forever . . ."; they are distinguished by "monotonous persistency . . . endless endurance" (60)—"Perhaps the overwhelming numerousness of the Forsytes frightened Mr. Galsworthy from utterly damning them" (61). Such assumptions, of course, complicate Lawrence's own series writing—in *The Rainbow*, *Sons and Lovers*, and *Women in Love*.
[12] Lawrence writes: "*The Man of Property* has the elements of a very great novel, a very great satire. . . . But the author has not the courage to carry it through. The greatness of the book rests in its new and sincere and amazingly profound satire. It is the ultimate satire on modern humanity, and done from the inside, with really consummate skill and sincere creative passion. . . . And then it fizzles out" (58). Lawrence thinks that satire falters within the novel, and then is entirely extinguished by the series: "The later novels are purely commercial" (69).

"sneaking, creeping, spiteful sort[s] of bitch[es]" (62). Lawrence hopes that the next generation, Jon and Fleur, will be "smothered in their own slime along with everything else. Which is a comfort" (72).

What's most remarkable about Lawrence's reading is that his own rhetoric seems to create the very nastiness he ascribes to Galsworthy. In part, incomparable backgrounds and understandable class antagonism may account for such invective. To Lawrence, the growing conservatism of the Forsyte saga necessarily reflected Galsworthy's own position. Increasingly "secure in comfort, wealth, and renown" (69), Galsworthy had already started out from upper-middle-class security anyway. Economic independence allowed him to write in the first place and gave him the poise and connections that made his so successful at it: he refused a knighthood, but accepted an Order of Merit; he was elected the first president of PEN, the international writers' organization; he received the Nobel Prize for literature in 1932. Though highly regrettable, it is not at all surprising, given Galsworthy's background, that, over the course of his long series of works, youthful rebellion against the status quo settled down into comfortable quiescence with it. Regrettable, not suprising, yet also not quite the whole story. For readings like Lawrence's simplify the trajectory of Galsworthy's series and ignore the complexities within it. They turn what is actually a series of repetitions going in circles from the start, an initial and direct acknowledgment of the attractions of quiescence always in tension with a dream of progression, into a steady devolution. Lawrence's attempts to force Galsworthy into one position so that he can occupy the other—conservative versus radical, hypocrite versus faithful—tell us more about Lawrence than they do about Galsworthy.

Complexity and troubling ambivalence of position actually seem to me to be the satirical point of *The Man of Property*—although Galsworthy was never comfortable with the term "satire," preferring "semi-satire" or "quasi-satire" for his own works precisely because critics insisted on a singleness of vision in what they defined as satire.[13] Jolyon's "Diagnosis of a Forsyte" is, like all his insights, ironic, directed as much against himself as against his cousin Soames. He knows, and keeps repeating, that "I'm a Forsyte myself" (*Man*, 2.10.203). He "saw Soames's side of the question too" (*Man*, 2.10.205), Galsworthy reminds us, just as Galsworthy goes on to do in the rest of his series. There's nothing *necessarily* redemptive about such irony, but it is (*pace* Lawrence) explicit and central in Galworthy's series: he is exploring the human impulse to want to have it both ways, to be unable, in fact, to do anything else. From the very start, the Forsyte saga, in its initial emphasis on Jolyon, is *about* someone who knows that he can't help but re-

---

[13] Gindin, 176. Galsworthy wrote to his sister, countering her objections about *The Man of Property*: "You would have a contrast so given as to enlist the reader on one side, and against the other. I don't feel like this" (Gindin, 164). As he wrote later to Edward Garnett: "In other words, this book [*The Patrician*], like *The M. of P.*, *The C. H.* and *Fraternity*, is simply the criticism of one half of myself by the other. . . . It is not a piece of social criticism—they none of them are. If it's anything it's a bit of spiritual examination" (Gindin, 177).

peat the very things he's critiquing. Rather than justify Galsworthy's conservatism, however, that insight gives us the tool with which to recognize it. In a sense, when Lawrence finds the Forsyte saga lacking, he's measuring it against its own standards, no matter now much he insists (that insistence forms the introduction to his essay) that he is not.

That rueful self-knowledge within the Forsyte saga, which certainly doesn't keep it from falling into all kinds of conventionalities about gender and class (to start with), still makes it preferable to me to writing like Lawrence's with its blind vituperation. Lawrence seems to me to scapegoat Galsworthy's recognition of his own limitations in order to deny any within himself: his vehement insistence on the very faults that Galsworthy confesses throughout to having (an odd trumpeting of the obvious for a writer so clever as Lawrence) is so high-pitched because it may be a desperate—doomed—attempt to free Lawrence from the same. Lawrence's bitter charges of sexism against Galsworthy (was there ever a greater irony?), for instance, function to permit the vehemence of his own conservative gender attitudes, through his language of "castration" and "bitches in heat." As Lawrence remarks, we do come to prefer Soames: not because (as Lawrence might have it) he is at least sexually honest when he rapes his wife, but because he can never completely shake off, even if he can never also fathom, his own limitations. Although, like Lawrence, I want to criticize the ultimate resonance of Bosinney and Irene's affair, my objections to it are not that Galsworthy didn't have the courage with it fully to assert heterosexual passion as the highest expression of "the free human individual" (55). If anything, in fact, the critique the series itself makes of Jon and Fleur's later affair seems to me (as a feminist critic) valuable because it actually repeats and brings to light the submerged self-serving character of the earlier liaison. To represent iconoclasm through heterosexual sex—extramarital or not—seems to me itself often highly conservative in gender terms.

Bosinney's and Jolyon's sexual conquests of the wholly passive Irene (supposedly beautiful—Beauty herself—in her passivity) are no less domineering than Soames's, as Jolyon recognizes: they are all part of "a world of men not wont to let beauty go unpossessed."[14] Shortly after he realizes that he too longs for Irene, Jolyon has a dream in which "he was not altogether himself, but Soames as well" (*In Chancery*, 3.3.574); reflecting later on the dream, he recognizes "the close encircling fabric of the possessive instinct walling in that little black figure of himself, and Soames" (*In Chancery*, 3.7.588). Because Jolyon recognizes himself in that double, ambivalent figure, Galsworthy implies that, aware of his identification with the hated Soames, Jolyon is a better partaker of Beauty incarnate because he is at least aware of the desire to contain it that is part of him. Jolyon and Irene's union replays and re-

---

[14] John Galsworthy, *In Chancery*, Book Two of *The Forsyte Saga*, 365–652; part 1, chap. 6, p. 414; all future references to this book will appear in the text.

vises her early relations with Bosinney as well, who is perhaps meant to perform, but never directly expresses, an epiphany like Jolyon's. Through his narrative repetitions within the series, Galsworthy seems to have written himself closer to his autobiographical source: Bosinney becomes a red herring; Jolyon, after all, is Soames's cousin. The relation between Jolyon and Irene should represent Galsworthy's ideal. Yet the affair between them, as well as that between Bosinney and Irene, remains disturbing partly because Galsworthy never fully disclaims his narrative's own possessiveness. Quite explicitly deciding to refuse Irene as a character any subjectivity of her own (the grand experiment of *The Man of Property*), depicting her only through others' eyes, may indicate the ways men see women, but it also partakes in them. Allegorizing Irene into Beauty converts her into the instrument and holding of the series, no matter how much Galsworthy is aware of the inescapable risks of wanting to possess beauty for our own purposes.

That Jolyon's own possessiveness reflects on Galsworthy as author too may explain why the narrative resorts to the violence of Soames's rape: its outrageousness and brutality work to obscure or at least mitigate the identification of Galsworthy's male figures both with one another, and with himself as author. In this, the series does try to have it both ways, yet it never forgets those identifications either. Jon and Fleur's arrested affair also exposes the gender inequity and patriarchal impulse that insist on male sexual domination of women. The gender dynamic of the novel becomes strained when Fleur, rather than her father, becomes the symbol of acquisitiveness. Fleur's pursuit and conquest of Jon—transforming him into the innocent ingenue—demonstrate just how difficult it is to flip conventions that way. Rather than revise, they actually expose and highlight the sexual double standard. Whether or not this was Galsworthy's intention doesn't matter; that reading readily presents itself to us because the emphasis of the series on duality allows us to interpret this way in spite of its author's intentions.

Like any series, the Forsyte saga is arranged and connected through repetitions like these, Soames and Irene's early conflict spinning out repeated and contested unions, in a long experiment of cause and effect. An experiment in cause and effect was Zola's definition of the naturalist novel;[15] for Galsworthy, such repetition seems expressly tied to the problem of determinism. The naturalistic bent of *The Man of Property*, its emphasis on natural forces as an overwhelming totality swamping and regulating any individual, suggests the series impulse already implicit within it, the compulsion to repeat and reflect something larger than any single novel. That the series takes over where naturalism leaves off may in fact explain why naturalism per se can fall away in Galsworthy's writing; only *The Man of Property* seems fully indebted to it. The narrative form of the series itself underwrites a vision that

[15] Emile Zola, "The Experimental Novel," in *Documents of Literary Realism*, ed. George J. Becker (Princeton: Princeton University Press, 1963), 162–96.

stresses the power of structural forces rather than individual will. Such a vision may explain why, over the course of the series, Jolyon, the ironist, falls out, to allow for concentration on Soames, the *eiron*, always bested by forces larger than he can understand. Just as in Jolyon's dream, within the narrative itself, as central figure merges into central figure, Jolyon does becomes Soames. That transformation emphasizes that even ironists are more completely eirons than they can ever fully appreciate; the series may come to prefer Soames precisely because none of us ever wants to be him.

The Man of Property inaugurates *The Forsyte Saga* by showing the powerlessness of Soames's will and the incidental injury that his stubborn hewing to it causes all around him. *The White Monkey*, the first novel of the second trilogy of the saga, repeats this theme: Soames loses his own private battle of wills with the shady manager, Elderson. Or rather, the story suggests the inadequacy of seeing the world in terms of individual volition at all. Soames never really wins or loses: Elderson, unpunished, levants to the Continent, Soames resigns from the Board, taking some of the blame unjustly, but without any of the dire consequences (lawsuits, imprisonment) that he's anticipated. The whole story, which would have furnished the plot for a Victorian triple-decker, simply drifts away in anticlimax midway through a novel that, driven by the series impulse, just keeps going.

The attempt by the individual to control his own destiny is within the series not central, but incidental. Part of Soames's pathos is that he is always trying unsuccessfully to make his own history, to assert his story as significant. His dim understanding that he never can doesn't prevent him from trying more and more desperate measures to do so anyway. But the demand for this kind of will power and conscious control over life may only be a cover story: Soames's rape of Irene in the spectacularly self-deluded attempt to make her love him reveals the depth of the irrational and aggressive drives lying behind—and put into play by—an insistence on conscious control. Asserting what is supposed to be his will actually releases what he doesn't recognize as his desires: to punish Irene brutally, but especially to keep himself in a position in which he can never win her, for *The Man of Property*— and the subsequent series—provides, if anything, a case study of the desire for the unattainable *because* it is unattainable (the post-modern understanding of desire itself, most familiar to us through Barthes and Lacan, who didn't, after all, invent it). What keeps Soames and the narrative going is "the fixed idea which has outrun more constables than any other form of human disorder"[16]—which is able to have its run, to keep repeating, precisely through the unconscious bargain that maintains it as fixed, that doesn't allow it completely to change, but just keeps repeating with a difference. Soames desires the woman he can never have because he doesn't want to have her.

---

[16] John Galsworthy, *To Let*, Book Three of *The Forsyte Saga*, 653–906; part 3, chap. 5, p. 861; all future references to this book will appear in the text.

In the Forsyte saga, the everyday provides the site for an over-emphasis on conscious will that allows unconscious discharge. In the midst of his fight with Elderson, Soames's second wife gives him a little book to read to help him sleep. Soames's lack of control over his own destiny has left him frantic; this book promises to provide him with the key to such control. It is a text detailing the theories of a noted public figure in the twenties—Emile Coué— a retired French pharmacist, whose accounts of the power of positive thinking had taken the high society of England by storm. Coué's method was simple: those wishing to effect change in their lives had merely to repeat, over and over, "every day in every way, I am getting better and better." Soames is surprised to find that "the theory, however extravagant, had somehow clung to him."[17] After repeating Coué's mantra in bed at night, he sleeps like a baby, and awakens the next day to "a curious sense of power" (*White*, 3.9.232). "'You know,'" his wife tells him, "'you are just the temperament for Coué, Soames'" (*White*, 3.9.232). The efficacy of his method, Coué argued, was that it allowed people to have direction of their own unconsciouses[18]—which, as Galsworthy tells us, "everybody now said, controlled the course of events" (*White*, 3.3.197). This method worked on the unconscious by fooling it, by adopting its own methods of indirection so that it didn't realize it was being controlled: you couldn't repeat directly what you wished, "for this, setting up a reaction, everybody said, was liable to produce" its opposite (3.3.197). Instead, you "le[ft] a thought" subliminally, drilling it in through mindless repetition every day until it "got into [the] subconscious" (3.2.189). Soames, so determined to control others, so miserable at being controlled, is indeed just the temperament for Coué. Some method to harness powers that he refuses to believe could remain intractable—just as he is always astonished at Irene's intractability—especially appeals to him. He dreams of "locks in the insides of men and women, so that their passions could be dammed to the proper moment, then used, under control, for the main traffic of life, instead of pouring to waste over weirs and down rapids."[19] And yet, or perhaps because of, his denial of the powers of the unconscious as ungovernable, Soames is more prey to them than any other character in the series.

Social critics suggest that Coué-ism became the rage in England because it

---

[17] John Galsworthy, *The White Monkey*, Book One of *A Modern Comedy* (*The White Monkey, The Silver Spoon, Swan Song*) (New York: Scribners, 1941), 1–291; part 3, chap. 9, p. 231; all future references to this book (abbreviated *White*) will appear in the text.

[18] See Emile Coué, *My Method Including American Impressions* (New York: Doubleday, 1923), and Emile Coué and J. Louis Orton, *Conscious Autosuggestion* (New York: Appleton, 1924). The book popularizing Coué's method was Charles Badouin, *Suggestion and Autosuggestion: A Psychological and Pedagogical Study Based upon the Investigations Made by the New Nancy School*, trans. Eden Paul and Cedar Paul (London: Allen & Unwin, 1920). Other imitators include James Alexander, *Thought Control in Everyday Life* (New York: Funk & Wagnalls, 1928).

[19] John Galsworthy, *Swan Song*, Book Three of *A Modern Comedy*, 577–899; part 1, chap. 13, p. 667; all future references to this book (abbreviated *Swan*) appear in the text.

offered an alternative to psychoanalysis, with which popular accounts of the time often lumped it, both simply just new fads. Dean Rapp's recent investigations of Coué-ism argue that "although like psychoanalysis it stressed the power of the unconscious, it provided an easy method for supposedly controlling it for one's own purposes, hence appealing to the desire for free will, as opposed to the determinism of the Freudians."[20] Coué's optimism that every day in every way we could triumph over any disappointment, mental or bodily, "advocated a remarkably unreconstructed form of the Victorian idea of progress" ("Better," 27)—precisely the idea of progress that the repetition compulsion, as well as the series impulse, complicate.

Coué so relied on the category of the everyday that he also appealed to it to authorize his method; he and his followers persuasively asserted the truth of their contentions by drawing on the rhetoric of common sense, proven by "numerous examples from everyday life" ("Better," 27). Even *The International Journal of Psycho-Analysis*—Freud's self-proclaimed "Official Organ"—admitted in its review of the most popular book of Coué-ism that it "is certainly written in a lively and interesting fashion."[21] This appeal to the everyday was also an appeal to a kind of empiricism that insisted on uncomplicated appearances; the attraction of Coué, the periodical press of the time recorded, was his "vast simplicity."[22] *The International Journal of Psych-Analysis* saw this instead as "the French passion for simplistic certitude, which so often creates the illusion of lucidity" ("Review," 88). For Freud, the everyday was not a commonplace realm of cognizance and certainty: *The Psychopathology of Everyday Life* had claimed it precisely as the dominion of the unconscious, a realm in which unrecognized forces held sway, determining the very reality we thought most free from them. In fact, in *The Psychopathology of Everyday Life*, Freud directly cited Galsworthy as a writer attuned to the oblique and infallible power of the unconscious. He credited Galsworthy, through his sensitivity to parapraxis in *The Island Pharisees*, with understanding how we try, through the everyday, to naturalize the unconscious, to make the irrational seem rational.[23] As Galsworthy writes in the Forsyte saga, "thoughts and yearnings, with which one lives daily, become natural, even if far-fetched in their inception." (*In Chancery*, 2.2.479).

Freud considered the strength of unconscious impulses swamping con-

[20] Dean R. Rapp, "'Better and Better—' Couéism as a Psychological Craze of the Twenties in England," *Studies in Popular Culture* 10 (1987): 17–36; 26; all future references to this essay (abbreviated "Better") will appear in the text.
[21] "Review of *Suggestion and Auto-Suggestion*, by Charles Badouin," in *The International Journal of Psycho-Analysis* 3 (1922): 87–88; 88; all future references to this essay (abbreviated "Review") will appear in the text. See also Ernest Jones's letter dismissing Couéism, "M. Coué and the Psycho-analysts," in *New Statesman*, April 15, 1922, 40.
[22] New York *Evening Mail*, January 5, 1923, quoted in Thomas Whiteside, "Better and Better," *New Yorker*, May 16, 1953, 101–25; 110.
[23] *The Psychopathology of Everyday Life*, in *Standard* 6: 132–33.

scious will so great that they ultimately extinguished individual identity. For him, the repetition compulsion was geared not to the personal gratifications promised by Coué, but to the surcease of individual personality altogether. Despite the promised advantageousness Coué-ism holds out for Soames, for his daughter, Fleur, who wants it to influence the gender of her child, and for the salesmen in the publishing firm that employs Fleur's husband, Michael Mont, the attractions of autosuggestion remain only temporary: as the series goes on, we learn that Coué becomes "comparatively out of fashion, since an American [presumably Dale Carnegie] . . . had found a shorter cut."[24] This is partly because, despite the fact that Fleur gives birth to the desired son (which is still not enough to make her happy), satisfaction in the Forsyte saga can never be fully realized. Despite his own dismissal of psychoanalysis, which he considered only a half-truth, Galsworthy's notion of repetition seems closer to Freud's than to Coué's.[25] Reflecting on his daughter, Fleur, near the end of the saga, Soames suggests one motive force for his own behavior, as well as for Galsworthy's narrative: "When you couldn't have what you wanted, yet couldn't let go; and drove, on and on, to dull the aching. Resignation . . . was a lost art, or so it seemed to Soames, as they passed the graveyard where he expected to be buried someday" (Swan, 3.12.859). The repetitions that carry us to that ending (and that grave) are also the only things that stave it off; Soames senses this only indirectly through another's loss. After losing her heart's desire, Jon, the first time, on the very brink of union with him, Fleur mechanically plays the gramophone over and over. "She had set that tune going again" Soames thinks. "Why—it was a mania! . . . It was as though she had said: "If I can't have something to keep me going, I shall die of this!" (To Let, 3.8.883). The Forsyte saga's own mechanical repetitions are also what keep it going—it would be nothing without them: not just the same plot it tells over and over (most notably epitomized in young Jolyon's letter to Jon, the most ritualistic of the innumerable distillations and summaries interwoven to form the saga), but also the saga's superficial, almost humoral, psychology familiar from soap-opera, and Galsworthy's particularly threadbare—melodramatic and self-important—style. Rather than spoiling his narrative, such involuntary and self-propelling elements provide its very substance and interest.

The Forsytes' conviction of their own extraordinary self-importance (Jolyon and Soames are the saga's central figures because they are the Forsytes who are not completely sure), their unthinking assumption of their sovereignty over the life around them, compels them not to recognize (an obliviousness always, ultimately, unhappy) that life as everyday—impersonal, un-

[24] John Galsworthy, The Silver Spoon, Book Two of A Modern Comedy, 293–575, part 1, chap. 2, p. 308.
[25] Galsworthy explicitly at least partially rejected Freud: "from the little I read of Freud, I think it's all very much the usual case of half-truths magnified into whole ones. . . . I have never made use of what little I know about psychoanalysis" (Gindin, 205).

characterizable, arbitrary. Galsworthy provides this alternative vision of the everyday in the texture of his narrative, through figures of class and gender: the anonymity of Gradman, Soames's clerk, the passivity of Irene, Soames's wife. Gradman, Galsworthy writes: "never missed that daily promenade to the Tube for Highgate, and seldom some critical transaction on the way in connexion with vegetables and fruit. Generations might be born, and hats might change, wars be fought, and Forsytes fade away, but Thomas Gradman, faithful and grey, would take his daily walk and buy his daily vegetable." (*To Let*, 2.5.792). Jolyon attempts to make his son Jon understand the significance of Jon's mother, Irene—the miracle of the accustomed, untrumpeted quality of her beauty, so that "she rise[s] from the foam [like Venus] . . . everyday" (*In Chancery*, "Interlude," 644). Locating the everyday in the unremarkable, however, doesn't protect Galsworthy from his own unthinking assumptions: in idealizing class and gender otherness, he can partially overlook the ways he contributes to the deprivations of those in such positions. When Michael Mont takes a worker from his firm, Tony Bicket, to lunch, he spends more on the meal than the man makes in a week: "I eat my conscience every day," Michael confesses to him (*White*, 2.3.118). Finally getting around to telling the story of such workers through the inclusion of the Bickets in the second trilogy doesn't absolve Galsworthy from his own participation in class injustice, though his lifelong practice of giving away half his income was at least more ameliorative than that of most people with his money and background. Giving Bicket a meal is not enough, as Michael ironically realizes; neither is his irony. Irony is no panacea for the ill of living in a world which needs revolution but offers only the most infinitesimal of changes. Irony can only be just another way of repeating what's already there. "An ironical world, his father had said," Michael thinks (on the last page of the saga). "Yes, queerly ironical, with shape melting into shape, mood into mood, sound into sound, and nothing fixed anywhere, unless it were that . . . instinct within all living things which said: 'Go on!'" (*Swan*, 3.16.889). Such repetitions, however, are the message of Galsworthy's series: with nothing fixed anywhere, because nothing is fixed anywhere, in spite of having nothing fixed anywhere, one goes on; instinct prompts us, whether we will or not.

The poignancy of human existence, as betrayed in narratives like Galsworthy's, rests in this knowledge—both conscious and unconscious, accepted and denied: control of our destiny eludes us; freedom from determination comes only in the death of the self. We take our existence itself from the very conventions—social, psychic, linguistic—which we may also hope to change. Our lives have no other meaning except in their terms. Whether we will or not, we can only repeat the things we have done before in the hope one day of doing them no longer—of putting other structures and determinations in place, evoking other behaviors, or (as Freud suggests) of simply ceasing altogether. The forces acting on us, however, are massive, complex, contradictory: their effects are by no means assured or predictable. Hence, the importance, and the attraction, of figures for this variable nexus, such as the series and the everyday.

Jacques Lacan, that oracular reader of Freud, says this another way: "Freud raises these same issues in the background of *Beyond the Pleasure Principle*. Just as life reproduces itself, so it's forced to repeat the same cycle, rejoining the common aim of death. . . . There is, in effect, something radically unassimilable to the signifier. It's quite simply the subject's singular existence. Why is he here? Where has he come from? What is he doing here? Why is he going to disappear? The signifier is incapable of providing him with the answer, for the good reason that it places him beyond death. The signifier already considers him dead, by nature it immortalizes him."[26] For Lacan, one's "personal little meaning—which is also heart-breakingly generic, human all too human"—ensnares us in an inescapable inability: we can never see beyond our position in a determining structure; that structure can never recognize our difference from the place (which abides) but that we only briefly hold in it.[27] Although we can theorize that difference, it remains in excess of any of our accounts. The Forsyte saga shows again and again, as any series does, how that excess, always excluded, yet gives rise to narrative. Jolyon and Soames may each suspect (one more, one less) that their own individual meanings really make no sense; still their own is the story both wish to communicate. The everyday, as I've been arguing, may be the site of the refusal of individual meaning, yet its own unassimilable character suggests it is also somehow the site for the excess of singular existence. As Galsworthy's narrator reminds the Forsytes: "that which is not imagined sometimes exists" (*Man*, "Interlude," 345). The obsessive repetitions of the series try to capture the story of a distinct self that cannot be imagined. Those repetitions become the incantations by which we hope, finally, though the invocations of sorcery or the dull chant of enlightenment, to make imagination and existence cohere. They give our lives the only meaning that they have, although it is not, as Marx well knew about history, ever the story we think it will be.

The interest to me of "the everyday" lies in the way such terms resist our attempts to control exactly what they mean. "The everyday" is the term I've chosen to examine specifically here, but all words and especially charged terms such as "women," "culture," "truth," and so on—work this way. I'm not suggesting that I think such terms are meaningless. Their meanings are simply not fixed, as the Forsyte saga demonstrates. They are generated by context, but a context we can never entirely map. They change, and yet per-

---

[26] Jacques Lacan, "The Hysteric's Question (II): *What Is a Woman?*" in *The Seminar of Jacques Lacan, Book III, The Psychoses 1955–56*, ed. Jacques-Alain Miller, trans. Russell Grigg (New York: Norton, 1993), 195–82; 179–80.

[27] Jacques Lacan, " 'I've Just Been to the Butcher's,' " in *The Seminar of Jacques Lacan*, 44–56; 54.

sist. They are always in excess of what we can capture. What eludes us are often the very meanings that contradict the ones we're sure of—but though we may be blind to those contradictions, they are still very much at play, molding the world in which we live and the decisions that we make about it. The utility of literary criticism is in keeping us aware of this subtle but powerfully effective register. Another way of saying this is that criticism makes us notice the rhetoric fueling politics—with the understanding that rhetoric isn't a veneer you can peel away to expose some unvarnished truth, and that politics is not some public sphere from which you can withdraw when you feel tired.

I've been interested in "the everyday' in particular because it is one of those terms we use to resist such an understanding of language, of meaning, of politics. We conjure "the everyday" like a charm; it becomes synonymous with Marx's "necessity" or Lacan's "real"—except that we forget, with the everyday, that those are markers we can never fully ken. We hope the everyday gives us direct and unmediated access to such realms. We'd like to think so. It's the stone we kick to reassure ourselves that we're here, we exist—that we know what existence means. Charm, stone—my own language too shows how "the everyday" radiates an insistent materiality, an overemphasis of referentiality. It operates as a figure of the literal.

This book focuses on tracing this term's resistance to understanding, on locating the complications of its meaning in its association with gender, on following the subtleties of its working through its manifestation in the series. "The everyday" and the series impulse in narrative are connected for me because, in representing wishes for the literal and the manifest, they nonetheless adumbrate the mysteries of the unconscious. That tension keeps the word and the form so absorbing and consequential. Though resistant to understanding, they seem especially available to analysis: as Freud said of his own kind of analysis, "an alliance has been made between the treatment and the compulsion to repeat."[28] He meant that psychoanalysis provides a carefully tended arena into which unconscious feelings may be transferred, enacted, and (by some miracle perhaps) worked through. That transference can happen, however, because the treatment mirrors the structure of the unconscious; Freud and Coué actually agree about that. What Coué misconstrues is the nature of that structure, not finite and masterable, but infinitely elusive, with its own returns and continuations, its endless backings and fillings. Freud's analytic theory, in its renowned interminability, unlike Coué's, is explicitly spun out of what resists it, what it seeks but can never fully know. I have hoped to follow that model: the resistance of the everyday, performed by the incessance of the series, is precisely what has made this project possible.

What my own unconscious promptings in writing it have been are not for

[28] Freud, "Remarks on the Theory and Practice of Dream-Interpretation," in *Standard* 19: 107–38, 118.

me to say, although, of course, I find them extremely interesting: my first study's emphasis on pessimism and power may have reflected that it was a book written for tenure. This one's stress on the drift of the everyday and the invariability of the series may come out of a different stage in my work life: the necessity, after tenure, of facing up to the fact that most of us work hard doing the same things again and again to no real end unless that round of toil itself becomes its own reward. I may want to repudiate the Frankfurt School's gloomy implication that the promise of the extraordinary, with its lure of exemption—whether money, fame, or political purity—works to mask the ache of the ordinary. I may, as an ordinary woman, as an ordinary critic and teacher, want to insist on the compensations of the everyday. Yet insisting on such compensations may still function as its own backhanded wish to pin down and transform the everyday. Who knows?

But my own acknowledgements in this book that it is impossible (for me, for anyone) to escape the desire to limit the everyday and, hence, to taste the real, are not meant to concede that I have failed in my critical project (its failures must fall on other fronts). I must for the sake of communication operate as if words have fixed meanings, even while continually questioning that premise. Because my project stresses the *process* of such questioning, what could be more rewarding than focusing on a term like the everyday or a form like the series? What distinguishes them from other terms and forms (which work the same way) is that they foreground repetition and ongoingness. They prompt me to insist on process. That process is tied to the struggle to resist repeating what we criticize in others, no matter how impossible completely ceasing to do so may be. No other project seems to me so interesting or difficult. The better world that criticism can help to inaugurate rests in the aid it gives ut to convert the Pharisees' prayer into an oath of human fealty and connection.

Hence, this book's constant attesting to the powers of the everyday and the series. I am stuck especially at the end of it by the efficacy of certain ways of repeating. Irony is one of them, but Teresa Ebert locates another in what she calls "the logic of the outrageous": "In this logic, sensationalizing, provocative, parodic assertions revive a nostalgia for the power of patriarchy, resurrect worn-out or discredited assumptions, stereotypes and practices, and represent them as natural and inevitable."[29] She elaborates "Marx's remark that history happens 'the first time as tragedy, the second as farce'" (12) in order to explore the rhetorical effect of going on too long, archaically, past exhaustion, well past when something's time is over. This form of repetition (one that my readers at this point may want to ascribe as much to this book as to any of the series it has treated) becomes nothing less than a kind of return of the undead. Ebert outlines it in trying to account for the force of re-

[29] Ebert, "The Politics of the Outrageous," *Women's Review of Books* 9 (October 1991): 12–13; 12.

cent assaults on feminism, such as Camille Paglia's: "She enlivens the commonplaces of patriarchy by turning them into farce, making them seem witty, original, and even fresh" (13). Such repetition translates what should be long-dead banalities into outrageous hyperbole so that "the 'outrageous' does the social work of rendering everyday violence natural and commonplace" (12). Overdoing the repetitions of the series, hyping the everyday, provide a highly effective political strategy. I would only stress that this power works *across* the political spectrum. The kind of camp Ebert charts as conservative takes on an entirely different valence in Judith Butler's emphasis on the radical possibilities of the iterative performances of gay drag.

The rhetorical threat of the series and the everyday therefore also provides their rhetorical promise; and vice versa. Using such tropes lies outside the categories of the conservative or progressive: Freud, who was almost more emphatically than anyone else both kinds of thinker at once, was a stunning cartographer of this power: the unconscious, always insidiously upsetting the everyday we think immune from it, making us repeat that which we're sure we'll never do, operates solely according to this logic. As it propels us powerfully to that longing for death we think we least desire, it also seems that, if repetition's power consists in pushing us past the banality of death, the issue of death as some kind of end may be moot. Galsworthy's novels, which themselves trouble terms like conservative and progressive (just as the death drive does on another register), seem to me importantly and emphatically about this unanswered and unanswerable question: just what might be the benefit of going on too long, impossibly long? The everyday is the place in which we try to imagine that performance. Whatever persists after our own individual deaths we tend to imagine in terms of our personal little meaning—human all too human—of the everyday: the dishes still washed, the sun rising and setting. . . . Freud and Galsworthy see that persistence as instinct in all narrative. It's the notion of the everyday as immanent, replete, in excess of any end (an excess that can remain mostly meaningless in our end-determined universe) that distinguishes the series from other forms of fiction.

Index

Chambers, Ross, 34n
Champion, Selwyn Gurney, 97n
Character, 167, 170
Charques, R. D., 184
Childers, Mary, 187
Christian, Barbara, 45, 180, 213, 216
Chtcheglov, Ivan, 128n
Class, 15, 18, 45, 91, 96, 169, 176, 179–
    187, 190–192, 200
Closure, 8, 11, 12, 37, 40, 41, 54–59
Cockshut, A. O. J., 97
Coetze, J. M., 15
Colby, Robert, 67n
Colby, Vineta, 67n
Collatrella, Carol, 13–14
Collins, Philip, 115n
Collins, Wilke, 50
Colonialism, 190. *See also* Imperialism
Commodity, 7, 10
Conflict, 17, 22, 26, 30, 75
Conrad, Joseph, 4, 47, 192, 207, 215, 222
Consensus, 32, 33
Consumer, 10
Context, 89, 91, 98, 100, 101, 105; inde-
    terminacy of, 107
Conventions, of speech, 106; narrative,
    57, 63
Critics: materialist, 9–11, 15, 174–178,
    183; minority, 80; poststructuralist, 17,
    18, 45
Cruse, Amy, 79n
Culler, Jonathan, 101, 103n, 106n
Culture, 6, 10, 11, 15, 19 22 ,23; anxiety
    over, 12; categories of, 7, 104; common,
    26, 27; as constructed, 88; differences in,
    14; fragmented, 27; mass, 52, 57, 71; as
    ordinary, 27, 31; patrilinear aspect of,
    24; relativism of, 105; revolutionizing of,
    20, 23; studies of, 15–18, 23, 28–37
Cunningham, Valentine, 64n

Dante Alighieri, 51
Darwin, Charles, 13
Debord, Guy, 136–137,140, 146n
de Certeau, Michel, 3–5, 45, 52, 130, 133,
    140–141, 156; *The Practice of Everyday
    Life*, 4, 140
Deleuze, Gilles, 45, 47, 54, 55–60
Deconstruction, 13, 31, 33, 86, 87
Defamiliarization, 20, 45, 54, 181, 190
Defoe, Daniel, 37; *Crusoe's Footprints*, 30;
    Robinson Crusoe, 37
de Lauretis, Teresa, 45, 68, 80
Derrida, Jacques, 30n, 31, 45, 86–89,
    101–106, 108, 189n, 211, 221
Desire, 66
Determinism, 221

Dickens, Charles, 3, 9, 10, 47, 50n, 51, 132
Difference, 17, 18, 20, 28; illusion of, 21;
    heterogeneity of, 28; of gender, 21; of
    gender and the everyday, 167
Doane, Mary Ann, 181
Dominance, 4, 11, 13, 30, 90, 126; female,
    114, 121; political, 32, 91; and race, 204
Donne, John, 100
Doubleness, 213
Doyle, Arthur Conan, 4, 36, 40, 44, 134–
    162
Dublin Review, 108
Dunbar, Paul Lawrence, 215
Duplessis, Rachel, 163
During, Simon, 35, 36, 86; *The Cultural
    Studies Reader*, 35, 36

Eagleton, Terry, 9, 48n
Ebert, Teresa, 235, 236
Echols, Alice, 144
Eliot, George, 3, 47, 5, 99; *A Mill on the
    Floss*, 99
Eliot, T. S., 100, 170
Everyday, the: defined, 19; as a category,
    33; as a construction, 96; as illimitable,
    105; maculinist aspects of, 143, 144; as
    obligation, 80
Expansiveness, 13, 14, 37, 42, 50
Extraordinary, the, 63–66, 70. *See also*
    Ordinary, the

Fascism, 171, 172, 177, 195, 210
Felman, Shoshana, 98n
Feltes, Norman, 9
Feminine, qualities of the, 71; eternal pas-
    sive, 56
Feminism, 15, 21, 29, 31, 34, 45, 46, 84,
    168, 187, 213, 216; and the everyday,
    144, 145; as a political position, 59
Fiction: African-American women's, 44, 45,
    212, 214–217; domestic, 49; realist, 79
Fielder, Leslie, 132, 133n
Fisher, Philip, 133, 159n
Fiske, John, 34n
Fitzgerald, Edward, 49
Fitzgerald, Penelope, 75n
Flaneur, 146, 147, 150. *See also* Walking
Fleishman, Avrom, 164
Flitterman-Lewis, Sandy, 59, 69
Foucault, Michel, 11–13, 90, 131n, 213,
    221
Frantz, Fanon, 45, 178, 202, 203, 206, 210
Freud, Sigmund, 4, 5, 45, 141, 219–221,
    233–236; *The Psychopathology of
    Everyday Life*, 4, 141, 230
Friedman, Ellen, 40n
Fuss, Diana, 174n, 181